VISUAL BASIC™
FOR WINDOWS™
DEVELOPER'S
GUIDE

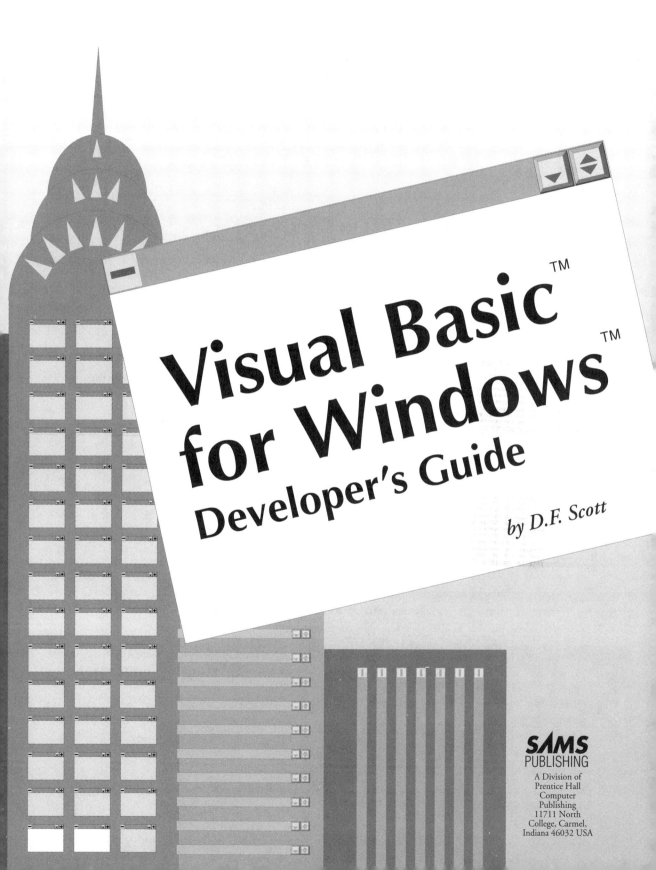

Visual Basic™ for Windows™
Developer's Guide

by D.F. Scott

SAMS
PUBLISHING

A Division of
Prentice Hall
Computer
Publishing
11711 North
College, Carmel,
Indiana 46032 USA

*For Jenny, who has taken her rightful place in the center of my life,
and believes in the adventure it is about to become.*

Copyright © 1993 by Sams Publishing

Trademarks

Screen reproductions in this book were created by means of the program Collage Plus from Inner Media, Inc., Hollis, NH.

*Composed in AGaramond and MCPdigital
by Prentice Hall Computer Publishing*

Printed in the United States of America

OVERVIEW

CONTENTS

Part II   From Concept to Ingenuity

Part III   Real-World Experimental Programming

ACKNOWLEDGMENTS

Whosoever would accept jade pendants
who has first heard source code growing in a cliff?

—Loosely paraphrased from Witter Bynner's translation of
The Tao of Life (Tao te Ching)

This book was born on the eve of a change of course in my life. I generally am not one to believe the reader should have a great deal of interest in the course of the author's life; but that change of course has played such a role in this book's production that the longtime reader may be able to spot its influences. I would like to acknowledge first those people who have put up with me during this transition period, and who are keeping my flame alive. Mom, I miss you, and I miss home. Dad, thanks for the faith and for your vision that has kept me alive.

The computer store I never failed to mention in previous acknowledgements, Info 1 Computers in Oklahoma City, is no longer. Sure, a software store took its place and moved to a new location, and the old location is now a day-care center. Yet the spirit of perserverance and stalwart dedication that Info 1 represented is still in search of a new home. Within my lifetime, hopefully soon, I shall give it one. I would like for Info 1's founder, John Hite, and my friends back home, Chris Hood, Charles Wagner, and Richard Kowals who kept that flame alive, to know that I am still dedicated to the old spirit of educating the individual while providing him with the service he seeks. INVENT1, the inventory control application that appears in this volume, would have been the new ordering and automation system for the store.

Special thanks go to the Acquisitions Editor, Greg Croy. How Greg managed to keep his patience and his mellow wits during times of chaos baffles me; I could not have done it.

My thanks to William and Pat Whitmer for letting me set up shop in their home for awhile. Generosity such as theirs is uncommon.

The "I1" logo which appears in the screen shots of the forms in the INVENT1 application was originally designed for Info 1 Computers by Christopher Hood.

ABOUT THE AUTHOR

D.F. Scott is an independent technical author, artist, musician, and poet living in Indianapolis, Indiana. He was technical editor of *The Computer Street Journal,* contributing editor of *ANALOG Computing* and *ST-Log* magazines, and a contributor to *Computer Monthly.* His regular series on alternative computing began appearing in *Computer Shopper* in 1985. Scott was also the moderator of the Computer Shopper Information Exchange. Currently, he is the author of several books on Visual Basic.

INTRODUCTION

To be a programmer is to be an idealist. It is to believe wholeheartedly that the way things work in an office, in a business, in a laboratory, or even in the abstract theaters of the mind itself is by nature explicable by means of a numerological language. Logically speaking, this cannot be altogether true; the entire global economy and scientific community will never be fully automated by the microprocessor. Yet every new concept in programming brings us somewhat closer to that ideal, the steadfast belief that It Can Be Done. We share more of our work with microprocessors than ever in our lives.

The concept of programming a computer through the use of a coded language predates the advent of the computer itself. The first publicly sold microcomputers relied on languages—mostly BASIC, at times Pascal—as the chief mechanism for processing instructions. What brought more people into computing in the 1980s, however, was not languages but packaged applications, such as spreadsheets or word processors. Although such packages may contain some sort of "macro" language that operates in the background, for the most part they operate using a push-button methodology of computing. New users are therefore given the impression that mastery of the art of computing requires simply a keen sense of what button should be pressed when.

Because shrink-wrapped application bundles cannot be pre-adapted to the specific needs of a particular buyer or office, buyers are expected to make their own adaptations to these packages. Adaptation in such instances cannot legitimately be considered programming. The act of adapting a software package to a large office environment whose methods and work habits have already been established can be compared to traversing a continent with the aid of a mint-condition road map written entirely in runes. As a private systems consultant, as a "sys-op" for a worldwide telecom network support group, and as a part-time "answer man" for the former Info 1 Computers, I made it my business to work with people who were just being introduced to computing, and who were trying to decipher on their own the mystery of how computing applied to them.

Here are some instances of how intelligent and well-meaning people I've met, without much to introduce them to the computer but the owner's manual and some tips from their friends, established their electronic office environment.

☐ A law firm had been keeping its time-based client accounts on a budget spreadsheet program capable of generating .WKS-format files. This program was incapable of generating sublists based on criteria from the main list; so the firm's client accounts receivable list had literally been typed, cell-by-cell, to a separate spreadsheet file. In search of greater functionality, the firm purchased a budget form-filler program for making out the bills; but that program was incapable of reading the addresses from the .WKS file. It was the job of the secretary to print the spreadsheet data regularly on a ream of tractor-feed paper, and hand-type the billing information into the form filler.

A friend down the hall pointed out that Lotus 1-2-3 could "print" the .WKS file to disk in an ASCII format; and using the DOS command TYPE, the secretary could look at the spreadsheet contents on the screen rather than have to waste all that paper. One can't operate the DOS prompt and the form-filler at the same time; so a friend in another office suggested the firm find some multitasking or task-switching software (this was prior to DOS 5). With that, the secretary could flip back and forth between the DOS prompt and the form-filler, reading information from the former and typing it into the latter. The secretary had come to Info 1 looking for that multitasker. As you might expect, I did not have to sell it to her.

A doctor's office was using WordPerfect to generate its billing statements. The secretary would open a bill template, type the individual entries from the filing cabinet records into the document, and save that bill as a separate file. Because DOS was capable of storing only 255 files per subdirectory, the secretary would create a new subdirectory each time the current one ran out of available entries. More importantly, though, each document was consuming considerable hard drive space. In an attempt to gain some of that space back, the office had been archiving its full subdirectories with PKZIP.

The office was looking for some way to make the relatively cryptic command structure of PKZIP more understandable to its temporary help, whose resumes list training in WordPerfect but not PKZIP. The office manager told me he had become frustrated with how computers have only generated more work for his office, and that before he chose to make the dive into computers, he didn't need a data compressor. I had the happy duty of telling him he didn't need one now.

A major New York magazine publisher had just purchased a set of Macintoshes for its layout department. Having decided the training costs for the layout staff were far too expensive, the corporate division ruled that its editorial offices would keep its existing set of non-networked PC/XTs exclusively for editing articles. The word processor of choice (seeing as how the choice had been made six years before) was XyWrite III, a capable program with few export filters and relatively little third-party support. As a result of unfortunate market obscurity, no program existed on either the Macintosh or XT platform that converted XyWrite's files to a format the Mac could read into Adobe Illustrator (this was before the Mac SuperDrive).

The XyWrite files were therefore saved to 3 1/2" diskette in ASCII format, because an XT program existed that translated DOS ASCII files into Mac ASCII files with a "false" resource header. All the converted files would have the same filename and icon, but that could be changed from the Finder. During translation, however, all the character formatting codes in the text for italics and underlining were lost; so a hard copy was made of the XyWrite file in advance, and then sent to Layout. This was so the layout artist could manually reenter the formatting codes into the Mac edition of the document through Adobe Illustrator. Because the solution to this problem involved both a change in the packaged software as well as calling in an on-site programmer, the solution was delayed until both XT and Macintosh systems were replaced completely.

People who are left entirely on their own to make sense of computing, with only a handful of self-contained DOS applications and their own stubborn ingenuity, often find themselves eventually tangled in a web of inefficiency. The very tangling of this web makes these people so afraid of computers that they are unwilling to try learning the basic principles they need to know to break themselves loose—the principles that would have steered them clear of the web in the first place.

This is where you come into the picture, as a programmer of job-specific applications and specific business solutions. Visual Basic isn't meant to be a development system for mass-produced software; to be honest, the Visual Basic interpreter is not powerful enough to handle the workload of a shelf-quality, adapt-it-yourself application. Its purpose in the office computing environment is for the production of small applications specifically adapted for well-defined tasks. It's possible to use Visual Basic for creating all-purpose utilities, and you see a few being constructed during the course of this book. Whereas assembly language lays down the foundation of the computing structure, and C and C++ act as the brick and stone masonry of computing's more visible superstructure, Visual Basic is part of the plaster and mortar that seal up the cracks and make straight and flush the interior of the office.

The development of a Visual Basic application is a construction process. In any book you might find on "do-it-yourself" home construction, room additions, or interior plumbing, you're given a thorough understanding of the tools you need for the job, given explicit instructions on how the job is generally performed, and shown detailed illustrations depicting the components of the job in progress. Sams' *Visual Basic for Windows Developer's Guide* will be quite similar in its approach.

Overview of the Book

A million tips and tricks does not a good programmer make. I could spend several hundred pages describing to you the proper use of butter, basil, and baking powder, and these things may be of some use to you in the kitchen at some point in your life. If you don't understand the process of cooking, no recipe or helpful hint will ever bake a casserole for you. Likewise, I could show you 101 Neat Things You Can Do with Scroll Bars. If your objective is to make an inter-office scheduling system, the greatest concentration of scroll bars ever to inhabit one program will not result in automation.

Visual Basic for Windows Developer's Guide deals with principles first, technique second, and Neat Things You Can Do third. The purpose for this specific prioritization is to fill a gap left by the dozens of books already published on the subject of Visual Basic. You may own all of them already, and are therefore inundated with text that concentrates on How-To. This book deals with **Why**.

Over the chapters to follow, you witness the evolution of Visual Basic procedures, modules, and full-scale applications. The histories at times transcend the boundaries of the chapters themselves. The reason for this is so you may be able to observe the creation of applications at the maximum level of detail possible, while focusing at times upon particular aspects that are the primary subjects of the chapters.

The Three-Part Plan

The book is divided into three primary partitions. Part I, "The Programming Process," deals with the decisions that are made in the development of a Visual Basic application. In this section, I reveal not only the successess but the fallacies and bad moves that can be made. It's quite easy to present the reader with a fully functional program, and in retrospect show you how all its wonderful features were implemented. Such a presentation lends itself to a paid party political broadcast, in that it assumes that I, as author, correctly perceived the problem at hand on first try, skillfully navigated the route through the event and general procedures, and gracefully polished the front-end panels, the result being a specimen of flawless execution. Flawlessness is a process, not a birthright. This book shows you not only the final product of the programming process, but the *initial* product, and the inefficiencies and errors I encountered along the way to the final goal.

Part II, "From Concept to Ingenuity," focuses more on the specific principles that lend themselves to better linguistic computing, rather than the broader, overall process detailed in Part I. Better management of memory, more direct communication with the user, and proper arrangement and management of data are all crucial goals to the overall betterment of programs. As in so many other aspects of life, stating the goal and *achieving* the goal are two processes with greatly differing results. Part II deals with the application of principle to programming.

In Part III, "Real-World Experimental Programming," I deal for the first time in perhaps several hundred thousand pages of programming tutorials, with the idea that programming can be fun, can be an art form, and can be an educational tool not only for the users of the programs but for the programmers as well. You study the logic of programming in greater detail, and see how scientific method can be applied to make programs smaller and more efficient. You also look at "artificial intelligence" in practice in board game programs, and you study how logical processes that appear to be making decisions may also be applied to real-world processes. One of the forgotten purposes of high-level language programs has been to model real situations, such as the daily operation of a bank or the minute-by-minute trading records of a large stock market, and play "what-if" with known mathematical trends. There are purposes to programming other than storing a Rolodex file and balancing a checkbook. Many of these purposes were considered quite common applications by the authors of the 1960s and early 1970s, although they have since faded from the textbooks. They are still applications in wide use today, just not as much in the public eye.

The Chapter Agenda

The first chapter, "Computing with a Language," begins by differentiating between computing with applications software such as 1-2-3 and Peachtree Accounting, and the use of a high-level programming language. The information here is especially helpful to you if you're programming for yourself or for your own office. A number of purchasers of Visual Basic—perhaps including you—were motivated to make that purchase by the overwhelming frustration they have felt in trying to make existing software packages applicable to their office environment. They bought Visual Basic believing that somehow, if they could just be patient enough to wade through the mountains of documentation, and the hours of trial-and-error, they might eventually be able to develop a program or system of programs that automates their office processes. For these people, Visual Basic is somewhat frightening. There are no step-by-step instructions for a programming language. In order to better comprehend Visual Basic, I draw parallels in the first chapter between it and written languages such as English.

In the second chapter, "The Structure of Visual Basic," I expand on this theme to discuss the grammar and phraseology of the language. BASIC—an acronym for Beginners' All-purpose Symbolic Instruction Code—uses much of the phraseology of the English language; if you look more closely at each instruction, however, there is always a simple object-operand structure that more closely approximates assembly language, though very heavily disguised.

The third chapter is an examination of the broader structure of a program, "The Application Model." The heart of an application is the part that takes the information it receives as data, and translates that data into a form the user can utilize as information. To comprehend how an application is constructed, you should first be introduced to a body of science called "information theory." This science deals with what parts of knowledge, language, and the work process can be represented using data. In a stock portfolio management application, for instance, the computer program itself has no inherent understanding of the forces driving world economics, and can make no predictions as to the future actions of the Federal Reserve regarding interest rates. Such a program, however, can make reasonable analyses based on the data you feed it. In this chapter, I begin to differentiate between information and data.

I address one of the most difficult and abstract subjects in the art of computing, "The Composition of Data," in the fourth chapter. Information theory is the study of *encoding*, and every computer program to some extent encodes data in a form that it (and sometimes only it) can utilize. Data is often the element of a program that is designed last; perhaps its modern role as an over-encountered afterthought explains why there is such an abundance of redundant data today. Data, like an application, can be structurally designed for efficiency, ease of access, and minimum redundancy. This process is perhaps more difficult to implement with respect to the Visual Basic interpreter, because it relies so heavily on the old mechanism for data access, one-datum-at-a-time. In a true multitasking system, the format of data is objectified so that multiple applications can make use of the same data without having to employ an export/import process. Microsoft has been rather enthusiastic recently about its implementation of objectified data; and in this chapter, you see the products of Microsoft's labor, both those that have been completed and those that are still in progress.

I then proceed to "The Goal of Automation," Chapter 5. In the business environment, it is the goal of the programmer to take some everyday work process and model it within the computer. This doesn't mean to create some new work process just so the office workers have greater opportunity to use a computer. This means to remove the responsibility for a work process from pencil and paper, and delegate it to the computer program. The intention of the programmer is to remove much of the tedium from the work process. The goal of the programmer is *automation.* To achieve this, you need to learn how to describe the work process on paper, using the English language rather than Visual Basic if necessary. You should practice describing what it is that goes on in the work process *without* using examples, metaphors, instances, overly explicit phraseology, or any of the other tools that make communication from one human to another human so effortless. The goal here is not to be deliberately vague, but to be completely *symbolic,* for high-level languages deal in algebraic symbology.

Chapter 6 concentrates on the "underside" of the programming process, "Development and Debugging." Throughout the book, you see how applications are developed using the "layering" concept, where one working function is added to another working function until the application becomes an integrated whole. This is a quite efficient method, but it is also prone to errors because it relies, for a time, upon a short-sided view of the purpose of the application. Tacking one short-sided vision onto another often results in errors, and that is perhaps the chief deficiency of this otherwise painless method of developing applications. Encountering errors is part of the natural course of programming. In fact, programs are made more efficient through a systematic plan of attack against errors and their more evil counterpart, bugs.

Moving to Part II, Chapter 7 deals with "Contexts, Scopes, and Relationships." Part of what is so confusing about Visual Basic to new programmers is the way definitions and declarations have varying levels of pertinence. A variable x to one module might not be the same x that appears in another module, though it can be. The form procedure for a dialog box may be called within an application far more often than once, though by varying the way in which it is called, the purpose for that dialog may be made more flexible and adaptable.

In this chapter, you learn about how applications can have interchangeable parts, and how you can use components you've already written to create entirely new applications for greatly varying purposes.

Chapter 8, "Communication with the User," focuses on the often conversational interchange between an application and its user, and how you as programmer can better facilitate this conversation. In the workstation model of computing, the time the user spends on a workstation is considered a "session." Graphic devices are employed in an application to complement the terms and numbers used to symbolize the messages being passed between human and machine, though an unrehearsed mixture of iconography and orthography can create input confusion (you learn about these two terms later). Although standards are currently being written to help define a common conversational vernacular among programs, these standards are often amended "on the fly" by software manufacturers, with toolbars and mouse gestures. Retroactively, these gestures become part of the standard, so perhaps a programmer should not rely upon published standards so much in defining how best to define the rapport between human and machine.

Chapter 9, "Engineering Original Devices," deals less with linguistic interaction and more with iconic and graphical interaction with a program. Modern electronic devices employ rows of buttons as their controls; thus in the simulation of those devices, graphical panels in Windows programs tend to use rows of buttons. Oftentimes true ingenuity involves a greater level of practicality, so perhaps we should strive to create more practical control devices for the user than push-buttons and drop-down lists. An original graphic control should be architecturally pleasing, though it should also appear physically tangible, as though it were a real device that the hand could touch.

Chapter 10, "The Windows Environment," introduces the instructions used by Visual Basic (and other Microsoft Windows applications as well) to communicate with Windows itself. Windows utilizes its own "language" for inter-application communication, called the Applications Program Interface (API). The Windows API is a series of libraries whose routines give you direct access to the graphical, data throughput, and functional facilities of Windows. This access is granted equivalently to Visual Basic, to C++, and to application packages such as Excel that utilize background languages.

A different use for the communications model is studied in Chapter 11, "Communication Between Applications." The Windows environment is designed so that applications will cease to be so arrogant that they take it upon themselves to be all things to all users. A Windows program is encouraged to share resources, tools, and the overall workload with other programs. A Visual Basic application may take advantage of the various "pipelines" given it by the Windows environment to act as an extension to another pre-existing Windows application.

Moving into Part III, Chapter 12 introduces you to "Algorithmic Logic." In any program, data represents *things* or objects in some way, whereas algorithms are well-structured procedures that represent *actions* or processes. An algorithm describes for the computer some real-world process, such as the selection of a record from a file based on nonspecific request criteria, or the sorting of a set of records. A procedure can be considered algorithmic when it utilizes reiterative procedural algebra—that is to say, when it uses symbological instructions, often repetitively, that employ math to perform a job that is not necessarily mathematical in the real world.

Programming was developed for situations in which the behavior of gaseous molecules, the condition of oilfield equipment parts over years of constant use, or the volatility in a country's gross national product after a particularly depressing election year can be modeled and explored. Simple formulas such as those used by a spreadsheet program will not work in such cases where procedural algebra is required.

The ill-named science of artificial intelligence is explored in the final chapter, "Making Programs Appear to Think." Here, we delve into decision-making algorithms, whose purpose is to determine the best course of action, the program having been given all forseeable options. An option is represented in a decision-making algorithm by the result of a calculation, which is not at all the process the human brain uses to perceive an option. An heuristic algorithm is an attempt to model the decision-making process as closely as possible (or as can be speculated) to human reasoning. It uses heuristics, or real-world rules represented by mathematical formulas. Perhaps for this reason, the most complex and involving programs a person can write are games, since the programmer is charged with the responsibility of defining the contents and boundaries of a small world whose rules are the laws of heuristic logic. I've often said that anyone who can conceive and thoroughly develop a workable, original game is quite capable, perhaps overqualified, to write an accounting program.

Finally, as an appendix for this book, I address the topic of "Documentation and Online Help." There is a law of uncertainty about the operation of mechanical devices that rivals Heisenberg's own. The more complex a mechanical device becomes—for instance, a construction crane or field harvester—the more likely a potential user is to readily discern the purpose of that device, though the less likely that person is to know how to use it. Conversely, however, the more simple a mechanical device is crafted to be—for instance, a tongue depressor or a shirt collar extender—the easier it is for someone to *use,* yet the more difficult it becomes for a potential user to discern what the heck it is. This segment of the book will deal with the topic of addressing the potential user through the use of the English language, just like we at Sams (try to) do every day.

You, the Reader

As the author, I have to make some assumptions about you, the reader. I assume you know some things about programming in Visual Basic, such as what a variable is; the difference between an expression of assignment and an expression of comparison; and the distinctions between a statement, a method, and a function. If you're unsure about these items, there may be some follow-up features along the way, but there won't be detailed discussions of the basics. May I suggest, if you need some refreshing, my colleague Bill Orvis' book, *Do-It-Yourself Visual Basic,* from Sams, or my own book, *Visual Basic By Example,* from Que.

Assuming you are a knowledgeable programmer, I address you, for the most part, as a programmer-for-hire or a consultant, or as the systems programmer for your company. You will be faced with development situations whose characteristics are not entirely under your control, and are subject not only to constant change but to misinterpretation. The people who may be employing you to write a problem-solving application for them might very well have a distorted view of the problem. The real solution to their problem might require a change of operating methodology on their part, and they may not want that change— they may prefer the comfort of the problem to the unfamiliarity of the solution. Rather than deal entirely with variables, objects, and procedures, I supplement the chapters with insight into the *programmer's decision-making process,* not just with regard to source code but to the client solution.

How This Book Works

To give you further insight regarding the double jeopardy of making a program that works right *and* satisfying your client, this book introduces segments called *Situation Blocks*. In these situations, the problem is attacked like a chess move: entirely logically, with regard to changing situations and the possibility of customer dissatisfaction with an otherwise perfect solution. You see how to mix original ingenuity with existing code you keep ready for such occasions, resulting in solutions to customer problems that prepackaged, shrink-wrapped software cannot solve. Each programming situation is discussed at length; but rather than stay on one topic for a hundred pages, I tackle each situation one piece at a time. Each situation is coded numerically, so when there is a stopping spot, I might put down Situation #3 for a while and come back to it later. When I do come back, I mark that spot with the header "Situation #3." There are plenty of things to talk about in the pauses.

This book may digress at times to cover particular programming techniques. For the simpler techniques, I might break for a paragraph to bring you a *Technique Note;* when I prefer to be more philosophical, I break for a *Principle Note.* For subjects that require further discussion and examples, the current discourse of the chapter pauses for a *Technique Capsule* that stands alone from the current discourse and acts as a miniature tutorial on the subject. You can pick out these mini-chapters by the way the layout sets them off from the rest of the text.

At times, a certain programming course or technique may take special advantage of a new feature of Visual Basic 2's Professional Edition. This package contains several custom controls, provided in the form of .VBX files, that add new devices to the Visual Basic toolbox. Many of these new features have not been documented by Microsoft in any great detail; therefore where necessary, I'll break in the midst of the text to show you a Technique Capsule, describing the operation of the extension .VBX controls.

If you read this book from front to back, you'll be taken on a tour through the scenic route of the programming process. Along the way, you'll stop to see some points of particular interest, though with one eye focused on the map. If you read it by scanning the margin notes for choice sections, you'll find elements of programming theory put into practice and described in summary, so you might be able to work your way through a bind in a hurry. If you're looking for a specific topic, you can use Sams' exclusive *Topic Finder* located in the back of the book. The Topic Finder shows a list of each margin note in the book, along with the number of the page where you'll find it. This list is arranged *by subject* rather than in alphabetical order like the standard index. After you've located the page number, you can find an identical listing of that topic along the left or right margin of the page. So however you choose to navigate this book, there are ways in which the layout and arrangement of topics can help you.

The Newer Nuances of Visual Basic

Throughout the course of this book, you will also be introduced through Technique Notes to the important new features of Visual Basic 2.0 for Windows Professional Edition (I could fill a lot of space with that title). You've probably read about many of these features, as a result of Microsoft's extensive advertising campaign, and perhaps by having simply read the box. I've chosen to temper my coverage of these features a bit, to not get overly excited by the term *new* like the ideal housewife of 1968 to a new detergent ad. Here are the more important new topics about which you'll be reading:

☐ The new implementation of the Visual Basic language enables you to declare variables that refer to specific objects. These object variables have properties just like graphic objects, although they can be as vague or as generic as you need them to be at any one time. Thus you can take any five scroll bars and align them, or set their values to zero, or arrange the contents of several text boxes within a form without referring to any one by name.

☐ The new watch debugging system enables you to monitor the status of variables during a program's run, as well as have the interpreter make complex evaluations of variables you're monitoring without affecting the course of the application.

☐ The new grid control—now a standard feature of all editions of Visual Basic—lets data be displayed in a tabular format, to complement the standard form style for which VB is already adept.

- [ ] With the new Object Linking and Embedding client control, it's possible to have a data document from a Windows application be displayed in its native format within a Visual Basic form and have the Windows application perform the document maintenance duties on behalf of the VB application.

- [ ] A prototype of Microsoft's Open DataBase Connectivity model is provided with Visual Basic, for users of Microsoft SQL Server to tinker with, though perhaps not to use for serious applications just yet. Using Structured Query Language to address data is a topic you'll see addressed here, and you'll also be given a general overview of Microsoft's intentions for the ODBC system.

- [ ] Visual Basic forms are now capable of linking directly with Windows' online help system, through a set of properties intrinsic to VB graphic objects that establish their relationship to the topics of an online help file. With Professional Edition, you can write this help file with a word processor and compile it to a form that the VB interpreter recognizes using Microsoft's Help Compiler.

To tackle the complexity of abstract thinking, of simulating possibilities, of wading through the multitude of errors, requires a large measure of idealism. Hopefully, through the course of this book, without losing sight of the fact that complexity makes for applicability, you can maintain the necessary spirit of idealism that is the mindset of the career programmer.

PART ONE

The Programming Process

COMPUTING WITH A LANGUAGE

1

Imagine for a moment the science fiction ideal of computing over the last half century. Notice, if you will, that in the pulp novels and in the movies, sci-fi writers have users speaking to computers. Icons are less powerful tools in sci-fi computing than words.

Programmers of the real world of the 1990s may be sold on the idea that icons and graphical layout are the basic tools for communicating with their users. The paid, professional dreamers of the modern age, however, still believe in the power of language as the key communication tool bridging humans and machines. Could it be that the fundamental building blocks of communication—the mental archetypes—are evolving more toward the word than the picture, and the software marketers really have it wrong? Are programmers who subscribe to iconography as their binding principle neglecting a far less confusing method of reaching the user?

In this chapter, you find two large-scale Visual Basic applications in their initial stages of construction. As you study them in detail, notice I'll be concentrating on those elements of high-level language computing that differ from using packaged software for the same purposes. Hopefully, you can begin to see why a language provides many unique and unduplicated methods for solving problems and automating tasks.

Why Use a Language?

The real purpose of Visual Basic is to generate unique problem-solving applications. Historically, the role of languages has not been to pick up the slack where packaged applications have left off. As you'll see later in this chapter, the high-level programming language constituted the first true user program for computers. The first packaged, do-it-all software applications found their way to the shelves at a time when computer hardware developers still thought all computer users were well on their way to becoming programmers. As limitless as the uses for shrink-wrapped software might appear, some substantial ground still remains virgin territory for the high-level language.

How a business can use a Visual Basic application.

Here are the chief reasons a business might prefer a custom-made application set built with high-level language rather than a software package:

☐ The way the business currently executes its work tasks cannot be properly automated by the current selection of prepackaged software.

☐ The way individuals in the business perform their jobs is subject to change, adaptation, and reassessment, for reasons ranging from management realignment to personal preferences. When the jobs change, the programs must change as well.

☐ Individuals not thoroughly trained to use computers can use a program with capabilities that can be augmented over time, as they learn more about computing. Spreadsheets and other software packages assume the users are the programmers and expect them to make adaptations on their own.

A corporation has the right to use software that is its own exclusive property, for reasons pertaining to competitiveness, market perception, and executive morale. If a corporation chooses to use secretive business strategies, it should not be forced to use the same mass-market software its competitors use.

Companies that deal with specific customers differently require a highly flexible software system. Packaged software tends to offer instructions about how a user's business should work rather than adapt to how a business does work.

Defining Visual Basic for Newcomers

Based on the way Microsoft markets Visual Basic, you might think it is just another customizable application. The company does emphasize the point-and-click philosophy of computing, as it does with Word for Windows and Excel. For customers who ask what Visual Basic is really for, the standard answer is that it's an instructional system for programming customized business applications. If you stick to the standard answer, you might be ignored like an incumbent politician. Instead, consider that even with the few hundred boxes of software on the shelf, there are countless office, business, scientific, and exploratory jobs yet to be automated by a computer program. If you learn how to express such jobs using an instructional language, you might fill some of the gaps left by the limitations of packaged software.

This answer causes a variety of responses—especially from users who might rather avoid being programmers. It's all a conspiracy; the big software manufacturers collude to prevent users from fully utilizing packaged software—so they must buy more software, so everyone is forced to be programmers, so manufacturers can sell more languages. Some think programming languages are useless and what people really want is power right out of the box. Those intrigued with the prospect of learning a high-level programming language often are users frustrated with productivity-in-a-box packages. They believe they know more than software manufacturers about how work is accomplished.

Visual Basic's real purpose in a business or office environment is to model the way paperwork and business transactions are ordinarily performed. A VB application can automate transactions to expedite and optimize everyday tasks, to make work less redundant and, perhaps, more enjoyable. In addition, a VB

The ideal purpose of Visual Basic in an office.

application should not create more work for the user. Some packaged software creates more work for the offices that use it; more time and effort is spent maintaining the computer system than running the business. Visual Basic programmers must avoid creating packages that require the time and cost of high maintainance; otherwise, there's no point in using it.

The most common misconception people have about Visual Basic—or any programming language—is that it's the backbone of an intelligent system. Probably due to confused marketing perceptions, people believe Visual Basic and other languages are inherently capable of studying problems, making analyses, and rendering conclusions. High-level programming languages are not intelligent; they do not describe anything to you. To be a fluent programmer, you should avoid the misconception that it is your role as programmer to speak to Visual Basic. As the author of Visual Basic applications, I try to refrain from thinking that I am communicating with Visual Basic.

The communications model of linguistic computing.

Figure 1.1 depicts the Communications Model of the High-Level Language (my terminology). The oval objects here represent parties in the conversation, and the arrow represents the transaction of the conversation. Telephone engineers use communications models to relate to hypothetical two- or multiple-party conversations. In this particular model, a communications model demonstrates a two-party conversation between the programmer and the user of the application.

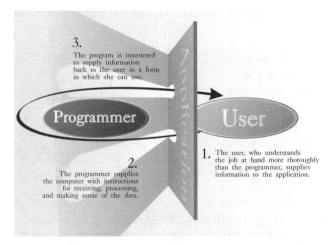

Figure 1.1. The Communications Model of the High-Level Language.

Notice the transaction starts and ends with the user; programmers logically act as a conduit for the passage of data between themselves and users. This is not a conversation between the program and the user or between the programmer and the program. The entire programming paradigm is a conversation between people. What is peculiar about this particular conversation is that you, the programmer, instruct the program in advance about how to respond to all queries to the user. You must anticipate all possible responses the users might issue to your appplication.

Figure 1.1 depicts the computer as a wall obscuring the view between programmer and user. As an author of programs, you may feel as though you're speaking to your user through a tape recorder. This is especially true in the case of Visual Basic—more so than with standard C++ or even QBasic—because of the system's revolutionary event mechanism. This system *can* make inputting data easier for the user. Recall, however, Newton's warning about the equal and opposite reaction. In computing, discretion about the course of the program is taken away from the programmer.

> **Principle Note:** When designing a program, imagine yourself interacting with the user rather than with the computer.

The following situation demonstrates the role of the high-level programming language in the (deferred) communication process between programmer and user:

Situation #1: The Retail Inventory Tracking System

Assume your client is a retail products store or chain of stores. This organization hires you to write a retail goods inventory, purchasing, and tracking system. The organization is small, so from time to time, the same person may purchase goods from suppliers or distributors, sell those goods, and analyze the sales history of those goods. The purchasing, invoicing, point-of-sale, and tracking modules, therefore, don't have to be entirely separate.

Users of this program need full access to every feature. They should be able to check inventory to see if a product is in stock, where it's located, and what its sales price is "on-the-fly." If a product is not in stock and a customer needs it right away, users should have the right to initiate the purchasing process now. At any time, users must be able to examine how sales are doing overall, for a specified category of products and for a particular product.

Situation #1 Goals.

Your goals for Situation #1 are as follows:

- ☐ The main inventory module maintains a database of all items for sale to the public.

- ☐ A customer list maintains information about customers with exclusive privileges and mail-order customers.

- ☐ The purchasing module maintains a list of the last-known costs offered by different distributors for each item. This enables buyers to determine the best deal at the current time.

- ☐ An invoicing and point-of-sale module makes instantaneous changes in the current inventory list.

- ☐ A sales tracking module shows users how particular goods are selling, accounting also for differing categories and brand names.

As promised in the introduction, you are on a detailed tour of the decision-making process for the programmer. Begin with decision number one: What is the most important and fundamental element of this program? Decide what element is most important and build this first. The Microsoft Programmers' Guide accompanying your copy of Visual Basic offers an explanation of how to build an application. The first thing it tells you to do is design the forms and windows. With all due respect to Microsoft, although this method can succeed, for the most part, it is a backwards way to work. Designing the front panels and the forms first might be advisable if it helps you determine *next* what elements of data belong to the program. Eventually, you should design the data on paper before you design the forms. Data is the most important part of the program, so you want to develop it at the beginning.

Technique Note: Design your global-scope data variables first, before you do *anything* else.

The data element that comprises the backbone of this program is the non-perishable inventory item. Study for a moment the characteristics of an item of inventory. (I like to use boxes of software as an example because I've been personally affiliated with that area of business.) Besides boxes of software, books, hardware, stereo components, and office furniture qualify as examples of this category. The essential characteristics of an item of inventory are its title, cost to the dealer, and shelf price. From the beginning, you come up against a crucial design decision: How do you define for the program "an item of inventory?" Is it a single box on the shelf, or is it a title that may contain one or more boxes for which space is reserved on the shelf?

Is It Bigger Than a Breadbox?

Here's the problem in detail: A box on the shelf may or may not have a specific serial number. If a manufacturer offers a special promotion for a limited number of items—say, a five-dollar rebate coupon inside specially marked and numbered boxes—you must record the serial number for it to appear on the customer's invoice. Then the customer can photocopy that invoice and send it to the manufacturer as proof of purchase. Furthermore, suppose a customer returns an item as defective. For the system to "unsell" this item and put it back in inventory, the serial number from the original invoice must be recorded somewhere. The purchasing department needs this serial number to return the item to the manufacturer (called a "return authorization" or "R. A." for short) for a refund or credit.

Items versus products; specifics versus indefinites.

Figure 1.2 shows the initial divisions taking place in the decision-making process. It appears you must distinguish between an item and a product, so you want two data files for these categories. An *item* is a particular object or box resting on the shelf, whereas a *product* refers to the title of a set of items. Although there are related elements for both categories, for efficiency's sake, keep redundancy to a minimum.

Admittedly Visual Basic is rather weak in the way it handles arrays of data in memory. The interpreter offers three data access schemes; two are applicable in the context of this program. The sequential-access scheme requires you, as programmer, to bring an entire array of data into memory, make changes or amendments to that data entirely in memory, and store that data in one lump sum back to disk when you are closing the file. Sequential access is a dangerous scheme when writing a Visual Basic application for networks. If two clients or peers along a network load the same data file into memory arrays and each peer makes changes to that data without seeing the other one's changes, the data file saved last overwrites the file saved first. This means half the changes are lost, and the file, in any event, becomes 100 percent invalid.

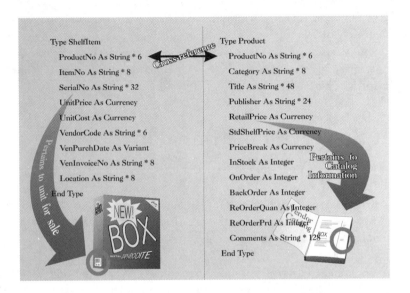

Figure 1.2. Five minutes into it, and already an identity crisis!

The random-access method is preferable when it is necessary to read one record at a time. Visual Basic makes its object-oriented syntax available to the programmer for use in variables. Microsoft has found it difficult to name the category of variables that are declared using the Type clause. In Visual Basic 1, Microsoft used the term *user-defined variables,* even though the programmer, not the user, does the defining. For Visual Basic 2, Microsoft has toyed with using the name *record variables,* because in Visual Basic's random-access data file scheme, these refer to constituent elements of data records. Because the variables do not comprise records, Microsoft may be ambiguous in its choice of terms. This volume, therefore, uses the term *composite variables* to refer to variable structures declared within a global or general module using the Type clause.

> **Technique Note:** When you have multiple data files with interrelated fields and face a choice between Visual Basic's sequential-access method and its random-access method, choose the random-access method.

The composite variable scheme enables you to address data fields in a record by subject first and field second, using the following syntax:

```
subject.field
```

From the point of view of a database engineer, the first term in the preceding reference is its subject because you can access all fields in each record using `subject` as a category. From the point of view of software engineers, however, the first term in the reference is the object; each field comprises a characteristic of a "thing," which, to address objectively, you must classify as an object. Feel free to be confused. This is an unresolved issue in the development of computing, and it is one of many you find in the course of this book.

In any event, you can utilize the structure of the `Type` clause in Visual Basic to begin to delineate between data tables and their constituent fields. In Figure 1.2, you see the distinction drawn between the sales item as a box on the shelf and as a product for sale. The first lines of code I wrote for the Visual Basic project INVENT1.MAK are my initial assessments for the structures of the two primary data files in this inventory system. I've added remarks that describe the role of each field in its composite variable.

```
Type ShelfItem
    ProductNo As String * 6        'Key field
    SerialNo As String * 32        'Number given the item
                                   ' by its manufacturer
    UnitPrice As Currency          'Shelf price given the item
                                   ' by merchant
    UnitCost As Currency           'Actual cost of the item set
                                   ' by vendor
    VendorCode As String * 6       'Code for the vendor that
                                   ' sold store this item
    VenPurchDate As Variant        'Date store purchased the
                                   ' item from vendor
    VenInvoiceNo As String * 8     'Invoice number of prior
                                   ' purchase from vendor
End Type
```

```
Type Product
    ProductNo As String * 6        'Key field
    Category As Integer            'Store-defined code for shelf
                                   ' category
    Title As String * 48           'Official title for the
                                   ' product
    Publisher As String * 6        'Store-defined code for
                                   ' product publisher
    RetailPrice As Currency        'Manufacturer-suggested
                                   ' retail price
    InStock As Integer             'Amount of product currently
                                   ' in stock (single-site)
    OnOrder As Integer             'Amount of product currently
                                   ' on order
    BackOrder As Integer           'Amount of product vendors
                                   ' placed on back-order
    ReOrderQuan As Integer         'Recommended reorder quantity
                                   ' on regular basis
    ReOrderPrd As Integer          'Store code for regular
                                   ' reorder
    Comments As String * 128       'Arbitrary comments from
                                   ' any user
End Type
```

All applications, to one extent or another, operate a database in memory or on disk, lest they be mere four-function calculators. The contents of a data file in memory are a table. To have organized contents, a table must contain a series of records of equal length. The order of the constituent variables in each of the previous Type declarations defines the length and structure of a record for the ShelfItem and Product data files. Each variable within the records constitutes a field for that record. Figure 1.3 shows how you can arrange the contents of a data table for the object variable ShelfItem, both as a record entry form and as a grid-style table like a spreadsheet. The fact that a spreadsheet is read in the grid style gives some the mistaken impression that a spreadsheet application can act as an efficient database or data file manager.

Notice now the construction of the two composite variables with respect to one another. Only one variable—ProductNo—is declared alike for both types. In this scheme, ProductNo contains a six-digit identification number that represents the title of the product—for the software store paradigm, say, Symantec Norton Utilities; for an art supply store, 10-qt. #2 turpentine; for a book store,

Quantum Reality by Nick Herbert. The store's purchasing department arbitrarily defines the product number sequence. Here, it is defined as a string because some importance may be applied later to the value of the individual digits. This is the key field that identifies the product across all data tables that refer to the product. Because it is the key field, which exclusively identifies the product and is expected to be unique across all entries, you do not have to share any other field between any two tables containing `ProductNo` as its key.

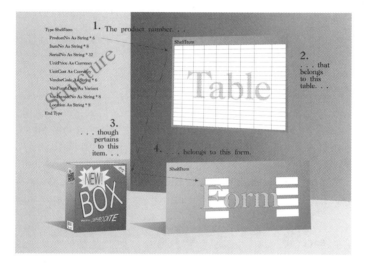

Figure 1.3. The dual identities of a data table.

The key field technique is crucial to the construction of any database or data file schema and is, therefore, the subject of this book's first breakaway technique capsule:

Technique Capsule: Key Data Fields

Definition: The key field is implemented in Visual Basic as a single, unique constituent element of a set of composite variables. The key field may contain numeric or alphanumeric data. By definition, it appears within more than one composite variable in the Visual Basic project. When a composite variable represents a data file to Visual Basic, the constituent elements declared within the `Type` clause each define a record for that data file. Each record of a data file relates to the same item or object. Generally in a record, one constituent element serves as an identifier—for instance, a person's Social Security number or an automobile's Vehicle Identification Number. You may use the same identifier for more than one composite variable, to represent the same person or item. This way, you don't have to store all the characteristics of the item you refer to throughout the Visual Basic project in memory in an overly large composite variable, or on disk in an oversized and cumbersome data file. You can also use a key field as an index field for sorting procedures.

Execution: Declare a set of composite variables within a general or global module using a `Type` clause. The purposes of these composite variables are related to one another, so their `Type` clauses each contain one—and only one—constituent variable whose name, definition, and declaration are equivalent. For style's sake, the key field is the first composite variable declared within those `Type` clauses that use the key field as their identifier.

Example: Suppose you're writing an application for a fast-lube car service establishment. The application uses two data files, one that contains a service record of all cars that have previously entered the garage and another with a list of prior invoices for each of those cars. You can use the Vehicle Identification Number, located on the dash or under the hood of most cars, as an identifier. Here's how the two `Type` clauses relating to records for the same auto might appear:

```
Type ServiceRecord
    VID As String * 36
    ServiceCode(16) As Integer
    ServiceDate(16) As Integer
End Type

Type Invoice
    VID As String * 36
    Number As String * 6
    EntryDate As Variant
    BillAmount As Currency
    Received As Currency
    PymtCode As Integer
End Type

Global CarHistory(1000) As ServiceRecord
Global CustomerHistory(1000) As Invoice
```

You can generate the first invoice for this customer using the contents of the data already being processed in the `ServiceRecord` file. Set the new key field for the `Invoice` file with this instruction:

```
CustomerHistory(newcar%).VID = CarHistory(thiscar%).VID
```

where `newcar%` is a pointer to the last record in the `ServiceRecord` file and `thiscar%` is a pointer to the current invoice record on the invoice form. (A pointer reflects the location of a record within a database or data file.)

Later in the application, suppose the accounting officer for this company pulls up the invoice record to see the services that merit such high charges. You can create a pointer to the car in question, thiscar%, with this instruction:

```
carno$ = CustomerHistory(thiscar%).VID
```

Now, you can use the variable `carno$` as a pointer to search for a match in the contents of `CarHistory(searchcar%).VID`.

Cautions: To properly implement key fielding in a data file, the contents of each entry in the key field must be unique. You may have to implement a safety feature in your applications to be sure no two key field entries are identical. To do this efficiently, you should enable your program to re-sort your data file each time a record is added, using the key field as the index field for the sort. This way, if two key field entries are identical, they appear next to each other after the data table is sorted.

For project INVENT1.MAK, the key field for many of the included composite variables is `ProductNo`, which pertains to the title or specific identity of a product on the shelf.

From the purchasing agent's point of view, several distributors may be competing for business by marking down prices below those printed in the current catalog. To make a purchasing decision, the agent must see the current catalog costs for each single item. Naturally, the purchasing agent receives calls from distributor agents marking these costs down even further. The nature of these special deals might not be classifiable as cost per box; they might be special markdowns for buying three of something, or one of item A along with two of item B. Already, many catalogs apply cost categories to every item to reduce the cost of that item if the total charge for an order is above a certain amount—say, $1,000. The cost of an item in today's nonperishable retail goods market is never fixed; in fact, it's highly variable. Somehow, you must be able to code the variability in costs, but for now, you can conclude that product cost is kept in a separate data file.

Inventing codes for storing information as data.

Could you use
a spreadsheet
instead?

While at this level of detail, pause for a moment to examine what you're doing and how different it is from working with a prepackaged application. In the 1980s, it was popular to use spreadsheet programs as database managers. A spreadsheet user writing an inventory "program" (read: set of loosely related macros) listed all the data fields related to a product of inventory on one sheet, one row per item, one column per field. In your model inventory application, you know you want a primary split between the item data file and the product data file, with some identifying fields shared and duplicated between the two files. Using a spreadsheet, those two files would either be two separate worksheets or two segments of one big sheet. Imagine the difficulty the spreadsheet user faces maintaining the relations between only these two tables or keeping track of the cell pointers for the different rows. Nothing further demonstrates the inefficiency of the spreadsheet as a business automation system than the flatness of its file format.

For now, put Situation #1 on the shelf: you come back to it in Chapter 3, "The Application Model." When you pick up the project again, you discover how to create and classify the various forms in the application. Later, you see how to design and use the project's more complex data structures.

The Universal Role of Language

Florian Coulmas, who teaches linguistics at the University of Dusseldorf, Germany, theorizes that the written language was invented as a way to symbolize money. In his brilliant 1989 examination of the evolution of textual symbology, *The Writing Systems of the World,* Coulmas presents evidence that the Sumerians of Asia Minor in 8000 B.C. used different shapes of stones as tokens representing monetary units. The Sumerians used soft clay tablets to record their market transactions, pressing each token into the clay so that each unique shape represented the value of the "coins" used in their transactions. Eventually they used sticks to "forge" the shape of the coins, and thus, written orthographic communication was born. Written text was needed to operate the accounting systems of the day.

An orthography, Coulmas defines, is a system of symbols that represents messages whereby the symbols and the messages have no direct meaningful link to one another. In Mayan cultures, a picture of a person might actually represent that person; but in the modern alphabet of the English language, p-e-r-s-o-n represents the abstract concept just as well, even though none of the six letters resembles (or is supposed to resemble) any part of the human form. In an orthography, the symbols rely on their positional relationship with one another to represent a message or a concept.

High-level languages employ indirect symbolism.

Visual Basic, because it borrows its terms and phraseology from the English language, cannot be considered an orthography, though it resembles one in the most important respect: it uses symbols to represent or model situations in which the symbol and the situation have no direct link to one another. It can be argued that algebra is rooted to Sumerian accounting. Algebra uses symbols to represent known and unknown values, as did the shapes of Sumerian coins. Visual Basic uses a combination of algebra and English to represent information as data and the changing relationships among the data elements as code.

Enter the Expressor!

For the next experiment with fully working applications, I'd like to present now the story of a programmable calculator application I created originally for another book. This discussion tends to be biographical, but I believe part of the total comprehension of programming is an understanding of the experience—what you think at first, what you attempt, where you correct yourself, when you become frustrated, and when you're satisfied that the work is, at last, completed.

Situation #2: The Expressor Mark Calculator

At some time as a professional programmer, you must develop a module that can be applied to nearly any application you write, and which also establishes your uniqueness and individual trademark. (If you use the following module in your applications, you'll be establishing *my* uniqueness and personal trademark, but a little free advertising wouldn't hurt.) The idea for the project for

Situation #2 stems not from an assignment, but from perserverence and pre-monition of problems yet to solve.

When users fill out a Visual Basic form, from time to time they may question what the value of a numeric entry should be. Often, they are compelled to pull up a pocket calculator and punch up a figure. The Microsoft Windows package offers a minimizable utility calculator which works well, though it doesn't really provide any extra functionality over and above a real desk calculator. Besides, users shouldn't be forced to work with just a calculator when they have a computer as their disposal.

The objective for Situation #2 is to create a module set that integrates into any business- or science-oriented project. It provides the user with a part-numerically, part-linguistically operated on-screen device that looks like a calculator but has the formula-solving features of an entire spreadsheet. The user can pull up this module set in the midst of another Visual Basic application or another Windows application, "dial" a formula that helps solve a particular, quick problem—a financial or a geometric problem, for example—and be presented with a verbally oriented representation of the chosen formula. Rather than press a mind-numbing series of buttons, the user can fill in the blanks. After the user solves the formula, the solution value appears in the calculator's readout and can be transferred to the main application. The effect is related to the entry of a formula (rather than a raw value) in a spreadsheet cell; the program solves for the formula and leaves the value in the cell. The Visual Basic module set, in effect, solves for a data field in a form.

My original objective for the Expressor project was somewhat foggy; in other words, I did not have a tremendously clear idea about what I was attempting to create. I doubt every novelist knows the precise plot of her book before she starts the first chapter. Likewise, I had a fairly clear idea of what my conclusion would be, without a great deal of insight as to how I would reach that conclusion. I knew that what I eventually wanted was a programmable calculator with some of the benefits of using Windows. I wanted it to be a calculator for users with a general comprehension of mathematical formulas—without having to memorize them beforehand. The Expressor would be less reliant on buttons and more reliant on language.

How the
Expressor
works.

Here's how it works. A series of slots on the face of the calculator act as its primary memories. The calculator maintains a list of memorized formulas whose variables have names, which also are memorized. When the user selects a formula to solve, the names for each of the constituent variables for that formula appear within the slots. Beside them, the user may enter values for the formula to solve (in later editions, the Expressor solves for ranges of values). The user may either use the standard calculator entry system to derive a value and then copy that value from the display to the memory slot or type that value in the slot directly. The objective of the application is to give the user a more verbal understanding of the formula.

Haven't We Done This Already?

A calculator is one of the test applications in Microsoft's Programmer's Reference for Visual Basic. I ignored that entirely, as well as the six dozen or so other calculator applications published in the competing texts on the subject of Visual Basic. If a more efficient method of operating a calculator were to be found, I would have to discover it—or stumble upon it—myself. By admitting this initial uncertainty, I am suggesting that it is possible to learn more about programming without the aid of tutorial texts; I run the risk of you putting this book down and experimenting with this notion.

In truth, if you intend to be an innovative programmer, each book you read on technique may hone your skills as a repeater of learned knowledge, though not necessarily as an innovator as well. The purpose of this history of my Expressor calculator project is not to give you yet another calculator to add to the Accessories group of your Program Manager, but to offer you the experience of an adventure in innovation. Definitely, I am painting an all too romantic picture about something that has little effect on world affairs (though I'm often tempted to mail certain world leaders a copy of the Expressor for use in tallying certain massive debts).

> **Principle Note:** When developing a large application from scratch, choose one part of the application you can make fully functional and concentrate on that, before you proceed to some other part.

Figure 1.4 depicts how the Expressor looked at birth—something like the cradle of a slim-line telephone. My first step in programming the Expressor was the very thing I said I wouldn't do: draw buttons first and assign code to them later. This is programming backwards; a programmer more accustomed to conventional BASIC creates the mathematics first and applies the special effects later. Visual Basic turns this backward thinking into an advantage. By drawing the buttons first and giving them .Name properties, the interpreter automatically prepares the framework for the procedures that govern their behavior.

Figure 1.4. The newborn Expressor, which, as of yet, is merely an echoer of digits.

Where does a
programmer
begin?

I have always programmed to make some small part of the project work completely and correctly *first*, partly for psychological reasons. I am reminded I know what I'm doing when I see something actually work. This renewal of self-confidence can save hours in supreme stupefaction over the enormity of the task at hand. Back in the '70s, before I read the *Creative Computing* magazine tutorials on programming, I tried to learn BASIC by intensely studying existing program listings printed on paper. Mind you, I did not own a computer at the time, so I was deciphering these program listings by comparing them to printouts and screen dumps of the output. At that time, BASIC programs had instruction numbers before each line—10, 20, 30 and so on. Because of this, the execution of programs often began, well, at the beginning, with the exception of certain subroutines generally tacked to the end of the program. (Notice Visual Basic programs often do not begin at the beginning, which is a fact reported in detail in later pages.)

Believing a program exudes from the brain as though it had a spout for such purposes, I made my first attempts at programming with one working element—the title page. I sometimes produced brilliant title pages, with my signature emblazoning the screen with blue laser light. Someplace on a set of rapidly decaying diskettes is a collection of dozens of title pages, resting suspended in a dust of chromium and confusion, in the Zone of Incompletion.

Programming
versus
sculpting.

To assume that every method and process for a large application is preconceived is as ludicrous as to assume a marble sculptor first imagines his model suspended in an eighteen-foot cube of marble and then with a chisel, works down to a perfectly polished, completed form. A true sculptor might use plaster to model his work in a miniature he can hold in his hands, add plaster to it gradually, and remove and replace an arm or an eyebrow to and from it at will. When he begins work on the actual marble, he may shape it so it starts to resemble the form he's modeling. Often, however, in an attempt to give a human form some semblance of life, the sculptor finishes some small part right at first—an eye, or a shoulder blade, or an outstretched hand. The rest of the form then eases into shape more easily when that one living piece reaches up from the depths.

Regardless of the distinctions Visual Basic draws among procedural contexts, variable scopes, and program modules, and despite its time-saving tools for designing forms, the interpreter gives you as programmer the rough equivalent of a chisel. With it, you attack the block of marble that is the Visual Basic project one piece at a time. It often makes more sense to work at first on the procedural level rather than the global.

The Core Context

For the usage model of the Expressor project, it made sense at first for me to give the buttons `.Name` properties, starting with the top row, of `Button7`, `Button8`, `Button9`, and so on. I wrote a procedure for `Button7` that placed the digit 7 in the upper readout, which was a label control I called `Readout`. Here's the first instruction I wrote for the entire project:

```
Sub Button7_Click ()
Readout.Caption = Readout.Caption + "7"
End Sub
```

From here, I started applying logic. I didn't want to allow the user to add digits forever; there must be some reasonable limit to the extent of the readout. I limited the readout to 19 digits (for reasons I have since forgotten) using the `Len()` function as follows:

```
Sub Button7_Click ()
If Len(Readout.Caption) < 20 Then
    Readout.Caption = Readout.Caption + "7"
End If
End Sub
```

> **Technique Note:** Indenting instructions typed in the midst of clauses—such as the previous If-Then clause—helps to identify the existence and extent of the clause. Tabs do not affect the execution of the Visual Basic program.

Avoiding premature and undue limitations.

For the decimal point button I named ButtonPoint, it makes sense to copy and paste the previous procedure into the Sub ButtonPoint_Click () framework. However, the number in the readout may be interpretable only if it contains no more than one decimal point. The program, therefore, has to know whether there's a decimal point or not. Logically, the procedure might attempt to convert the alphanumeric contents of the Readout label to a numeric value using the Val() function. In the event of failure or an error, it invokes an error-trap routine that assumes one too many decimal points in the display. Certainly, at this stage, ButtonPoint can be the only culprit preventing the textual contents from being successfully converted to a value, because every other character that can be sent to Readout now is a digit. Besides being cumbersome to implement, another type of character at some future date in the Expressor's development may prevent Val() from translating Readout.Caption to a numeric value—for instance, a hexadecimal digit such as "C."

> **Technique Note:** Whenever possible, assume your program is capable of doing more than it does now. Avoid limiting the extent of your logic to the present capabilities of the program.

Flag variables.

Furthermore, a constant reevaluation of the contents of Readout.Caption hampers the effectiveness of the program. Its behavior becomes a bit paranoid, constantly asking the interpreter, "Is this a number now? How about now? How about if we add this?" and so on. Instead, it's easier if the program is told once that there's one decimal point in the readout "and don't add another one there, please."

In Visual Basic, when the purpose of an instruction is really to ask the interpreter about the status of something in your program, the response you receive from the interpreter is purely symbolic. It is up to you as programmer to develop the code for this symbolism. In other words, the response to "Is the box red or white?" or "Which user is online at the moment?" will be phrased by the interpreter using a code developed by you. However, if the answer to a question you pose may be phrased as yes or no, true or false, on or off, the code for the response already exists, and the interpreter already recognizes it.

Whatever symbolism you choose to use, there is one overall rule that applies to the symbology: Since the number of possible symbols is both finite and integral, the variable you use for representing the response symbol will be an integer variable. Because the number of possible responses is always whole (you can't have half an answer), you don't need any fractional storage space for the variable. A variable that represents a yes/no or true/false answer—in other words, a binary state—is a flag variable.

Technique Capsule: Flag Variables

Definition: A flag variable is an arbitrarily named term whose value at any one time in the program represents a binary state. In such cases, a binary state may be equivalent to a true/false state, a yes/no answer, an either/or response to a comparison, or any other situation requiring a one-state-or-the-other representation. A flag variable is independent of any graphics objects currently existing within any form in the Visual Basic project.

Execution: The most common method available to the programmer of Visual Basic 2 for representing true/false states is to use the language's pairs of internal constants: True and False, On and Off, or Yes and No. In each pair, the numeric value of the former constant is always -1, and the value of the latter constant is always 0. In cases where the explicit use of -1 and 0 is not descriptive enough, you may choose instead to declare constants within the declarations section of the module, or within the global module, if present. Here are some example declarations:

```
Const BLACK = -1
Const WHITE = 0

Const IN = -1
Const OUT = 0
```

Declaration of a flag variable pertinent to True/False, BLACK/WHITE, and IN/ OUT cases might appear as follows:

```
Static state As Integer
Dim side As Integer
Global direction As Integer
```

Assign a value to a flag variable in the traditional fashion of an expression of assignment:

```
state = True
```

You can use a flag variable in an expression of comparison:

```
If side = BLACK Then
    .
    .
    .
End If
```

A flag variable is useful in any type of conditional clause:

```
Select Case direction
    Case IN
        .
        .
        .
    Case OUT
        .
        .
        .
End Select
```

Cautions: A flag variable is most useful if its declared scope is broader than local. Because a strictly local variable reinitializes upon the execution of End Sub or Exit Sub, its value—if it is declared numeric—resets to 0. As a flag variable, 0 has meaning, so the initialized value of a numeric local variable always is False or No. If the flag variable is not formally declared with Global, Dim at the modular level, or Static at the procedure level, Visual Basic 2 gives it the default type of Variant. This means the flag variable appears to have no value whatsoever (not even zero) until an instruction explicitly gives it a value. When a noninitialized and nondeclared flag variable is invoked in a logical comparison, such as If Not State Then—even and especially if State does not equal anything—the logical expression Not State evaluates True, just as if State = 0, or False, or No.

There is a danger in using LEFT and RIGHT as constants with the Const statement, because these words also are reserved keywords in the Visual Basic vocabulary. Left and Right are part of the Left$() and Right$() functions (the $ is now optional in all string functions), and the .Left property is part of the coordinate system for graphics objects.

The flag variable I created for Sub ButtonPoint_Click () is point_lock, whose value may be set to True or False. Surmising only this procedure makes use of point_lock, I declared it to be Static. Here's how the procedure first appeared:

```
Sub ButtonPoint_Click ()
Static point_lock As Integer
If point_lock = False Then
    Readout.Caption = Readout.Caption + "."
    point_lock = True
End If
End Sub
```

This procedure remembers the value of point_lock. (In this context, it is the only procedure that does.) After the conditional clause is executed once, it cannot be executed again until some other procedure sets point_lock to False. Conceivably, this can be the procedure for the Clear button, or whatever instruction differentiates between the end of input for the previous value into the readout and the beginning of the next value.

This brings up the next problem: How can the program know when one number ends and the next one begins? Evidently some signal can be sent with the function buttons: when the user of a calculator presses "plus" or "times," it must mean she's through entering the current value into the display.

At first, I toyed with the idea of invoking a variable ready as a flag variable, to be set to True when an entered value has been properly terminated. I tried the following with success:

```
Sub Button7_Click ()
If Len(Readout.Caption) < 20 and ready = False Then
    Readout.Caption = Readout.Caption + "7"
Else
    Readout.Caption = "7"
End If
End Sub
```

The addition to the second line makes it impossible to add "7" to the current value unless ready = False. If a procedure attached to the mathematical function buttons sets ready to True, the next "7" typed clears the readout except for the first "7" digit in the value.

Rethinking this process led me to the following conclusion: why make two comparisons with the If-Then statement, joined with And, when you can make one instead? If ready is a tally of the number of characters in the readout (previously represented by Len(Readout.Caption)) and the value of ready is positive (non-zero), it must be accepting new input. If the user, pressing a function button, terminates value entry, the _Click procedure for that button can signal that termination by setting ready to 0 (or False, but because ready never sets to True, this syntax might appear cumbersome).

> **Technique Note:** You can consider a variable a *virtual flag* if its positive/zero value can represent a true/false binary state.

After implementing variable ready as a virtual flag, the procedure appeared as follows:

```
Sub Button7_Click ()
If ready < 20 Then
    Readout.Caption = Readout.Caption + "7"
    ready = ready + 1
Else
    Readout.Caption = "7"
    ready = 1
End If
End Sub
```

After I completed the Sub ButtonPoint_Click () procedure, it appeared as follows:

```
Sub ButtonPoint_Click ()
Static point_lock As Integer
If point_lock = False And ready < 20 Then
    Readout.Caption = Readout.Caption + "."
    point_lock = True
```

```
    ready = ready + 1
End If
assess_readout
End Sub
```

The presence of `assess_readout` is the result of an idea whose full benefit had yet to come to fruition in Expressor I. In Visual Basic, any term on a line by itself that is not part of the machine's existing vocabulary is considered to be a call to a procedure; you may use the keyword `Call` to identify a procedure call, as in `Call assess_readout`.

Originally I had written in this position the instruction `readout_value = Val(Readout.Caption)`. The purpose of this instruction is to translate the caption of the text box into a real value for the sake of the program. I moved the instruction into procedure `Sub assess_readout ()` with the idea that, eventually, the value conversion process becomes far more detailed than a single instruction, especially if numeric base conversion is someday implemented (in Expressor III, it was). My hope was to eliminate redundancy in the source code of the program; I saw no reason for having eleven event procedures, each with several instructions that performed the same purpose.

As it turned out, I never really developed `Sub assess_readout ()` for Mark I, but left it in nonetheless. Here is the entire procedure:

```
Sub assess_readout ()
readout_value = Val(Readout.Caption)
End Sub
```

If I had stopped the project at Mark I, I might have taken out this procedure and placed its single constituent instruction where I originally wrote it. Frankly, the procedure isn't entirely necessary in the current context of the program. The presence of `Sub assess_readout ()` did pay off, however, in successive editions of the Expressor: leaving the hooks in made the program easier to upgrade later.

Technique Note: When programming for the future, put in the "hooks" for later procedures now, even if the contents of these procedures are presently relatively empty. Call this methodology "planting early."

Eliminating Redundancy, Repetition, and Redundancy

Control arrays.   The easiest way to program is not necessarily the most efficient way. There are 10 number buttons in the Expressor program, the nonzero types each having identical behavior. Cut-and-paste with the code editor might appear to be the solution here for replicating the instructions that define their uniform behavior; through a clever manipulation of object-oriented syntax, however, you can use one procedure to define the behavior for all nine positive-value buttons.

You generally first see control arrays used in option and check sets, usually within a frame control. All the indicatable objects within the frame receive the same .Name property, but each individual object has an exclusive subscript in the form of an .Index property that identifies the object specifically. You can extend control arrays, however, to include and encompass regular command buttons.

Technique Capsule: Non-Option Control Arrays

Definition: A non-option control array is a set of related graphics objects within a form that are not option dots or check boxes. By definition, the .Index properties of the objects in a non-option array have some pertinence to the program other than to identify the control. You can use the .Index to send some value to the interpreter that represents, for instance, a selection from a classical numeric menu or a cell in a small grid.

Execution: Control arrays are not variables; thus, they are not dimensioned. When the first graphics object (control) in the array is drawn on the form, the object receives all the properties that distinguish this array. You then copy the object to the Windows system clipboard, using Edit/Copy. It is crucial at this point to indicate (surround by eight indicator nodes) the graphics object acting as the container for this control array—the form itself or a frame within that form. You can indicate the form itself, outside the objects within it, by clicking on its background. Upon selecting Edit/Paste, successive objects in the control array—clones, if you will—appear within the formerly indicated collector or "parent" object.

Example: Assume you have six command buttons in a control array called FrontMenu. Each button on the form precedes a listing for a selectable division of the program, such as Accounts Receivable or Purchasing. The following procedure can send control of the program to the chosen division:

```
Sub FrontMenu_Click (Index As Integer)
Select Case Index
    Case 1
        accounts_receivable
    Case 2
        accounts_payable
    Case 3
        purchasing
    Case 4
        sale_tracking
    Case 5
        payroll
    Case 6
        customers
End Select
```

Example: In a library catalog search program, a 10x4 grid of text labels acts as a selector control for enumerated categories in the Dewey Decimal System. The Dewey System is divided into 10 main categories of nonfiction subjects, numbered 000, 100, 200, and so on. Subcategories in the Dewey System are represented as 001, 150, 290, and so on. In the 40-button control array, there are 10 columns for each category and four rows designating subcategories in increments of 25. Each book category receives its own data file in the program, ordered by Dewey number, so the subcategory increments can help the file pointer search for a particular record.

The arrangement of the buttons in this example is tabular, thus two-dimensional, whereas the shape of a control array in Visual Basic is one-dimensional. You can determine the category and subcategory increments mathematically as follows:

```
Sub Dewey_Click (Index As Integer)
    category = CInt(Index / 10) * 4 - 1
    subcategory = 100 / (Index Mod 10)
    filespec$ = LTrim$(Str$(category)) + "00"
    subcat$ = LTrim$(Str$(subcategory))
    .
    .
    .
End Sub
```

In this example, the contents of `filespec$` are set to the "hundreds" category for the chosen Dewey topic, by deriving the single digit character from the Index of the array and adding the characters `00`. Later in the program, an instruction may use `filespec$` as the filename for a data set being loaded into memory with the `Open` statement. The contents of `subcat$` may then be used to point to a particular subdivision of the data file.

Cautions: Under normal conditions, you may choose names for variables in Visual Basic arbitrarily. The Visual Basic interpreter is notoriously confused when the word `Index` in the `Sub` procedure declaration line is changed to some other name. Although `Index` acts like an integer variable for the sake of the procedure, `.Index` is also a property, and you can address a property without its antecedent when the object being referred to by the property is the topic object of the event procedure. In the previous example, `Index` refers to the antecedent object `Dewey` without stating so explicitly. For safety's sake, leave the term `Index` as it is.

By taking off the positively numbered buttons drawn in the Expressor form thus far and replacing them with a control array called `ButtonPos`, I was able to define these buttons' behavior with a single event procedure, listed here:

```
Sub ButtonPos_Click (Index As Integer)
If ready > 0 Then
    If ready < 20 Then
        Readout.Caption = Readout.Caption
    + Right$(Str$(Index), 1)
        ready = ready + 1
    End If
Else
    Readout.Caption = Right$(Str$(Index), 1)
    ready = 1
End If
assess_readout
End Sub
```
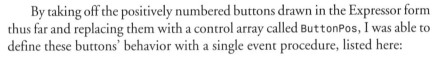

I used the expression `Right$(Str$(Index), 1)` rather than `"7"` or `"8"` or `"9"`. With the non-option control array, arithmetic determines for me what value the program must use at any one time.

The zero key behaves differently from the positively-numbered buttons in one important respect: when the readout is "clear," it already contains a zero. If the user presses the zero key at this time, the readout should not show "00."

Entry of further zeros by the user should now be disabled until there's an absolute value in the readout. Therefore, I used the text of Sub ButtonPos_Click () as a model, copying the text into the framework of Sub Button0_Click () and amending it as follows:

```
Sub Button0_Click ()
If ready > 0 And ready < 20 Then
    Readout.Caption = Readout.Caption + "0"
    ready = ready + 1
End If
assess_readout
End Sub
```

The key addition here is the comparative expression ready > 0 to the If-Then clause. It allows only the instructions within the clause to execute if there's already one real digit in the readout—in other words, not just a zero. When the readout has just a zero in it, the value of ready is zero, as though there are no digits in the readout at all. Pressing a positive digit key triggers the first instance of the instruction that renders ready positive, ready = ready + 1. With ready now positive, you can execute the conditional clause in the preceding procedure. Notice, Sub Button0_Click ()'s version of ready = ready + 1 is protected from being executed unless the condition ready > 0 solves true, and that can happen only if ready was incremented earlier.

At this point, you have a functional program. It accepts input from the keypad simulated on the front panel and echoes that input to a readout. This functional program really doesn't do anything—that is, anything useful—but it works, and you can save it. This is the first main layer in the development of the Expressor application. Feel free now to stop, fix yourself a sandwich, watch your screen saver plot its warp speed starfield, and contemplate the next layer of development.

The Birth of the Application

The computer has yet to fulfill the mission for which it was created. Historically, it has resulted in more work for the people who use it, rather than a reduction of the workload. The reason for this has more to do with the integration of the machine into the workplace: there continues to be an overall lack of understanding of the computer's capabilities and limitations.

The first languages were user programs.

The original objective of the first developers of computers was to allow *users* *(read: programmers)* to communicate with the computer via a language. Having a nonprogrammer use the computer by means of an *application* came late in the conceptual development of computing. In the 1960s, the development of the *user program* greatly accelerated. Back then, the user program performed the role of both the operating system and the application. In other words, not only did the program handle the task of acquiring input from the user, but the low-level interactions with core memory as well. The early developers, however, didn't see the role of the user program as being dual at this point. They saw it as a means to cover up the low-level logic that comprised the everyday lexicon between human and machine, with high-level linguistic terms.

COBOL (COmmon Business-Oriented Language) became one of the more successful user programs of its day, though FORTRAN (FORmula TRANslator) became one of the primary models for the first edition of BASIC. IBM sold FORTRAN to its 1960s customers with the premise it was part-algebra and part-English, and that communicating with the computer for an ordinary businessperson eventually could become second nature.

The idea that language isn't necessary to achieve proper human/computer interaction is a relatively recent one. The idea began circulating about 1981, with the advent of VisiCalc, the first modern spreadsheet program. It gained popularity in 1984 after Apple's agressive Macintosh marketing campaign convinced computing newcomers that language wasn't altogether a necessary tool—that graphical symbology can be far more efficient.

Suddenly, language was something to fear, even shun. Common User Access is a standard for the appearance of graphical applications from the user's point of view; this standard is ongoing and officially the product of a consortium of software manufacturers—though some of those manufacturers tend to disagree. CUA has convinced software manufacturers and thousands of programmers that symbology is the key and that the process of input to a computer can be divided into two user events, which I call *disclosure* and *directive*. The CUA application presents the user with a form for entering data elements into fields in sequence or at random. This selective input of data is disclosure. Directive is then the process of the user giving the program a command or a response to an option. Menus and buttons are the primary tools here, and where appropriate, CUA prefers you to use symbological icons for your buttons.

Granted, the *U* in CUA presumes the standard deals only with computer users, who are widely seen as different people altogether than computer programmers. However, the role of Visual Basic—a piece of software designed for programmers—in the work environment is not extraordinarily different from the role of Excel or Access or even the more task-specific applications such as PerForm Pro and Quicken. These are programs designed for users, yet to varying degrees, the users must adapt these programs to their specific work environments—to find an application for them.

In the older sense of the word, some modern applications—especially Excel, 1-2-3, and database management systems such as FoxPro—are *programmed* by their users. Because the Windows editions of these programs interact so tightly with the Windows environment, the joining of application and environment might be the modern equivalent of the user programs of the 1960s. Whenever designers of a software package have extended its capacity to be customized by users so that they can create original applications for it, however, they have employed background languages. It appears disclosure and directive are not the only two elements of communication between human and machine; at some point in the process, there must be description. Only through a language can there be complete communication between the user and software.

THE STRUCTURE OF VISUAL BASIC

The objective of this chapter is to demonstrate the unique composition of the Visual Basic programming language. Visual Basic is the product of three decades of evolution. The history of BASIC can be likened to the history of the written English language, which itself is a product of genius, circumstance, colloquialism, and conquests. This chapter may give you a greater appreciation of the power of language to express a concept, even when that language is bound by the laws of procedural algebraic syntax.

2

I'm Afraid I Can't
Do That, Dave

One of the primary fears held by the previous generation of computer users was that, at some time, computers might become intelligent and efficient enough to coalesce eventually, form some sort of alliance or political party, and on their own, seize control of the world, rendering everyone pawns of the computer. The fear that pervades computer users today transcends from the computer to the programmer. Today, people believe the operation of the computer might eventually become so complex (and thereby inefficient) that the skill level needed to process a simple business form will, in time, confound even the most able office workers, rendering them pawns of the computer.

The older fear has yet to die off completely, but individuals' growing experience with the microcomputer has led them (correctly) to conclude it is no more capable of seizing control of world affairs than is a similar coalition of microwave ovens or trash compactors. The newer fear is far more rational and justified, though equally as paranoid. We programmers who have followed the development of computing from the first high-level programming languages to Visual Basic and have concluded computing has somehow grown progressively simpler, are kidding ourselves. Because the tools for operating a computer are now more tangible and comfortable to the computer user (clicking an image of a button with the mouse, for instance, rather than punching infinite holes in a paper card with a straight pin) the workload of the computer has grown proportionally over time. Both users and programmers continue to conceive new applications for it almost daily, having been inspired by its exponentially growing capabilities. It takes an idealist to believe the computer can possibly perform to everyone's expectations.

The programmer's role in 1953 was to define a mathematical formula as a problem, feed it into the computer with some device that sets the proper circuits to on or off, and wait to see whether the machine renders a result or blows a tube. If you've studied assembly language programming, you'd be surprised at the degree of resemblance between today's assembly language and the programming systems of 1953, such as EDSAC. The mechanism of a logical processor is simple; by Newtonian standards, a computer is perhaps the simplest of all conceivable machines. The principle of assembly language, therefore, is quite simple—there's a virtual one-to-one correlation between what you want the machine to do and the term you use to make it do it. As to the question of what the EDSAC programmers could do with their computer, the answer is, not much. The machine using EDSAC was about as functionally capable as a modern programmable calculator.

The Smash Hit That Flopped at Its New York Debut

In the early 1950s, the computer was a formula solver and a tabulator. It could have kept records if there had been a storage mechanism capable of maintaining a practical database. At that time, however, the long-playing album was a miracle of science. When the computer finally became fast enough to solve formulas, NBC Television gave an RCA model its American premiere in November 1960 before a live audience. It sat under glass on the lower floor of the RCA Exhibition Hall on 49th Street in New York City making predictions about the Kennedy-Nixon race while Huntley and Brinkley "spoke" to it from Studio 8H in Rockefeller Center. Based on results from the precincts tabulated thus far, the RCA unit predicted Kennedy to win one hour and Nixon the next.

What the television audience saw was the face of the RCA model and a superimposed predicted final tally that represented the entire output of the machine. What the public did not see was the people feeding vote tallies into the machine through what was then a rather sophisticated input device—a row of toggle switches. What the public also did not see was the computer actually shutting down (that's right, a fatal error) before the night was over. Bugs in the machinery or not, there is this to consider: Training an ordinary office worker to use the RCA's toggle switches, after the initial apprehension subsided, was actually easy. All the RCA did was render the result of a linear mathematical formula; that was as much application as the machinery of the time could handle. Still, the myth must be disproven that computers have grown easier to use over the years. They have not.

The same formula used to predict the outcome of the election in 1960 could be easily programmed into a 1-2-3 spreadsheet. I say "easily" because by now, we're more accustomed to computers, and simple linear formulas are the order of the day for programmers, even with something as low-level as 1-2-3. Think back, however, and replace that 1960 RCA computer with a 486DX2 running Windows and 1-2-3. Could the same trainer teach the same ordinary office worker to operate the 486 with results at least as successful as on that night in November?

Now, while you're pondering that question, consider the ordinary office worker of 1960 and place that person beside the ordinary office worker of 1993. Is one office worker so much more evolved a specimen that more complex machinery is by nature less confusing to her than to the less-evolved office worker? Are people in general simply more *compatible* with technology today than they were three decades ago? These questions presume humans must evolve somehow to catch up with technology. It rings with the echo of the early fear that computers evolve like species, perhaps with plans of world domination. Actually, it is technology's duty to adapt to human beings, not through evolution but through reconstruction. This is the job of the programmer—you.

Machines are not subject to the laws of social Darwinism. More often, they are products of the laws of capitalism and marketing. A measure of supply-and-demand thinking governs every program you write. In this business, however, your clientele, your public, cannot know what to demand unless you supply a sampling—an exhibition, if you will—of the future. You invent what your customers will eventually want. You might be clairvoyant, or you might choose to be an idealist.

Adding the Functionality Layer

Symbological programming languages existed before computers themselves were actually able to interpret the symbology. As an alternative to flowcharting, a type of pseudocode language was developed in the late 1950s, called ALGOL—ALGOrithmic Language. Programmers used this language on paper only to correlate their thoughts; they later restructured these thoughts into assembly language themselves. IBM's FORTRAN was the first language whose symbols bore a one-to-one correlation with symbols a computer program could comprehend—or, to be more precise about the terminology, parse. The more capable computers of the early '60s were capable of performing the parsing themselves, while lower-order models actually had FORTRAN programmers refer to a book which denoted which holes needed to be punched into a card to represent their instructions. In any event, human beings were the first programming language interpreters, and in a strange way they were the precursors of Visual Basic.

As language systems have developed, the symbology used to phrase instructions has become less and less directly symbological and more expressive. A thorough understanding of the programming process includes a study of direct and indirect representations of functionality and the benefits and shortcomings of both.

Situation #2: The Expressor Mark II Calculator

To demonstrate the exclusive role of language in computing, I pick up now where I left off in Chapter 1, "Computing with a Language." What must be added at this point to the Expressor Mark I are the four-function buttons on the right side of the calculator's input panel. There are two models of operation for the modern pocket calculator. The most common model is algebraic notation or "TI notation," (named after Texas Instruments, which made it popular). The less common model is used by heavy-duty scientific programmable calculators—most notably, those made by Hewlett-Packard—and is Reverse Polish Notation (RPN).

Calculator notations.

The difference between the two relates to the order in which the user presses the buttons on the keypad—that is, the time at which the functions those buttons refer to are actually executed. Figure 2.1 demonstrates the differences between the two notations, with respect to a simple mathematical formula.

Because of Visual Basic's design, clicking a command button activates an event procedure that performs the function of that specific button. The immediate problem with implementing algebraic notation is that clicking a button must initiate an event procedure for some other button—namely, the function button previously pressed. If no function button was pressed yet, well, nothing happens. The event is put in a holding queue until the next function button is pressed.

RPN does not present this problem, because clicking Enter causes addition to happen now and clicking X causes multiplication to happen now. RPN is obviously more suitable to the natural structure of Visual Basic; therefore, I chose to utilize RPN first, and quite frankly, it's the easiest method to implement.

Although it might appear to the user that a calculator is solving for a large equation, actually its program is extremely simple. Whether it uses TI or RPN notation, the calculating program remembers only two values—the one currently in the readout and the one in the previous readout. For the Expressor, I chose to call these values `readout_value` and `combine_value`, respectively. I made this decision before completing the button routines, and I wrote the following declarations in the general declarations area of the global module EXPRESOR.GBL:

```
Global readout_value As Double, combine_value As Double
Global ready As Integer
```

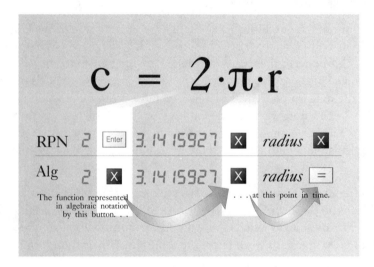

Figure 2.1. Instantaneous and delayed reactions.

What's a Global For?

Planning
ahead with the
global module.

A rational question you might ask at this point is, why did I implement a global module in a single-form, single-module application? Logically, a variable declared with modular scope in the general declarations area of EXPRESOR.FRM would have the same overall scope as a global variable for the project. Again, my reasoning related to planning for the future. I wanted graph and table plotting features at some future date. I estimated early that these three variables would be pertinent to any extra modules I might add later. (By the way, I guessed wrong about `ready`, the variable that represents the number of user-entered digits in the readout. I only needed it for the calculator form, so I later moved the declaration to the modular level and edited it to read Dim ready As Integer.)

My first implemented function was addition. Here's how the event procedure looked upon completion:

```
Sub Enter_Click ()
assess_readout
readout_value = readout_value + combine_value
combine_value = readout_value
Readout.Caption = Str$(readout_value)
ready = 0
End Sub
```

This procedure works the way any calculator works: the calculator keeps one value in its memory—the one I call combine_value—besides the value it holds in its readout. When a function is invoked, it uses the display value as the *operand* and the combine value as the object of the function. When the function is completed, the result displays in the readout, and that readout value *becomes* the combine value. This process is shown in the preceding BASIC code with little else to cloud it. I set ready = 0 at the end of the procedure so that if the user presses a digit key now, the readout immediately clears; the program at this point believes no real digits are in the readout. Some might call this clever programming, others "lying;" in any event, the scheme works.

The next two procedures use a less clever technique:

Cut-and-paste as a legitimate technique.

```
Sub Minus_Click ()
assess_readout
readout_value = readout_value - combine_value
combine_value = readout_value
Readout.Caption = Str$(readout_value)
ready = 0
End Sub

Sub Times_Click ()
assess_readout
readout_value = readout_value * combine_value
combine_value = readout_value
Readout.Caption = Str$(readout_value)
ready = 0
End Sub
```

This technique is pure cut-and-paste, and it demonstrates the power of the modern programmer's code editor program. Only the operators in these two routines have been changed. The division operation required only minor modification:

```
Sub DividedBy_Click ()
assess_readout
If readout_value <> 0 And combine_value <> 0 Then
    readout_value = readout_value / combine_value
End If
combine_value = readout_value
Readout.Caption = Str$(readout_value)
ready = 0
End Sub
```

Avoiding division by zero.

The Visual Basic interpreter does not allow the use of the value 0 as the denominator for any mathematical operations involving division, because there is no real answer. If you try dividing by zero or by a variable whose value is zero (or by an uninitialized variable) you receive a "Division by Zero" error. This is why the division instruction is encased here inside a conditional clause; rather than tell the Expressor's user, "You're wrong, you used a zero in division, go home and sulk," I prohibited the operation from proceeding. The lack of explanation might confuse the user, but anyone who tries division by zero must be confused anyway; confirming for that person that he's confused is not the role of an application, but more for a self-help book.

Implementing the four functions of the calculator took less than half an hour of thinking and execution. I could brag and admit this scheme worked right on the first try; however, this is a book about the reality of programming, and the reality here—as it is with many more complex programs—is that the primary function of the program is often the easiest part to implement.

The easiest function to implement thus far was the percent button, whose event procedure appears as follows:

```
Sub Percent_Click ()
readout_value = readout_value / 100
Readout.Caption = Str$(readout_value)
ready = 0
End Sub
```

If you've used the percent button on a real calculator, you know you can multiply a number by 45%, which can be entered as [4][5][%] rather than [.][4][5], although the two sequences result in the same entry in the readout. All the percent button does is adjust the value in the readout, having nothing to do with combine_value. This is why you don't find that variable in this procedure.

Strangely enough, it took me more time to implement the readout-clearing event procedures than it did the percent button.

```
Sub ClearAll_Click ()
Readout.Caption = "0"
readout_value = 0
combine_value = 0
ready = 0
End Sub


Sub ClearEntry_Click ()
Readout.Caption = "0"
readout_value = 0
ready = 0
End Sub
```

Procedure Sub ClearAll_Click () pertains to the "C" (clear) button, whereas procedure Sub ClearEntry_Click () pertains to the "CE" (clear entry) button. The clear-entry button erases only the readout, but does not forget the current combine value. The clear-all button makes the calculator forget everything pertinent. What took these procedures longer (by a few minutes) to implement was the question of where to place the ready = 0 instruction. I actually had the idea of maintaining a global flag variable function_on that would register true when a function button is being pressed. I later eliminated this flag variable, realizing ready always can be made to equal zero precisely whenever function_on registers true.

Technique Note: To eliminate redundancy, take time to study the status and flag variables you've created thus far, to see if their purposes at any time parallel one another. If they do, you might be able to eliminate some redundant variables entirely, or else redeclare their scopes to be more localized to a procedure.

You now have another completed layer, and the Expressor Mark I is now a calculator. Its linguistic functionality comprises the next layer, but for now you can save the project and take another of those sandwich/starfield/contemplation breaks so pertinent to the programming process.

The Structure of Assembly, or the Assembly of Structure

Machine
language
defined.

While you're on break, here's something to contemplate: Assembly language is a rudimentary way to symbolize the logical computing procedures of the central processor. The principle behind machine language—which is really assembly language without the added abbreviations—is profoundly simple. In fact, here it is: every logical path etched by the manufacturer into the silicon of the CPU is numbered. For a logical operation to take place, such as addition or the transfer of a value between internal registers, a predetermined set of electrical signals is sent down these numbered paths. The pattern of each electrical signal set is itself numbered, and the value of that number is equal to 2 to the power of each path containing a signal, added together. The resulting value is the numerological symbol for a logical operation. The set of all such values constitutes the language of the CPU. That, in a nutshell, is machine language.

If assembly language is as uncomplicated as raising etched electrical paths to the power of two, what is the point of BASIC? With assembly, your course of action is practically decided for you in advance by the mechanism of the processor. With BASIC, your choice of methodologies is arbitrary. The answer to this question is simple, but not easy: Human beings are baffled by excessive simplicity. This is not a defamation of humankind; to the contrary, this is an explanation of how our minds managed to evolve in the first place.

Any machine in the modern work environment must be complex enough for its user to negotiate its operation with ease. "Easy" and "simple," thus, are not synonymous in this context. From this axiom comes one of the primary principles of all programming: the simpler one makes the mechanism of his program, the more difficult it becomes for its user to apply it to his everyday work with ease. Take the classic example of the mismarketing of database management software during the 1980s. Customers used to compare the dBASE III database manager with its $800 price tag to some name-address-zip code "database manager" with its $39.95 price tag and ask, what's the difference? If both manage databases, why not buy the cheaper product? I've become a veteran of the fine art of answering this very question.

The inquisitive customer could not have known beforehand that one product prints mailing labels on cheap printers, whereas the other was built to supplement large operating systems. You could argue the el-cheapo database manager was the simplest product to devise, from the programmer's view. Handling successive individual lists guaranteed to contain only three lines of data, without having to bother with all that algorithmic comparison stuff, is no problem. You learned that in Chapter 1. Now, place yourself in the position of C. Wayne Ratliff, the inventor of dBASE and its original database format. Imagine what work it must be for a person such as Ratliff to conceive a program applicable to a multiplicity of tasks, a mere fraction of which might presently be conceived.

On the other side of the equation, place yourself in the role of the buyer of the $39.95 database manager. Here is a person who wants to maintain the mailing list for his company. In time, he'll spin off a company division and will want a separate list. This means, of course, installing the program once again in a different subdirectory and remembering to keep the filenames of each list generated separate from one another—so one list doesn't cancel the other out. Who's doing the management of the database now, the program or the user? Obviously, this cheap-but-simple program is not easy, because it is not applicable. The more complex program will eventually be the easiest for its users.

Crafting Unique Functionality

It's time to add something to Situation #1 to make this mere calculator into the unique Expressor I'd like for it to be. I want the user to see specific formulas it's capable of solving described in English, allowing her to simply fill in the blanks. The names of formulas programmed into the Expressor appear in a list box called CalcList. To solve a formula, the user first dials the name of this formula from the list control.

The textual contents of CalcList are assigned to it during the _Load event for the startup form. Here's the procedure:

```
Sub Form_Load ()
CalcList.AddItem "Surface Area of RC Cylinder"
CalcList.AddItem "Volume of RC Cylinder"
```

```
CalcList.AddItem "Zone Area of Sphere"
CalcList.AddItem "Force of Earth/Body Attraction"
CalcList.AddItem "Doppler Shift Transmitted Freq."
label$(0, 0) = "Radius of right circular cylinder"
label$(0, 1) = "Height of cylinder"
label$(1, 0) = "Radius of right circular cylinder"
label$(1, 1) = "Height of cylinder"
label$(2, 0) = "Radius of sphere"
label$(2, 1) = "Height of zone"
label$(3, 0) = "Mass of Earth"
label$(3, 1) = "Mass of body in Earth's grav. field"
label$(3, 2) = "Radius of Earth"
label$(3, 3) = "Distance of body above Earth's surface"
label$(4, 0) = "Observer velocity"
label$(4, 1) = "Source velocity"
label$(4, 2) = "Observed frequency"
label$(4, 3) = "Velocity of wave"
End Sub
```

I picked a set of five formulas out of the blue for the initial tests of the project. The array variable label$() contains descriptions for each of the parameters in the five formulas. When the user chooses a formula from CalcList, the Visual Basic interpreter determines the number of the chosen item in the list and responds by placing the corresponding label$() descriptions in the five slots belonging to the control array ParamText(). The following procedure performs this maneuver:

```
Sub CalcList_Click ()
For n = 0 To 4
    ParamText(n).Caption = label$(CalcList.ListIndex, n)
Next n
Clear_Params
End Sub
```

The first item in the VB list box is numbered 0, the second item 1, and so on. To correspond with this legendary offset, the first dimension of the two-dimensional array label$() is numbered 0. The .ListIndex number for the formula list is made to correspond directly to the first dimension of label$().

In the list box for this panel, the number of the current choice from this list is the .ListIndex property setting for the list. That property may be used to point to a set of parameter descriptions for the slots just above the list. CalcList.ListIndex is a pointer to the first dimension of the array label$(), which acts as the set number for each batch of parameter descriptions. label$ (1, *n*) refers to a description—such as "Velocity of wave"—that appears in set number 1. A few spaces are added to the end of the text so some space separates the text from the right side of the slot.

> **Technique Note:** Make the index numbers of related arrays and list controls correspond exactly. Otherwise, you must use a formula to convert the index of one array to the index of another when drawing relations between the two arrays.

The labels, now in their respective slots, point the way for the user to fill in the blanks. The array of blanks is called Param(), and they require no event procedures in order to work. The user can type entries in the blanks, or can transfer the result of the calculation currently in the readout to a specific blank, using one of a series of buttons in yet another control array called StoreBank(). The procedure for this is nothing more than a textual transfer, as shown here:

```
Sub StoreBank_Click (Index As Integer)
param(Index).text = Readout.Caption
ready = 0
End Sub
```

Here you see the major selling point for the entire utility—describing calculator formulas in English rather than with cryptic algebra and buttons—implemented in 19 setup instructions and six operational instructions. That's it. Once again, the most functional element of an application can be the smallest.

The formula-solving scheme at this stage in the Expressor's evolution is somewhat temporary. The setup for now is this: When the user presses the Apply Formula button, the _Click event procedure for that button acts as a multiplex branching hub leading to a set of Function procedures that solve the selected formula and render the result to the readout. Here's the temporary hub procedure:

```
Sub ApplyFormula_Click ()
For in = 0 To 4
p(in) = Val(param(in).Text)
Next in
```

```
ndx = CalcList.ListIndex
Select Case ndx
    Case 0
        solution = surf_area_rccyl(p(0), p(1))
    Case 1
        solution = volume_rccyl(p(0), p(1))
    Case 2
        solution = zone_sphere(p(0), p(1))
    Case 3
        solution = force_att(p(0), p(1), p(2), p(3))
    Case 4
        solution = dopp_shift(p(0), p(1), p(2), p(3))
    Case Else
        Exit Sub
End Select
Readout.Caption = Str$(solution)
End Sub
```

The array p() was declared modular at the beginning, so all the Function procedures that solve the particular formulas don't have to have the p() array passed to them—something of a redundant act.

Select Case is often preferable to multiple GoTo statements.

When I first developed this procedure, I utilized an old-style multiple branch with the On-GoTo statement. I began programming in BASIC in 1978, so I've written enough GoTos to create a pattern in my brain, an irreconcilable manual branching pattern that modern programming methodology doesn't help me overcome. In this particular instance, I revised the scheme using the arguably more efficient Select Case clause. Still, I'm not one to entirely discard GoTo and defend it whenever I can. So when I do find a legitimate use for it, you'll be the first to know.

You're at another end-of-layer pause now. The Expressor Mark I seems to be functioning adequately. Other programmers tend to call these moments "success"; I call them "dinner." I realize what time it is and decide to eat, or perhaps get some sleep. In any event, the way I gloat is by waxing philosophical.

The Evolution of Visual Basic's Phraseology

When John Kemeny and Thomas Kurtz created the BASIC programming language in 1964, they originally intended to make BASIC interpreters easy to write, by giving each BASIC instruction a uniform syntax. This syntax, in principle, would be based on the structure of assembly language. As you look at Visual Basic source code now, you probably see little resemblance to assembly language; frankly, if you did see a resemblance, chances are great you might not be reading this book now, but rather a guide to Turbo Pascal.

Assembly languages date back to about 1947 and have since been constructed amazingly similar to one another. Nearly all assembly languages ever conceived break instructions into two parts, whose syntax appears as follows:

Assembly language syntax.

```
opcode     [operand]
```

The term opcode in this syntax is an early word for *command* and is short for *op*eration *code*. In assembly language, an opcode might tell the CPU to perform such things as fetch a byte from an index register, add a comparison value to the CPU's accumulator, or jump to some other instruction in the program. The operand, when present, refers to some specific register of the CPU. Later in the development of microprocessors, the operand in an assembly language instruction could refer to an address of memory, or even to a specific undeclared value. The resulting instruction bore the syntax of a simple English-language sentence, where opcode acted as the verb and operand the object. The subject, to borrow a phrase from English grammar, was always an "understood you."

Believe it or not, early BASIC borrowed this same syntax from assembly language. John Kemeny (who later became the president of Dartmouth College) was working prior to 1964 on a standard for assembly languages called DARSIMCO for DARtmouth SIMplified COde. At the same time, Thomas Kurtz at another office of the college was working on a project to make ALGOL into a real programming language.

You can see where the paths of these two men converged. Both Kemeny and Kurtz believed then—and still believe—in maintaining a fundamental simplicity of instruction syntax. For this reason, they followed the opcode/operand syntax in the first editions of BASIC. Each instruction was on a line by

BASIC borrows its primary syntax from assembly.

itself and was divided into two parts: the operation code first, followed by the terms of that operation. The general syntax of the following old-form instructions, therefore, had the same two-part breakdown:

```
10    LET B = 5
20    LET A = A + 5
30    GOTO 670
```

Respectively, these instructions fetched a value into a variable, added a value to an accumulative variable, and jumped to some other instruction. The focus of the sales pitch for BASIC in the late 1960s was hardware manufacturers, such as General Electric, who might want to distribute the language with their machines; it stated a high-level programming language was now not much more trouble to implement than a low-level language such as pure assembly.

Distinction between low- and high-level languages.

What do I mean by low-level and high-level languages? These are early terms that still work well in describing the type of reasoning required for the *human* to interpret a programming language. In a low-level language such as an assembly language, the symbology employed resembles more the way the computer or central processor receives instructions. In a high-level language such as BASIC, COBOL, or C, the symbology employed resembles more the way a human receives and responds to instructions. The interpreter or compiler for a high-level language requires at least one extra symbological "pass" of reinterpretation before the computer may understand what instructions it's being given.

Not long into the development of BASIC at Dartmouth College, Kemeny and Kurtz added functions to the language, for a type of embedded instruction. The syntax of this instruction was still two-part, though it resided in the operand section of the larger body of the instruction, as in this example:

```
50    C = INT(2 * 3.1415927 * R)
```

Here, INT() is an embedded instruction in its own right, whereas the expression between the parentheses acts as the embedded operand. To make it easier for the second edition of the BASIC interpreter to recognize embedded instructions, the first function terms were limited to three letters, followed immediately by a left parenthesis or a string identifier. Thus, the interpreter could easily identify INT(), SQR(), VAL(), and STR$(). The embedded instruction led to the first real grammatical distinction between terms in the BASIC programming language, that is, between statements and functions.

So why are BASIC and Visual Basic such complex syntactic affairs today? What happened to the simplicity of the primary structure developed at Dartmouth? Theoretically, when Microsoft created the first high-level language interpreter for microcomputers with its Altair 8080 BASIC in 1976, authors Paul Allen and Bill Gates broke down the elements of each instruction line encountered by the interpreter—that is, statements, line numbers, semicolons, and enclosed strings—into *lexemes,* similar to the way elements of spoken language are divided into rudimentary sounds or phonemes.

The lexeme model of the interpreter.

The program for the Altair 8080 BASIC interpreter became the model for future editions of Microsoft BASIC; all Microsoft's BASIC interpreters used the lexeme model for deciphering or parsing a BASIC instruction. Using this model, it becomes more efficient, from the interpreter programmer's point of view, for the BASIC programmer to describe as many command instructions as possible using the fewest lexemes. Microsoft therefore encouraged BASIC program writers to embed functions within other functions, to place multiple statements on one instruction line, and to expand the capabilities of IF-THEN so that a group of contained instructions were rendered dependent upon a condition being met, rather than only one instruction.

The problem with this early model of efficiency is it produced a number of source code entanglements that were not easily resolved. Customers in the early 1980s began complaining that Microsoft BASIC was, on the whole, illegible. Also, BASIC's inventors, Kemeny and Kurtz, were not at all pleased with Microsoft's "unauthorized" revisions to their otherwise pristine language. In a massive restructuring effort, Microsoft developed its first QuickBASIC compilers to allow for the elimination of line numbers and, therefore, the optional droppage of the GOTO statement, which was so often held responsible for the "spaghetti code" that pervaded that era.

Modern BASIC and Visual Basic are so unlike its ancestors primarily because the definition of efficiency has changed several times over the last three decades. To keep current with the changing definition of "efficiency," BASIC had to change too. In the late 1980s, Microsoft started adding object-oriented syntax to the language to achieve some sort of simplicity in the language's structure. Any professional programmer can tell you that Visual Basic is not a truly object-oriented language, for reasons that could consume another chapter. The simple referential syntax of object-orientation is appealing, however, and finds its home in Visual Basic. The syntax is this:

The addition of object-oriented syntax.

```
object.{operation ¦ characteristic}
```

Each object-oriented reference is divided into *two* parts (sound familiar?) representing the verb and object you find in an English-language sentence. If you don't see the historical irony in this, then the term "full circle" must not mean much to you.

Property Settings for Expressor Mark I

What follows is a list of the important properties and attached procedures for each graphic object in EXPRESOR.FRM, the form module for the Expressor Mark I. This list was generated using MicroHelp's programmer's aide product, VBXRef.

```
Form: EXPRESOR.FRM
   General Procedures:
       assess_readout Clear_Params dopp_shift force_att
➡surf_area_rccyl
       volume_rccyl zone_sphere


       BackColor           &HFF8080
       Caption             Expressor
       ForeColor           &H808080
       FormName            Form1
       Icon                (Icon)
       LinkTopic           Form1


       Active Form Event Procedures
        Form_Load


   Control Type: Label
       Control Name: ParamText(00)
       Alignment           1 - Right Justify
       BackColor           &HFFFFFF
       Caption
       CtlName             ParamText
       ForeColor           &HFF0000
       TabIndex            5
```

```
Active Control Event Procedures
    <None>

Control Name: ParamText(01)
Alignment           1 - Right Justify
BackColor           &HFFFFFF
Caption
CtlName             ParamText
ForeColor           &HFF0000
Index               1
TabIndex            33

Control Name: ParamText(02)
Alignment           1 - Right Justify
BackColor           &HFFFFFF
Caption
CtlName             ParamText
ForeColor           &HFF0000
Index               2
TabIndex            34

Control Name: ParamText(03)
Alignment           1 - Right Justify
BackColor           &HFFFFFF
Caption
CtlName             ParamText
ForeColor           &HFF0000
Index               3
TabIndex            35

Control Name: ParamText(04)
Alignment           1 - Right Justify
BackColor           &HFFFFFF
Caption
CtlName             ParamText
ForeColor           &HFF0000
Index               4
TabIndex            36

Control Name: Readout
Alignment           1 - Right Justify
BackColor           &HFF0000
```

```
        Caption              0
        CtlName              Readout
        FontName             Courier
        FontSize             15
        ForeColor            &HFFFFFF
        TabIndex             0

        Active Control Event Procedures
            <None>

Control Type: TextBox
     Control Name: Param(00)
        BackColor            &HFFFF00
        CtlName              Param
        TabIndex             10
        Text                 0

        Active Control Event Procedures
            <None>

     Control Name: Param(01)
        BackColor            &HFFFF00
        CtlName              Param
        Index                1
        TabIndex             29
        Text                 0

     Control Name: Param(02)
        BackColor            &HFFFF00
        CtlName              Param
        Index                2
        TabIndex             30
        Text                 0

     Control Name: Param(03)
        BackColor            &HFFFF00
        CtlName              Param
        Index                3
        TabIndex             31
        Text                 0
```

```
    Control Name: Param(04)
    BackColor              &HFFFF00
    CtlName                Param
    Index                  4
    TabIndex               32
    Text                   0

Control Type: Command Button
    Control Name: ApplyFormula
    BackColor              &H400000
    Caption                Apply Formula
    CtlName                ApplyFormula
    TabIndex               16

    Active Control Event Procedures
     ApplyFormula_Click

    Control Name: Button0(09)
    BackColor              &H400000
    Caption                0
    CtlName                Button0
    FontName               Courier
    FontSize               9.75
    Index                  9
    TabIndex               2

    Active Control Event Procedures
     Button0_Click

    Control Name: ButtonPos(01)
    BackColor              &H400000
    Caption                1
    CtlName                ButtonPos
    FontName               Courier
    FontSize               9.75
    Index                  1
    TabIndex               1

    Active Control Event Procedures
     ButtonPos_Click
```

```
Control Name: ButtonPos(02)
BackColor          &H400000
Caption            2
CtlName            ButtonPos
FontName           Courier
FontSize           9.75
Index              2
TabIndex           17

Control Name: ButtonPos(03)
BackColor          &H400000
Caption            3
CtlName            ButtonPos
FontName           Courier
FontSize           9.75
Index              3
TabIndex           18

Control Name: ButtonPos(04)
BackColor          &H400000
Caption            4
CtlName            ButtonPos
FontName           Courier
FontSize           9.75
Index              4
TabIndex           19

Control Name: ButtonPos(05)
BackColor          &H400000
Caption            5
CtlName            ButtonPos
FontName           Courier
FontSize           9.75
Index              5
TabIndex           20

Control Name: ButtonPos(06)
BackColor          &H400000
Caption            6
CtlName            ButtonPos
FontName           Courier
FontSize           9.75
```

```
Index              6
TabIndex           21

Control Name: ButtonPos(07)
BackColor          &H400000
Caption            7
CtlName            ButtonPos
FontName           Courier
FontSize           9.75
Index              7
TabIndex           22

Control Name: ButtonPos(08)
BackColor          &H400000
Caption            8
CtlName            ButtonPos
FontName           Courier
FontSize           9.75
Index              8
TabIndex           23

Control Name: ButtonPos(09)
BackColor          &H400000
Caption            9
CtlName            ButtonPos
FontName           Courier
FontSize           9.75
Index              9
TabIndex           24

Control Name: Button_Point(10)
BackColor          &H400000
Caption            .
CtlName            Button_Point
FontName           Courier
FontSize           9.75
Index              10
TabIndex           3

Active Control Event Procedures
 Button_Point_Click
```

```
Control Name: ClearAll
BackColor          &H400000
Caption            C
CtlName            ClearAll
TabIndex           7

Active Control Event Procedures
 ClearAll_Click

Control Name: ClearEntry
BackColor          &H400000
Caption            CE
CtlName            ClearEntry
TabIndex           6

Active Control Event Procedures
 ClearEntry_Click

Control Name: DividedBy
BackColor          &H400000
Caption            /
CtlName            DividedBy
TabIndex           15

Active Control Event Procedures
 DividedBy_Click

Control Name: EditCut
BackColor          &H400000
Caption            Cut
CtlName            EditCut
TabIndex           9

Active Control Event Procedures
 EditCut_Click

Control Name: Enter
BackColor          &H400000
Caption            Enter
CtlName            Enter
TabIndex           12
```

```
Active Control Event Procedures
 Enter_Click

Control Name: Minus
BackColor            &H400000
Caption              -
CtlName              Minus
TabIndex             13

Active Control Event Procedures
 Minus_Click

Control Name: Percent
BackColor            &H400000
Caption              %
CtlName              Percent
TabIndex             8

Active Control Event Procedures
 Percent_Click

Control Name: StoreBank(00)
BackColor            &H400000
Caption              <<
CtlName              StoreBank
TabIndex             11

Active Control Event Procedures
 StoreBank_Click

Control Name: StoreBank(01)
BackColor            &H400000
Caption              <<
CtlName              StoreBank
Index                1
TabIndex             25

Control Name: StoreBank(02)
BackColor            &H400000
Caption              <<
CtlName              StoreBank
Index                2
TabIndex             26
```

```
Control Name: StoreBank(03)
BackColor          &H400000
Caption            <<
CtlName            StoreBank
Index              3
TabIndex           27

Control Name: StoreBank(04)
BackColor          &H400000
Caption            <<
CtlName            StoreBank
Index              4
TabIndex           28

Control Name: Times
BackColor          &H400000
Caption            X
CtlName            Times
TabIndex           14

Active Control Event Procedures
  Times_Click

Control Type: Combo Box
    Control Name: CalcList
        BackColor          &HC00000
        CtlName            CalcList
        ForeColor          &HFFFFFF
        Style              2 - Dropdown List
        Text               CalcList

    Active Control Event Procedures
      CalcList_Click
```

Rethinking an Existing Structure

A single-form Visual Basic application generally is a utility program, because, logically, it has the capacity to perform only one primary accessory function.

An example of a utility that performs an accessory function is a calculator project such as the Expressor Mark I.

To make a utility into an application, the extent of the utility's functionality must be expanded so there is more than one computational engine. In this chapter, you see the Expressor I utility become the Expressor II application with the addition of a graphing feature. This graph is a real image file that can be exported to another Windows application that can use such an image, for example a word processor. In an application, the functionality is extended into multiple uses that can be charted hierarchically, whereas, the functionality of a utility is *uniplex*—having only one true function.

Figure 2.2 shows the Expressor in its fully-modified Mark II state.

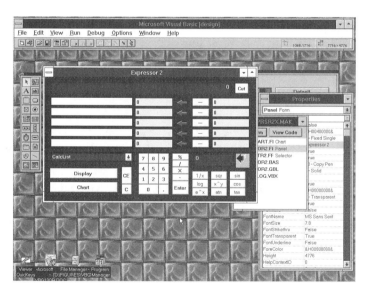

Figure 2.2. Like laundry soap, this product becomes new and improved in minutes.

Yes, It Does Come with Directions

The new Expressor panel works like this: To solve for a particular formula, the user chooses that formula from the list box. A set of parameter descriptions shows up in the same five white slots that described the formula parameters in Expressor I. The user can solve the formula for any single set of known values two ways. He may type each parameter for the formula beside its associated description, or he may use the RPN calculator to find the value of one parameter and transfer that value to the appropriate slot by clicking the raised purple arrow beside that slot. After the user enters the parameters, he clicks the Display button. The calculator readout then shows a result value for the formula.

The Expressor solving for ranges of values.

To solve for a range of values, however, the user now has available to him the new charting mechanism integrated into Expressor II. To select which parameter acts as the range for the chart, the user clicks one of the buttons beside the parameter slot currently marked "- - -." This causes the button to read "x>>," meaning the parameter box to the right of the "x>>" button will contain the maximum value in the range. The parameter to the left of that button will contain the minimum value. For instance, one of the formulas added to Expressor II is a simple sine wave function. To solve for all angles between –360° and 360°, the user enters –360 in the parameter slot where he would normally enter values for the Display button. He then clicks the "- - -" to the right of that parameter, making it an "x>>" button (only one button can have the "x>>" range marker in it). If a value currently appears in the main readout, it is copied to the maximum range slot; this is a regular text box, though, whose contents can be replaced by the user overtyping them.

After the user has entered the parameters and chosen and defined the charting range, a chart for the formula results for all values in the range is brought to the screen by the user clicking the Chart button. The chart form is displayed momentarily, but it might take a minute for it to show any values (in other words, it's not as fast as Excel just yet). The chart, complete with axis tick marks and intermediate values along each axis, soon appears.

Here are those procedures belonging to the Expressor II panel form:

EXPRESR2.FRM

General Declarations:

```
Dim label$(15, 4)
Dim point_lock As Integer
Dim readout_value As Double, combine_value As Double
Dim ready As Integer
Dim solution As Single, V2 As Single
```

The array variable `label$()` now contains as many as 15 sets of parameter descriptions, which display within the parameter slots whenever a formula is chosen from the list. Variable `point_lock` is still a flag that keeps the user from entering two decimal points to a number. The `readout_value` and `combine_value` also operate as they did before, with `readout_value` made equal to the number currently being entered into the display and `combine_value` made equal to the previous number.

Variable `ready` is a register that determines whether the next digit or symbol entered clears the contents of the display. This register is set to zero whenever a function button is pressed on the panel; `ready` separates one entire value from the next so that two sequences of digits don't become mixed. Variable `solution` is a receiver for the results from the calculating module of this program, which is `EXPRESR2.BAS`. Finally, `V2` retains the memory value displayed in the second, smaller digital display on the panel.

Event Procedures:

```
Sub Form_Load ()
Load Chart
CalcList.AddItem "Surface Area of RC Cylinder"
CalcList.AddItem "Volume of RC Cylinder"
CalcList.AddItem "Zone Area of Sphere"
CalcList.AddItem "Force of Earth/Body Attraction"
CalcList.AddItem "Doppler Shift Transmitted Freq."
CalcList.AddItem "Escape Vel. of Body From Earth"
CalcList.AddItem "Strength of Grav. Force"
CalcList.AddItem "Simple Sine Wave"
CalcList.AddItem "Parabolic Function"
CalcList.AddItem "Length of Median of Triangle"
CalcList.AddItem "Period of a Compound Pendulum"
CalcList.AddItem "Period of Circular Earth Orbit"
label$(0, 0) = "Radius of right circular cylinder"
label$(0, 1) = "Height of cylinder"
label$(1, 0) = "Radius of right circular cylinder"
label$(1, 1) = "Height of cylinder"
label$(2, 0) = "Radius of sphere"
label$(2, 1) = "Height of zone"
label$(3, 0) = "Mass of Earth"
label$(3, 1) = "Mass of body in Earth's grav. field"
label$(3, 2) = "Radius of Earth"
label$(3, 3) = "Distance of body above Earth's surface"
```

```
label$(4, 0) = "Observer velocity"
label$(4, 1) = "Source velocity"
label$(4, 2) = "Observed frequency"
label$(4, 3) = "Velocity of wave"
label$(5, 0) = "Gravitating mass"
label$(5, 1) = "Radius of Earth"
label$(6, 0) = "Mass of gravitating object"
label$(6, 1) = "Mass of orbiting body"
label$(6, 2) = "Radius of Earth"
label$(7, 0) = "Coefficient"
label$(7, 1) = "Angle"
label$(8, 0) = "Coefficient"
label$(8, 1) = "Variable"
label$(8, 2) = "Exponent"
label$(9, 0) = "Length of side 1"
label$(9, 1) = "Length of side 2"
label$(9, 2) = "Length of side 3"
label$(10, 0) = "Radius of gyration about pivot"
label$(10, 1) = "Distance from pivot to ctr. gravity"
label$(11, 0) = "Radius of orbit"
label$(11, 1) = "Mass of object being orbited"
xslot = -1
End Sub
```

In this Sub Form_Load () event procedure, the array variables are painstakingly seeded ("pre-seeded?") so that the list box and parameter slots can display the proper text at the proper time.

The basic four arithmetic functions are as they were in Mark I, as well as the percent function that divides the readout_value by 100. Along with those, I added the following new arithmetic and trigonometric functions:

```
Sub Reciprocal_Click ()
assess_readout
If readout_value <> 0 Then
    readout_value = 1 / readout_value
    Readout.Caption = Str$(readout_value)
    ready = 0
End If
End Sub

Sub Logarithm_Click ()
assess_readout
```

```
If V2 <> 0 And readout_value <> 0 Then
    lg = Log(readout_value) / Log(V2)
    readout_value = lg
    combine_value = readout_value
    Readout.Caption = Str$(readout_value)
    ready = 0
End If
End Sub

Sub NaturalLog_Click ()
assess_readout
If readout_value <> 0 Then
    lg = Log(readout_value)
    readout_value = lg
    combine_value = readout_value
    Readout.Caption = Str$(readout_value)
    ready = 0
End If
End Sub

Sub Root_Click ()
assess_readout
If readout_value <> 0 Then
    pwr = Sqr(readout_value)
    readout_value = pwr
    combine_value = readout_value
    Readout.Caption = Str$(readout_value)
    ready = 0
End If
End Sub

Sub PowerRaise_Click ()
assess_readout
pwr = readout_value ^ V2
readout_value = pwr
combine_value = readout_value
Readout.Caption = Str$(readout_value)
ready = 0
End Sub

Sub Arctangent_Click ()
assess_readout
```

```
rads = readout_value * (PI / 180)
readout_value = Atn(rads)
Readout.Caption = Str$(readout_value)
ready = 0
End Sub

Sub Sine_Click ()
assess_readout
rads = readout_value * (PI / 180)
readout_value = Sin(rads)
Readout.Caption = Str$(readout_value)
ready = 0
End Sub

Sub Cosine_Click ()
assess_readout
rads = readout_value * (PI / 180)
readout_value = Cos(rads)
Readout.Caption = Str$(readout_value)
ready = 0
End Sub

Sub Tangent_Click ()
assess_readout
rads = readout_value * (PI / 180)
readout_value = Tan(rads)
Readout.Caption = Str$(readout_value)
ready = 0
End Sub
```

Both the Sub Logarithm_Click () and Sub PowerRaise_Click () functions borrow the value of a second parameter in variable V2 (a tribute to Dr. von Braun). The user can find this value in the new SecondValue text box, which acts as a visible memory for the calculator. The user can transfer any value appearing in the readout by clicking the swerving purple arrow; this is also a text box, so he may type a parameter here as well.

To raise the value of the readout to a power, the user enters that power into this second text box. This value becomes the value of variable V2, by virtue of the following procedure:

```
Sub SecondValue_Change ()
V2 = Val(SecondValue.Text)
End Sub
```

Suppose the number 2 is in the readout and 3 is in the second value box. By clicking the "x ^ y" button, the readout displays 8 or 2^3 (two raised to the third power). Using the second memory in this way takes the place of five or six buttons reserved for squaring, cubing, or raising to the fifth or twelfth powers. Now suppose the user wants to find the fifth or twelfth root of a value. He enters the root number in the display and presses the reciprocal button (1 / y). The reciprocal of the value entered is now in the display. It can then be transferred to the second value display by the user clicking the swerving arrow. He enters the radicand (3 for third root, 12 for twelfth, and so on) into the display, and then clicks the "x ^ y" button. The result is the calculated value of x ^ (1 / y), which is the same concept as finding the yth root of x.

The following routine handles the placement of the main display value into the second display:

```
Sub Store2nd_Click ()
SecondValue.Text = Readout.Caption
V2 = Val(SecondValue.Text)
End Sub
```

The Slow March of Progress

Remember a certain one-instruction procedure from the Expressor Mark I— it appears here in its Mark II edition:

```
Sub assess_readout ()
readout_value = Val(Readout.Caption)
End Sub
```

Notice, I made an entire Sub procedure for one instruction when it takes one instruction to call the procedure. During the original design of the Expressor, I wanted to leave opportunities for hooks for future expansion of the program and didn't want to have to re-edit the entire program mechanism. The procedure call assess_readout is already in place in all the arithmetic function's _Click procedures. To add a process to this program that takes place after each button click, I could simply add that process to the Sub assess_readout () procedure without having to rewrite my button routines.

Some excuse, huh? Did you buy it? As you can see, I haven't added any new processes to this "Watch This Space" procedure. It's no matter, though; the program isn't hurt by my leaving this hook. In fact, for programming technique, I still advocate implementing such hooks—as long as programs remain modular—to leave open a path for new ideas. If you have any ideas for this procedure, you might consider mailing them to me.

> **Technique Note:** Continue to justify the means by which you planned ahead, even when the reasons are not readily evident.

The next procedure, Sub CalcList_Click (), is triggered whenever the user appears to have made a selection from the formula list. It acquires the parameter descriptions set earlier in the Sub Form_Load () procedure, and it places them into the appropriate parameter slots. Next, the parameter value areas themselves are cleared.

```
Sub CalcList_Click ()
For n = 0 To 4
    ParamText(n).Caption = label$(CalcList.ListIndex, n) + "    "
Next n
Clear_Params
End Sub
```

The previous procedure places a call to Sub Clear_Params (), as follows:

```
Sub Clear_Params ()
For pl = 0 To 4
Param(pl).Text = ""
ParamTo(pl).Text = ""
Next pl
ClearAll_Click
End Sub
```

Remember, two quotation marks next to each other stand for "empty contents," and to empty a text box, you have to set its contents to a state of emptiness using an equation such as Param(pl).Text = "".

For the Expressor Mark II, I replaced the five buttons in the array StoreBank() with a control array of picture boxes with the same name. For the .Picture properties, I used a purple left-pointing arrow from the Visual Basic icon library shipped with the product.

To the right of StoreBank() are some drab gray buttons, used to select the parameter that is represented by the x-axis in the chart. The control array routine that handles those buttons is as follows:

```
Sub AxisSelect_Click (Index As Integer)
If ParamTo(Index).Text = "0" Or ParamTo(Index).Text
   = "" Then
   ParamTo(Index).Text = Readout.Caption
End If
ready = 0
Select Case AxisSelect(Index).Caption
Case "---"
   If xslot = -1 Then
      AxisSelect(Index).Caption = "x >>"
      xslot = Index
      For correct = 0 To 4
         If correct <> Index Then
            AxisSelect(correct).Caption = "---"
         End If
      Next correct
   End If
Case "x >>"
   If xslot = Index Then
      AxisSelect(Index).Caption = "---"
      xslot = -1
   End If
End Select
End Sub
```

Here is this same routine in pseudocode:

```
Procedure for clicking on one of the axis
  selection buttons:
If the text slot beside the button that was clicked
  on either contains a "0" or is blank, then
    Place the contents of the main readout inside
      this slot.
End of condition.
The main readout is assumed to contain all the
  digits in an entire value.
Examining the text within the button itself for a
  moment,
```

```
Supposing that button had only "---" in it,
    Then if we haven't chosen an x-axis range, then
        Place the "x>>" marker in this button.
        We'll say the x-axis range is here.
        Looking at all the rest of the buttons,
            For some other button than this one, then
                Make every other button read "---."
            End of condition.
        Examine the next button.
    End of condition.
On the other hand, if there's already a "x>>" here,
    Then if it's because this already was the chosen
      axis slot, then
        Put the "---" back in this button.
        Say there is no slot anymore.
    End of condition.
End of supposition.
End of procedure.
```

At this point, the Expressor Mark II is ready for the implementation of a charting module that displays results for a range of possible input values in the included formulas. I pick up that part of the modification in Chapter 3, "The Application Model."

THE APPLICATION MODEL

3

By now, you've probably read about a dozen "first books of computing," most of which have probably attempted to answer the question "What does a computer do?" with another question: "What would you *like* it to do?" While working in one aspect or another of the computing business for the last sixteen years, I've heard the first question all too often. My response, at times, must sound like "What do you *expect* it to do?" I try to elicit from the questioner some picture, however sketchy, of her work environment. If I know what she does, I can tell her what her computer can do.

Computers Have No Brains

The computer's real purpose in the work environment is to act on behalf of the user for those jobs that require an inordinate amount of the user's time, patience, and diligence if she works on her own. People tend to believe a computer *substitutes* for people. In reality, it doesn't take the place of a person if the computer is fulfilling its proper role in the workplace. In many work environments, the computer does indeed eliminate certain jobs, but only to the limited extent to which those jobs were developed in the first place. Corporations do fire employees and hire computers, but keep an eye on those corporations and watch the confusion that soon ensues in the ranks. Computers cannot replace people because only people can have an understanding of the job at hand. The appropriate role of the computer in the workplace is to promote the user to a higher level of work, giving that person more time and better judgment criteria for making decisions and planning strategies for the future.

Computers require people as their primary source of input. Therefore, the programs used by computers should be designed to be integrated into the environment of human beings. Of course, there are adaptations that people must make in order to accept technology in their lives, but this acceptance is a matter of psychology. Businesspeople learned to accept the incursion of the stock ticker and the telephone into their offices during the first half of this century. If you look at what was written then about those devices, you find the same fears associated with computing technology today.

The communications model of computing.

The telephone was adapted to the current work environment through extensive ergonomic planning by its redevelopers. Alex Bell's project was planned as a mechanical device to carry variations in sound waves along a chemically treated metal plate over an electrically charged wire. It was not planned as a device for you to dial an 800 number and order a copy of the Democrats' economic plan. The telephone is seemingly indispensable not because of the original genius of its mechanics, but because thousands upon thousands of people since 1876 have modeled new uses for it—in a sense, new *applications*. The most useful applications for the telephone have been modeled by their developers in advance on paper, using charts. These developers may as well be programmers.

What Bell Labs Gave Us

What made the telephone truly work—not mechanically, but environmentally—was a gradual incorporation of the *communications model* within the world telephone service. This model is an understanding of how parties exchange information, put into words and graphs using a method first developed at AT&T Bell Laboratories. In the 1960s, the same Bell Laboratories began incorporating the communications model into its understanding of how computing should work—environmentally, not mechanically. Today, the best software incorporates the "telephone" model of how information changes hands between parties.

The computer, like the telephone, is a medium of transfer. It provides the stage for an ongoing communication between two parties—the programmer and the user. The language between the two parties is one of exchange: the programmer supplies the user with *functionality*, and the user responds with *information*. Combining the two, then, the programmer resolves the conversation by supplying the user with *more information*. During their existence in the computer, these units of transaction are "packaged," if you will, as *data*.

This is the modern communications model of computing. All transactions that take place between programmer and user follow this model. This may answer the question "What does a computer do?" for the career or novice programmer. For the user who's simply trying to get another day's work done in approximately a day, this model doesn't help her compute any more than a thorough comprehension of signal switching station technology helps a person get her quarter back from a pay phone. To answer the user's questions, a programmer must first place himself in the role of the user—to assume her situation, to presume how she does her job. What does this person really *want* from a computer, and by contrast, what does she *need* from it?

Planning the Modules

In this chapter, you study how a programmer determines the hierarchical order of forms in a Visual Basic project so that the user can navigate easily among forms in the application and still maintain her sanity.

Situation #1: The Retail Inventory Tracking System

Look ahead now at the plan for this project's various modules. Figure 3.1 shows one of the forms being utilized by this project. This form pops up whenever the user searches for a product at the request of a customer. This should give you an idea not only of the appearance, but also the capabilities and limitations of a form module in this project.

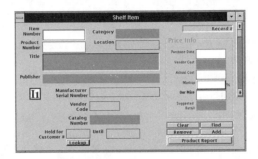

Figure 3.1. The shelf item form in its formative stages.

In order to determine what other composite variables require declaration at this point, it's necessary to decide *now* what forms will be used for the entry and display of data during the course of the program. The following list describes my initial interpretation of the various form modules for Situation #1:

A form is necessary to register the entry of an item (or set of items) into inventory.

Another form is necessary to create a new product entry in the inventory list. Conceivably, this could be the same form used by the person looking for a specific product entry in inventory.

At least one form is necessary for processing restock orders from wholesale vendors.

One form handles the entry of new customers into the invoicing list scheme.

A similar form is necessary for the entry of new vendors into the vendor list. This will perhaps be the least-invoked form in the set.

A large form will be required for entering invoices at the point of sale.

A similar form is necessary for entering purchase orders from customers recorded in the existing customer list.

Visual Basic 2 now allows multiple forms to be collected together under one "umbrella" form using a feature that has been part of Windows for quite some time, the Multiple Document Interface (MDI). When you use a Windows MDI application, the program's main window can contain several *child windows*, each of which represents a document or form currently under construction. The style of each child window can be identical to one another; so in the new VB2 scheme, a child form being designed for an MDI application can represent the style of several duplicate forms in the VB application.

Technique Capsule: Multiple Form Instances

Definition: The Microsoft Windows Multiple Document Interface allows a two-tiered hierarchical structure of windows in an application. With MDI employed, windows that contain documents or forms can be grouped together inside the application's main window. This main window is the *parent window*, and its constituents are *children*. This nomenclature was first adopted by MIT for its windowing environments in the late 1970s.

The Visual Basic 2 interpreter allows for the creation of one central MDI parent window per project. You then can enroll another form already existing within the project as a child window model at design time, by setting the `.MDIChild` property for that form to `True`. More than one instance of a form enrolled as a child can appear in the designated parent form at the same time. Each instance can be minimized and maximized by the user within the area of the parent form designated as its workspace.

Execution: To add an MDI form to the current project, select New MDI Form from the VB control window's File menu. The new form appears forthwith. Note that fewer properties pertain to an MDI parent form than to a standard form. The area currently contained in the MDI form window is the workspace for all child forms in the application, and is considered the workspace for the entire application.

To add controls to the MDI window as you do for a standard form, you first must give the MDI window a type of platform upon which controls can rest. This platform is supplied in the form of a picture box. Regardless of where you draw the perimeter of the picture box, it will appear later along the top of the

MDI form workspace. From this point on, any graphic object you place within the area of this upper region behaves like an object placed in a standard form. You do not place graphic objects in the lower region of the MDI form; this space is for the display of child forms. There are now two divisions of the MDI form: the upper control region and the lower workspace region.

To make an existing form recognizable as a child form by the VB interpreter, at design time, set the form's .MDIChild property to True using the Properties window. When the MDI form is loaded into the workspace, each form in the project whose .MDIChild property is set to true appears in the workspace area of the MDI parent window in the state designated by the initial setting of its .WindowState property.

Normally, you give a form a .Name property at design time and bring it into the Windows workspace by means of the Load statement or the .Show method. You can bring another instance of an existing MDI child form into the workspace of the MDI form with, of all things, the Dim statement, using the following syntax:

```
Dim instancename As New childformname
```

After you execute this syntax of the Dim statement (which is somewhat taxed these days), instancename becomes the object name of the child form currently in the MDI form workspace. In this example, instancename is an example of an object variable, which is operated somewhat like a composite variable, except that it is not invoked with the Type clause, and its components are the properties of a standard graphic object.

The instruction instancename.Show brings the child form instance into the MDI form workspace; instancename is now addressable as an object. The childformname is the .Name of the original or prototype form you give it at design time, using the conventional Properties window. The MDI child form is the only type of Visual Basic graphic object that can receive its instance name at runtime.

Example 1: A travel agency wants a VB application for setting up flight, hotel, and transportation reservations for its clients. The main form that shows the client's travel itinerary is registered as the MDI parent form. Alternate forms are necessary for the application to display more than one instance of plane departure and arrival information, the location of available lodging, and the make and location of rental cars. These child forms have the .Name properties of Flight, Hotel, and RentACar, respectively. The .MDIChild properties for each of these forms is set to True. The following instructions create second instances of these child forms:

```
Dim FlightPlan As New Flight
Dim Reservation As New Hotel
Dim Automobile As New RentACar
```

At this point, the three second-instance child forms are enrolled in the Visual Basic project, but are not yet officially *loaded*—which means they are not part of the Windows workspace. The next instruction brings the child form FlightPlan into this workspace, but does not show it yet:

```
Load FlightPlan
```

The following instructions bring the remaining two dimensioned forms into the Windows workspace and into the MDI parent form's workspace, and make them visible as well:

```
Reservation.Show
Automobile.Show
```

Once the user maximizes a child form using the standard window maximizing control, its size can expand to fill the entire workspace region of the parent form—that is, the entire area below whatever control region might have been drawn into the parent form.

Example 2: Object variables, like composite variables, can be dimensioned for single-dimension arrays in order that you may place multiple instances of a single designed form into the MDI parent workspace at one time. The syntax for the array instruction is as follows:

```
Dim instancename(numforms%) As New childformname
```

An instruction with this syntax will place the number of forms represented by numforms% within the MDI parent form. So say the program in the first example is revised so that five hotel reservation forms may be displayed all at once. First, a global declaration is necessary to keep track of how many instances of a form are currently active. This will be placed within the declarations section of one of the general modules.

```
Global ReservInstance As Integer
```

Next, here's the instruction which dimensions the object variable array:

```
Dim Reservation(1 To 5) As New Hotel
```

The `.Show` method works only on individual instances of a graphic object, so a loop clause is required to bring all five into the parent workspace, such as the one below:

```
For inst = 1 To 5
    ReservInstance = ReservInstance + 1
    Reservation(ReservInstance).Show
Next inst
```

At the time the `.Show` method is invoked for one of the forms in the object array, before `Next inst` is executed, control is passed to the `Sub Form_Load ()` procedure for the new form instance. Because five copies of the same source code process will soon be running simultaneously, each copy will need some identification index passed to it indirectly. Forms don't pass parameters between each other, so a form-level variable representing the form instance index will need to take its value from a global variable, dimensioned within the general declarations area of the form module, as below:

```
Dim Instance As Integer
```

When `Sub Form_Load ()` executes, the form-level variable `Instance` specific to that form is given a copy of the current `ReservInstance` number that is global to the application, as shown in the fragment below:

```
Sub Form_Load ()
Instance = ReservInstance
.
.
.
End Sub
```

Now `Instance` for each form will contain a value that is the only truly trustworthy distinguishing element for referring to a form as an entity rather than to all forms in the array as a whole.

Cautions: Any form that is invoked by means of the `Dim` statement, whether or not it is an MDI form, is given the name of the object variable stated by the `Dim` statement, *not* the `.Name` property of the model form drawn at design time. Conceivably, `Dim` can be used to generate entirely new forms and control contents without any of them having to be designed beforehand using the Visual Basic form designer. Be careful, therefore, not to confuse the `.Name` property for a model form with its true name.

An MDI parent form, by default, is not the start-up form for a VB application. If the parent form is to be the main or start-up form in the application, you must register it so manually by selecting **P**roject from the VB **O**ptions menu and choosing the parent form name from the list box that follows.

In Microsoft's documentation for the MDI, its programmers suggest that every window used in an MDI application—with the exception of dialog boxes—be within the boundaries of the parent window. Besides dialog boxes, this leaves one parent form and the rest children, but no independent windows. This is Microsoft's suggested structure, though it is not mandatory. Within a Visual Basic application, you can have one MDI parent form along with several independent standard forms.

Blast Precedent!

Because the suggested structure seems to make sense, why would you want to have both parent and independent forms in the same MDI application? Wouldn't such an arrangement confuse the user about which part of the Windows workspace contains the application? Indeed this is a danger, although there might be cases in which using an independent form is preferable to subscribing entirely to the Microsoft MDI application model:

Blending MDI with non-MDI elements.

☐ The workspace, or client area, in the MDI parent form may not provide adequate space on low-resolution screens for a large input panel or for a document or picture represented to scale on-screen.

☐ An independent form can represent a utility for the user, such as a certain linguistic calculator you might have read about.

☐ In an application containing a large number of form modules encompassing many realms of functionality, giving every form equal footing in a parent window might cause an overabundance of active controls, leading to confusion on the part of the user. Granted, MDI child windows can be minimized; but three or four active customer forms, nine slips showing available hotel rooms, a handful of reserved standby plane tickets, a customer invoice, and a list of phone numbers all in one workspace does not make for wonderfully organized computing.

The problem you face at the moment, in tandem with the design of the data, is the division of jobs in the application. Other guides to Visual Basic programming would have you start drawing graphics objects in forms now. By doing so, you'd hopefully be able to determine which command functions belong to what module by shuffling their associated buttons among the forms on the screen. This programming method works, if you enjoy countermanding yourself over and over. I call this method "trickle-down programming."

The two-tiered MDI structure.

The primary deficiency in the MDI model of the application is that it is restricted to a two-tiered structure. Every conceivable form is corralled into one encompassing fence, and whether minimized or maximized, every form appears to have an equal role. Granted, Microsoft's name for the system is appropriate; a multiple document interface implies a system that is not meant to be structured for multiple hierarchical tiers, but for equally structured blank sheets of paper. So certainly Microsoft must plead guilty to the charge of truth in advertising.

Figure 3.2 is a hierarchical divisional chart for all the modules for Situation #1. Within the list that appeared in Chapter 2, I regimented the modules into three divisions—Inventory Control, Sales, and Utility. Notice the non-uniform way I drew the boundaries encompassing the three divisions.

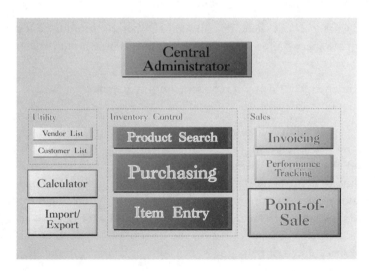

Figure 3.2. A realistic hierarchical module chart.

If I were writing this inventory control system purely for DOS, each module—represented in Figure 3.2 by a labeled rectangle—would probably be a program in and of itself. At the top of the hierarchical chart for the DOS edition of this program, a menu program would serve as a sort of foyer, from which the user would choose to enter a program module the way he might traverse a museum—into one annex and back out to the foyer again.

Instead, I've chosen to corral modules *variably,* with regard to the following:

- [ ] The varying degree of relationship the modules should have to one another at runtime.

- [ ] The ways data will be shared between the modules.

- [ ] The extent to which certain modules are made available to nonmanagerial or otherwise unauthorized users.

To explain: In the Inventory Control division, the Purchasing, Product Search, and Item Entry modules may all be of equal interest to the user—presumably the purchasing agent—at the same time. Therefore, it makes sense that these three modules be made available to the user simultaneously—enrolled, for instance, in an MDI parent window.

In the Sales division, however, the Point-of-Sale module should be set off from the Invoicing and Performance Tracking modules. Salespersons or other nonmanagerial employees will probably not be using the other modules in the set; to these users, the Point-of-Sale module (POS) is the only part of the program they ever need to see. Therefore, it might be more efficient to construct a direct route to POS to give this module special treatment.

In the Utility section, the Vendor List and Customer List modules are well suited for an MDI system, where several instances of these forms in the workspace might be sensible. Below the division's boundary perimeter in the process model, however, are two modules that should be treated separately: a pop-up calculator (which is a segue to the Expressor) and an import/export module that may not need a form associated with it—data transfer can take place in the background.

"Central Administration" is my term for my combination of the main start-up form—the MDI parent form corral for all nonindependent form modules—and a data control system should this application ever become installed on a network. You might recall from Chapter 1, a database is in danger of being

Defining a role for the MDI parent form.

rendered meaningless if it is being written to simultaneously from a single source by more than one client or peer. Because the default "Form1" is not an MDI parent, you must manually make the Central Administrator the start-up form using the method described earlier.

The model I've drawn for Situation #1 is something of a hybrid between the way DOS applications have conventionally been constructed and the professed Windows application model. Figure 3.3 diagrams these two models. The left partition shows the DOS model of the application, arrived at, mostly, by default. The DOS memory model is still limited to (only!) 640K of program space, so DOS application authors are generally inclined to write programs as separate *overlays* linked together by a central menu program.

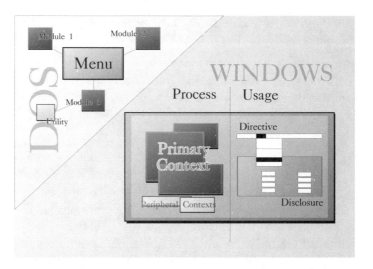

Figure 3.3. The DOS and Windows models of the application.

The Microsoft Windows model of the application compels programmers to give the user equal access to all modules at all times, so there isn't this entry/exit symbology that pervades the DOS model. I've walked through Windows applications with new Windows users who had become accustomed to the DOS model; the questions they ask most often are, "Where am I? What am I *in*?" These people had used DOS applications for so long that they thought multimodule overlaying was the way all programs are written. They would navigate a Windows application for the first time like a blind person accustomed to walking in a museum and suddenly finding herself in the center of a coliseum.

Probably by now, some of these users have grown accustomed to the Windows system of overlapping and tiling and maximization. I must, however, emphasize the word *some*. People have grown familiar with the way microcomputer programs work the same way they've grown familiar with the layout of their offices and houses in their respective countries, or even in their states or provinces. The issue here is one of *architecture*.

Earlier I referred to the frontispiece of a DOS program acting as something of a foyer; later, I mentioned how DOS users are accustomed to asking, "What am I *in*?" In order for users of an application to imagine just what it is they're doing, they often picture themselves inside an ethereal building. The DOS prompt becomes a corridor and subdirectories become the various compartments and offices in an executive complex. To be able to predict how users might imagine touring your own applications, you might need to adopt an attitude that is partly Carl Jung, partly Frank Lloyd Wright, and partly Rimsky-Korsakov.

Modeling an application is a skill akin to architecture. You, as a programmer, can spend 100 percent of your development time designing the database and calculative portions of your program, and expect the user to have already provided the necessary data for these portions. To think this way—to borrow a term from my editors—is to forget your audience. To operate a program, a user needs boundaries, regulation, and organization—even if these concepts are held entirely in his mind. To render unto the user the semblance of organization, you must paint a picture for the user, to make him feel like a part of himself occupies a common space with the program's tools.

This is why users feel comfortable with the DOS model of the application. Though it is restrictive from a programmer's view and places too much overhead in the importing/exporting of data, the DOS model often gives the impression that each module is a room. Giving a Windows application to a DOS user often makes him feel lost at first. By contrast, giving a DOS application to a person accustomed to working on a Macintosh or with Windows might give that user an allegorical feeling of claustrophobia. The feeling an application gives the user of openness or of snugness is exactly that—a *feeling*. This feeling is crucial to the user's ability to navigate the application and find the features he wants without the aid of a road map.

No matter how open or closed you make your applications, it's crucial you do the following:

1. Provide the user with navigational aids so he can easily find his way around.

2. Plan routes the user takes to transfer between functions or modules, so that there is a clear and memorizable usage process with which the user may easily grow familiar.

Where the Engines Go

So far you're still in the conceptual stage of programming. Notice, no actual source code has been added to Situation #1 since the beginning of this chapter. Earlier, it was ascertained that the application can maintain as many as 11 types of form modules, as shown in Figure 3.2. In a large application such as this, you as programmer separate the *engine* of the program—the parts that do the actual calculation and processing of the data—from the input mechanism. In other words, with several hundred buttons and controls on 11 forms, it probably isn't efficient design technique to place the main body of the source code in event procedures. An event procedure responds to only one event. With perhaps a few hundred buttons in the entire project, chances are that the functions those buttons perform will become duplicated. You might choose to cut and paste routines for those functions from the dozen or so _Click event procedures that do the same thing. It would be far more efficient, however, to place the routine for that function *once* within a general procedure in a separate module, and have all the _Click event procedures requiring that function to branch to the general procedure.

> **Technique Note:** For large applications, place the often-used process-ing functions—such as data retrieval, calculation, and sorting—in general procedure modules separate from the form modules. This reduces the overall size of the source code.

In small applications in which a major calculation routine is called by only one button, it makes sense to place that routine in an event procedure in a form module. In the Expressor, for instance, the calculation-ending routine need appear only in procedure `Sub Equals_Click ()`; addition need happen only in `Sub Plus_Click ()`, and so on. Notice, though, how the Expressor project is being constructed. No hierarchical module charts have been drawn, like the one for the inventory control system INVENT1 shown in Figure 3.2. The Expressor is a pushbutton application—more to the point, it is officially a utility and by some programmers' definitions, not an application at all.

For INVENT1, the next job is to consider where to place the "engines." Based on the chart I've drawn, it makes sense to create three general modules for the Item/Product Control, Sales, and Utility sections. This way, each general module contains instructions pertaining to only one category of the overall job; if one category of operations in the application has any future upgrades, the upgraded routines can be placed within one file. An office worker then can install this file in place of the existing file. Table 3.1 shows a list of the projected filenames for the major modules belonging to INVENT1, not counting custom controls and supplementary nonstandard dialog boxes.

Table 3.1. The projected modules for the INVENT1 project.

Name	Description
INVENT1.MDI	Central Administrator
INVENT1.GBL	Global Module
INVOICE.FRM	Invoicing
CUSTMRID.FRM	Customer List
SHLFITEM.FRM	Product Search
VENDORID.FRM	Vendor List
PRODUCT.FRM	Product Search
POS.FRM	Point-of-Sale
IMPORTEX.FRM	Import / Export
TRACKING.FRM	Performance Tracking
PURCHSNG.FRM	Purchasing

continues

Table 3.1. continued

Name	Description
ITEMNTRY.FRM	Item Entry
EXPRESOR.FRM	Calculator
INVCTRL1.BAS	Inventory Control Engine
INVSALS1.BAS	Sales Engine
INVUTIL1.BAS	Utility Engine

Some auxiliary filename extensions.

A bit about the filename extensions: Global modules are no longer necessary for global definitions in Visual Basic 2, though I still find them useful in large applications. You could place the global variable declarations at the front of any one of the three general modules—the last three in the list with the .BAS extension—though the choice would certainly be arbitrary. I tend to place the extension .GBL rather than the default .BAS extension on global modules. The .MDI extension was my idea (I won't claim it exclusively, though) and perhaps it'll catch on.

Modeling a Real Job for Computing

Here's the status of Situation #1 so far: The primary data set structures are established, but there are several more sets to design. The identity and interrelationship of the important modules in the project have been ascertained. Now is a good time for you to place yourself in the role of user and imagine how this program can best be operated. Again, no source code is being written here, but take heart. You are not wasting time.

What does a reasonable, intelligent person expect to do when he sits down to use this program? Rather than bungee jump right into the first line of source code, imagine what it actually is like to use this program. Along the way, you see me taking notes.

To make INVENT1 more like a turnkey program, install its main icon in the StartUp group of the Windows Program Manager. With that done, the Central Administrator window pops up forthwith. The first order of business is to have the user identify himself. For security reasons, the application should be able to keep track of who logs on and off the system. This helps management deter employees from tampering with the data files. If there is a network online, you could let it handle the log-on and system security functions, but for this model, I've chosen to assume such a system is not in place.

The security role of a Central Administrator form.

Taking notes: Point 1. A security system performs log-on and log-off operations for the user.

From here, what happens? Assume your user is the purchasing agent for a retail establishment. The inventory acquisition process begins with purchasing. Before the shelves are stocked, the inventory system has no idea what type of product to add, so the purchasing agent uses INVENT1 to make a list of items to purchase for restock from wholesale vendors.

Here's the problem: In many non-perishable retail merchandise industries, more than one vendor competes for a retailer's or reseller's business with competitive pricing. Generally, vendors publish a catalog, whether it be semiannually, quarterly, or monthly. In highly volatile businesses, vendors publish their catalogs on microfiche and, in the book distribution business, online via modem.

The Outgoing Part of the Process

I have never come across a packaged inventory control system that does not assume one vendor always offers only one cost for a product at any one time. Every purchasing agent knows a vendor catalog offers *at least* one cost—which itself is variable and subject to change without notice—and then updates for those prices are mailed or faxed weekly. Even then, the vendor's dealer representative calls twice a week to validate or update those prices. Even with all that variance, the purchaser is not held to any one of those stated costs. The purchaser and dealer representative may make a separate deal over the phone, and that deal might not have anything to do with any one specific product, but instead with rounding off the total dollar amount for the order to the next lowest $100.

So in order for INVENT1 to become a realistic program to be used in realistic circumstances, it must address the following three questions: How much *does* the reseller pay for the product; how much *should* he pay for it; and how much *did* he pay? The vendor catalog can even serve to exacerbate the problem rather than solve it. One catalog may offer a three-tiered price system where the cost of a product is reduced if the dollar amount of the total order exceeds a certain amount. Some vendors actually have more than one catalog—one that contains the main dealer costs, and others that contain lower costs that the vendors promise to the resellers if they maintain a certain purchasing commitment level throughout the quarter. To top it all off, dealer representatives frequently offer the reseller's purchasing agent great deals on unpublished products—generally products too new to be printed in catalogs.

Taking notes: Point 2. The price of an item on the shelf may be fixed, but the price of a product is always variable.

If the INVENT1 programmer decides the dealer cost for each product is the price the reseller last paid for it, then if there are more copies of that particular product still in stock at the time of the current order, the dealer cost is changed retroactively. As a result, the daily performance reports do not reflect a correct profit margin on the day the older items are sold. However, if the purchasing module has the user enter every conceivable cost for every product, this replication of data only creates more work for the user, by having him replicate everything he reads in the catalogs. However, dealer costs offered by the various vendors must be recorded somehow because the cost a dealer's representative offers a vendor during a "special offer" phone conversation is generally lower than the cost in that vendor's catalogs.

The part of the job cross-referencing most benefits.

The *automative* solution is somewhere in between, as a part of the existing job, not an addition to it. A quick recap of the lowest dealer costs thus far recorded for a product might be the most help to the purchasing agent in this situation. This way, the purchaser can cross-reference offers made by other vendors at the same time he's on the phone with one. Each time a vendor makes an offer or a catalog price that is worth noting, that offer is entered into the product list at the purchasing agent's convenience. The purchasing agent never stops using hard-copy catalogs, so it's not reasonable to expect the purchaser to spend his valuable time entering costs into the computer, especially when they'll become outdated in a minute or two. (One of the key words in this paragraph is "cross-reference." Keep that word in mind, hyphen and all.)

So here's the model that appears to be taking shape: The purchasing agent keeps the INVENT1 purchasing module running on his personal console. When a good price—or a notable price—is known, the purchaser enters it into the module. When the purchaser is negotiating a price or determining what needs to be ordered for restock, the purchasing module shows an assessment of the best prices entered into the data set thus far. The module does not replace catalogs; doing so would be asking for too much busy work from people who need the computer to *reduce* their workload.

The Incoming Part of the Process

The morning following the day the order was placed, the parcel service arrives with incoming inventory. INVENT1 isn't an accounting system (at least not yet), so it can be assumed the check for the C.O.D. packages has already been written. Now, there are several boxes to unload. Each box has a packing list and an invoice in a pouch on its outside lid. The purchasing agent must check the list against the contents of the box. Assuming each list item actually is in the box, the agent now enters the items received in the official inventory list.

At this point, the job should be fairly easy. The invoice lists only one price for the amount the dealer actually paid for the product. Not only does this cost become registered as the cost of the item (or the "box," or the "package") but also as a legitimate cost of the product. When the purchaser investigates the product later for best prices, this crucial price—the one actually paid—comes up.

Taking notes: Point 3. Each time items are checked into inventory, the dealer costs (vendor prices) paid for those items go into the product record.

When an item is registered as being in inventory, it is given a unique item serial number for the dealer's use only. This serial number acts as an identifier when the sales clerk punches up the item on the point-of-sale module.

The purchaser has two ways he might register the incoming items as belonging to inventory. He could read each item on the invoice and individually enter the product name and pricing data for each item into the Item Entry module. However, if he uses INVENT1 to compile the contents of an order, he could instead tell the Item Entry module that the contents of a specific order did arrive, and then check off those items placed on back order or missing from the shipment.

To automate the process further, the application could prompt the purchasing agent to select certain items for restock from the existing list. This list may then be updated when the agent receives information about new products from the wholesale vendor. Each order is retained within a special list that keeps track of pending invoices. Assuming the order is intact when it arrives, each item is checked in automatically by "checking off" the invoice; otherwise, items not arriving are marked. The pending invoice is still retained within its data set until the non-arrivals arrive.

Taking notes: Point 4. The contents of a vendor order should be kept in a separate list, recallable when items are later entered into inventory.

Notice that the process model of the purchasing job has been devised in anticipation of coming events. Rather than ask only the common questions "What happens now?" and "What happens next?" the process model being devised has sought to ask a broader question, temporally speaking: "How does what happens next affect what happens later?" When you as programmer broaden your own *time focus*, as I call it, you help eliminate redundancy in the work process of your user.

Broad and
narrow
time focus
compared.

To explain: A common application with what I call a *narrow time focus* approaches the purchasing job like this: It asks the user to enter new products into the inventory list immediately. When the user orders a product, he enters a number in the on-order field for each product list. When the product arrives, he updates the on-order field with a zero and the in-stock field with the number of arrivals.

Indeed, many purchasing applications are written this way; but ask yourself as a programmer with insight into the way non-programmers do their jobs, what *work* does this model accomplish? Does the program perform a function on behalf of the user, or vice versa? Suppose the purchaser needs a list of everything ordered on a given day. An application written with the narrow time focus method must compile this list at the time of query, after looking at the on-order fields for each inventory item. Assume the user is asked to search for separate listings of each product at the time of initial purchaser consideration, at the time of order, at the time of acquisition, and at the time of sale. The user must do all the referencing. Notice also, in the narrow time focus model, the product list and the item list are the same list.

In the broad time focus model you're striving for, the user enters products into the purchasing module at the time of first consideration—when the purchaser is introduced to the product. This entry creates a record in the products list as well as in the items list. The status of an order is compiled by the application at this point, and the user can cross-reference this status using the product list. Once the order-in-progress status is listed as "received," the in-stock status of each item received is automatically updated in the items list, unless the user countermands that process. There is an interconnection, a communication in existence between each data list, resulting in a minimization of input necessary to operate the program. The item list relies on the product list for its titles and identities; the invoice list also relies on the product list.

Figure 3.4 is a sketch depicting the routes a user might take through an application to cross-reference an element of data not currently on-screen.

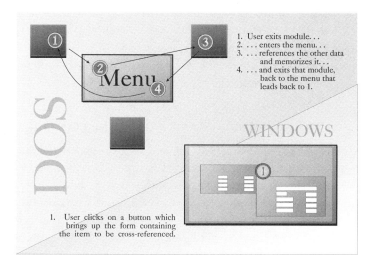

Figure 3.4. Cross-referencing in DOS and in Windows.

The chief benefit of using the Windows model of the application for broad time focus applications is that, for data files containing interrelated elements, their associated forms can be made to call each other directly. In the DOS usage model depicted in the left panel of Figure 3.4, the user must exit one module before entering the next. Without some type of overlapping of the data records displayed on-screen, direct cross-referencing of data elements appearing in two or more records is rendered at least cumbersome, if not impossible. In strict DOS programs, in order to reference an element of data pertinent to the current form, the user probably must exit the current screen to access another screen containing a field for that element. This exit and reentry process takes the application out of one overlay program and into the next, which involves the closure and reopening of data files and the subsequent dropping and reestablishment of variables and data pointers.

In the Windows usage model on the right panel of Figure 3.4, you find a fair degree of overlap has been represented symbolically. By "overlap" in this context, I'm not referring to the union of window borders, but the sharing of resources and data between active forms in the application. Overlap enables the user to retrieve a data element pertinent to one form window from within another, while both forms are active and on-screen. This can be considered a progressive usage model, except for the danger of forcing the user to perform the same steps to accomplish the same cross-reference—that is, close one window, go back to the main window (Central Administration), and open another one. So each form window should be configured to link directly to all other forms that display related data. Later in the book, I investigate unique ways to present cross-referencing options.

Taking notes: Point 5. Each major form in the application should be capable of accepting cross-referenced data directly from another form.

Here's one way to implement cross-referencing, using two of the three forms in the Inventory Control collective context. In this part of the discussion, I've jumped ahead to the form design portion of the project, though it was necessary to illustrate my point. Figure 3.5 shows the inventory product entry form and the item entry form. Remember the distinction between the concepts of *product* and *item:* the former refers to a produced or published title, whereas the latter refers to a specific shelved item, box, or package.

On each form is a button that calls up the other form. When a user reading the Product Display form clicks Shelf Report, for instance, the Shelf Item form is displayed. At startup, it shows the item most recently checked-in that has the same product title as the one in the Product Display window. This is a cross-reference operation for the user who is searching through the product list, has a product on-screen, and wants to know how many of that product are currently in stock.

Likewise, a button marked Product Report appears on the Shelf Item form. When the user clicks this button, the data for the product associated with the item in the Shelf Item window appears immediately. This, too, is a cross-reference. The main reason I didn't put all the data from both forms in Figure 3.5 in one big window is because the user will not be needing all the data at all times. The secondary reason is because the user can employ these two forms for purposes other than purchasing. For instance, the Shelf Item form may be used by the point-of-sale module, and the Product Display form may be used by the Invoicing module. Had both forms been sewn together, half the amalgamated form would remain unused during a cross-reference, wasting valuable screen space.

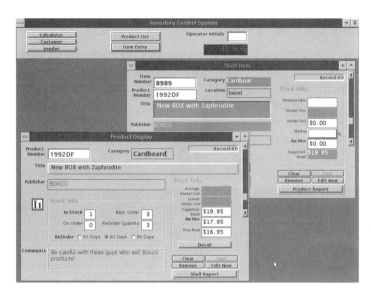

Figure 3.5. Two forms whose paths frequently cross.

Form Sculpting

While Figure 3.5 is still fresh in your mind, I'd like to digress for a moment to address a form appearance feature recently made available in the Professional Edition of Visual Basic 2. Here, Microsoft includes several custom controls as .VBX files that can be added to the Visual Basic toolbar. One such file, THREED.VBX, adds six controls to the toolbar. This file is a sampling of the features of a software package called 3D-Widgets, by Joe Modica and Joe Dour of Sheridan Systems.

The 3D Panel control.

In the two forms in Figure 3.5, I used one of these controls, Sheridan's 3D Panel, to make some text boxes appear raised above the form level or to give some text boxes and buttons an enclosing ridge or ditch.

The 3D Frame control.

The other 3D-Widget control used by the two forms in Figure 3.5 is the 3D Frame control. This frame operates and behaves much like the standard Visual Basic frame, though it offers the added illusion of a small ridge or indentation in the form. You can designate whether the frame is to be inset or raised by setting the frame's `.ShadowStyle` property to `0` or `1`, respectively.

Technique Capsule: Graphics Control Beveling

Definition: A graphic object can be made to stand out (or in) from the rest of the form, giving that object a particularly special status among its peers, by enclosing it within a 3D Panel. This is one of the controls added to the Visual Basic toolbar by the custom control file THREED.VBX. The panel acts much like a frame control in the standard VB toolbar; although through a specific property setting, a control placed anywhere within the boundaries of the panel can be made to snap like mercury to the boundaries of the panel. This way, the control appears to have its own extraneous bevel. The intended effect is to give the newly bordered control special status, helping the user not only to find the control but to determine its relative importance. This enhances the entire appearance of the form.

Execution: To make the 3D Panel control available to your VB project, from the File menu of the VB control window, select Add File. From the item selector that follows, choose THREED.VBX. The control identifier button shown above appears in the toolbar shortly.

Before drawing the control you mean to accentuate, use the 3D panel button in the toolbox to draw the control's surrounding border. While positioning the panel, treat it as though you're drawing the control itself. Text will appear in the panel by default, signifying that the panel also can double as a bordered label. To clear this text, set the panel's `.Text` property to a null string.

The 3D Panel acts like a frame not only by Visual Basic's definition, but also by the dictionary definition. Indeed, the panel utilizes a kind of moulding, as depicted in Figure 3.6. The frame has three "planes," consisting of an outer and inner bevel separated from one another by the official panel border. The widths for both bevel planes in pixels (not twips) are set using the single property .BevelWidth; the pixel width of the border area is set using the .BorderWidth property.

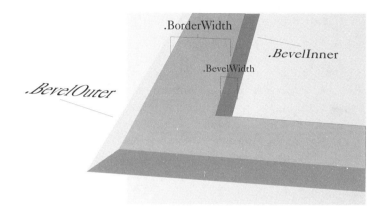

Figure 3.6. A cross-section of the 3D Panel's frame moulding.

Microsoft Windows gives its graphics controls a raised or lowered appearance by placing lighter and darker gray shading along their edges. The effect relies entirely on an optical illusion that makes your eye believe a light is shining on the computer screen from the upper-left. For 16-color and most 256-color Windows screens, the three-dimensional illusion of the 3D Panel appears to work best if the .BackColor of the form is set to light gray; however, the illusion may work well in pastel for 32-bit color Windows screens.

The direction of the carving for the innermost bevel is addressed using the .BevelInner property; likewise, the outermost bevel is addressed using .BevelOuter. The possible settings for both of these properties are as follows:

Setting	Effect
0	None (entirely transparent)
1	Inset (lighting hits the lower right)
2	Raised (lighting hits the upper-left, as with a command button)

To make a control in a 3D Panel snap to its inner boundaries automatically, set the panel's .AutoSize property to 3 - AutoSize Child to Panel. When the panel is set to the proper position, size, and shading, you then enter a control in the panel as you would into a standard VB frame. With .AutoSize set to 3—regardless of the position of the control you drew in the panel—the control's borders will automatically expand to fit just within the inner bevel of the panel.

Suggestions: Setting the panel's .BevelInner property to 1 - Inset and its .BevelOuter property to 2 - Raised, and placing a command button within that frame while its .AutoSize property is set to 3, will cause the button to appear sunken into the form. If you've ever studied closely the remote control on a TV or VCR, the "protected" buttons—the ones you don't want to press accidentally—often are sunken into the panel in a similar way. Sinking a Visual Basic command button in this manner, therefore, might give the user the impression these are protected buttons to use with care. Setting .BevelOuter to 2 and .BevelInner to either 0 or 1 conversely gives a command button within the panel the appearance of added importance, over and above the usual buttons in the standard plateau.

The Proper Context

The definition of context in a VB application.

End of digression. I've often written about the differences between *scope* and *context*. The latter isn't a subject usually covered in detail by Microsoft's texts on Visual Basic. Scope is a characteristic of variables which, as you know, is determined at the point of declaration.

Context is a characteristic of instructions that is determined by the positioning of those instructions within the application source code. Each form module contains a section for general procedures as well as event procedures, and the appearance of general procedures in a form module is identical to that of a general procedure in a general module (at the risk of sounding redundant). However, whereas a procedure in a form module can call and pass parameters to a procedure in a general module, the same does not hold true for the converse.

Collective and auxiliary contexts distinguished.

The concept of context is somewhat vague—certainly more so than scope—though it becomes clearer after a thorough examination of the computing job. Look at the previous discussion about how a retailer's purchasing agent does his job and how the INVENT1 application might automate that job. At one point, the term *collective context* refers to the three form modules in the Inventory Control section of the application.

In a large application such as INVENT1, individual jobs being automated tend to distinguish themselves. Different users have different usage profiles, and these profiles can be drawn onto the hierarchical model for the application, like the model in Figure 3.2.

In the hierarchical model for INVENT1, it's easy to identify the Product Search, Purchasing, and Item Entry form modules as belonging to a collective context. Yet the purchasing agent may be using other modules from the other collective contexts—for instance, the Vendor List module from Utilities and the Performance Tracking module from Sales. You therefore might draw a *peripheral context* linking the Inventory Control section and these two other modules. The purchaser may not have to access the Customer Invoicing module, however, unless he happens to have a dual role in the company. Even if he does wear two hats, it's unlikely he'll ever wear both at once, so it's safe to differentiate the purchasing agent and the salesperson as separate users, even if they are the same person.

As the programmer of a large application, in Visual Basic or any other language, you should plan in advance for modules and procedures that share data (especially through cross-referencing) to be part of a collective context. Modules and procedures whose jobs are only slightly related to one another, though whose domains in the process model may partly intersect, should be planned as part of a peripheral context. Why?

☐ Jobs shared by all modules in a collective context can be represented by one general procedure addressable by all modules in that context.

☐ Data shared by modules that tend to link to one another should be prepared for parameter passing or for scope sharing.

☐ The job of programming the application can be better planned if you know the interrelationships between procedures and modules in advance. This way, you can better structure what layer of the program to build first and what layer to build next. Contexts help define layers in the programming process.

Is There Such a Thing as a Common User?

This chapter has focused upon planning a large application to be utilized by specific users. The optimum models of the application professed by software manufacturers have focused in large part upon what they call the *common user*. After such an in-depth examination as the one featured in this chapter, can we, in good faith, conclude that such a thing as a common user even exists? Some responses to this question deal with how users commonly communicate with machines, as well as with one another.

The first concept people have historically formulated about the role of the computer is that they can walk up to it, feed it the situations of their daily lives and business routines, and that the computer will organize those routines, set them right somehow, and spout forth something on a spool of ticker tape that gives their lives a greater degree of organization. This concept assumes users can talk to the computer—not by voice perhaps, but through some other type of language. Sensible people who have never seen a microcomputer work do not imagine multiple spreadsheets with variable-border-length cells and implicit macros.

The modern shrink-wrapped software application package does little to respond to the initial expectations of these rational, intelligent people. All an application—any application—does is assimilate data, reorganize it, and display it in the same or some other form. Think about it—a word processor is a storage system for character patterns, and a so-called "desktop publishing" program is a word processor with graphics. The core engine mechanism is the same—data in, data out. The common spreadsheet application, at the core, is a tabular data recorder with a calculator built in. Dan Bricklin's original 1970s prototype for VisiCalc was programmed in 8K AppleSoft BASIC. Think about it—the core of a spreadsheet is a small program, and the rest is *bulk*. The other categories of applications—contact management, business accounting, personal accounting, "Happy Birthday" banner printing—primarily have data-in/data-out engines.

The data input mechanisms for these categories of programs are in the process of being standardized by consortiums of manufacturers and by other companies that believe in the pertinence of the standardization process. In North America and Europe, the standardizational goal for data input is *Common User*

Access. CUA is based on the idea that users tell the computer what they want by pointing to it, and that people can communicate data to the computer by indicating and filling in the appropriate box like one fills out a tax return. The idea here is that all communication can be reduced to pointing to menu entries or icons and filling in the appropriate blanks. This is, in a sense, the Unified Field Theory of computing—that users can point-and-click anything they want done. It assumes that all computing is a data-in/data-out process.

The CUA standard forgets the principal assumption and primary need of new computer users. These people assume there is some sort of *language* linking human and machine. They are taught about the power of the mouse later, and in the teaching, they often conclude that their first impressions of computing were incorrect, that perhaps all of computing can be described symbolically. "All you do," says the Microsoft slogan in the television ads, "is point and click."

Common User Access.

You and I know better. The problem with this approach is not that computing is, for some reason, supposed to be more difficult than point-and-click. We know that if every computing function were represented by the point-and-click methodology, computing would, in fact, be a more *difficult* process. A program must have more efficient means for acquiring data and commands from the user than mere buttons and switches. If point-and-click were the only means of communication open to the programmer, it would therefore follow that the more processing power the application was given, the more buttons would have to be employed in order for the user to access that power. A panel full of hundreds of buttons is a far more confusing computing device than even a DOS prompt.

How then do you, as the programmer of a large application, utilize Visual Basic, a language whose professed methodology is primarily based upon point-and-click? The key to writing a large application, in Visual Basic or any other language, is extensive preplanning—laying a more solid foundation, if you will. If you're counting instruction lines, not much source code is written during this period. If you're examining the programming process holistically, you are writing every instruction in the application *now*, in the planning stage.

THE COMPOSITION OF DATA

The most neglected element of the programming process in texts, lectures, and tutorials is the design and construction of data. On the surface, the subject sounds about as much fun as a detailed Government Accounting Office study of the federal budget. Perhaps for that reason, we who teach programming and want to hold your attention tend to skip the subject, leaving it for appendixes or books we might later write.

On behalf of all who've skipped the dreaded topic, it's time to bring data forth and examine it under a

4

microscope. The common assumption is that data is magically generated in a fully manageable state when the application has been fully developed. The truth is, programmers of large-scale applications conceive the structure and format of their data first. It is easier at that point to design the application around the completed data structure—the same way it's easier to build a house by erecting the wooden frames and attaching wall panels to them.

The Development of Data

The modern microcomputer application is a communications device. To borrow some concepts from Marshall McLuhan, a man who understood communications in a more philosophical light, the application program is the medium, and the data is the message. The two are distinct and separate concepts, and for that reason, it is important to note that an MS-DOS computer does not know what data is. The only code that has meaning to a DOS machine is the executable code that comprises a program. If it's not executable—in other words, if it's garbage—to the DOS machine, it must be data. Therefore, anything the operating system or BIOS level of the computer cannot by nature understand is assumed to be data.

A data file works only if it has meaning to the program that uses it. The program is a product of people; it is entirely up to these people—the programmers—to design and assemble the structure of data, either from scratch or by following some preconceived format. You, as a Visual Basic programmer, need not understand machine language to know that the interpreter constantly is breaking the Visual Basic source code into executable machine code. You should, however, create a precise structure for your data files, lest they become long, meandering streams of undistinguished characters.

One of the primary mistakes commonly made by instructors in teaching the art of computing is that they teach people how to construct programs without addressing how to construct data. Data is that part of the computing machine that makes it go. Yet all too often, instructors choose to focus on more tangible subjects such as loop clauses and far pointers, and they touch on, if not ignore altogether, the fact that if you cannot organize data, you cannot program. Data is an esoteric topic with respect to computing—the way the construction of blood corpuscles is esoteric with respect to the discussion of good health. Because it is such a misunderstood topic, data has been the chief sticking point that has hampered the development of computing.

Visual Basic is certainly the most advanced commercial form of the BASIC programming language; however, in all its graphical glory, its methodology for handling data is much the same as Microsoft introduced for TRS-80 Level II BASIC in 1979. By itself, it can be argued, Visual Basic is ineffective for programming an application that manages handfuls or large amounts of data. Perhaps this is why half of the add-on products for Visual Basic available now are sets of dynamic link libraries and custom controls for the creation and manipulation of data records and databases. Visual Basic is data-deficient, but with the addition of database-handling libraries, it can be an extraordinarily versatile front end for a database assistant manager or even for a full-scale system.

How Data Developed

The text you are reading now is data. The file my word processor produced while I was writing this chapter was not composed solely and specifically of the alphanumeric characters on this page. Someplace in the data file—generally in the header—is a segment of even more data that explains to the word processor how this text is supposed to be formatted. This segment of data often is called formatting information, and sometimes the components of such segments are called instructions.

Here is where the distinction between program code and data code becomes fuzzier. To interpret the rest of the data in the file, some programs, such as word processors and database management systems, require some type of instructional segment to explain the data. You can read this passage because you know where the spaces are between words and because you know what to do when you reach the end of a line. A word processor must be told what margins are and what spaces are. During programming, the word processor must be "trained," in a sense, to recognize the messages from the data file—What are spaces? What are margins? To make data meaningful—to make it into *information*—you must program the application to recognize the meaning in it, often from scratch. When you realize that every time a word processor is loaded into memory and launched, it must relearn the definition of "word," you begin to see where "scratch" is on the scale of understanding.

What gives data its meaning?

A program that organizes records—related bits of information about people, items of inventory, or corporate accounts—needs much more training about how elements of data are associated with one another. You may at some time write a person's name and phone number on a slip of paper. Although you might forget where you put that slip of paper, you won't forget, once you find it, to associate the phone number with the person's name. They are, after all, on the same slip of paper. A computer program cannot make similar assumptions. Unless the program operates a modem, it probably won't know what "phone number" is. It can be taught to associate one element of data with another, by virtue of the relative placement of the two elements in the file, or by the length of those elements in characters (reserve 40 or so characters for the name and 13 for the phone number, for instance), or even by the appearance of the contents.

If you're entering data into a database, you don't have to be as concerned as the programmer of the database management system (DBMS) about how this data is interpreted by the program later. If you're the programmer of the DBMS, your chief concern is the formatting of the data—how to isolate the data from the garbage and associate related elements of data with one another.

Modern DBMSs for PCs (dBASE IV, Paradox, Oracle, B-Trieve) use what are generally described as procedural languages. These languages give their programmers the ability to instruct the DBMS about how to create the data records and tables, how to structure the tables, what elements of data to associate with other elements, and how to respond to commands from the user. Visual Basic is also a procedural language, though its vocabulary does not have many instructions for organizing data.

The correlation between forms and records.

When displayed on a form, as in the inventory item forms in Chapter 3, "The Application Model," data appears organized. A data display form is a window—to borrow the term's older meaning—in a portion of the data file. The file you're peering into is divided into records, and this form displays one record at a time. Objectively, a record is a collection of related data elements. For you and me, the "partition" for this record might as well be the border of the form window. For the program behind this form to know where each record begins and ends, there must be a kind of logical partition, if not a visible one. One of the most important elements of data file structuring is determining the answer to this dilemma: Do you let the data file supply its own partitions—its own fenceposts—between records, or do you have the program supply those partitions on behalf of the file? Put another way, what do you deem responsible for deciding where—amid the long list of characters—records and fields begin and end: the program or the data file?

The question has much to do with the advances in data-storage technology through the years. The first diskettes sold for use with microcomputers—

especially the first Apple IIs—were hard sectored. Magnetic signals that acted as fenceposts were written to the disk during manufacturing. These signals defined for the computer where a sector began and ended. Today, MS-DOS writes similar fenceposts to soft-sectored diskettes for the first time during formatting; in fact, this is part of what formatting is all about.

If you let the program decide where records begin and end when written to disk, give the records fixed lengths so the program later knows where the records begin and end. This way, if you know each record is 128 bytes, you don't have to put beginning and ending signals in your data file. You know that to read the fifth record, you start at character number (5 * 128).

Sequential Access Versus Random Access

Figure 4.1 symbolizes this perennial quandary graphically. Panel 1 shows a small, four-item-per-record standard sequential access data file as it might appear on disk. Between each item are those partitions introduced earlier that tell the data manager program reading the file that each field begins and ends at this point. When the program sees this partition, it knows to stop mapping the field into memory, but here's the clinch: The partition tells the program that the field has ended, but not where. The only way you can use ordinary sequential access to find record #67 is to do the following: Have the program start at record #1 and read into memory the number of fields in one record until the end of that record. Then the program would be at record #2, so the program should repeat this process 65 more times until it reaches the beginning of record #67. The process is akin to scanning an audio tape for a particular song: without the aid of automatic music search, you must touch the fast-forward and play buttons again and again, until you find the song you want.

Panel 2 of Figure 4.1 shows the random access method at work on a data file with exactly the same contents. Here, you find no partitions between fields. The data manager program is endowed with a method of mathematically predicting where records and fields begin and end because it knows the precise length of a record. Each record has exactly the same length, so if each record is 62 bytes long, to find record #357, the program knows to start at byte #22134 in the file. It doesn't have to read 356 records first, just to forget them all, to reach the 357th. The downside of random access is that each field in every record must have as many bytes reserved for it as the maximum possible or foreseeable field in that record. For example, if you're keeping track of a collection of old record albums (remember vinyl?) and you have a record whose Title field has 64 reserved characters, you use all 64 characters in the field containing the title "Hair."

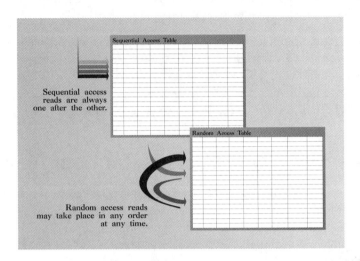

Figure 4.1. Standard sequential and random access methods compared.

Technological applications of random access.

The advent of diskette technology made random access possible. Again, the data in its file was written and read by the computer in a long stream, and it was up to the program that used the data to interpret its meaning. Yet it wasn't specifically necessary here for the program to read the data file from beginning to end in sequence or to use indexes as aids for retrieving data. Records in a random access file are numbered; it's easy for the computer to pull record #68, followed by record #12 and #79. The term *random access* in this instance means the same as it does in the term *Random Access Memory.* Data stored in memory is read into a register through a numeric address or some symbol (such as a variable) that stands for an address.

In Chapter 1, "Computing with a Language," you saw how Visual Basic mixes object-oriented syntax with the random access model in an example constructed for Situation #1, the retail inventory tracking system. Granted, Visual Basic does not have a highly structured native language for data access, but the objectified data model provides Visual Basic with its most versatile system for data access. Visual Basic *will* have a highly versatile model for database management when Microsoft's Open DataBase Connectivity (ODBC) becomes fully operational. At this writing, the version of ODBC that shipped with the Professional edition of Visual Basic 2 is equipped for use only with Microsoft's SQL Server, a data distribution system for local area networks and workgroups.

Is Random Access Progressive or Regressive?

The sequential data access model always assumes the next record to be read will be the one immediately following the previously read record. The random access model appears quite different because it enables you to read any specified record at any one time. Suppose, though, you were to have a procedure in your Visual Basic application search for a record, or for any number of records, containing a specifically named field. If the Structured Query Language (SQL) were an inherent part of Visual Basic, this request would be no problem. With the standard random access model, however, would the interpreter have to pry into each record in search of the specified field?

Think about this question from the perspective of a professional programmer; and if you already are one, put on your best programmer's hat. You can ask Visual Basic to retrieve a record only by virtue of its position in the data file. If you use random access to address that position by number, then that number is not necessarily one of the fields in that file. Many programs read a record into memory, check one field of that record for the wanted contents, and if they're not found, dump that record and read the next. This process continues until the field contents are finally found. Random access or not, this search method is actually quite sequential, so the benefits of random access go right out the window.

Implementing a query with the random access model alone.

Again, common sense gives you the solution when programming precedent does not. When you search for a word in a dictionary or a name in a telephone directory, you're able to find it because the entries are sorted. The key to finding a record in a set is to sort the set. The next question is, when should this set be sorted?

In Chapter 1, I introduced the concept of the key field, and I mentioned it would prove to be important in sorting operations. Suppose your application was employed to search for a specific record number, and that number does not refer to the record number in the file, but to the contents of the key field. If the sequence of the records stored in the data file on disk is not sorted by the key field contents, each key field can be loaded into an array in memory, and that array then can be sorted. There is now a sorted array; what's next? If the search process merely starts at the beginning of the array and plows through record after record toward the end, what has all this sorting accomplished? In some cases, especially where a key field that appears in the beginning of the data file shows up at the end of the sorted array, the purpose of sorting is actually defeated.

Situation #1: The Retail Inventory Tracking System

Here the problem of searching for a specific record is applied to the Inventory Control project INVENT1, picking it up from in Chapter 3, "The Application Model." In Chapter 1, the record structure for the two main data sets are constructed and declared in the INVENT1.GBL global module. The data types are declared ShelfItem and Product in the first two Type clauses in the global module. Once again, look at these two clauses:

```
Type ShelfItem
    ProductNo As String * 6          'Key field
    ItemNo As String * 8             'Secondary key field
    SerialNo As String * 32          'Number given the item
                                     '  by its manufacturer
    UnitPrice As Currency            'Shelf price given the
                                     '  item by reseller
    UnitCost As Currency             'Actual cost of the item
                                     '  set by vendor
    VendorCode As String * 6         'Code for the vendor that
                                     '  sold reseller this item
    VenPurchDate As Variant          'Date reseller purchased
                                     '  the item from vendor
    VenInvoiceNo As String * 8       'Invoice number of
                                     '  purchase from vendor
    Location As String * 8           'Store code for physical
                                     '  location of item
End Type

Type Product
    ProductNo As String * 6          'Key field
```

```
    Category As Integer            'Reseller-defined code for
                                   '  shelf category
    Title As String * 48           'Official title for the
                                   '  product
    Publisher As String * 6        'Reseller-defined code for
                                   '  product publisher
    RetailPrice As Currency        'Manufacturer-suggested
                                   '  retail price
    PriceBreak As Currency         'Allowed minimum negotiated
                                   '  price
    InStock As Integer             'Amount of product currently
                                   '  in stock (single-site)
    OnOrder As Integer             'Amount of product currently
                                   '  on order
    BackOrder As Integer           'Amount of product vendors
                                   '  placed on back-order
    ReOrderQuan As Integer         'Recommended reorder quantity
                                   '  on regular basis
    ReOrderPrd As Integer          'Store code for regular
                                   '  reorder
    Comments As String * 128       'Arbitrary comments from
                                   '  any user
End Type
```

In the two preceding Type clauses, the common field ProductNo is the key field, and the same key field identifies the same product for both composite variables. That is, each record of an item on the shelf contains a product identification field that relates that record to the specific and unique product. Only one record in the product list contains this product ID; otherwise there's confusion.

Suppose a procedure in INVENT1 is searching for a specific record in the Product data table, based on the contents of its product identification field. Here's how to make the application search more efficiently for that product, in a rough English-language sketch of the operation:

The Sort-Search-Retrieve query simulation method.

1. Create two arrays in memory with identical lengths and subscripts to one another. One array contains the product ID field contents, and another contains the actual Visual Basic random access record number for the record with the ID field. Give a unit variable the target for the search.

2. Have an algorithm sort in ascending order the product identification field array in memory numerically or alphabetically. During an array sort operation, the locations of two entries in the array are swapped with one another, and swapping continues until the array is sorted. While swapping proceeds, the corresponding positions of the Visual Basic record number array are swapped as well, as shown in Figure 4.2. When the product ID array is sorted, the record number array certainly won't be, though the latter array continues to reflect the location in the random access data file where each product record is found.

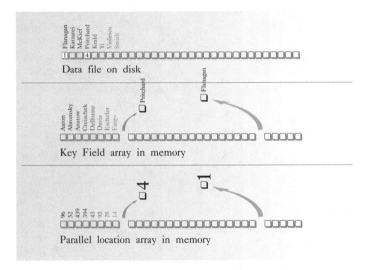

Figure 4.2. The ID field array and product number arrays, before and after the sort.

3. The search operation begins in the middle of the product ID array, as shown in Figure 4.3. If the first array element searched is not the target (slang term: *scored a miss*) because the array is sorted, the search procedure "knows," at least, whether the target ID falls before or after the current element. Assuming the target falls earlier, the search procedure jumps back half the distance in the array between the beginning and the current element. The element arrived at is then tested, and the back-or-forward jump process is repeated for smaller jump amounts until, eventually, a hit is scored. Although this process might sound tedious, it

takes fewer tries on the average to find an element with this method, than by starting at the beginning and testing each element down the list one at a time.

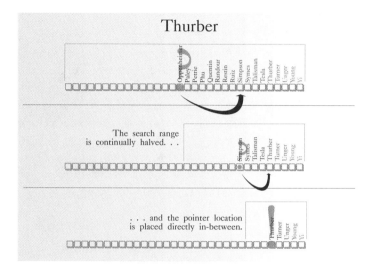

Figure 4.3. Bouncing about the record ID array.

4. When the target ID field is found, have the procedure record its array subscript. Next, retrieve into a unit variable the value from the second array with the same subscript number as that from the target ID field. This record number is the Visual Basic data file location of the whole record bearing this record number.

5. Give the data-reading procedure this record number. The Get # statement in this procedure will load the record components composite variables using the conventional random-access process. The contents may then be displayed in the form on-screen.

Algorithms-in-a-Box

Because so many applications require routines such as sorting and unit retrieval, I keep ready-made procedures on hand for copying into a general module. Such procedures are called *algorithms*; the term comes from an Arabic term meaning "repetitious math." The purpose of an algorithm in modern computing is to simulate or model repetitious real-world procedures as procedural algebra—the mathematical heart of a high-level programming language. Sorting a list, picking the top ten elements from any number of lists, or deciding which shipping route is the most efficient between cities in North America are processes that fall in the category of algorithms.

There will be entire chapters on this subject in this book, so there won't be too much digression from the topic of data. The structure of data and of algorithms, however, do bond with one another, especially at the point where sorting is employed. Configuring the processes for sorting and searching for sorted elements might seem tedious. The truth is, in programming it helps to plagiarize oneself. I copied my best sort algorithm to the Inventory Control general module and adapted it in about one minute. You will see this sort procedure again and study it in detail, but for now, I want to introduce you to the sort algorithm and give you a brief rundown about what's happening:

```
Sub qsort (dta() As Variant, locat() As Integer,
➡   arraylength As Integer)
Dim i As Integer, j As Integer, b As Integer, 1 As Integer,
➡   t As Integer, r As Integer, d As Integer
k = 1                    'initial subdivision number
p(k) = 1                 'left boundary of subdivision
w(k) = arraylength       'right boundary of subdivision
l = 1                    'left boundary of array
d = 1                    'search direction
r = arraylength          'right boundary of array
Do
toploop:
    If r - 1 < 9 Then GoTo bubsort
    i = 1
    j = r
    While j > i
        If dta(i) > dta(j) Then
            t = dta(j)
            dta(j) = dta(i)
            dta(i) = t
            d = -d
        End If
        If d = -1 Then
            j = j - 1
        Else
```

```
            i = i + 1
        End If
    Wend
    j = j + 1
    k = k + 1
    If i - 1 < r - j Then
        p(k) = j
        w(k) = r
        r = i
    Else
        p(k) = 1
        w(k) = i
        l = j
    End If
    d = -d
    GoTo toploop
bubsort:
    If r - 1 > 0 Then
        For i = 1 To r
            b = i
            For j = b + 1 To r
                If dta(j) <= dta(b) Then b = j
            Next j
            If i <> b Then
                t = dta(b)
                dta(b) = dta(i)
                dta(i) = t
            End If
        Next i
    End If
    l = p(k)
    r = w(k)
    k = k - 1
Loop Until k = 0
End Sub
```

You study this algorithm in detail in Chapter 13, "Making Programs Appear to Think." For now, here's a summary of the activity in this procedure. The array that's sorted here is dta(). This array has local scope and Variant type, so any other procedure in the project can feed this procedure an array of strings or numbers or even calendar dates, and Sub qsort () will sort it in ascending order.

Roughly, here's the way `Sub qsort ()` (also known as QuickSort) works. If the array is likened to books on a shelf, the sorter is given right and left hands. The left hand starts at the beginning of the shelf and exchanges books (or data elements) with the first right-hand book—counting from the right backward—whose title belongs before the left-hand book. Both hands pick up their books and swap them with one another. The count then flips directions, and with the right hand staying where it is, the left hand starts counting forward until it finds the first book that belongs after the right-hand book. Those two are swapped, and the direction of the count flips back.

Eventually, the two hands collide. At that point, the element is divided into two subarrays, and the swapping process starts over with those smaller subarrays. Even with the smaller arrays, the hands collide again, and another pair of subarrays is created. (Now you know why algorithm means repetitious math.) When a divided subarray has become so small that it isn't worth apportioning left and right hands for—say, five or six books—the subarray is sent to a "bubble-sorter" (yes, that's the name of it), and the small group is perfectly sorted from left to right. At some point, every book will become part of a subarray, and it is the small-group sorting of the subarrays that eventually makes the entire shelf perfectly sorted.

Back in `Sub qsort ()` now, the second array, `locat()`, carries the Visual Basic number for the record containing each data element. When QuickSort swaps two elements of `dta()`, it swaps the corresponding elements of `locat()`. After `dta()` is sorted, `locat()` registers the location in the random access file of the record containing each sorted ID field.

Technique Note: Legitimate use for `GoTo` #1—The `GoTo` statement can be used to fork a procedure into two parts whose paths do not converge again, as they might following the end of a conditional clause.

After `Sub qsort ()`, the record-finding process continues to the binary search procedure (another procedure from my personal library adapted to the present purpose).

```
Sub bsearch (dta() As Variant, locat() As Integer,
➡   arraylength As Integer, s As Variant)
```

```
i = Int(arraylength / 2)
l = 1
r = arraylength
Do While t <> s
    t = dta(i)
    Select Case True
        Case t = s
            Exit Do
        Case t < s
            l = i
        Case t > s
            r = i
    End Select
    i = l + Int((r - l) / 2)
Loop
End Sub
```

Notice some similarity in the structure between the sort and search algorithms. Both perform their functions by dividing their arrays into two parts repeatedly. Both rely on the postulate that in an ascending sorted array, a lesser-valued element falls earlier in the sequence than a greater-valued element.

Declaring the Dependent Data Structures

At the end of Chapter 3, the INVENT1 application was left in this state: the application model was drawn on a hierarchical chart, and collective and peripheral contexts were determined for the various modules. Although I discussed how a purchasing agent might use this application every day, I also took notes for future reference when the data sets are constructed. These notes read as follows:

1. A security system performs log-on and log-off operations for the user.

2. The price of an item on the shelf may be fixed, but the price of a product is always variable.

3. Every time items are checked into inventory, the dealer costs (vendor prices) paid for those items go into the product record.

4. The contents of a vendor order should be kept in a separate list, recall-able at the time items are entered into inventory.

5. Each major form in the application should be capable of accepting cross-referenced data directly from another form.

Implementing the security system.

Consider each of these points in sequence. The security system is part of the Central Administrator form and is the first thing a user sees when booting INVENT1. For the Administrator to identify a user who's an employee in a company with a handful of people on the payroll, all that's needed is the employee's initials. When the company makes a crucial change to inventory—for example, when it removes a product from the list or reduces its price—a signal of that change, along with the user's initials, is recorded and sent to an auxiliary data file. For the Security system (part of Central Administration, the MDI parent and start-up form), there are two random access data file definitions, as follows:

```
Type Security
    Initials As String * 3
    LogInDate As Variant
    LogInTime As Variant
    TimeOn As Variant
End Type

Type Alteration
    Initials As String * 3
    AltCode As Integer
    AltTime As Variant
End Type
```

Visual Basic 2 is now capable of storing dates and times as valid variables, as long as those variables are declared implicitly (without using a declarative statement) or declared using the Variant data type. This enables the inclusion of specially considered elements in composite variables.

Accounting for extreme variance in informational value.

As you saw in Chapter 3, there is no single way for the reseller to determine how much a product would cost were it purchased from a vendor, nor is there a fixed method for the reseller to determine how much to charge a customer. It isn't reasonable to expect the reseller's purchasing agent to spend countless hours copying figures from vendor catalogs when the offers made by those catalogs might be beaten tomorrow by those same vendors' dealer representatives over the phone. On the other hand, the purchaser needs INVENT1 to keep track of the costs he has been offered by the various vendors to that point.

Figure 4.4 shows the Vendor ID form for this application. I wrote a data file format for vendors and then drew this form; but admittedly, during that time, I remembered certain other fields which should be included. For this reason, I then amended the data file format.

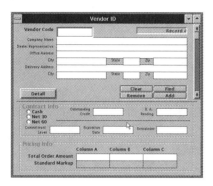

Figure 4.4. What a purchaser needs to know about his vendor.

The Detail button on the Vendor ID form allows only the uppermost vendor address portion of the form to show at first, and reveals the lower detail portion only on demand. The composite data type associated with this form is declared as follows:

```
Type Vendor
    Code As String * 6                'Vendor key code
    Name As String * 48               'Name of vendor corporation
    DealerRep As String * 32          'Name of key contact person
    OffAddress As String * 50         'Address where the money
                                      '  is sent
    OffCity As String * 20
    OffState As String * 5
    OffZip As String * 10
    DelAddress As String * 50         'Address where all the
                                      '  returns are sent
    DelCity As String * 20
    DelState As String * 5
    DelZip As String * 10
```

```
    TermsCode As Integer          'Code for reseller payment
                                  '   contract terms
    Commitment As Currency        'Minimum purchase commitment
                                  '   if any
    CommitDate As Variant         'Time when commitment
                                  '   runs out
    CommitRdr As Currency         'What's left to be spent
                                  '   toward commitment
    OutCredit As Currency         'Outstanding credit coming
                                  '   from vendor
    RAPending As Currency         'Credit that would be coming
                                  '   from returns
    OrderBreak(3) As Currency     'Per-order milestone for
                                  '   achieving price breaks
    Markup(3) As Single           'Corresponding percentage of
                                  '   price break
End Type
```

When a reseller first begins a business relationship with a vendor, the vendor may at first require the reseller to pay for orders with cash up front. Over time, as the vendor trusts the reseller, the vendor might relax the payment terms, generally to *Net 30,* which means payment in full is due in 30 days. The TermsCode field of Type Vendor refers to the type of payment agreement currently in effect.

Some vendors offer special price breaks to resellers if they can make a commitment to purchase goods valued at a certain dollar amount over a three-month or perhaps one-year period. The Commitment field refers to the total amount of this commitment, if one exists. CommitDate is the day the commitment is scheduled to be met, and CommitRdr refers to the amount remaining to be purchased before the expiration date.

In Chapter 3, I mentioned that some vendors use multiple pricing tiers to encourage resellers to purchase more items per order. One common enticement method is a three-column system, where small orders are tallied in Column A, medium-size orders in Column B, and larger orders in Column C. Resellers are likely to use flat-rate, across-the-board markdowns from suggested retail, where Column A is 33 percent, B is about 35 percent, and C is about 38 percent. Where vendors use such markdowns, the component arrays OrderBreak() and Markup() tally them.

Now, across-the-board markdowns might not be guaranteeable, so it makes sense to have a pricing detail form list the possible costs for each item. Figure 4.5 shows this subordinate form, which was not originally planned in the hierarchical chart for INVENT1. The Detail form is an extension of the Product Display form, and would appear beside it if the user clicked the Detail button.

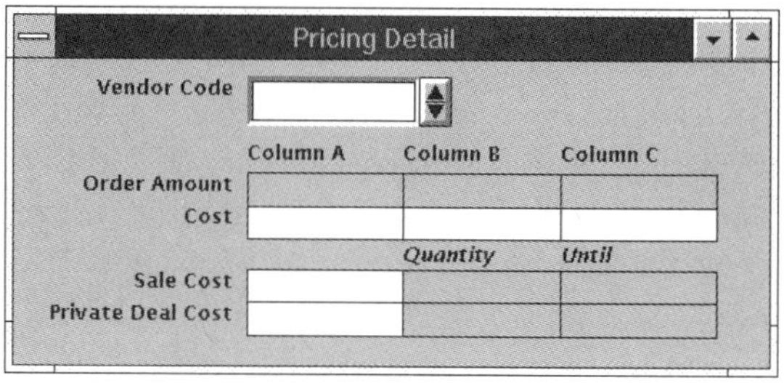

Figure 4.5. Whatever happened to your old-fashioned red-tag sale?

To resolve the issue of storing cost breakdowns in detail without forcing the purchaser to enter the entire contents of every catalog, I created a separate composite variable type that keeps records for only those products the purchaser deems important. Each catalog record includes a copy of the six-character ProductNo key field, tying it to the product it refers to. Here's the structure of the catalog record:

```
Type VenCatalog
    VendorCode As String * 6        'Code created by reseller
                                    '  for associated vendor
    CatalogNo As String * 12        'Unique catalog number for
                                    '  product
    ProductNo As String * 6         'Key field for product
    Cost(3) As Currency             'Cost breakdown in vendor
                                    '  catalog
    SaleCost As Currency            'Vendor special
    SaleBreak As Integer            'Required order quantity
                                    ' for special offer
    SaleDate As Variant             'Expiration date of special
    PrivateCost As Currency         'Separate deal offered by
                                    '  vendor via phone or fax
    PrivateBreak As Integer         'Required order quantity for
                                    '  separate deal
```

```
      PrivateDate As Variant          'Expiration date of private
                                      '  deal
      PackageOrderNo As String * 6    'Cross-reference to
                                      '  combination order number
End Type
```

If the three-column cost breakdown differs from the standard structure recorded in the vendor profile, the Cost() array records the individual breakdown. The catalog costs may be overridden in two cases—costs from a special offer or from a bargain struck between the purchaser and the vendor's dealer representative over the phone. Both costs are treated individually. When a purchase is registered through the Purchasing module, the program assumes the reseller is paying the lowest price offered by that vendor for the given quantity, unless otherwise stated.

This leads to another point from my notes in Chapter 3. There I concluded the vendor cost list should be updated each time a purchase is entered into the system and the cost paid by the reseller falls below the lowest cost listed in the VenCatalog table.

Believe it or not, the way to implement Point #3 is to address Point #4—the need for a separate vendor purchase file. Here's the structure for a reseller purchase:

```
Type Purchase
      VendorCode As String * 6
      OrderDate As Variant
      OurInvoiceNo As String * 16
      Purchaser As String * 3
      Quantity(100) As Integer
      ProductNo(100) As String * 6
      ProductCost(100) As Currency
      DelivStatus(100) As Integer
      ShipCost As Integer
      ShipRoute As Integer
End Type
```

The Purchaser field is a reference to the initials of the current user, entered through Central Administration. Visual Basic 2 now enables you to enter arrays as components of composite variables, but unfortunately these arrays cannot be dynamic arrays—only static. If dynamic arrays were allowed, I could have added one more component—NumItems—for the number of items ordered, and invoked a procedure to use `NumItems` to `ReDim` (redimension) the dynamic arrays containing the items ordered. Because only static arrays are allowed, I chose 100, a reasonable maximum number of orderable items. Unfortunately, this results in a lot of wasted space.

Because the concept of a customer-placed order to the store is so similar to the concept of a store-placed order to its wholesale vendor, I used `Purchase` as a model structure for the composite variable for customer orders, shown here:

```
Type CustOrder
    CustCode As String * 6
    OrderDate As Variant
    OurInvoiceNo As String * 16
    PONo As String * 16
    Purchaser As String * 3
    Quantity(32) As Integer
    ProductNo(32) As String * 6
    ProductCost(32) As Currency
    ProjectPrice(32) As Currency
    DelivStatus(32) As Integer
End Type
```

Recalculative and Cross-Referencing Fields

One goal of data structuring is to *create* as much overlap as possible. Where information is stored once within a data file, that same information should not have to be stored yet again in a separate file in use by the application. Information in this instance—as is the case with all areas of database planning—is the vital message the data is conveying to the user by way of data.

Certain fields in the Shelf Item and Product Display forms for INVENT1 convey the same information to the user. For instance, the "Our Price" and "Suggested Retail" fields in both "Price Info" frames should read identically for a product in one form and an associated shelf item in the other.

I could have made `RetailPrice` a component variable for both the `ShelfItem` and `Product` tables. Even though there would have been redundancy, I would have avoided having to make the Shelf Item module cross-reference the `Product` table for certain data elements. This would have meant loading one array with the product code ID fields and another array with the number of the records containing those fields, then sorting the arrays, performing a binary search, and retrieving the record whose number is pointed to by the location array. This is all quite a lot of trouble to save a slice or two of disk and memory space, so why bother?

The problem with the question "Why Bother?" is that it's contagious. It spreads like a virus through the ambition centers of the programmer's mind, rendering the perseverance regions paralyzed and eventually mutating the programmer into a short-sighted spouter of inconsistent, convoluted code. Making INVENT1 do the sort, search, and retrieval process, rather than only declare a redundant field, might mean an extra expenditure of time in milliseconds; however, the tighter, though distributed, data structure I've created here is more efficient. It maintains as closely as possible a one-to-one ratio of information content to data. The goal of the designer of data is to represent the most information with the least amount of data in the tightest possible region of space attainable.

Redundancy in a data table or schema (set of related tables) increases the possibility of inconsistency, and therefore of error. The key field method ensures related data records absolutely address one another; after the sort, search, and retrieve process is done, only the related data record is pulled from the table, so there can be no error. I realize this sounds like a campaign promise, but think of it like this: The computer excels more at math than it does at maintaining lists of data. The more math you use to help in the data-storing process, the more capable the computer should be of doing the job. Relating data elements to one another is, in an especially well-rephrased manner, mathematical in nature.

Technique Note: As a general rule, the more math you use in representing data and relating data elements to one another, the more reliable the database becomes.

Using Data That Works

The way Visual Basic normally handles data files, characters are read to and written from what is really, for all intents and purposes, an ASCII document. Later, when a VB program is employed to read this document, it must somehow be taught how to recognize what parts of the document are meaningful, and what parts are merely a bunch of spaces. The objective of dataset and data file management libraries is to make the meaningful part of the data more recognizable.

The way information is made meaningful to people is by patterning and positioning. Part of the reason people purchase interpreters such as Visual Basic is to be able to apply layout techniques to data in ways that they themselves can define. Visual Basic's standard equipment makes it easy for data to be laid out like a form; using the 0GRID.VBX control, it may also be displayed in a row/column tabular format, like a spreadsheet. Data makes more sense to us displayed either of these ways than as an endless stream of characters, although the computer application will store data in character streams.

So the first way we make data more meaningful—more *informational*—is by augmenting its accessibility. Rather than reading the entire stream from beginning to end each time, the application should be able to point to a specific record or field. The next way we make data more useful is by giving it structure and identity. The most common structure given to data stored in MS-DOS machines is the .DBF file format, which was originated for the first dBASE programs by C. Wayne Ratliff back in 1979. Ratliff's original intention was to write a football statistics manager; but on the whole, his objective had always been to encode the structure of data along with the data, and store that with the file. This way it would not be entirely up to the program that reads the data to interpret it; the structure would not have to be defined entirely by the program. Instead, the program reads a set of indexes and maps, and deduces the structure from that.

Ratliff made this structure work for CP/M and MS-DOS computer systems—which, in his day, rarely contained an excess of 64K of RAM, and sported hard disks only as a luxury. The MS-DOS file structure to which we are still somewhat bound retains the same general constraints today, with multi-gigabyte CD-ROM systems at our disposal, as it did during the days when 360K was, to put it briefly, a lot. MS-DOS still treats all files as equals. A program is a file, a resource header is a file, an overlay is a file, and a database is a file. In the dBASE structure, an index is a file too.

During the development of DOS, few thought there would ever be a need to distinguish executable from non-executable code. In fact, one of the early selling points of DOS was the fact that this distinction was *not* made. Because so many businesses initiated their databases using the then-young dBASE structure on their 64K machines of old, and along the way added record after record to their tables, even though computer hardware and most applications managed to evolve beyond the amoebic stage, the structure of the dBASE file stayed about as resilient as the structure of algebra and trigonometry. Today, the basics of the old .DBF format are in the public domain—which means anyone can write a database manager using .DBF—and in deference to all the DBMS manufacturers *other* than Borland, the format is now referred to broadly as *xBase* format.

So, rather than having to find new ways to structure data, most of the time database programmers are looking for new ways to interpret the *same* data, without having to change the foundation of the huge databases already generated. With Visual Basic assuming the role of what one writer called "the dream database front-end," what is required now is a real data management engine running in the background. Since ODBC has proven itself to be, shall we say, "under construction," I've chosen to provide you instead with a data management system that really works; namely, Terry Orletsky's *vxBase,* which is contained in its entirety on the demo disk included with this book.

Applying vxBase

The way to think about dynamic link libraries is not as a series of small programs with individual function calls chained together, but as the mechanism of a large program with function calls that act as hooks into the system. vxBase is a full-scale database management program for xBase files, using Clipper-style indexes (Clipper is a DBMS development system manufactured by Nantucket Software). The vxBase library calls are modeled after Clipper's procedural language, which itself was modeled heavily after dBASE III.

In the xBase format, each .DBF file contains code that represents the structure of a *table*—which is a set of related records whose fields and field names correlate exactly. The contents of a database table may be listed on a grid, with each row of the grid containing a single record of data, and each field name apportioned its own column. There is a great deal of simplicity to the .DBF file structure that makes it readily comprehensible by the database programmer, if not entirely adaptable to every foreseeable application. A .DBF file is based on streams of characters, like most other files in MS-DOS. The greater portion of that file which contains the records are stored in sequence adjacent to one another. Each record has a fixed length in characters; so it is ridiculously easy to generate a table-format report with perfectly aligned rows and columns, for a .DBF file whose records are *n* characters long, by printing *n* characters of the file starting at record 1, generating a carriage return and line feed, and printing the next *n* characters.

Outside the Bounds of DOS

To effectively program in vxBase, it would help you to have had some experience programming with Clipper or, in lieu of that product, dBASE III Plus. The database-devoted DLL functions in vxBase parallel those of the older dBASE, the most obvious exceptions being that all vxBase DLL calls are preceded by the letters vx; a number of calls have been expressly created for the purpose of handling graphics and displays. Of course, many of the dBASE procedural commands such as DO CASE and SAY were dropped, to account for the fact that Visual Basic provides that same functionality, perhaps to a greater extent.

To give you an idea of the dynamics of the system, I'll take you on a tour of Terry Orletsky's test application, also included with the demo disks. It is actually a parts inventory system for an aircraft brokerage house, such as the one Orletsky's colleague runs in Alberta. First of all, before loading any application that uses vxBase, whether an uncompiled Visual Basic project or an .EXE file, you must first load a special program into memory called VXLOAD.EXE, whose main purpose is to drive the DLLs on behalf of *vxBase*. This way, if something goes wrong, VXLOAD will know to clear the DLL from memory; sometimes VB will leave it in memory even if you've cleared the interpreter from memory.

The Aircraft Brokerage Test Application

After you've loaded VXLOAD.EXE into memory, its "VX" icon appears in the corner of the screen, letting you know the database management system is officially active. Here's the `Sub Form_Load ()` procedure for the test application's startup form, as written by Terry Orletsky:

```
Sub Form_Load ()
    FromExitButt = True
    ' register the task with the vxbase multitask list
    ' ------------------------------------------------
    vxInit
    ' we are using enhanced controls so
    ' set system gray to dark gray
    ' -----------------------------------
    vxCtlGraySet
    ' increase number of handles
    ' for the task from 20 to 32
    ' --------------------------------------------------
    If vxSetHandles(32) < 32 Then
        MsgBox "Not enough Handles"
        Unload VXFORM0
    End If
    Call vxSetLocks(False)
    j% = vxCloseAll()
    FromExitButt = False
End Sub
```

All the proper DLL function declarations appear within the global module of the application. `vxInit()` officially registers this VB task with vxBase—a way, in a sense, of "logging in." Later, `vxSetHandles()` checks to see if enough file handles are available for this task; otherwise, the task might not be able to cross-reference the necessary number of data files. `vxSetLocks()` here disengages automatic record locking. One of the problems programmers of multiuser databases must face is the fact that one current image of the data must be maintained for all systems that may access the data, at all times. Without record locking, if two users load an image of a database table simultaneously, and both make their own respective additions to the table, one user's changes might override the other's when they are both saved back to the same source file location. The `False` setting above means the DBMS assumes, for the most part, you're on a single-user system. Next, `vxCloseAll()` is used like a "reset" directive to vxBase, closing any open data files if they may happen to be resting unattended somewhere in the system. Again, another element of the dynamics of multitasking databases rears its ugly head.

When the aircraft brokerage test program loads into the workspace, after the title form is a simple menu form, much like the vertical database applications of old. Skipping over the menuing procedures, assume you're going into the aircraft inventory screen.

At this point, a procedure call is placed to this general procedure in the module VXBMOD.BAS:

```
Sub AircraftOpen ()
' open aircraft file
' ------------------
   AircraftDbf = vxUseDbf("d:\vbasic\vxbtest\aircraft.dbf")
   If AircraftDbf = FALSE Then
      MsgBox "Error Opening aircraft.dbf. Aborting."
    End
   End If
   Aircraf1Ntx = vxUseNtx("d:\vbasic\vxbtest\aircraf1.ntx")
   Aircraf2Ntx = vxUseNtx("d:\vbasic\vxbtest\aircraf2.ntx")
' Declare Aircraft Table
' ----------------------
   Call vxTableDeclare(VX_RED, ByVal 0&, ByVal 0&, 0, 1, 6)
   Call vxTableField(1, "Type", "c_cat", VX_FIELD)
   Call vxTableField(2, "Description", "left(c_desc,20)", VX_EXPR)
   Call vxTableField(3, "Code", "c_code", VX_FIELD)
   Call vxTableField(4, "Price", "c_price", VX_FIELD)
   Call vxTableField(5, "Year", "c_year", VX_FIELD)
   Call vxTableField(6, "TTSN", "c_ttsn", VX_FIELD)
End Sub
```

The vxUseDbf() function parallels the USE command in dBASE because it specifies a database table file to be opened. In the previous access modes we've studied thus far, some variant of the Open keyword had been specified to declare a data file open; here, vxUseDbf() fulfills the same purpose. Access to a .DBF file is bidirectional unless the vxUseDbfRO() function is used instead; in that case, the file could not be altered or written to.

The index files used by vxBase are in the Clipper, not the dBASE, format because, commented Terry Orletsky, "they're faster and smaller than dBASE .NDX files." The vxUseNtx() instructions declare as open two index files, both of which refer back to the contents of the main aircraft data file.

The next section is the real surprise of this program. vxBase does *not* use any custom controls or THREED.VBX for its three-dimensional output; the three-dimensionality portion of the package is actually a special graphics feature supplied for vxBase by programmer Ray Donahue and integrated into the system by Terry Orletsky. The vxTableDeclare() function sets up what is called a *browse list*. It's not a graphic object, mind you, but a separate window that is opened with this function. Within the function, the VX_RED constant sets up a red column head with 3-D text. The vxTableField() functions then set up respective columns for each field, using the field names passed to it in the third parameter.

From here, the program passes control to this procedure (comments by Terry Orletsky):

```
Sub BrowseAir ()
    ' Browse Aircraft File
    ' Called from VXFORM1 OpenAircraft_click and VXFORM6.AirBrowse
    ' -------------------------------------------------------------
    ' Select Aircraft File
    ' --------------------
    j% = vxSelectDbf(AircraftDbf)
    j% = vxSelectNtx(Aircraf2Ntx)
    ' Open a browse table no editing capabilities
    ' -------------------------------------------
    AircraftReturn = 0  ' declared as GLOBAL so VXFORM6 can
➥ interrogate
    ' Disable menu items
    ' ------------------
    VXFORM1.OpenCust.Enabled = FALSE
    VXFORM1.OpenAircraft.Enabled = FALSE
    VXFORM1.LinkBuyToSell.Enabled = FALSE
    VXFORM1.LinkSellToBuy.Enabled = FALSE
    VXFORM1.PackFiles.Enabled = FALSE
    Form6Active = TRUE  ' true so will be true when browse up
' Execute the browse routine (will use table declared in VXFORM0)
' --------------------------------------------------------------
    Call vxBrowse(VXFORM1.hWnd, AircraftDbf, Aircraf2Ntx, FALSE,
➥ TRUE, FALSE, 0, "Aircraft On File", AircraftReturn)
    Select Case AircraftReturn
        Case BROWSE_ERROR
            MsgBox "Error in AirCraft Browse!"
```

```
            VXFORM1.OpenCust.Enabled = TRUE
            VXFORM1.OpenAircraft.Enabled = TRUE
            VXFORM1.LinkBuyToSell.Enabled = TRUE
            VXFORM1.LinkSellToBuy.Enabled = TRUE
            VXFORM1.PackFiles.Enabled = TRUE
            Form6Active = FALSE
            Exit Sub
        ' user closed browse with sys menu
        ' -----------------------------
        Case BROWSE_CLOSED
            j% = vxSelectDbf(AircraftDbf)
            j% = vxClose()
            VXFORM1.OpenCust.Enabled = TRUE
            VXFORM1.OpenAircraft.Enabled = TRUE
            VXFORM1.LinkBuyToSell.Enabled = TRUE
            VXFORM1.LinkSellToBuy.Enabled = TRUE
            VXFORM1.PackFiles.Enabled = TRUE
            Form6Active = FALSE
            Exit Sub
        ' the only other choice is the user double-clicked
        ' a record or pressed the enter key, thereby requesting
        ' a full display on VXFORM6
        ' ----------------------------------------------------
        Case Else
            VXFORM6.Show
    End Select
End Sub
```

The vxSelectDbf() and vxSelectNtx() routines tell vxBase that the database-related instructions to follow pertain to these specific table and index files, in case more happen to be open at the time—for instance, the customer or parts file. After some of the menu selections are disabled, the vxBrowse() function places the *browse object,* as Orletsky calls it, into the currently open window. This object is a window unto itself, positioned to look like an MDI child window, although it is not really the child of the main menu window, so it can be moved about independently of the menu.

Internal Expressions

As fascinating as the vxBase browse control is, perhaps the most fascinating part of this DBMS library package is the way it evaluates arithmetic expressions passed to it as strings, independently of Visual Basic. A great majority of the arithmetic and string-handling functions of dBASE III are supported by vxBase; thus in cases of library functions where a field name is required, you may choose to substitute a vxBase arithmetic expression. The form of these expressions can be gratifyingly complex.

For instance, in one of the previous procedures, you saw the expression `"left(c_desc,20)"` used in place of the lone field name `c_desc`. This function is similar to Visual Basic's `Left$(term$, 20)`, although it refers to a setting for an entire field of data entries, not to a VB variable. Notice the presence of quotation marks; VB is passing vxBase a formal string or string variable, so when a real VB variable isn't being specified, the quotation marks are required. Remember, `c_desc` is not a VB variable in this instance, but a vxBase field name, referring to a set of related entries rather than a single string.

You may also embed a logical condition within a vxBase function, as though you were invoking an `If-Then-Else` clause. For instance, suppose you want the Totals column in the browse table to contain only positive values, and to leave blanks wherever a specific total is zero or below. You could pass the `vxTableField()` function the following expression:

```
"if(total<0,total,'')"
```

Notice the doubled single-quotes between the double-quotes... okay, I'll rephrase that. Notice the two single-quotes between the two quotation marks. Like doubled double-quotes, they signify an empty or null string; but because they are passed as part of a VB string between double-quotes, they are converted to single-quotes. (Actually, some dBASE versions prefer single quotes in expressions anyway.) The expression above is phrased like a function with three parameters, the first being the arithmetic condition being tested ("Is the total greater than zero?"). The second parameter represents the "true side" of the mini-clause; in this case, `total` by itself simply means please display the total. The `''` null string as the third parameter—the "false side" of the mini-clause—means please leave the field empty if the expression test fails, and the total is zero or negative.

The author of vxBase has asked me to remind you that, because the product is shareware, if you choose to use vxBase in your business, please purchase a registered copy through his company, vxBase, Ltd. The registration fee and process is listed in the files on the demo disks accompanying this book, and the registration address is listed in an appendix. In exchange for the fee, you will be sent a full instruction manual, along with a working copy of Terry Orletsky's data utilities program *DataWorks.*

Data in Memory

After they are loaded into memory, what do arrays and sets of data actually *do?* In INVENT1 the records would appear to rest in memory at the spot where they are loaded, and they would wait to be updated or sorted. The type of data schema the INVENT1 project utilizes is not entirely indicative of the way all tables, arrays, or structures are created or utilized. Each field in the INVENT1 structure is representative of some name or characteristic of a thing, like an adjective modifies a noun.

An entirely different way to conceive a data array is more *geometrical* than lexical. The next example demonstrates the use of data arrays in modeling mathematical functions.

Situation #2: The Expressor Mark Calculator

Picking up from Chapter 2, "The Structure of Visual Basic," it is the intention of the Expressor Mark II project to give the user access to a charting module. The original purpose of the Expressor Mark I was to solve one formula and display its results in a calculator-style readout. Mark II will solve this same formula for a range of values whose minimum and maximum values are entered into the Expressor's front panel. This module will take the linguistic formula currently displayed on the panel, solve for that formula several hundred times rather than one, and plot the results on a separate x/y chart form.

The design of the chart form is a quite simple affair, graphically speaking. Basically it's a lot of blank space with a few controls along the lower edge, as shown here:

```
Form: EXPCHART.FRM
General Procedures:
    <None>
```

```
        AutoRedraw         True
        BackColor          &H40
        Caption            Expressor Chart
        FormName           Chart
        LinkTopic          Form2

        Active Form Event Procedures
            <None>

    Control Type: PictureBox
        Control Name: ChartArea
        AutoRedraw         True
        BackColor          &H40
        BorderStyle        0 - None
        CtlName            ChartArea
        FontBold           False
        FontName           Helv
        FontSize           7.78125
        ForeColor          &HFFFF

        Active Control Event Procedures
            <None>

    Control Type: Label
        Control Name: ChartLoad
        Alignment          2 - Center
        BackColor          &HFF
        Caption            Load
        CtlName            ChartLoad
        ForeColor          &H0
        TabIndex           5

        Active Control Event Procedures
         ChartLoad_Click

        Control Name: ChartSave
        Alignment          2 - Center
        BackColor          &HFFFF
        Caption            Save
        CtlName            ChartSave
        ForeColor          &H0
        TabIndex           4
```

```
Active Control Event Procedures
 ChartSave_Click

Control Name: Cutter
Alignment            2 - Center
BackColor            &HFFFF00
Caption              Copy
CtlName              Cutter
ForeColor            &H0
TabIndex             2

Active Control Event Procedures
 Cutter_Click

Control Name: FlipPanel
Alignment            2 - Center
BackColor            &HFF00
Caption              Panel
CtlName              FlipPanel
TabIndex             3

Active Control Event Procedures
 FlipPanel_Click

Control Name: Prnt
Alignment            2 - Center
BackColor            &HFF00FF
Caption              Print
CtlName              Prnt
ForeColor            &H0

Active Control Event Procedures
 Prnt_Click
```

Defining Expressor II's Contexts

The way the Expressor has been designed thus far, the Function procedures performing the formula calculations have been constructed in the EXPRESR2.BAS general module. These same function procedures will be called for the charting module of Expressor II, though I intend to leave the Function procedures where they are now. The chief reason the charting procedures are placed in EXPRESR2.BAS rather than in EXPCHART.FRM is the procedures receive some of their data inputs from the main panel form, and a procedure in one form module cannot call a procedure in another form module directly. So the Expressor panel cannot turn to the chart and say, "Hey, chart, here's something for you to plot"; the two form modules live in different worlds and are not on speaking terms. A general module can act as mediator between two forms, as a conduit for data being exchanged between them. It bridges the contexts between two form modules whose own contexts would otherwise be limited to their respective module boundaries.

The charting module is by far the largest and most complex procedure dealt with thus far, so rather than print it on a ream, I'll present it here in bite-size chunks.

EXPRESR2.BAS

General Declarations:

```
Dim xi(50) As Single, yi(50) As Single, xln(50)
➡  As Single, yln(50) As Single
Dim charty(1000)
```

Figure 4.6 depicts the Expressor chart drawing area. Rather than use the GRAPH.VBX extension control shipped with VB2 Professional Edition, I've chosen to have this procedure draw an original, completely framed and "ticked" x/y chart. The results from this original procedure will be unique and more adaptable to the potential purposes of other applications.

Here is a description of the work performed by the Expressor charting mechanism in summary: The main picture box in the chart form contains a rectangular field that in turn contains the function chart. The area of this rectangular plotting field is entirely variable and can be stretched to fit snugly beside the surrounding text. The field is divided into 1,000 long, tall columns. Each column represents a range of possible values along the y-axis. The formula the user selects through the Expressor Panel form (the calculator) is executed 1,000 times. The value of each result is stored in the array charty(1000). Each time the formula is solved, a point is plotted in one of the columns, counting one by one from the left. The greater the charty() value, the higher the plotted point; the lesser the value, the lower the point.

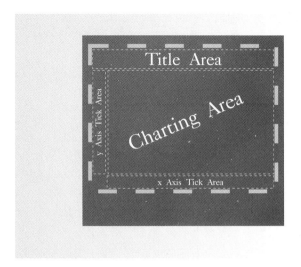

Figure 4.6. The Expressor chart field in its newborn, empty state.

On the Expressor panel form, the user enters maximum and minimum range values. The range between them is divided into 1,000 equal parts. The column on the extreme left represents the solution to the equation when solving for the minimum value; the column on the extreme right represents the solution when solving for the maximum value. Each column in the chart represents a value interval equal to 1/1000 of the difference between the maximum and minimum column values. In other words, the width of each column is 1/1000 of the total distance between the left and right values along the x-axis.

As the procedure assesses the chart's appearance, it extracts from each of the 1,000 columns the highest- and lowest-valued solutions for the chosen formula. These values become the maximum and minimum for the range represented by the y-axis of the chart. The maximum and minimum values are represented at the extreme upper and lower points of each column. Representative tick marks are placed at regular intervals along the left and lower borders of the chart rectangle, denoting the value of certain points along the two axes. As many as 50 tick marks indicate the values along the left and bottom of the chart. The representative values for the x- and y-axes' tick marks are stored in the array variables $xi()$ and $yi()$; the location of these tick marks on the chart form are represented in the array variables $xln()$ and $yln()$.

Here is the procedure that draws these wonderful charts.

General Procedures Area, Part 1:

```
Sub CreateChart (xmin As Single, xmax As Single,
➡ xslot As Integer)
Chart.Show
Chart.ChartArea.Cls
title$ = Panel.CalcList.Text
Chart.ChartArea.FontSize = 16
Try:
If Chart.ChartArea.TextWidth(title$) >
➡ Chart.ChartArea.Width Then
    Chart.ChartArea.FontSize = Chart.ChartArea.FontSize
➡        - 1
    GoTo Try
End If
```

The header for the procedure accepts the minimum and maximum range values xmin and xmax as parameters, along with their slot of origin on the panel xslot. The chart is shown, so the user will know her program has not crashed. The title for this chart, title$, is taken directly from the name of the formula chosen from the panel's drop-down listbox. A routine then determines what point size to use for the title text by starting with 16 points, utilizing the .TextWidth() method to see whether the title in title$ fits inside the space of ChartArea, and if not, reducing the point size by 1. Yes, I used GoTo. I hope you're not too shocked. A tech editor might comment I could or should have used a Do-Loop clause instead, but I sometimes tend not to. I learned to program in old BASIC, so I'm used to GoTo; and with all due respect to the conservative movement in programming to stamp out GoTo in our lifetimes, I still believe the statement does the job.

Pen-style plotting to a picture box.

As you read the rest of this procedure, try to imagine this chart as being plotted with a mechanical pen. This pen is on an armature whose gears not only determine but also record the position of the pen. The current coordinates of the pen may be stated as (CurrentX, CurrentY). If anything is to be drawn or printed to the form, it appears here. Thus when text or lines are plotted, in your mind picture this pen moving like a mechanical plotter. The pen position starts, by default, at (0, 0)—the upper-left corner.

Part 2:

```
Chart.ChartArea.ForeColor = 65535
Chart.ChartArea.CurrentX = (Chart.ChartArea.Width / 2) -
➥   Chart.ChartArea.TextWidth(title$) / 2)
Chart.ChartArea.Print title$
Chart.ChartArea.FontSize = 8.25
Chart.ChartArea.CurrentY = Chart.ChartArea.CurrentY + 100
charttop = Chart.ChartArea.CurrentY
Chart.ChartArea.CurrentX = 0
```

Imagine the mechanical plotter has just picked up a bright yellow (#65535) ink pen. The chart's title will be centered in the middle of the form. Imagine now the mechanical arm moving along the x-axis (horizontal) to the center and then back to the left for a distance half the projected width of the title. Remember, the `.TextWidth` method can project the width of text before it is printed. This is the old Gregg Beginners' Typewriting method for centering a title on a page, put into practice in BASIC.

After the title is printed, the font size is reduced to 8.25 points—the font size for the tick marks. The `.CurrentY` gear for this analogetic armature is moved down 100 twips. The coordinate position of `Chart.ChartArea.CurrentY` at this point is recorded as variable `charttop`. The procedure now has a place marking the extreme upper edge of the chart. This chart has a variable size; it consumes as much space as it can, but leaves just enough for the text around it, no matter what the text's size will eventually be. Next, the pen is moved back to the left edge of the chart. This is the virtual equivalent of a "carriage return." Figure 4.7 depicts the course the virtual armature-driven pen has taken thus far.

After awhile, you plot tick marks and values to the point where the armature rests now. For the nonce, it's time to invoke the formula-solving mechanism for the 1,000 columns.

Part 3:

```
frmula = Panel.CalcList.ListIndex + 1
intval = (xmax - xmin) / 1000
For in = 0 To 4
    p(in) = Val(Panel.Param(in).Text)
Next in
If xmin = xmax Then
    Panel.Show
    Exit Sub
End If
```

Figure 4.7. How variables coalesce to model a virtual pen.

The index number of the formula being solved is extracted from the Panel form. By the way, full references must be placed to the form and its subordinate graphic object—for instance, `Panel.CalcList.ListIndex` and `Chart.ChartArea.CurrentY`—because these references appear in the middle of a general, non-form-specific procedure. When specifying all graphic objects in a general procedure, you must specify their absolute source—which is often called the *parent object.*

The range of values being plotted is representable as (xmax - xmin). This range is divided by 1,000 to obtain `intval`, an interval value. This value can be interpreted as the "width" of each column in the plot, not geometrically as much as numerically. If the geometrical width of the plot is represented by the y-axis extending between the left and right sides of the plotting area, then 1/1000 of this extent is representable by the plot made by one pixel. The standard parameters of the formula are retrieved into the array variable `p()`. The whole procedure may be aborted now if there's no difference between the minimum and maximum values—in which case, an erroneous plot would be generated if it continued.

Part 4:

```
For pval = xmin To xmax Step intval
    p(xslot) = pval
```

```
    charty(px) = calculate(frmula)
    If px = 0 Then
        ymax = charty(px)
        ymin = charty(px)
    Else
        If charty(px) > ymax Then
            ymax = charty(px)
        End If
        If charty(px) < ymin Then
            ymin = charty(px)
        End If
    End If
    px = px + 1
Next pval
```

This is the most crucial loop in the procedure. Because `intval` is equal to 1/1000 of the distance between the minimum `xmin` and the maximum `xmax`, this loop is executed exactly 1,000 times. This is the case no matter how small or great the difference between `xmin` and `xmax`, because the `Step` value has already been determined to be `intval`. The current count of this loop is kept in `pval`; for each of the 1,000 columns in the plot, `pval` represents at some time the relative value for that column.

Variable `xslot` is passed to this procedure as a parameter. It retains the slot location of the minimum and maximum range values on the panel. For now, the `p()` value for the parameter that has the range associated with it is fed the current value of `pval`. The call to `Function calculate ()` is the same call placed in Expressor Mark I when the user clicks the Apply Formula button on the calculator panel; so the charting mechanism works, in effect, as though it were clicking Apply Formula a thousand times. Each solution is stored in the array `charty()` at the position numbered `px`. Variable `px` keeps count of the current column number, from 0 to 999. At the end of the loop, this count is manually incremented before the program moves to the next column.

The conditional clause checks whether the loop clause is plotting for the first column—`px` = 0. If it is, the conditional clause may conclude this first column contains both the largest and the smallest solution values seen thus far.

Part 5:

```
dif = ymax - ymin
hght = Chart.ChartArea.Height - charttop - 100
yticks = Int(Chart.ChartArea.Height / 450)
```

```
intervaly = hght / yticks
For plt = 0 To (yticks - 1)
    yi(plt) = ymax - ((dif / (yticks - 1)) * plt)
    If yi(plt) < 1 Then
        pl$ = Format$(yi(plt), "0.######")
    Else
        pl$ = Format$(yi(plt), "###############.##")
    End If
    Chart.ChartArea.Print pl$
    Chart.ChartArea.CurrentX = 0
    Chart.ChartArea.CurrentY = Chart.ChartArea.CurrentY
        + intervaly - 200
    w = Chart.ChartArea.TextWidth(pl$)
    If w > wide Then
        wide = w
    End If
Next plt
```

The loop clause in Part 5 is complete and deals with yet another range, that being the one between the highest value of the result ymax and the lowest value ymin. The total height of the region in ChartArea that will contain the actual chart is the .Height of ChartArea minus the charttop value found earlier, minus 100 for extra margin. This measurement is stored as variable hght.

The ticks along the left side of the chart area denote the relative value of a point plotted along the y-axis. The number of ticks that it is reasonable to display, given the current size of the chart, is estimated by taking the entire height of the chart and dividing it by 450. Next, the entire height of the chart area, represented by variable hght, is divided into the same number of intervals (intervaly) along the y-axis as tick marks. Each height interval here does not represent charted value, mind you, but size for the sake of plotting tick values to the correct coordinates on the chart.

The plt loop counts as many ticks as there are along the left side, but subtracts one from that figure because the initial loop clause value is zero and not one. The value of each tick along the y-axis is stored in the array variable yi(). At the top of the chart, the tick mark should register the highest value found so far, represented by ymax. For the first iteration of the loop, plt = 0, so ((dif / (yticks - 1)) * plt) also equals zero. Therefore, nothing is subtracted from ymax at the first iteration, and the first tick mark registers the maximum value.

In later iterations, for all values where plt > 0, a value interval is calculated as equal to dif / (yticks - 1). This is the interval in value (not size) for the space between y tick marks. This interval is multiplied by plt, which keeps track of the number of intervals counted from the top thus far. The result is a value which is subtracted from ymax to obtain the value of the tick mark at the current interval. This value is stored in yi(plt).

Notice the graphics portion of the plotting routine does not want to know how big yi(plt) is, but how wide it is. A string variable pl$ is initiated for containing the textual form of the value of yi(plt) for the current interval. If this value is less than 1, extra decimal spaces are plotted, as represented by the six pound signs after the decimal point in the format descriptor "0.######". If the value is more than 1, as many as 16 digits before the decimal point are plotted, followed by as many as two decimal places.

The contents of pl$ are plotted to the chart (although you don't see the chart yet), and plotting this string naturally moves the pen toward the right. After the plot is completed, however, .CurrentX is moved back to the extreme left edge of the chart area, and .CurrentY is moved down relative to the amount of the size interval intervaly minus 200 twips for margin. This is the print position for the next tick value. Figure 4.8 tracks the route taken by the pen since Figure 4.7.

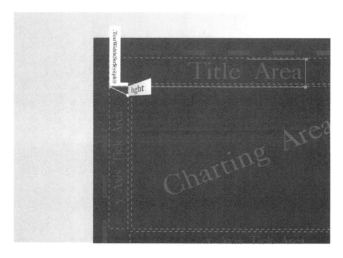

Figure 4.8. Journey through the geometry of imagination.

A variable w is used to calculate the width of the number just printed, and another variable wide keeps track of the widest number printed thus far. This width is remembered for the sake of the first instruction in the next part of the procedure:

Part 6:

```
chartleft = wide + 100
tick = charttop
For plt = 0 To (yticks - 1)
    Chart.ChartArea.Line (chartleft - 100, tick) -
➡       (chartleft - 1, tick)
    yln(plt) = tick
    tick = tick + intervaly
Next plt
```

Variable chartleft now contains the point representing the extreme left edge of the actual chart. This margin accounts for the widest number printed thus far along the left side, plus 100 twips for extra margin.

Next, a variable tick is set initially to the y-axis coordinate of the twip at the top of the actual chart area. This variable is used to plot a small line emanating from the extreme left edge of the chart, and pointing to the tick value already printed to the chart.

Part 7:

```
chartbottom = tick - intervaly
w = Chart.ChartArea.TextWidth(Str$(xmax))
chartright = Chart.ChartArea.Width - (w / 2)
wdth = chartright - chartleft
yaxlin = Chart.ChartArea.CurrentY + 150
dif = xmax - xmin
xticks = Int(Chart.ChartArea.Width / 1100)
intervalx = wdth / xticks
For plt = 0 To xticks
    xi(plt) = xmin + ((dif / xticks) * plt)
    If xi(plt) < 1 Then
        pl$ = Format$(xi(plt), "0.######")
    Else
        pl$ = Format$(xi(plt), "###############.##")
    End If
    Chart.ChartArea.CurrentX = chartleft + (intervalx
➡       * plt)
```

```
    tick = Chart.ChartArea.CurrentX
    xln(plt) = tick
    Chart.ChartArea.CurrentY = yaxlin
    w = Chart.ChartArea.TextWidth(pl$)
    Chart.ChartArea.CurrentX = Chart.ChartArea.CurrentX
➥       - (w / 2)
    Chart.ChartArea.Print pl$;
    Chart.ChartArea.Line (tick, yaxlin - 99)-(tick,
➥       yaxlin - 50)
Next plt
```

Now the tick-marking process starts again, but this time sideways. The routine in Part 7 is modeled after the y-axis routine, but was adjusted to account for the x-axis. Notice the values of chartbottom and chartright are computed right away. The bottom of the chart is where the last tick mark was placed for the y-axis. The right edge of the chart is figured by taking xmax, the string length of the maximum value along the x-axis, dividing that in half, and subtracting the result from the width of the entire ChartArea. This roughly centers the final x-axis tick mark beneath the extreme right edge of the actual plot area.

A minor difference between the x- and y-axes routines is one plt loop plots both the tick value and the tick mark for the horizontal axis. Each tick value is centered beneath its tick mark.

Part 8:

```
Chart.ChartArea.Print
pmt$ = RTrim$(Panel.ParamText(xslot).Caption)
Chart.ChartArea.CurrentX = (Chart.ChartArea.Width / 2)
  - (Chart.ChartArea.TextWidth(pmt$) / 2)
Chart.ChartArea.Print pmt$
Chart.ChartArea.Line (chartleft, charttop)-(chartright,
  chartbottom), QBColor(0), BF
Chart.ChartArea.Line (chartleft, charttop)-(chartright,
  chartbottom), QBColor(8), B
For ypt = 1 To yticks - 2
    For xpt = 1 To xticks - 1
        Chart.ChartArea.PSet (xln(xpt), yln(ypt)),
          QBColor(2)
    Next xpt
Next ypt
```

Beneath the chart, the text that describes the parameter whose range is being plotted is retrieved from the `Panel` and centered beneath the actual chart area. Next, the area to contain the chart proper is painted entirely black and then given a gray border. The `ypt` loop places faint green points marking the intersections of the interval lines inside the chart.

Part 9:

```
intspcx = (chartright - chartleft) / 1000
If ymax - ymin <> 0 Then
    ratioy = (chartbottom - charttop) / (ymax - ymin)
Else
    ratioy = chartbottom - charttop
End If
For plot = 0 To 999
    Chart.ChartArea.PSet (chartleft + (intspcx * plot),
➥        chartbottom - ((charty(plot) - ymin) * ratioy)),
➥        QBColor(10)
Next plot
End Sub
```

Finally, it's time to plot the 1,000 solution values to the formulas that were loaded into arrays eons ago. The number of twips between `chartright` and `chartleft` is divided by 1,000 to obtain an interval value equal to the width of each column to be plotted. Then the aspect ratio between `chartbottom` and `charttop` is figured, but only in the instances when there's a rational difference between `ymin` and `ymax`—if the graph doesn't show a flat horizontal line. If there is a flat horizontal line, there's no use trying to divide the total chart height by zero because that would cause an error in the program.

In the final loop, a bright green point is placed in each column at a horizontal position equal to `chartleft` plus the column width times the number of the column; and at a vertical position equal to the solution value for the column minus the minimum possible value—in order that the minimum value appears at the top of the chart—times the aspect ratio.

End of procedure. Here's the procedure that calls the new charting module when the user clicks the Chart button:

```
Sub ShowChart_Click ()
If xslot = True Then Exit Sub
If CalcList.ListIndex = -1 Then Exit Sub
xmin = Val(Param(xslot).Text)
```

```
xmax = Val(ParamTo(xslot).Text)
CreateChart xmin, xmax, xslot
End Sub
```

This procedure is exited If xslot = True—which means, if the user didn't select a value range for the chart—or If CalcList.ListIndex = -1—if the user didn't select a formula. The minimum and maximum range values being plotted are retrieved from the text boxes and placed in the variables xmin and xmax. These two, along with the index of the slot they came from, are passed to the procedure CreateChart, which plots this chart practically by itself.

Property Settings for Expressor Mark II

Here's a list of the important properties for Expressor Mark II's start-up form, again generated by MicroHelp's VBXRef:

```
Form: EXPRSOR2.FRM
General Procedures:
    assess_readout Clear_Params

    BackColor          &H400000
    BorderStyle        1 - Fixed Single
    Caption            Expressor 2
    ForeColor          &H808080
    FormName           Panel
    Icon               (Icon)
    LinkTopic          Form1

    Active Form Event Procedures
     Form_Load

Control Type: PictureBox
    Control Name: Store2nd
    BackColor          &HFF8080
    CtlName            Store2nd
    Picture            (Icon)
    TabIndex           49
```

```
Active Control Event Procedures
 Store2nd_Click

Control Name: StoreBank(00)
BackColor          &H400000
BorderStyle        0 - None
CtlName            StoreBank
ForeColor          &HFFFFFF
Picture            (Icon)
TabIndex           44

Active Control Event Procedures
 StoreBank_Click

Control Name: StoreBank(01)
BackColor          &H400000
BorderStyle        0 - None
CtlName            StoreBank
ForeColor          &HFFFFFF
Index              1
Picture            (Icon)
TabIndex           45

Control Name: StoreBank(03)
BackColor          &H400000
BorderStyle        0 - None
CtlName            StoreBank
ForeColor          &HFFFFFF
Index              3
Picture            (Icon)
TabIndex           46

Control Name: StoreBank(05)
BackColor          &H400000
BorderStyle        0 - None
CtlName            StoreBank
ForeColor          &HFFFFFF
Index              5
Picture            (Icon)
TabIndex           47
```

```
Control Name: StoreBank(06)
BackColor              &H400000
BorderStyle            0 - None
CtlName                StoreBank
ForeColor              &HFFFFFF
Index                  6
Picture                (Icon)
TabIndex               48

Control Type: Label
Control Name: ParamText(00)
Alignment              1 - Right Justify
BackColor              &HFFFFFF
Caption
CtlName                ParamText
FontBold               False
FontName               Helv
FontSize               7.78125
ForeColor              &HFF0000
TabIndex               15

Active Control Event Procedures
    <None>

Control Name: ParamText(01)
Alignment              1 - Right Justify
BackColor              &HFFFFFF
Caption
CtlName                ParamText
FontBold               False
FontName               Helv
FontSize               7.78125
ForeColor              &HFF0000
Index                  1
TabIndex               33

Control Name: ParamText(02)
Alignment              1 - Right Justify
BackColor              &HFFFFFF
Caption
CtlName                ParamText
```

```
FontBold            False
FontName            Helv
FontSize            7.78125
ForeColor           &HFF0000
Index               2
TabIndex            34

Control Name: ParamText(03)
Alignment           1 - Right Justify
BackColor           &HFFFFFF
Caption
CtlName             ParamText
FontBold            False
FontName            Helv
FontSize            7.78125
ForeColor           &HFF0000
Index               3
TabIndex            35

Control Name: ParamText(04)
Alignment           1 - Right Justify
BackColor           &HFFFFFF
Caption
CtlName             ParamText
FontBold            False
FontName            Helv
FontSize            7.78125
ForeColor           &HFF0000
Index               4
TabIndex            36

Control Name: Readout
Alignment           1 - Right Justify
BackColor           &H800000
Caption             0
CtlName             Readout
FontName            Courier
FontSize            12
ForeColor           &HFFFFFF
TabIndex            0
```

```
Active Control Event Procedures
    <None>

Control Type: TextBox
   Control Name: Param(00)
   BackColor              &HFFFF00
   CtlName                Param
   ForeColor              &H0
   TabIndex               1
   Text                   0

   Active Control Event Procedures
       <None>

   Control Name: Param(01)
   BackColor              &HFFFF00
   CtlName                Param
   Index                  1
   TabIndex               3
   Text                   0

   Control Name: Param(02)
   BackColor              &HFFFF00
   CtlName                Param
   Index                  2
   TabIndex               5
   Text                   0

   Control Name: Param(03)
   BackColor              &HFFFF00
   CtlName                Param
   Index                  3
   TabIndex               7
   Text                   0

   Control Name: Param(04)
   BackColor              &HFFFF00
   CtlName                Param
   Index                  4
   TabIndex               9
   Text                   0
```

```
Control Name: ParamTo(00)
BackColor            &HFFFF00
CtlName              ParamTo
Text                 0

Active Control Event Procedures
    <None>

Control Name: ParamTo(01)
BackColor            &HFFFF00
CtlName              ParamTo
Index                1
TabIndex             4
Text                 0

Control Name: ParamTo(02)
BackColor            &HFFFF00
CtlName              ParamTo
Index                2
TabIndex             6
Text                 0

Control Name: ParamTo(03)
BackColor            &HFFFF00
CtlName              ParamTo
Index                3
TabIndex             8
Text                 0

Control Name: ParamTo(04)
BackColor            &HFFFF00
CtlName              ParamTo
Index                4
TabIndex             10
Text                 0

Control Name: SecondValue
BackColor            &H800000
BorderStyle          0 - None
CtlName              SecondValue
FontName             Courier
FontSize             12
```

```
    ForeColor              &HFFFFFF
    TabIndex               43
    Text                   0


    Active Control Event Procedures
     SecondValue_Change

Control Type: Command Button
    Control Name: ApplyFormula
    BackColor              &H400000
    Caption                Display
    CtlName                ApplyFormula
    TabIndex               24


    Active Control Event Procedures
     ApplyFormula_Click


    Control Name: Arctangent
    BackColor              &H400000
    Caption                atn
    CtlName                Arctangent
    FontBold               False
    FontName               Helv
    FontSize               7.78125
    TabIndex               55


    Active Control Event Procedures
     Arctangent_Click


    Control Name: AxisSelect(00)
    BackColor              &H400000
    Caption                - - -
    CtlName                AxisSelect
    FontBold               False
    FontItalic             True
    FontName               Tms Rmn
    FontSize               7.78125
    TabIndex               38


    Active Control Event Procedures
     AxisSelect_Click
```

```
Control Name: AxisSelect(01)
BackColor            &H400000
Caption              - - -
CtlName              AxisSelect
FontBold             False
FontItalic           True
FontName             Tms Rmn
FontSize             7.78125
Index                1
TabIndex             39

Control Name: AxisSelect(02)
BackColor            &H400000
Caption              - - -
CtlName              AxisSelect
FontBold             False
FontItalic           True
FontName             Tms Rmn
FontSize             7.78125
Index                2
TabIndex             40

Control Name: AxisSelect(03)
BackColor            &H400000
Caption              - - -
CtlName              AxisSelect
FontBold             False
FontItalic           True
FontName             Tms Rmn
FontSize             7.78125
Index                3
TabIndex             41

Control Name: AxisSelect(04)
BackColor            &H400000
Caption              - - -
CtlName              AxisSelect
FontBold             False
FontItalic           True
FontName             Tms Rmn
FontSize             7.78125
```

```
Index              4
TabIndex           42

Control Name: Button0(09)
BackColor          &H400000
Caption            0
CtlName            Button0
FontName           Courier
FontSize           9.5625
Index              9
TabIndex           12

Active Control Event Procedures
 Button0_Click

Control Name: ButtonPos(01)
BackColor          &H400000
Caption            1
CtlName            ButtonPos
FontName           Courier
FontSize           9.5625
Index              1
TabIndex           11

Active Control Event Procedures
 ButtonPos_Click

Control Name: ButtonPos(02)
BackColor          &H400000
Caption            2
CtlName            ButtonPos
FontName           Courier
FontSize           9.5625
Index              2
TabIndex           25

Control Name: ButtonPos(03)
BackColor          &H400000
Caption            3
CtlName            ButtonPos
FontName           Courier
```

```
FontSize            9.5625
Index               3
TabIndex            26

Control Name: ButtonPos(04)
BackColor           &H400000
Caption             4
CtlName             ButtonPos
FontName            Courier
FontSize            9.5625
Index               4
TabIndex            27

Control Name: ButtonPos(05)
BackColor           &H400000
Caption             5
CtlName             ButtonPos
FontName            Courier
FontSize            9.5625
Index               5
TabIndex            28

Control Name: ButtonPos(06)
BackColor           &H400000
Caption             6
CtlName             ButtonPos
FontName            Courier
FontSize            9.5625
Index               6
TabIndex            29

Control Name: ButtonPos(07)
BackColor           &H400000
Caption             7
CtlName             ButtonPos
FontName            Courier
FontSize            9.5625
Index               7
TabIndex            30

Control Name: ButtonPos(08)
BackColor           &H400000
```

```
Caption             8
CtlName             ButtonPos
FontName            Courier
FontSize            9.5625
Index               8
TabIndex            31

Control Name: ButtonPos(09)
BackColor           &H400000
Caption             9
CtlName             ButtonPos
FontName            Courier
FontSize            9.5625
Index               9
TabIndex            32

Control Name: Button_Point(10)
BackColor           &H400000
Caption             .
CtlName             Button_Point
FontName            Courier
FontSize            9.5625
Index               10
TabIndex            13

Active Control Event Procedures
 Button_Point_Click

Control Name: ClearAll
BackColor           &H400000
Caption             C
CtlName             ClearAll
TabIndex            17

Active Control Event Procedures
 ClearAll_Click

Control Name: ClearEntry
BackColor           &H400000
Caption             CE
CtlName             ClearEntry
TabIndex            16
```

```
Active Control Event Procedures
 ClearEntry_Click

Control Name: Cosine
BackColor           &H400000
Caption             cos
CtlName             Cosine
FontBold            False
FontName            Helv
FontSize            7.78125
TabIndex            57

Active Control Event Procedures
 Cosine_Click

Control Name: DividedBy
BackColor           &H400000
Caption             /
CtlName             DividedBy
TabIndex            23

Active Control Event Procedures
 DividedBy_Click

Control Name: EditCut
BackColor           &H400000
Caption             Cut
CtlName             EditCut
TabIndex            19

Active Control Event Procedures
 EditCut_Click

Control Name: Enter
BackColor           &H400000
Caption             Enter
CtlName             Enter
TabIndex            20

Active Control Event Procedures
 Enter_Click
```

```
Control Name: Logarithm
BackColor            &H400000
Caption              log
CtlName              Logarithm
FontBold             False
FontName             Helv
FontSize             7.78125
TabIndex             50

Active Control Event Procedures
 Logarithm_Click

Control Name: Minus
BackColor            &H400000
Caption              -
CtlName              Minus
TabIndex             21

Active Control Event Procedures
 Minus_Click

Control Name: NaturalLog
BackColor            &H400000
Caption              e ^ x
CtlName              NaturalLog
FontBold             False
FontName             Helv
FontSize             7.78125
TabIndex             52

Active Control Event Procedures
 NaturalLog_Click

Control Name: Percent
BackColor            &H400000
Caption              %
CtlName              Percent
TabIndex             18

Active Control Event Procedures
 Percent_Click
```

```
Control Name: PowerRaise
BackColor            &H400000
Caption              x ^ y
CtlName              PowerRaise
FontBold             False
FontName             Helv
FontSize             7.78125
TabIndex             53

Active Control Event Procedures
 PowerRaise_Click

Control Name: Reciprocal
BackColor            &H400000
Caption              1 / x
CtlName              Reciprocal
FontBold             False
FontName             Helv
FontSize             7.78125
TabIndex             54

Active Control Event Procedures
 Reciprocal_Click

Control Name: Root
BackColor            &H400000
Caption              sqr
CtlName              Root
FontBold             False
FontName             Helv
FontSize             7.78125
TabIndex             51

Active Control Event Procedures
 Root_Click

Control Name: ShowChart
BackColor            &H400000
Caption              Chart
CtlName              ShowChart
TabIndex             37
```

```
Active Control Event Procedures
  ShowChart_Click

Control Name: Sine
BackColor            &H400000
Caption              sin
CtlName              Sine
FontBold             False
FontName             Helv
FontSize             7.78125
TabIndex             56

Active Control Event Procedures
  Sine_Click

Control Name: Tangent
BackColor            &H400000
Caption              tan
CtlName              Tangent
FontBold             False
FontName             Helv
FontSize             7.78125
TabIndex             58

Active Control Event Procedures
  Tangent_Click

Control Name: Times
BackColor            &H400000
Caption              X
CtlName              Times
TabIndex             22

Active Control Event Procedures
  Times_Click

Control Type: Combo Box
  Control Name: CalcList
  BackColor            &HC00000
  CtlName              CalcList
  ForeColor            &HFFFFFF
  Style                2 - Dropdown List
  Text                 CalcList
```

```
Active Control Event Procedures
 CalcList_Click
```

A Starter Set of Expressor II Functions

The procedure that's to bring about all this marvelous stuff is the `Sub main ()` procedure for the first general module. As you can see in the following listing, that claim is hard to believe:

```
Sub main ()
Panel.Show
Load Chart
End Sub
```

I won't be dividing this procedure into parts.

As I stated before, the charting routine places 1,000 calls to function `calculate ()`, which solves for the chosen formula in the panel's list box. This function procedure acts primarily as a switchboard, as is obvious from the following listing:

```
Function calculate (frmula As Integer)
Select Case frmula
    Case 0
        calculate = surf_area_rccyl(p(0), p(1))
    Case 1
        calculate = volume_rccyl(p(0), p(1))
    Case 2
        calculate = zone_sphere(p(0), p(1))
    Case 3
        calculate = force_att(p(0), p(1), p(2), p(3))
    Case 4
        calculate = dopp_shift(p(0), p(1), p(2), p(3))
    Case 5
        calculate = escape_velo(p(0), p(1))
    Case 6
        calculate = grav_force(p(0), p(1), p(2))
    Case 7
        calculate = sinewave(p(0), p(1))
    Case 8
        calculate = parabola(p(0), p(1), p(2))
    Case 9
        calculate = median(p(0), p(1), p(2))
```

```
    Case 10
        calculate = perpendulum(p(0), p(1))
    Case 11
        calculate = circorbit(p(0), p(1))
End Select
End Function
```

The procedure receives the formula by number and then directs the call by number to the proper branch, using the Select Case clause to direct the way. Each Case branch takes the program to a completely unique function routine, though the return value is shuttled through the same variable calculate back to the calling body of the program—in this case, your charting module.

Here are some Function procedures whose operational parameters were established in Chapter 2:

```
Function circorbit (radius, mass)
circorbit = (4 * PI ^ 2 * radius ^ 3) / (GRAV * mass)
End Function

Function dopp_shift (vo, vs, fo, c)
dopp_shift = ((c + vo) / (c - vs)) * fo
End Function

Function escape_velo (mass, radius)
escape_velo = Sqr((2 * GRAV * mass) / radius)
End Function

Function force_att (men, mbd, r, y)
force_att = -GRAV * ((men * mbd) / ((r + y) ^ 2))
End Function

Function grav_force (M_object, m_orbiting, radius)
grav_force = (GRAV * M_object * m_orbiting) / (radius
  ^ 2)
End Function

Function median (side1, side2, side3)
median = (Sqr(2 * (side2 ^ 2 + side3 ^ 2) - side1
  ^ 2)) / 2
End Function
```

```
Function parabola (coefficient, variable, exponent)
parabola = coefficient * variable ^ exponent
End Function

Function perpendulum (ko, r)
perpendulum = (2 * PI * ko) / (Sqr(gracc / r))
End Function

Function sinewave (coefficient, angle)
rads = angle * (PI / 180)
sinewave = coefficient * Sin(rads)
End Function

Function surf_area_rccyl (r, h)
surf_area_rccyl = (2 * PI) * r * h
End Function

Function volume_rccyl (r, h)
volume_rccyl = PI * (r ^ 2) * h
End Function

Function zone_sphere (r, h)
zone_sphere = 2 * PI * r * h
End Function
```

By the way, the constants PI, GRAV, and gracc are declared in the global module with these instructions:

```
Global Const PI = 3.1415927
Global Const GRAV = .000000000066732    'gravitational constant
Global Const gracc = 9.80665            'acceleration of free fall
                                        '  in m/s^-2
```

If you plan to add functions that use constants to Expressor II, you might want to add more to this list. In any event, to add your own functions to Expressor Mark II, do the following:

In the Sub Form_Load () procedure of EXPRESR2.FRM, add the name of the formula at the end of the list of formulas in the CalcList.AddItem segment of the procedure. This is how you will see the name of the form in the drop-down listbox, as well as at the head of the chart.

☐ Your formula can have as many as five parameters, indexed from 0 to 4. Add the names of these parameters to the end of the `label$()` list, starting with parameter #0—represented by the second dimension in this two-dimensional array variable. The first dimension value is equal to the next available formula following the final one in the list.

☐ You might have to rewrite the `Dim Label$()` declaration in the general declarations area of EXPRESR2.FRM if you have more than 16 functions in the list now.

☐ In the `Function calculate()` procedure in EXPRESR2.BAS, add another `Case` to the list at the end of the `Select Case` clause whose number corresponds to the formula number in `CalcList`. This `Function` procedure acts as a switchboard that takes the program to your personalized function routine.

☐ Enter your own branch routine below the `Exit Function` statement. This is a single line in the syntax `solution = function_name$(params)`, where `function_name$` is a name of your choice, and `params` contains a list of references to the `p()` global array, containing the parameters for your function.

☐ At the end of this routine, type the function declaration for your personal function. This can contain variables with names of your choosing within the parentheses, as long as they can be represented with single precision. After you press Enter, the Visual Basic interpreter creates a frame for your function, automatically giving it an `End Function` instruction.

☐ Your function can contain as many instruction lines as necessary, as long as the name of the variable returning a value to the calling body of the application and your function name are the same.

Because Visual Basic is a relatively weak language for handling data, using it as a teaching tool for understanding how data works is at times a job akin to training novice auto mechanics about the combustion engine using weed whackers in place of automobiles. No matter how you program, the design and format of your data is the key factor to the success of your application. Visual Basic merely makes you conceive data using its more rudimentary elements—record location, for instance.

Other options for building Visual Basic databases.

The most exploited category of Visual Basic add-on products is database management libraries. Software Source's VB/ISAM MX enables you to set up indexed sequential-access databases using tried-and-true methods subscribed to by mainframe programmers for decades. Pioneer Software's Q+E Database/VB lets the Visual Basic application access data files in the dBASE .DBF format and soon will add other formats to that repertoire. Coromandel's DB Controls sets up the format of a data record for you automatically while you're drawing the form, and Blue Rose Software's DataBasic enables you to use a proprietary format to set up databases with tremendous access speeds.

Plug Away

Several third-party packages enable you to access data using the Structured Query Language rather than Visual Basic. By far, SQL (often pronounced "sequel") is a superior data access language, yet to be surpassed by any proprietary or standardized procedural access system. Because this book is not about third-party packages, you won't find details about them here. I explore in depth third-party packages along with SQL in my book *Extending Visual Basic* from Sams Publishing.

THE GOAL OF AUTOMATION

5

It is written that the force that triggered the Industrial Revolution of the first half of the 20th Century was automation. The probable truth is that it was the ingenuity of an inspired few that engineered the industrial shift in North America, and later in Europe, from handcraftsmanship to assembly-line automation. At that time, the definition of *automation* was considered to be the implementation of machines as tools for tasks previously undertaken by people, in such a way that the entire work process became scheduled, accelerated, and better organized. People and machines became partners in the execution of the chief industry of the early 20th Century, manufacturing.

The chief industry currently emerging in North America is *information*, as the hub of the world's manufacturing recenters itself in Southeast Asia. We are seeing large corporations emerge as the world's primary information suppliers; and, if the history of this chief industry continues to parallel the history of the last one, the new information providers, the capitalists of the information industry, will become challenged by an ever-growing coalition of socialized information providers—that is, believers in knowledge for the people. In order for information to survive and prevail as an industry, it needs the brainpower of capitalists and large corporations to build its infrastructure; but to distribute it to the masses and make people aware of the power of information requires the guts and shade-tree ingenuity of the users' groups, bulletin board systems operators, and shareware authors.

The definition of *automation* need not change much, even though the industries to which that term applies are undergoing substantial metamorphoses. In the new information industry, the computer can act as a hand-in-hand partner with people in planning, analysis, and management. It need not replace people in order to work; before 1929, automation created jobs, took people off the streets, and even built new cities.

Three ways to provide automation.

I realize you may not want to integrate something that sounds like part of a manifesto in your Visual Basic personal accounting or inventory control programs. Yet the automation concept works in computing because it reminds programmers to strive not to replace the role of the user in the workplace, but to *assist* that user. The first way this can be accomplished is by removing tedium from the work process; by having the application assume the repetitious, mentally taxing, and paper-overloaded processes in the office.

The second way to achieve automation is by presenting the office worker with *alternative methods* for accomplishing everyday tasks. The goals and products of these jobs do not change, but the means to achieve them do change. The third way is for the application to reprocess the data given it by the user and present the informational products of that reprocessing and algorithmic recalculation in such a way that the user may see new meaning in that data.

Igniting the Engines

In Chapter 4, Situation #1, the INVENT1 project, you saw the structure of its underlying data using Visual Basic's random-access model. The necessary tools and the infrastructure of the application are in place. It's time now to make this application somewhat operational.

Situation #1: The Retail Inventory Tracking System

One drawback of the Visual Basic random-access data model is that you often find yourself searching for synonyms when configuring names for variables and types. You see, when you make the initial Type declarations in the global module or general declarations section, you generally think of one name for each category of records in your data tables, as demonstrated by the following example:

```
Type VenCatalog
    VendorCode As String * 6       'Code created by reseller
                                   '  for associated vendor
    CatalogNo As String * 12       'Unique catalog number for
                                   '  product
    ProductNo As String * 6        'Key field for product
    Cost(3) As Currency            'Cost breakdown in vendor
                                   '  catalog
    SaleCost As Currency           'Vendor special
    SaleBreak As Integer           'Required order quantity for
                                   '  special offer
    SaleDate As Variant            'Expiration date of special
    PrivateCost As Currency        'Separate deal offered by
                                   '  vendor via phone or fax
    PrivateBreak As Integer        'Required order quantity for
                                   '  separate deal
    PrivateDate As Variant         'Expiration date of private
                                   '  deal
    PackageOrderNo As String * 6   'Cross-reference to
                                   '  combination order number
End Type
```

I now have one name for referring to catalog listings. This is one of the data tables that will be utilized by the ShelfItemID form. The purchasing agent will use this data to determine the amount spent for a specific package. (Notice a synonym pair here, "shelf item" and "package.") Later in the global module, a record variable Catalog() is declared As VenCatalog. The term Catalog() now refers to a record in the VenCatalog table; in effect, it's a pointer, acting in place of the internal pointer maintained by Visual Basic's sequential-access model.

I shouldn't blame Visual Basic for situations that my self-proclaimed ingenuity might manage only to exacerbate. Later, in order to identify the Visual Basic file channel number with something more memorable than a numeral, I declare a constant CatalogItems as referring to data channel #3, which is reserved exclusively for the VenCatalog table and is held open throughout the run of the application. Next, I declare the term CatalogFile as a constant *string* that can stand in place of the filename for the VenCatalog table. Now, I wasn't forced to add more like-sounding terms to the already near-homonymous vocabulary of the INVENT1 application. You will see, however, that even though I must keep track of all the slight variations in my terms (for instance, is it the *table* that has the "Ven" in it or is it the *form name?*), the constant declarations make many instructions more legible to the human reader. Supposedly, this is one of the benefits of using high-level languages.

If you've ever wired your home or office for cable television or for multiline telephones, you've had experience with splitting several lines, routing them to the various rooms, and distributing the signal from the main trunk to individual stations or receivers. In short, you've networked. In computing, distributing the data structures and variables among the various contexts of INVENT1 is a process similar to networking. In Chapter 3, you saw the main Type declarations for the random-access tables. The next step is to declare record variables, as follows:

```
Global Listing(8) As Product
Global Package(8) As ShelfItem
Global Catalog(8) As VenCatalog
Global Supplier(8) As Vendor
Global Order(8) As Purchase
Global Request(8) As CustOrder
Global Client(8) As Customer
Global LogOn As Security
Global MajorChange As Alteration
```

A record variable, you might remember, is the object for the sake of object-oriented references to the data in each record. A random-access `Get #` instruction, for example, takes three parameters. The first is the channel number for the open data file, the second is the record number being read, and the third is the record variable. Here's a legitimate access of the catalog listing file:

Employing a record variable.

```
Get #3, RecordNo, Catalog(table)
```

Next, I chose to declare multipurpose constant terms. My original idea was to let names stand in place of data file channel numbers. Later, I realized other numerals could benefit from the same type of aliasing, in the same order. It makes sense that one set of constant declarations be applied to all cases, as follows:

Declaring constants for data channel names.

```
Global Const Products = 1
Global Const Packages = 2
Global Const CatalogItems = 3
Global Const Customers = 4
Global Const Vendors = 5
Global Const Employees = 6
Global Const Purchases = 7
Global Const CustomerOrders = 8
```

Now each data channel has a name, so the access of the catalog listing data file may now read like this:

```
Get CatalogItems, RecordNo, Catalog(table)
```

The constant terms may also serve to identify what I call *table routes*. These routes apply to array variables that will represent characteristics of all the data files—for instance, the number of valid records in a data file and the record currently being displayed. These array variables are declared next in the global module, as follows:

Using instance arrays to route certain records to MDI children.

```
Global Total(8) As Integer
Global Current(8, 8) As Integer
Global ActiveInstance(8) As Integer
```

The INVENT1 application has eight major data files; the channel names for all eight have already been declared. (The ninth instance is not a major one.) It only makes sense to use the same naming pattern for the channel number as for the table routes. The array variable `Total()` maintains the total number of valid records (notice the qualifier "valid" again) for each open data file. Once `Total()` has been declared, I can now use the term `Total(CatalogItems)` to refer to the total number of records in the VenCatalog table. Notice how legible this reference is; it certainly beats using Total(3).

Relating Instance Variables, or the Pointer Sisters

Because INVENT1 is a Multiple Document Interface application, it can utilize more than one instance of a form whose .MDIChild property is set to True. I set an arbitrary limit of eight for the number of instances of any one form type. With as many as eight forms of the same type accessing the same data file, separate file pointers should be maintained for each form. After all, it's pointless to duplicate the same form eight times if all eight instances can show only the same record. If there are eight customer ID forms showing within the parent, with different customer records displayed within each form, it is therefore said there are eight *instances* of customers showing.

Structuring the instance pointer variables

I created an array variable Current() to be two-dimensional; the first dimension refers to the data file and the second to the particular instance that applies to each form. With Current() in place, each duplicated MDI child form now has its own independent file pointer. A separate array variable ActiveInstance() keeps track of how many instances of pointers are currently active for each data form. When a new duplicate form becomes active, that form reads a record at some location other than the point where the first form is reading. Every time such an "otherness" is created, the ActiveInstance() value for the data file being read is incremented. The value is then fed to the new instance of the active form, in order to distinguish what it's reading from what its sister form may be reading.

By the way, that access to the vendor catalog file now reads like this:

```
Get CatalogItems, Current(CatalogItems, Instance),
➥   Catalog(Instance)
```

The next order of business is to establish aliases for the fixed filenames required by the INVENT1 data file system. This application works with only one set, or schema, of data files. Unlike a spreadsheet, with this application the user will not be closing the active data set from the menu bar and opening another one. Because the names for the data files are, characteristically speaking, constant, constants may be declared for them as follows:

```
Global Const ProductFile = "d:\invent1\products.i1"
Global Const PackageFile = "d:\invent1\packages.i1"
Global Const CatalogFile = "d:\invent1\catitems.i1"
Global Const CustomerFile = "d:\invent1\customer.i1"
Global Const VendorFile = "d:\invent1\vendors.i1"
Global Const EmployeeFile = "d:\invent1\employee.i1"
Global Const PurchaseFile = "d:\invent1\venpurch.i1"
Global Const CustOrderFile = "d:\invent1\custordr.i1"
```

With these constant declarations in place, the instruction that initiates the catalog file reads as follows:

```
Open CatalogFile For Random As CatalogItems
```

Granted, the slightness of the variations in all these terms may become confusing at times, but look at how this instruction would read without the alias terms to help it:

```
Open "d:\invent1\catitems.i1" For Random As #3
```

Finally, in the global module, I've placed the following declarations:

```
Global PrID$(), PrNam$(), PrX() As Variant, PrLoc() As Integer
Global PaID$(), PaNam$(), PaX() As Variant, PaLoc() As Integer
Global CaID$(), CaNam$(), CaX() As Variant, CaLoc() As Integer
Global CuID$(), CuNam$(), CuX() As Variant, CuLoc() As Integer
Global VeID$(), VeNam$(), VeX() As Variant, VeLoc() As Integer
Global EmID$(), EmNam$(), EmX() As Variant, EmLoc() As Integer
Global PuID$(), PuNam$(), PuX() As Variant, PuLoc() As Integer
Global CoID$(), CoNam$(), CoX() As Variant, CoLoc() As Integer
```

For the most part, the main field required for sorting is either the key field or the title/name field, here shown by the -ID$() and -Nam$() arrays. There might be future cases when some field other than the ID and name fields will be sorted. Thus, in anticipation of all possible cases, I've created all-purpose arrays suffixed with -X() and declared with type Variant. The -Loc() arrays are the record location arrays, which will be sorted along with the array being searched.

Notice these are dynamic arrays; even though these array variables are continually reloaded with contents, I don't have to invent some near-unrealistic maximum boundaries for them any more, thanks largely to the new way Visual Basic 2 treats dynamic arrays.

Declaring
arrays for the
sort-search-
retrieve
method.

In Chapter 3, you read about the sort-search-retrieve method of simulating a database query. In summary, to find a record in a database file where one field matches a unique name, such as an ID field, two arrays are created. One array contains the ID field contents for each record in the file, and the second contains the record numbers. While the ID field array is sorted, the record number field is concurrently jumbled, but the sort helps the search algorithm find the wanted record more quickly and efficiently. After the appropriate field is found in the array, the corresponding element in the record number array points to the location of the wanted record in the data file.

The preceding group of eight instructions declares pairs of dynamic arrays which, at the time of sorting, will be redimensioned using ReDim for precisely the number of records in their associated data files. With the dynamic array system in place, the sorting utility arrays will be no longer than is absolutely necessary at the time—there won't be leftover null-valued array elements.

Technique Capsule: Size-to-Fit Arrays

Definition: A dynamic array variable, when declared, initializes only the title of the array, but gives it no associated elements yet. Before a dynamic array variable can receive values or string contents, it must first be given storage elements to work with—in short, the array variable needs its array. The ReDim statement is used to give a dynamic array variable true upper- and lower-array boundaries, and it can be invoked more than once for any given dynamic array.

Utilizing a new syntax for Visual Basic 2, the Preserve qualifier used with ReDim may be used to resize a dynamic array without reinitializing any of the values contained in it. The upshot of using ReDim Preserve is that an array need no longer be declared for an arbitrary amount of elements the programmer might deem a reasonable maximum.

Execution: Historically, when a programmer has declared an array that might, during the course of the application, contain any number of names, he has thought ahead to how many possible names the array may contain in its lifetime and declare the array for that amount, as in the following example:

```
Dim TotalNames$(10000)
```

Using the original dynamic array technique, the array was initialized by the programmer first and later given an array whose length was equal to the number of names, as follows:

```
Dim TotalNames$()
   .
   .
   .
ReDim TotalNames(numnames%)
```

Notice the amount of elements given the dynamic array is defined here by a variable `numnames%`. Because an instance of just a variable by itself within an instruction is counted as an expression, the `ReDim` statement may only appear in the midst of a procedure, not within a declarations area. The scope of the dynamic array, however, remains the same as it was at initialization. Thus if a dynamic array is declared `Global`, then a `ReDim` instruction appearing within a procedure leaves the array global in scope and allows the values and boundaries of the dynamic array to be maintained even after execution of `End Sub`.

The problem with the structure in the previous example is that the value of `numnames%`, when transmitted to the dynamic array `TotalNames()`, must remain fixed if the array is to continue to keep a list of names. If one name more than `numnames%` must be added to the list, the dynamic array can be redimensioned with `ReDim`, but the names previously held in the array must be reloaded. To do this, you must have another array full of contents with which to reload this array, thus defeating the purpose of a dynamic array.

With Visual Basic 2, you can add (or remove) elements to the dynamic array using the `ReDim Preserve` instruction without altering the contents of the existing array elements. Dynamic array maintenance, thus, is divided into three stages, among which the number of names variable is free to change, as shown in the following example:

```
Dim TotalNames$()
   .
numnames% = fixed_amount
   .
ReDim TotalNames(numnames%)
   .
numnames% = numnames% + additions
   .
ReDim Preserve TotalNames(numnames%)
```

The final statement in the preceding code changes the number of elements in the `TotalNames()` dynamic array, without disturbing the current contents of the array. The list of names now is free to be expanded on-the-fly, without its existing contents being nullified by the interpreter and reloaded by the program.

Example: Suppose a newsletter publisher uses a Visual Basic application to keep track of subscribers. Perhaps for psychological reasons, this publisher doesn't want to limit the number of entries in the subscriber list to an arbitrary maximum.

At the beginning of the source code, the programmer of the publisher's subscriber list application has declared the structure of the subscriber table in a Type clause as type Subscribers. This structure undoubtedly contains names, addresses, and such questionable, though often-used characteristics as median family income and political affiliation. The next order of business is to declare a record variable with this type of structure. In this case, the declaration appears in the global module:

```
Global Reader As Subscribers
```

Because the application must access only one subscriber record at a time, regardless of the number of subscribers in the list, Reader doesn't have to be declared as an array variable. (Important note: Record variables such as Reader cannot be declared as dynamic arrays, only as static.)

The Len() function now has a dual use in Visual Basic. Its second and lesser-known use is to determine the length of a stored record in a random-access data file. Rather than figure the fixed record length of a complex record structure on a calculator, it instead may be determined using Len(). You now can use this function in the Open instruction for the subscriber data file. In fact, you use the term Len twice, though both instances have different meanings for this instruction.

```
Open "SUBSCRIB.DAT" For Random As #1 Len = Len(Reader)
```

The LOF() function returns the length in bytes of an open data file being pointed to by its channel number. By dividing the length of the file in bytes by the length of each record, you obtain the number of records in the data file. The expression for this example looks like this:

```
NoRecs% = LOF(1) / Len(Reader)
```

This demonstration shows you a resizable dynamic array in action; so now that all of this background information is out of the way, you finally can focus on the subject of declaring the dynamic array that contains the names of each subscriber in the global module as follows:

```
Global ReaderName$()
```

Later in the program's run, when the value of NoRecs% is determined, you can make the dynamic array operational with this instruction within a procedure:

```
ReDim ReaderName$(NoRecs%)
```

You now have an array whose number of elements exactly matches the number of records currently in the data file. Along the way, however, assume the program adds records to the end of the subscribers file. (If the data file is to be sorted in memory, independently of the data file in its stored state, there's no reason to insert records in the middle of a data file.) The program keeps track of how many records should be in the data file during the addition process. So if NoRecs% has just been incremented, the following instruction tacks on another element to the ReaderName$() array without disturbing it:

```
ReDim Preserve ReaderName$(NoRecs%)
```

At this point, a name can be added to the array, either before or after the record is saved to the data file.

Moving from Data Definition to Procedures

Returning to the INVENT1 application, the eight sets of dynamic arrays to be used in the sort operations have been declared. The global module is complete, and the next step is to devise the mechanism for acquiring, storing, displaying, and cross-referencing data. When that is done, you can consider the application operational.

The startup form for this application is manually set to the MDI Parent form, which is given the form .Name of Central. For the next procedure to work, this instruction was added to the declarations section of Central:

```
Dim t(8) As Integer
```

The first actual executing procedure, therefore, is not a Sub Form_Load () procedure as is the standard convention, but Sub MDIForm_Load (). This procedure's job is to open the data files and to fully initialize the self-resizing dynamic arrays. Here's the listing of the procedure as it currently appears:

Opening data channels using declared constants.

```
Sub MDIForm_Load ()
Open ProductFile For Random As Products Len = Len(Listing(1))
Open PackageFile For Random As Packages Len = Len(Package(1))
```

```
Open CatalogFile For Random As CatalogItems Len = Len(Catalog(1))
Open CustomerFile For Random As Customers Len = Len(Client(1))
Open VendorFile For Random As Vendors Len = Len(Supplier(1))
Open EmployeeFile For Random As Employees Len = Len(User)
Open PurchaseFile For Random As Purchases Len = Len(Order(1))
Open CustOrderFile For Random As CustomerOrders Len =
➡    Len(Request(1))

Total(1) = LOF(Products) / Len(Listing(1))
Total(2) = LOF(Packages) / Len(Package(1))
Total(3) = LOF(CatalogItems) / Len(Catalog(1))
Total(4) = LOF(Customers) / Len(Client(1))
Total(5) = LOF(Vendors) / Len(Supplier(1))
Total(6) = LOF(Employees) / Len(User)
Total(7) = LOF(Purchases) / Len(Order(1))
Total(8) = LOF(CustomerOrders) / Len(Request(1))

For tl = 1 To 8
    ActiveInstance(tl) = 1
    For tl2 = 1 To 8
        If Total(tl) > 0 Then
            Current(tl, tl2) = Total(tl)
        Else
            Current(tl, tl2) = 1
        End If
    Next tl2
Next tl

For arr = 1 To 8
    t(arr) = Total(arr)
Next arr
ReDim PrID$(t(1)), PrNam$(t(1)), PrX(t(1)), PrLoc(t(1))
ReDim PaID$(t(2)), PaNam$(t(2)), PaX(t(2)), PaLoc(t(2))
ReDim CaID$(t(3)), CaNam$(t(3)), CaX(t(3)), CaLoc(t(3))
ReDim CuID$(t(4)), CuNam$(t(4)), CuX(t(4)), CuLoc(t(4))
ReDim VeID$(t(5)), VeNam$(t(5)), VeX(t(5)), VeLoc(t(5))
ReDim EmID$(t(6)), EmNam$(t(6)), EmX(t(6)), EmLoc(t(6))
ReDim PuID$(t(7)), PuNam$(t(7)), PuX(t(7)), PuLoc(t(7))
ReDim CoID$(t(8)), CoNam$(t(8)), CoX(t(8)), CoLoc(t(8))
```

```
For arr = 1 To Total(Products)
    Get Products, arr, Listing(1)
    PrID$(arr) = Listing(1).ProductNo
    PrNam$(arr) = Listing(1).Title
    PrLoc(arr) = arr
Next arr
For arr = 1 To Total(Packages)
    Get Packages, arr, Package(1)
    PaID$(arr) = Package(1).ItemNo
    PaNam$(arr) = Package(1).SerialNo
    PaLoc(arr) = arr
Next arr
For arr = 1 To Total(CatalogItems)
    Get CatalogItems, arr, Catalog(1)
    CaID$(arr) = Catalog(1).CatalogNo
    CaNam$(arr) = Catalog(1).VendorCode
    CaLoc(arr) = arr
Next arr
For arr = 1 To Total(Customers)
    Get Customers, arr, Client(1)
    CuID$(arr) = Client(1).Code
    CuNam$(arr) = Client(1).LastName
    CuLoc(arr) = arr
Next arr
For arr = 1 To Total(Vendors)
    Get Vendors, arr, Supplier(1)
    VeID$(arr) = Supplier(1).Code
    VeNam$(arr) = Supplier(1).Name
    VeLoc(arr) = arr
Next arr
For arr = 1 To Total(Employees)
    Get Employees, arr, User
    EmID$(arr) = User.Initials
    EmNam$(arr) = User.LastName
    EmLoc(arr) = arr
Next arr
For arr = 1 To Total(Purchases)
    Get Purchases, arr, Order(1)
    PuID$(arr) = Order(1).InvoiceNo
    PuNam$(arr) = Order(1).OurPurchCode
    PuLoc(arr) = arr
Next arr
```

```
For arr = 1 To Total(CustomerOrders)
    Get CustomerOrders, arr, Request(1)
    CoID$(arr) = Request(1).OurInvoiceNo
    CoNam$(arr) = Request(1).PONo
    CoLoc(arr) = arr
Next arr
End Sub
```

Seven of the eight record variables referred to in the Open statements at the beginning of Sub MDIForm_Load() are array variables, dimensioned for eight record units apiece for each possible instance of an MDI child form. The Len() function requires an existing record variable, so it cannot accept just a reference to an array such as Listing() for its parameter. Thus, the (1) subscript is added for the array variables, though I could just as easily have used (8) or (5).

The next set of eight instructions readies the Total() array for the maximum number of records in each data file, obtained using the LOF() / Len() formula introduced earlier. These instructions must be written individually, separately from a loop because, for the second syntax of the Len() function, the record variable being referred to must be addressed explicitly. No declared constant can replace the name of a variable.

Next comes a loop wherein the first ActiveInstance() of each set of eight forms is made ready by setting the instance number for each data file to 1. The Current() two-dimensional array provides pointers to all data files being used by all active MDI child forms. These values are initialized to the Total() value for each data file, which is the numeral address of the last record entered in the file.

The eight loop clauses that follow the Open instructions are necessary to load the dynamic arrays for sorting. It would be nice to create a double-nested loop, with the outer loop bounded by For arr = 1 To 8. This won't work, however, because of the differing structure of the eight record types. There's no uniform ID field title or name field title, and there really can't be if the record variable structures are identified uniquely by the different forms. So there's a fair degree of source code expended for these instructions, though it is necessary under the circumstances.

The Exploded View

Figure 5.1 shows the distribution system for data in this application. The system is divided into five vertical sections. The primary data tables are in Section 1. Their structures are declared using the Type clauses in the global module. The data distribution in this model proceeds from left to right. In Section 2, the data tables are all assigned file channels. The Current() pointer system helps span the incoming data from the apportioned channels to as many as eight instances, as shown in Section 3.

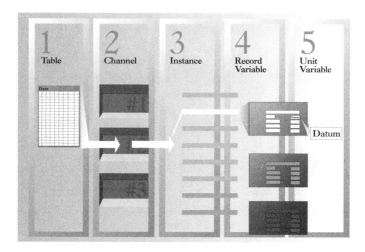

Figure 5.1. The trunk-to-node distribution model of data for INVENT1.

In Section 4, the data in each instance is retrieved into record variables. From there, each record is split into fields, and the values or contents of those fields are assigned to standard unit variables in Section 5.

Before you get the impression that the distribution system outlined in Figure 5.1 also represents a sort of time line, this figure does not represent the steps programmers use to conceive data elements. In other words, I didn't decide on the names for all these data files first, then give them channel numbers, and at the end ask, "Now, what shall I name all the fields in these record variables?" Truth is, the time line is closer to the reverse. Basing my initial models on two other inventory control programs I had used before, I had originally drawn the product-related and item-related data as part of the same structure.

Writing the data fields created thus far on paper, I realized the following: Each box or package on the shelf has its own peculiar characteristics, including, most obviously, its individual serial number. A chief complaint about inventory control systems is that several boxes of the same product purchased at different times from different vendors can each have costs that sometimes differ wildly. The system, however, keeps track of only one cost and one vendor source. The authors of this system appear to believe the reseller picks only one source for a product, and when another vendor offers a more competitive dealer price, the old source data is no longer valid.

The "visible record" versus the real record.

I decided there's a primary division between the product data and the package/item/box data. At times, the *visible record* of a product—the part the user sees on the form—relies on the data in the shelf item file, and vice versa. Therefore, you must express this crossover and sharing of data relationally. You must devise a "machine" that can trigger the automatic access of supplemental related data when necessary. The user does not see which data is primary and which is supplementary, but sees only the visible record.

Making the Invisible Visible

Preparation for drawing process models.

At this point, you may have read enough regarding data models to think this book is about dBASE. Now it's time to start drawing process models. For an application to automate a job, you must satisfactorily answer these questions:

☐ Have you anticipated all the rational actions the user might take at this time?

☐ Have you anticipated all the *irrational* actions the user might take at this time?

☐ Does the program respond well to the rational actions and cancel out all the irrational ones without patronizing or bullying the user?

☐ Have the steps the user must take to perform the major tasks been optimized so that the application knows what the user currently is doing and, thus, doesn't need to be constantly informed and reinforced?

Hit Any Key to Continue

A DOS hard-coded, flat-file database management program I once used (thankfully only once) worked like this: A form was displayed on the screen, and each field in the form had a number beside it. To place an entry in the field, the user first chose a command. This included, for example, F1 for Save Form, F2 for Clear Form, F3 for Update Field, and other uses for the remaining function keys *any* reasonable user might readily decipher—such as F9 for "reordinate"—functions that seemed born for the function keys to which they were assigned (Sarcastic? Me?). If a user wasn't capable of spotting that right away, then evidently he doesn't understand the subtleties of DOS hard-coded, flat-file database management programs and may need to take a course to comprehend it all. After all, this is the information age!

At any rate, suppose F4 stood for Enter Field—I don't really remember what stood for what, so maybe I need to go back to school. Up would pop a menu obscuring the form I was trying to look at, asking me which field number I wanted to update. I entered the field number, pressed Return, and a blinking cursor would appear in the field I chose. I'd type a datum in the field and press some key *other* than Return (probably F12) to get the cursor *out* of the field and back in the menu. Next, I typed F1 to save the updated form.

I suppose this program might serve other purposes—perhaps updating some other field on *another* form? So I pressed whatever function key loads another form, for example F18. Up would pop a menu asking me which form I wanted to load, and there were so many forms in this list that I had to scroll through the menu with the down-arrow key. No problem, only a few thousand forms, but I'd know the one I wanted when I saw it. After finding it, I pressed Return—not some cheap Return substitute—and the chosen form entered the screen. Now it was time to tell the program I wanted to enter new data into this form, so I typed whatever function key stood for Update Field (I don't recall which one just now).

This program must have been a documentation writer's dream, because it's a model of simplicity. One procedure loads a form into the screen—press F1, scroll through the list, press Return, and it's there. From the programmer's view, this must have been a breeze to write. At any time during the program's run, the user can do only a handful of things. The user is carefully steered through each operation like a remotely guided robot. There's no room for error, because the user can't goof. By simply entering and reentering the same commands, the work is done without hassle. All the manufacturer of this software needs now is a magazine review that says, "Does the job! We give it a rating of 9.487234!" and the job of producing a program is complete. It has to sell, because the reader of this review has even been told to want this program.

The Downside of Simplicity

What's wrong with this picture is what was wrong with most commercial programming in the 1980s. The software producers assumed it was the duty of the user to comply with whatever operational procedures were imposed upon her at the time, and to adapt her work process to fit this operationally perfect program. Because the program *works,* thought the author, the user would naturally be compelled to learn its operation by rote, and be happy to plow through the function keys day after day, minute after minute *simply* because it gets the job done.

What's *really* wrong with this picture is its inherent simplicity. It has been incorrectly assumed that programs should be built *simply,* and that the more menus, choices, and clearly marked function keys a program has, the simpler it will be to operate. This notion has been entirely disproven by Microsoft Windows. The best and brightest Windows applications are those that anticipate the user's actions, leave her free to adopt her own procedures based on several ways to work, and give her visible tools that so obviously represent the task they help perform that the correlation is almost archetypal.

This has made life quite a bit more difficult for the programmer, who has had to stop asking, "What *must* the user do?" and ask instead, "What *might* she do?" What makes Microsoft Windows (and the other windowing systems and environments that preceded it) so appealing to users is *freedom of movement.* The key to implementing this freedom has been the event-driven program mechanism. Microsoft's implementation of event-driven programs is hardly original, and it is perhaps less technically proficient than other systems in its product category. The key to its appeal, however, is the ease with which the user can move about the program and adopt her own methods for operating it. Where there are restrictions, they are well-padded, and they are presented without the line-in-the-sand attitude so prevalent among DOS programs of the 1980s. Where in a Windows application do you find the "DO NOT!" warnings and the patronizing "Did you remember to...? (Y/N)" inquiries?

The Event-Driven Mechanism

Visual Basic is one of the few BASIC implementations that successfully uses the event-driven mechanism. As you know, there is a point in time when all the Visual Basic instructions that can be executed have been executed, and the application rests in limbo waiting for the user to trigger an event procedure. Few other implementations of BASIC can rest in limbo, or rest at all, except with the invocation of the INPUT statement. If you're unfamiliar with INPUT, or merely in need of a blast from the past, here is how such an instruction looked:

User input before the era of events.

```
530  INPUT "What do you want to do now";UR$
```

INPUT was the chief mechanism for acquiring any response from the user. Its limitations were these:

☐ INPUT would be executed only when the program got around to it; meanwhile, the program was busy and didn't have time to listen to the user. The statement was invoked when the *program* was ready to do so, not when the user cared to issue a command.

☐ The type of response INPUT would acquire was always fixed—such as the previous string variable. Therefore, restrictions were placed on that response. A function key, for instance, could not replace a textual response for the previous example. Further, if UR was a value variable and not a string, the user could respond only with a number, and the inevitable error-trap routine would punish the user had he not entered a number.

☐ The way the application would recognize the user's command was always after-the-fact. When the user clicks a command button or drags an icon over a region, Visual Basic recognizes these actions as unique commands that trigger only one response. The programmer defines only the response. An old BASIC application could not at all recognize the contents of UR$ in the previous example as a command unless, later, the application had instructions to decipher them, such as IF UR$="U" THEN GOTO 6500 or ON VAL(UR$) GOTO 6500, 6520, 6550....

Conventional programming flowcharts represent the user input portion of the program as a diamond, which is eventually pointed to by the routing arrows. The program represented by such a chart goes about its business and then, at the appropriate moments, gathers input from the user. The result of this input might branch the program in as many as three directions, and early programmers' guides noted users might be limited to no more than three choices. The reasons for this might have to do with the early definitions of simple operation, or with the fact that a diamond had only three points remaining after the input routing arrow consumed one for itself.

Scoring High in the Compulsory Figures

The process model of the event-driven application does not resemble a flowchart in any appreciable means. Moreover, you can compare it to the patterns left in the court by an ice skater—frequently looping, though always meeting again someplace in the middle. Figure 5.2 depicts a process model for the ordinary MDI child form in the INVENT1 application.

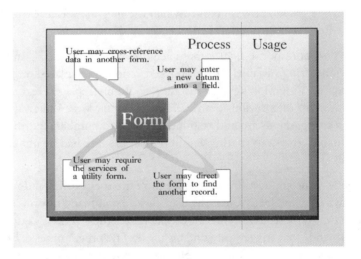

Figure 5.2. A process model fit for Tai and Randy.

You read about the communications model of the application in Chapter 3. The model pertains to the interchange of data between the user and the application. The process model deals with only half of the communications circuit, beginning with the acquisition of data and commands from the user, processing and calculation of the data, and the presentation of the result in a fashion the user can interpret readily as information.

Notice, this cloverleaf pattern shows no absolute sequence of user events. The user rarely does this first, that next, and then something else afterward as a standard course of events in an event-driven application. The user merely proceeds to operate the program. This operation isn't a choice from a menu, but an execution of the user's prerogative. All the user's possible actions for operating a form, when that form is active, are available now, unless some are purposefully or temporarily disabled by the programmer. The user, at all times, can press any buttons, enter data in any fields, and select from the menus the form makes available.

Because this operation has no absolute sequence, you can't flowchart what the user is supposed to do next. In the old DOS process model, the user practically had to beg the program's permission to do anything, even though it was time for it to be done. In the event-driven process model, the application waits on the user hand-and-foot, if I may be allowed this anthropomorphism.

Here's how I devised the process model for INVENT1. As much as possible, the user input is centered towards the MDI child forms. The panel on the MDI parent is necessary only to log in the user and to select a form. After logging in, the user starts the first product form by clicking the Product Listing button. Figure 5.3 shows this form in the midst of its parent window.

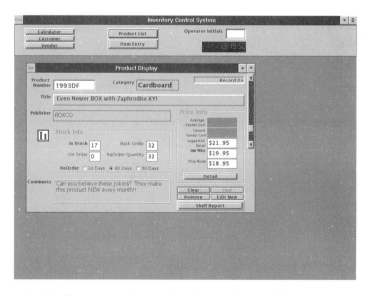

Figure 5.3. Finally putting the product form where it belongs.

Here are the major property settings for the Product Display form:

Listing 5.1. PRODUCT.FRM. Property Settings.

```
Form ProductID
    BorderStyle      =   1  'Fixed Single
    Caption          =   "Product Display"
    Height           =   5328
    Left             =   1200
    MDIChild         =   -1  'True
    Top              =   2244
    Width            =   8328

    SSPanel Panel3D8
      BevelWidth     =   3
      Height         =   2652
      Left           =   7920
      Top            =   0
      Width          =   252

      VScrollBar RecordShown
        Height       =   2580
        LargeChange  =   10
        Left         =   36
        Max          =   1
        Min          =   1
        TabIndex     =   43
        Top          =   36
        Value        =   1
        Width        =   180

    SSPanel Register
      Alignment      =   4  'Right Justify - MIDDLE
      BevelOuter     =   1  'Inset
      BevelWidth     =   3
      Caption        =   "Record #"
      Font3D         =   1  'Raised w/light shading
      FontBold       =   -1  'True
      FontItalic     =   0   'False
      FontName       =   "Lucida Sans"
      FontSize       =   7.8
      Height         =   252
```

```
      Left            =   6000
      Top             =   120
      Width           =   1812

SSPanel Panel3D7
      AutoSize        =   3   'AutoSize Child To Panel
      BevelOuter      =   1   'Inset
      BevelWidth      =   2
      Height          =   252
      Left            =   6600
      Top             =   3960
      Width           =   1212

      CommandButton Find
         Caption         =   "Find"
         FontBold        =   -1   'True
         FontItalic      =   0    'False
         FontName        =   "Lucida Sans"
         FontSize        =   7.8
         Height          =   204
         Left            =   24
         Top             =   24
         Width           =   1164

SSPanel Panel3D6
   CommandButton Remove
      Caption         =   "Remove"

SSPanel Panel3D4
   CommandButton Add
      Caption         =   "Add"

SSPanel Panel3D2
   CommandButton Clear
      Caption         =   "Clear"

SSPanel Panel3D3
      AutoSize        =   3   'AutoSize Child To Panel
      BevelInner      =   2   'Raised
      BevelWidth      =   2
      BorderWidth     =   2
      Height          =   372
```

continues

Listing 5.1. continued

```
        Left              =      5400
        Top               =      4440
        Width             =      2412

        CommandButton ShelfReport
            Caption       =      "Shelf Report"
            FontName      =      "Lucida Sans"
            FontSize      =      7.8
            Height        =      228
            Left          =      72
            Top           =      72
            Width         =      2268

    Begin SSPanel Panel3D1
        BevelWidth        =      3
        BorderWidth       =      0
        Height            =      400
        Left              =      960
        Top               =      750
        Width             =      6852

        TextBox ProductTitle
            BorderStyle   =      0    'None
            FontBold      =      -1   'True
            FontItalic    =      0    'False
            FontName      =      "Lucida Sans"
            FontSize      =      9.6
            Height        =      324
            Left          =      120
            TabIndex      =      2
            Top           =      36
            Width         =      6696

    TextBox ProductCategory
        FontName          =      "Lucida Sans"
        FontSize          =      10.8
        Height            =      372
        Left              =      3960
        TabIndex          =      1
        Top               =      240
        Width             =      1500
```

```
SSPanel SSPanel1
   AutoSize         =   3   'AutoSize Child To Panel
   BevelOuter       =   1   'Inset
   BevelWidth       =   2
   Height           =   396
   Left             =   960
   Top              =   240
   Width            =   1548

   TextBox IDField
      FontBold      =   -1  'True
      FontName      =   "Lucida Sans"
      FontSize      =   10.8
      Height        =   372
      Left          =   24
      TabIndex      =   0
      Top           =   24
      Width         =   1500

SSFrame SSFrame1
   Caption          =   "Price Info"
   FontBold         =   0   'False
   FontItalic       =   0   'False
   FontName         =   "Lucida Sans"
   FontSize         =   10.8
   Height           =   2652
   Left             =   5400
   Top              =   1200
   Width            =   2412

   MaskEdBox AverageCost
      BorderStyle   =   0   'None
      Enabled       =   0   'False
      FontName      =   "Lucida Sans Typewriter"
      FontSize      =   9.6
      Format        =   "$#,##0.00;($#,##0.00)"
      Height        =   336
      Left          =   1080
      Top           =   360
      Width         =   1068
```

continues

Listing 5.1. continued

```
MaskEdBox LowestCost
    Enabled        =   0    'False
    Height         =   336
    Left           =   1080
    Top            =   720
    Width          =   1068

MaskEdBox PrPriceBreak
    FontBold       =   -1   'True
    FontItalic     =   0    'False
    FontName       =   "Lucida Sans Typewriter"
    FontSize       =   9.6
    Format         =   "$#,##0.00;($#,##0.00)"
    Height         =   336
    Left           =   1080
    TabIndex       =   50
    Top            =   1800
    Width          =   1068

MaskEdBox OurPrice
    Height         =   336
    Left           =   1080
    TabIndex       =   49
    Top            =   1440
    Width          =   1068

MaskEdBox ListPrice
    Height         =   336
    Left           =   1080
    TabIndex       =   48
    Top            =   1080
    Width          =   1068

SSPanel Panel3D5
    AutoSize       =   3    'AutoSize Child To Panel
    BevelWidth     =   2
    Height         =   252
    Left           =   240
    Top            =   2280
    Width          =   1932
```

```
     CommandButton PriceDetail
          Caption           =    "Detail"
          FontName          =    "Lucida Sans"
          FontSize          =    7.8
          Height            =    204
          Left              =    24
          Top               =    24
          Width             =    1884

     Label Label11
        Alignment           =    1  'Right Justify
        Caption             =    "Price Break"
        FontBold            =    0    'False

     Label Label6
        Caption             =    "Average Vendor Cost"

     Label Label8
        Caption             =    "Lowest Vendor Cost"

     Label Label9
        Caption             =    "Suggested Retail"

     Label Label10
        Caption             =    "Our Price"
        FontBold            =    -1   'True

  TextBox PubName
     FontBold         =    0    'False
     FontItalic       =    0    'False
     FontName         =    "Lucida Sans"
     FontSize         =    9.6
     Height           =    372
     Left             =    960
     TabIndex         =    3
     Top              =    1320
     Width            =    4212

  SSFrame SSFrame2
     Caption          =    "Stock Info"
     FontBold         =    -1   'True
```

continues

Listing 5.1. continued

```
FontName      =    "Lucida Sans"
FontSize      =    9.6
Height        =    1596
Left          =    960
Top           =    1800
Width         =    4212

SSOption ReOrderWhen
    Caption       =    "90 Days"
    FontBold      =    0    'False
    FontItalic    =    0    'False
    FontName      =    "Lucida Sans"
    FontSize      =    7.8
    Height        =    192
    Index         =    3
    Left          =    3000
    TabIndex      =    46
    Top           =    1320
    Width         =    852

SSOption ReOrderWhen
    Caption       =    "60 Days"
    Index         =    2
    TabIndex      =    45

SSOption ReOrderWhen
    Caption       =    "30 Days"
    Index         =    1
    TabIndex      =    44

TextBox NumInStock
    FontBold      =    -1    'True
    FontName      =    "Lucida Sans Typewriter"
    FontSize      =    9.6
    Height        =    336
    Left          =    1320
    TabIndex      =    4
    Top           =    456
    Width         =    396
```

```
TextBox NumBackOrder
    Height          =    336
    Left            =    3360
    TabIndex        =    6
    Top             =    456
    Width           =    396

TextBox NumOnOrder
    Height          =    336
    Left            =    1320
    TabIndex        =    5
    Top             =    840
    Width           =    396

TextBox NumReOrder
    Height          =    336
    Left            =    3360
    TabIndex        =    7
    Top             =    840
    Width           =    396

Label Label4
    Caption         =    "ReOrder"

Label Label7
    Caption         =    "In Stock"

Label Label13
    Caption         =    "Back Order"

Label Label12
    Caption         =    "On Order"

Label Label14
    Caption         =    "ReOrder Quantity"

PictureBox Picture1
    Height      =    408
    Left        =    396
    Picture     =    I1.ICO
```

continues

Listing 5.1. continued

```
        Top             =   1872
        Width           =   408

SSPanel SSPanel5
        BevelInner      =   1   'Inset
        BorderWidth     =   1
        Height          =   828
        Left            =   960
        Top             =   3600
        Width           =   4212

        TextBox PrComments
           BorderStyle  =   0   'None
           FontBold     =   0    'False
           FontName     =   "Lucida Sans"
           FontSize     =   9.6
           Height       =   756
           Left         =   120
           MultiLine    =   -1   'True
           TabIndex     =   8
           Top          =   36
           Width        =   3972

    Label Label1
        Caption         =    "Product Number"

    Label Label16
        Caption         =    "Category"

    Label Label2
        Caption         =    "Title"

    Label Label3
        Caption         =    "Publisher"

    Label Label15
        Caption         =    "Comments"
```

Working with Multiple Sub Form_Loads

Each new MDI child form is passed a number that represents its instance number, so it knows how many copies there currently are of itself, and remembers not to confuse its own file pointer with the pointers belonging to any copies. The variable `instance` holds the instance number, which is declared in Listing 5.2.

General declarations:

```
Dim Instance As Integer
Dim Loader As Product
```

Here, `Loader` is a separate record variable to be employed in the sorting procedures, described later in this chapter.

General Procedures:

To change the contents of a field in the form, the user places the cursor within that field and types the new contents. The user is free to move the cursor about the form, either with the mouse or with the Tab key. Because the `.TabIndex` properties for each field are organized in advance, the cursor doesn't jump wildly from one field to another across the form when the user repeatedly presses Tab.

Devising Implied Commands

Every time the user makes a change to a field, the change is recorded in the current record variable. This is an input concept borrrowed from Macintosh programs (especially a model devised for HyperCard). The user doesn't have to press an Update button for the changes to be recorded. Now, for each field the interpreter recognizes two events that can be used as indicators of a change in the field values. The `_Change` event for a text box—the standard graphics object for including editable fields—takes place when an alteration is made to the contents of the text box. `_Change`, however, is recognized for any alteration, so if a user types a 26-letter name in a title field, the event procedure `Sub Title_Change ()` will be executed 26 times.

In creating the various forms for this application, I imported a generic, ready-made form, `NameForm`, which I'd written the previous year. The form's model used the record of a person's name and vital information; I revised it to account for the differences in the record structure. The `NameForm` model enabled the user to enter and change records without clicking commands from

Plagiarizing oneself again.

buttons or menus. It was a simple type-and-go operation. Paging through existing records was done with a scroll bar.

Making use of the _LostFocus event.

The original NameForm recognized a change in the record through the _Change event procedures for each text field. Although it achieved the desired effect, it was inefficient, especially if I later chose to implement an Undo button. The _LostFocus event for a text box is recognized when the cursor leaves the text box. When the user clicks another text box or a button, the _LostFocus event procedure for the graphic object that previously contained the cursor (and thus held the focus) is executed once only, regardless of how many characters have been typed.

For INVENT1, when the record is ready to be saved, the contents of the text fields are held within a record variable Listing(), declared earlier as having the composite variable type Record. This record variable is currently being held in memory, but it isn't truly a record until it's saved to disk. Two user actions can trigger this. Clicking the Add button adds one entry to the self-sizing dynamic array. Also, the paging device at the right of each major form is a vertical scroll bar called RecordShown. Moving the scroll bar saves the currently displayed record to its proper position, regardless of whether there were any changes in that record.

```
Sub Form_Load ()
tl = Total(Products)
ReDim Preserve PrID$(tl), PrNam$(tl), PrX(tl), PrLoc(tl)
Instance = ActiveInstance(Products)
If tl > 0 Then
    RecordShown.Max = tl
Else
    RecordShown.Max = 1
    Register.Caption = "New File"
    Exit Sub
End If
ShowRecord
End Sub
```

The ReDim statement at the beginning "fixes" the sort arrays by setting them to their proper lengths. The Instance number is a major variable throughout most major references to the contents of a record. If you could pass a parameter to a form when you start it with the Load statement or .Show method, Instance would most certainly be the parameter passed between the parent and

child windows in this application. The maximum parameter of the scroll bar is
set, and control is passed to a procedure Sub ShowRecord ().

```
Sub ShowRecord ()
If LOF(Products) >= Len(Listing(Instance)) Then
    Get Products, Current(Products, Instance), Listing(Instance)
    IDField.Text = LTrim$(Listing(Instance).ProductNo)
    ProductTitle.Text = LTrim$(Listing(Instance).Title)
    ProductCategory.Text = LTrim$(Listing(Instance).Category)
    PubName.Text = LTrim$(Listing(Instance).Publisher)
    PrPriceBreak.Text = Str$(Listing(Instance).PriceBreak)
    NumInStock.Text = Str$(Listing(Instance).InStock)
    NumOnOrder.Text = Str$(Listing(Instance).OnOrder)
    NumBackOrder.Text = Str$(Listing(Instance).BackOrder)
    NumReOrder.Text = Str$(Listing(Instance).ReOrderQuan)
    ListPrice.Text = Str$(Listing(Instance).RetailPrice)
    PrComments.Text = LTrim$(Listing(Instance).Comments)
    If Listing(Instance).ReOrderPrd > 0 Then
        ReOrderWhen(Listing(Instance).ReOrderPrd).Value = True
    Else
        For w = 1 To 3
            ReOrderWhen(w).Value = False
        Next w
    End If
    RecordShown.Value = Current(Products, Instance)
    Register.Caption = "Record #" + Str$(Current(Products,
    ➥Instance))
End If
End Sub
```

Way back in the midst of Sub MDIForm_Load (), all the Current() instance
data pointers were set to the last record in the file. So when Sub ShowRecord ()
begins execution, the value of Current(Products, Instance) is set to the last,
and probably latest, data record in the Products file. Sub ShowRecord () does
not address this last variable explicitly (by number) because the procedure is
designed to be used on demand for whatever happens to be the current record.

All the text fields in this form that have direct bearing on a field variable in
the Products data file are loaded with field contents. Next, the scroll bar value
is set to reflect the record currently shown. From here, execution of the application passes into that wonderful state of limbo so characteristic of the event-
driven model.

In all honesty, I developed Sub ShowRecord () before I redeveloped Sub Form_Load (); so I suppose I've proven you don't have to write a program from front to back. Sub ShowRecord () contains no math or complex structure, though with Sub Form_Load (), I spent a few more minutes toying with the order of events and removing redundant instructions it shared with ShowRecord concerning the scroll bar.

The application can now accept textual input from the user without executing Visual Basic instructions. For each field in the products form, a _LostFocus event procedure handles the enrollment of the field contents in the record variable. There's not much to these event procedures, with a few exceptions. For the most part, only one instruction is contained in the framework, as the following example shows:

```
Sub PubName_LostFocus ()
Listing(Instance).Publisher = PubName.Text
End Sub
```

Because the Suggested Retail and Our Price fields contain prices, it would be nice to keep a dollar sign present before each value in the text fields and to maintain two digits following the decimal point. In the past I have written routines to convert the format of the digits in a text field for dollar amounts, but Microsoft's Professional Edition of Visual Basic 2 contains a new custom control that performs such maintenance functions on behalf of its programmer.

Technique Capsule: Self-Formatting Numeric Text Fields

Definition: The masked text box control is provided to Visual Basic by way of the file MSMASKED.VBX. Once installed, the file adds this tool to the Visual Basic toolbar.

The purpose of the masked text box control is to allow for automatic reformatting of uniformly formatted data, such as dollar values, times, and dates. The appearance and major characteristics of a standard text box are borrowed here, though there are two other exclusive properties of importance.

Execution: The .Format property for a masked text box specifies the character arrangement for its contents. The setting of .Format does not affect the setting of the .Text property for the masked text box, though the appearance of the control's contents is affected. The .Format property is set to a string of characters that follows the Microsoft descriptor language for field formatting, utilized by Visual Basic's Format$() function and by Microsoft Excel. When set, a secondary property, .Mask, imposes limitations on the appearance of each character that appears in the masked text box, in corresponding order from left to right. If one of the characters in the .Mask setting is set to a pound sign, #, the corresponding character in that field's .Text setting must be a digit to be displayed.

Example: Suppose the .Text property for a masked text box is continually set to the current time by the Time$ internal variable. From the Visual Basic properties window, the .Format property for the masked text box can be set to hh:mm AM/PM. Although Time$ generally is rendered in 24-hour format, the AM/PM specification tells the interpreter to translate the time to 12-hour format. The preceding zero in hours numbering from one to nine o'clock is removed.

With the masked text boxes in place in the Price Info frame of the Product Entry form, I was able to keep their _LostFocus event procedures simple, as in the following example:

```
Sub ListPrice_LostFocus ()
Listing(Instance).RetailPrice = Val(ListPrice.Text)
End Sub
```

I didn't have to write any wild and cumbersome conversion routine to keep double-digit values in the text box and a dollar sign at the front, yet I'm still able to keep RetailPrice declared As Currency. The Val() function alone converts the text in the box to a Currency value.

I constructed this interactive form module to reduce the amount of commands the user must give the form to enter records. When the user types data over an existing record, the application assumes the user is updating the current record. There is no update button, in other words. The procedure that updates the current form—transparently to the user—is the change event for the scroll bar. When the user says, "Next form, please," the current record variable is stored to the Products file, as shown in the following event procedure:

```
Sub RecordShown_Change ()
Put Products, Current(Products, Instance), Listing(Instance)
```

```
Register.Caption = "Record #" + Str$(RecordShown.Value)
Current(Products, Instance) = RecordShown.Value
ShowRecord
End Sub
```

This procedure is quite simple: the record is stored using the Put # instruction. (There's no pound sign in the previous instruction because the record channel number was replaced by the declared constant Products.) The record number register is updated, the current record pointer is set, and execution branches to Sub ShowRecord (). From there, the program again goes into limbo, waiting for something to happen.

The user can also store a record by telling the application that it is indeed a *new* record, to be tacked to the end of the old one. For these directions to be divulged requires the services of a command button (at last). For that job, the following procedure is written:

```
Sub Add_Click ()
tl = Total(Products) + 1
ReDim Preserve PrID$(tl), PrNam$(tl), PrX(tl), PrLoc(tl)
Put Products, Current(Products, Instance), Listing(Instance)
Current(Products, Instance) = tl
Total(Products) = tl
RecordShown.Max = RecordShown.Max + 1
RecordShown.Value = RecordShown.Max
ClearForm
End Sub
```

The major difference here is that at the beginning of the procedure, the sort arrays are stretched with the array-resizing technique introduced earlier in this chapter. The parameters for the scroll bar then are reset to fit the expanding array length.

There's nothing terribly exciting about Sub ClearForm () . Listing it here only demonstrates the need for a single text box clearing instruction for Visual Basic.

```
Sub ClearForm ()
IDField.Text = ""
ProductTitle.Text = ""
ProductCategory.Text = ""
PubName.Text = ""
AverageCost.Text = ""
```

```
LowestCost.Text = ""
ListPrice.Text = ""
OurPrice.Text = ""
PrPriceBreak.Text = ""
NumInStock.Text = ""
NumOnOrder.Text = ""
NumBackOrder.Text = ""
NumReOrder.Text = ""
PrComments.Text = ""
End Sub
```

One necessary command button, Remove, calls a procedure that removes a record from the file.

```
Sub Remove_Click ()
If Current(Products, Instance) < Total(Products) Then
    For mve = Current(Products, Instance) To Total(Products)
        Get Products, mve + 1, Listing(Instance)
        Put Products, mve, Listing(Instance)
    Next mve
End If
ClearForm
If Current(Products, Instance) = Total(Products) Then
    Current(Products, Instance) = Current(Products, Instance) - 1
End If
If Total(Products) > 1 Then
    Total(Products) = Total(Products) - 1
Else
    Put Products, 1, Listing(Instance)
End If
ShowRecord
End Sub
```

In the random-access model of Visual Basic, the only way to remove a record from a file permanently and keep the file intact—without a bunch of holes appearing in it like an unpacked dBASE file—is to count every record following the removed one and walk it back one notch. The first loop clause in Sub Remove_Click () has the honors. The first record moved back overwrites the one currently displayed and, so in effect, deletes it. The next conditional clause following the call to Sub ClearForm () ensures the current instance record pointer is not pointing to a record number that's now one unit beyond what the new total number of records will be. The final clause ensures one record is always in the file, even if it's an empty one. The clause does this by reducing the total number of records if and only if the number is greater than one; if the only record is an empty one, it is saved at position one. It's extremely unlikely that the user of this product will delete every item in his inventory—regardless of what used car dealership ads tell you. Assuming that in the current economy this one-in-a-billion chance ever does come about, though, this clause is necessary to avoid a bug in the future—when the program tries to delete a nonexistent record from a nonexistent file.

Keep in mind that this application is still in a formative stage. As development of this application progresses, you will most likely need to amend some of these procedures, especially `Sub Remove_Click ()`. If a listing of a product is removed, it's necessary to remove or tag for removal all shelf items currently listed in inventory with that product number. Consider how the user of this application might want the program to work in this instance.

Suppose the product listing is removed because a product's name and catalog number change. It might be more efficient for the user to update the specifications for the current record. However, should you force a user to think in any particular way? The user might think the proper way to work is to delete the current record, add a new one, and attach the old inventory items to the new product listing. Would the user necessarily appreciate it if the items belonging to the old product were automatically deleted, and he were to find out only when it was too late? On the other hand, does the programmer want a bunch of inventory items in the `Packages` data file having no products associated with them?

These reflect the types of questions a programmer asks himself as he proceeds under the premises of layered programming. You might think it is more efficient to put all these questions on paper ahead of time. You would be correct in saying the programmer *should* indeed try to indicate the normal and abnormal processes for using the program and the types of questions a user might ask before you write the first source code instruction. The truth is, though, you as programmer will definitely find yourself asking new questions altogether as the programming process proceeds. Attempting to answer everything in advance is like trying to navigate a garden maze from the outside. You can't expect to recognize immediately all the shrubbery you might encounter along the way.

Where Is the Automation in All This?

At last, I'm at the point where this application can be made to do at least one of the things it will be employed to do in the workplace—besides storing and recalling records. The sort-search-retrieve engine needs to be adapted to the current environment.

As it is with so many of my applications under construction, I start at the end and work back toward the beginning. Because the simulated-query procedure is entirely the same for every form I use, with the exception of a few identifiers, it makes sense to give the sort and binary search procedures a global context.

The way Visual Basic 2 has restructured its contextual definitions, you no longer have to separate global declarations from the rest of the project within a global module. General procedures in a general module automatically have global context unless declared otherwise using the `Private` qualifier. So it would seem the sorting and binary search procedures, which require global context, can be tacked to the end of whatever I'm currently calling the global module; therefore, I can have a global procedures module. Theoretically, this is possible, but not at the time of this writing, apparently because of the declaration of dynamic arrays used in this module. Dimensioning a dynamic array for modular or global scope within the declarations section of INVENT1.GBL, and then using `ReDim` later in the module, results in a "Subscript out of range" error, even though the subscript boundaries of a dynamic array cannot be traversed during redimensioning. Apparently, the interpreter still maintains some of the old distinctions between the global and general module, although they are supposed to be removed.

Why not try to make a global procedures module?

I therefore had to choose one of the general modules as the repository for global procedures; and because the Inventory Control module is the most important of the set of three, I placed it there. This placement of the source code in a module, or any other general module, does not affect the global context of these procedures.

With the different names and lengths I've given to the sorting arrays declared in the global module, it becomes necessary to declare a set of generic arrays within the procedure declarations. This way, the generic arrays may receive parameters passed to them, along with the contents of whatever arrays were doing the passing, regardless of their names.

The sorting procedure now looks like this:

```
Sub qsort (dta() As String, locat() As Integer, arraylength
➡  As Integer)
Dim i As Integer, j As Integer, b As Integer, l As Integer,
➡  t As Variant, r As Integer, d As Integer
ReDim Preserve dta(arraylength), locat(arraylength)
ReDim p(arraylength), w(arraylength)
k = 1                      'initial subdivision number
p(k) = 1                   'left boundary of subdivision
w(k) = arraylength         'right boundary of subdivision
l = 1                      'left boundary of array
d = 1                      'search direction
r = arraylength            'right boundary of array
Do
toploop:
    If r - l < 9 Then GoTo bubsort
    i = l
    j = r
    While j > i
        If dta(i) > dta(j) Then
            t = dta(j)
            x = locat(j)
            dta(j) = dta(i)
            locat(j) = locat(i)
            dta(i) = t
            locat(i) = x
            d = -d
        End If
        If d = -1 Then
            j = j - 1
        Else
            i = i + 1
        End If
    Wend
    j = j + 1
    k = k + 1
    If i - l < r - j Then
        p(k) = j
        w(k) = r
        r = i
    Else
```

```
            p(k) = l
            w(k) = i
            l = j
        End If
        d = -d
        GoTo toploop
    bubsort:
        If r - l > 0 Then
            For i = l To r
                b = i
                For j = b + 1 To r
                    If dta(j) <= dta(b) Then b = j
                Next j
                If i <> b Then
                    t = dta(b)
                    x = locat(b)
                    dta(b) = dta(i)
                    locat(b) = locat(i)
                    dta(i) = t
                    locat(i) = x
                End If
            Next i
        End If
        l = p(k)
        r = w(k)
        k = k - 1
    Loop Until k = 0
End Sub
```

The generic arrays to which I refer are dta()—the array that will actually be in a sorted state when all this is done—and locat(), the parallel array that receives the locations where the records with the sorted fields can be retrieved from the data file.

The Algebraic Description of QuickSort

Earlier in this book, I used the left-hand/right-hand analogy to describe what's happening in the QuickSort routine. Allow me to be more literal in this description of the sorting process, and mind you, this is my implementation of QuickSort, not my invention. (I did optimize the standard procedure, as you see momentarily.) Figure 5.4 depicts an unsorted array and the way the variables are used to divide and conquer it. I used single-letter variables in my sort algorithms in deference to the more classical style, though notice I used remarks in the preceding variable declarations to help you determine the purpose of these variables.

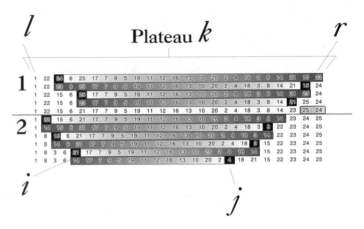

Figure 5.4. A demonstration of sorts. Part 1.

At first, QuickSort perceives the unsorted array as one vast plateau of numbers or, in this case, characters. This single plateau is numbered 1, and the plateau number for this application is k, as shown in Figure 5.4. The initial boundaries of the array, left and right, are assigned to variables l and r. Because QuickSort eventually subdivides the larger array, a pair of integer arrays keeps track of the left and right boundaries of the subdivisions, however many there finally are. There never can be more subdivisions than units in the larger array, so the arrays p() and w() can be dimensioned safely for arraylength units. I added one variable to the classic procedure, d. It stands for the direction of the current swap and saves you from writing the same swap clause twice.

The way algorithms work is by repeating the same mathematical process over and over until the objective is complete. Often, the algorithm cannot know in advance how many iterations of the work loop it must undergo before the job is completed; however, at least it does know that moment when it arrives. For Visual Basic, the Do-Loop clause is most convenient for algorithms of this nature, because the conditions necessary for exiting the loop can be loosely stated—in this case, when the condition k = 0 is met, for reasons you see in a moment.

When the main body of the loop starts, variable i represents the "left hand" and variable j the "right hand." The left-hand entry swaps lower-ordered entries with the right; from that point, the right-hand entry swaps higher-ordered entries with the left. Remembering to think symbolically, notice some distance between i and j in Figure 5.4, Panel 2. There's no reason to swap the values pointed to by i and j if there's (little or) no distance between the two. Thus, While j > i (while there's distance between the two entries), you can make comparisons; otherwise, generate a new subdivision and reset the left- and right-hand boundaries.

The swap takes place if i points to an element greater in value (or alphanumerical order) than the element j points to. In the classic algorithm, t is employed as a temporary variable that retrieves the j value immediately before the i element is set to the j value. The i element then is set to the value in the temporary value. The directional variable d then is negated, so if it equaled 1 (forward), following the swap, it equals -1 (backward).

Suppose the swap hasn't taken place yet. The directional variable d is tested to see which direction you're going. Your objective is to determine whether to move the right-hand test unit back (j = j - 1) or the left-hand unit forward (i = i + 1). After one hand or the other is moved, Wend is executed, and the swap test takes place again, unless the two hands collide—an event depicted in Figure 5.5, Panel 1.

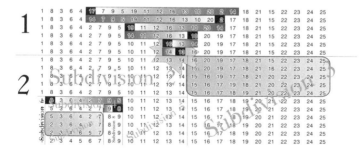

Figure 5.5. A demonstration of sorts. Part 2.

At this time, the entire array has yet to be fully sorted, although all the values to the *left* of the collision point between i and j are lesser in value than all those to the *right* of that collision point.

When the `Do-Loop` exits after `i` and `j` have collided, the algorithm places a partitional division that divides the previous array `#k` into two subarrays or subdivisions. The next condition tests whether the collision point is closer in value or content to element `1` or element `j`. The aim is to determine which is the larger segment—the one to the left or to the right of the collision point—and assign the left and right boundaries for that segment to `p(k)` and `w(k)`, respectively. The directional variable then is swapped, and using the dreaded `GoTo` statement, program execution proceeds back to a point immediately below the `Do` instruction.

If the subdivisions were allowed to be divided indefinitely, this algorithm would actually not know where or when to stop. For this reason, immediately after the `Do` instruction, a test checks to see whether there's too small a distance between left and right boundaries—in this case, less than 9—to bother with creating another subdivision. If `r` and `1` are too close, execution proceeds to a routine marked `bubsort` that performs a BubbleSort operation (a different type of algorithm) on subdivisions of eight elements or less. Each time a bubble sort completes, one subdivisional count is removed from variable `k`. When `k` equals zero, this is an indicator that all the subdivisions were broken down to eight units or less, and were all bubble sorted. You learn about the bubble sort algorithm in detail in a later chapter.

> **Technique Note:** Visual Basic can evaluate string contents with the same operators it uses to evaluate numeric values. Therefore, `"A" < "Z"` evaluates true, and if a$ starts with an earlier letter than b$, `a$ < b$` also evaluates true. Because of this, you can use the same program model with an algorithm that sorts or otherwise evaluates string contents as you use with numerical values.

The only reason to sort the arrays in memory is because when using an algorithm that searches for an item, searching within a sorted array gives the search algorithm one more piece of information than it would have had in an unsorted array when the element being searched is the wrong one. The algorithm, with one simple conditional test, concludes that the element being searched for falls before or after the one that just failed the test. This before-or-after test results in a binary state; that is why this algorithm is called a binary search. Here is how I implemented the standard binary search for INVENT1:

```
Function bsearch (dta() As String, locat() As Integer,
➥   arraylength As Integer, s As String, over1 As Integer)
➥   As Integer
i = Int(arraylength / 2)
l = 1
r = arraylength
Do While t <> s
    t = RTrim$(dta(i))
    Select Case True
        Case t = s
            Exit Do
        Case t < s
            l = i
            i = i + Int((r - l) / 2)
        Case t > s
            r = i
            i = i - Int((r - l) / 2)
    End Select
Loop
If over1 = True Then
    n = 1
    For d = -1 To 1 Step 2
        m = i
        Do
            m = m + d
            If dta(m) = dta(i) Then
                n = n + 1
                If d = -1 Then
                    i = i - 1
                End If
            Else
                Exit Do3
            End If
        Loop
    Next d
    over1 = n
End If
bsearch = locat(i)
End Function
```

You're already familiar with the generic arrays dta() and locat(). The contents being searched for are declared to be s. I modified this procedure so that

if over1 is set to True, the procedure is told to search for more than one instance of the same contents. The number of instances found would then be
returned to the calling body of the application through over1 again, because
the variable was passed by reference rather than by value.

The binary search algorithm is related to the QuickSort concept, although
it's far simpler. Figure 5.6 demonstrates the binary search algorithm's primary
principle. The search starts in the middle of the array, and it's unlikely the
contents searched for turn up on first try. Variable i represents the element being
searched, and t contains the value or contents of the array at i. Variable s represents the target element. Again, l and r represent the left and right boundaries for the portion of the array being searched.

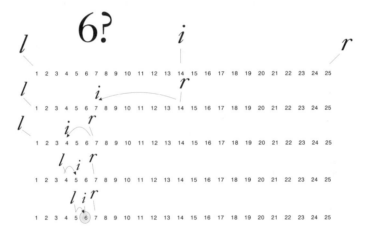

Figure 5.6. Homing in on the target.

The value of i always is set to an element directly between l and r. The
Select Case clause knows how unlikely a match between search contents and
target is, so it tests for t = s only as the first Case. If the found value is greater
than the target, the left boundary is placed where the search element is now,
and the searched element pointer i is set halfway between the new left and right
boundaries. If the found value is less than the target, the *right* boundary is
reset.

This would normally be where the algorithm ends. Repeated execution will
eventually yield the target contents, although my additions will first look immediately to the left of pointer i and then immediately to the right of it to search

for repeated instances of the target contents. If identical contents are found immediately before the location pointed to by i, then i is scooted back one notch. When the procedure is exited, i points to the first instance of the target contents in the array, and the variable passed to over1 will contain the number of instances of the target starting at i and proceeding forward in the array.

As I've stated before, the majority of the time you spend programming will be directed toward debugging. The previous sorting and searching procedures are in themselves somewhat flawless (well, okay, *mostly* flawless... well...). Nevertheless, in trying to integrate them with the rest of this application, I encountered flaw after flaw for hours. I even managed to crash the Visual Basic interpreter once or twice (or sixteen hundred times). So if you would, stay with me in this discussion of automation while I proceed to Chapter 6, "Development and Debugging."

DEVELOPMENT AND DEBUGGING

The concept of debugging is generally presented to the reader in something akin to an appendix, as a sort of mop-up operation. Any veteran programmer knows "development" and "debugging" are, in this business, synonymous. At the point where conceptualization, diagram-drawing, and process modeling ends, the errors and bugs begin.

6

Distinguishing between errors and bugs.

An error in computing is nothing major, except in cases where the error continues to make itself known after the programmer deems the product complete. Errors are trappable, and the Visual Basic interpreter can stop execution to tell you something is wrong. A bug, according to professional programmers, is far more serious. The bugged program can go about its business once the bug is encountered, but it will go about in something akin to the way a sick child crosses a rope bridge over a torrential river in a wind storm. It's not so much a matter of *if* the program is going to crash, it's a matter of *when* the program is going to crash. At times you have to stop the program manually; at others, expect to give your crashed application the three-finger salute.

The Visual Basic interpreter tells you what's wrong when an error condition is trapped. You can write an error-trapping routine for a procedure—provided the error occurs within the procedure—that responds to problems such as a file you're trying to open not being available or a subscript in memory to which you're trying to assign a value not being dimensioned. Errors are hardly worth writing about; bugs are another matter. A bug throws the program's normal course off track, and at first, neither the interpreter nor you have any idea why.

Revealing the Command-Line Interpreter

Using the Immediate Panel to converse directly with the VB interpreter.

The operating environment of Visual Basic is unique for an old reason: It has kept a command-line interpreter, now in the form of the Immediate Panel in the lower portion of the Debug Window, for communicating with the interpreter itself while the application is in break mode. You can speak to this window in BASIC—in some cases, abbreviated BASIC. To a limited extent, you can have the interpreter change the operating conditions of the Visual Basic application while it is in stasis. Although Visual Basic 2 has dramatically improved its debugging features with the addition of watchpoints (now called "watch expressions"), the Immediate Panel of the Debug Window is by far the most useful feature you can use. If you've ever programmed in C, you will wish your compiler had such a conversational device.

Situation #1: The Retail Inventory Tracking System

It would be somewhat embarassing if it weren't so deliberate: I must show you some bugs in my code to demonstrate the process of debugging. I'll begin with a problem I encountered while tweaking the binary search routines for INVENT1. The problem is that the sort procedure and the search procedure both work. At some point, the application generates a blank ID field. Because blanks fall before characters in the ASCII code, the sort procedure takes this blank ID field—which wasn't entered deliberately—and places it at the beginning of the array, shifting all the legitimate entries down one. When the search algorithm encounters the blank entry in the first slot—by name dta(1)—it literally hangs (gets stuck). The objective is to keep the Products module from generating blank records that lead to blank entries at the top of the sorted array.

Clue #1

While the search routine hangs itself, I press Ctrl-Break to stop the endless soul searching and bring up the Debug Window. Polling the window for the current contents of dta(1), the command-line interpreter responds with a blank line. However, when I give the Debug Window the instruction ?"*"dta(1)"*" (the ? is shorthand for Print), the CLI responds with two asterisks separated by six spaces. Six spaces is the fixed length of the product ID field Listing(Instance).ProductNo.

The old between-the-asterisks trick.

Now begins the great detective mystery. I want to know just when the contents of dta(1) become "   " (quotation marks mine). Because I operated the module and entered one field in the Products file already, I know the ID number in the first record is 01234. When does one of my instructions change the state of things?

Trying the Watch System

To find out, I set the interpreter's watch system to break when the expression dta(1) = "   " first evaluates true. My thoughts were that, at the time of the automatic break, the hazy-line instruction pointer would be sitting atop the perpetrator instruction.

If you've never set a watch expression, here's how I went about it: From the control window's Debug menu, I selected Add Watch. In the dialog panel that followed, I typed the expression `dta(1) = "      "` (the spaces before and after the = are unimportant) and set the option dot for "Break When Expression Is True." After I clicked OK, the Watch Panel of the Debug Window (the upper portion, above the Immediate Panel) showed my watch expression, along with a reading of its current evaluative status. Now, if the expression evaluates true, when I break the program manually or when the watch system breaks it for me, the end of the watch line should read -1; otherwise, it should read 0 for false.

As a programmer in this situation, I long for the time when this expression evaluates false (0). The problem is that I want the cause of this bug to show itself, so I actually want the expression to evaluate true (−1) so I can finally eradicate this bug. Like a district attorney, I need this vital evidence so I can conclude my case.

Clue #2

So here I am waiting for the blank entry to cause the watch system to break the module's execution. The module never broke. I waited for about a minute (which in 486DX2/50 time is quite a while; galaxies can be constructed in such time) and then I had to break the program manually again. When I quizzed the CLI `?dta(1)`, however, once again I received a blank line; and when I tried my between-the-asterisks trick, once again I was met by six spaces between two asterisks. Is the watch system malfunctioning? Is it susceptible to the same type of prioritization that is characteristic of Windows event procedure handling? For instance, drawing instructions are often put on hold by Windows while the Visual Basic interpreter processes mathematical instructions. Could the watch mechanism be put on hold as well?

Clue #3

In the logical language of Visual Basic, if the expression `a > 5` evaluates true, the Debug Window instruction `?a>5` makes the CLI respond with a -1, for logical true. The expression I gave the watchpoint system was `dta(1) = "      "`, with regular spaces between the quotation marks. Is it possible this instruction evaluates false? I quizzed the CLI with `?dta(1)="      "`, and it responded with a 0, for logical false. Apparently, the watchpoint system works just fine; the expression I gave it was false.

In case you're wondering whether I'm paranoid, I always tell programmers to suspect everything else before blaming themselves. Some people are trained to believe success means no errors and an error in programming is failure. Many error conditions and bugs occur in programming. If you equate success with eternal flawlessness, you need to seriously recondition your way of thinking now. In fact, let me be the first to postulate that errors make for better programs, because their presence helps you adjust the program's structure to make it more efficient.

Clue #4

Using the instruction `?asc(left$(dta(1),1))`, I ask the Debug Window CLI, which characters appear to be spaces? Its response is a simple `0`. This explains why the watch expression didn't stop the program's run. The ASCII value of a standard space character is 32, not 0. To engage the watch system, you must be able to type the expression that breaks the program, and you can't type an ASCII character number 0 on the keyboard. Can you use the `String$()` function to feed ASCII zeros mathematically to the watchpoint system? I tested this idea by quizzing the CLI `?dta(1)=string$(6,0)`. The response was `-1`—yes, it works.

ASCII zeros used as padding characters.

Clue #5

I edited the watch expression to read `dta(1) = String$(6, 0)`. I ran the application, and again it hung at the search procedure. I broke it manually and once again quizzed the CLI `?dta(1)=string$(6,0)`. The answer, again, was `-1`. The watch system was not breaking the program, so it would seem apparently Windows does prioritize the watch system behind repetitious calculations such as algorithms.

Watch system aside, you can see the system is generating a bad record somewhere. Could the problem be with the instructions that call the search procedure? The Find button on the Product Display form (PRODUCT.FRM) has this event procedure:

```
Sub Find_Click ()
id$ = RTrim$(IDField.Text)
If Total(Products) > 1 Then
    SearchForRecord id$
End If
End Sub
```

Obviously, there's no reason to have the interpreter start searching for a record unless there's more than one record to search for. That's the reason for the preceding conditional clause. The other procedure that places the call to `Sub SearchForRecord ()` is the event procedure for the ID field losing the focus. My idea here was for the user to be able to type in a unique product number and without doing anything else, have the record with that number magically display itself. This number would be displayed upon the record number field's loss of the focus, as shown here:

```
Sub IDField_LostFocus ()
If ProductTitle.Text = "" Then
    If Total(Products) > 1 Then
        id$ = RTrim$(IDField.Text)
        SearchForRecord id$
    End If
Else
    Listing(Products).ProductNo = LTrim$(IDField.Text)
End If
End Sub
```

One of the conditions for starting the search process is if the Title field on the form is empty, a possible signal that the user isn't updating an existing procedure. The next condition that must be met, understandably, is when there is more than one record in the `Products` file. The product number entry should not be considered a formal entry if it is actually accessing an existing record (keep this in mind for a moment).

Both these procedures conditionally branch here:

```
Sub SearchForRecord (id$)
Put Products, Current(Products, Instance), Listing(Instance)
ReloadArrays
qsort PrID$(), PrLoc(), Total(Products)
spot% = bsearch(PrID$(), PrLoc(), Total(Products), id$, False)
Current(Products, Instance) = spot%
ShowRecord
End Sub
```

The `Sub SearchForRecord ()` procedure starts by placing the current record in the file, before executing the procedure that loads the sort arrays with the proper values:

```
Sub ReloadArrays ()
For arr = 1 To Total(Products)
    Get Products, arr, Loader
    PrID$(arr) = Loader.ProductNo
    PrNam$(arr) = Loader.Title
    PrLoc(arr) = arr
Next arr
End Sub
```

If you think you've seen this routine before, you have an excellent memory. It first appeared in the `Sub MDIForm_Load ()` procedure, when all eight sort arrays were loaded with these values. Go back to `Sub SearchForRecord ()` for a moment. Notice, `Sub IDField_LostFocus ()` doesn't assign the contents of `IDField.Text` to `Listing(Instance).RecordNo` unless the user is not searching for a record, yet when `Sub SearchForRecord ()` starts, the first instruction executed is the `Put #` instruction. (I still write the pound sign for identification purposes even though the sign is overwritten by the constant `Products`.) If the product number field isn't assigned to the record and the record is written to the file, the interpreter must be sending an empty field to the record—mustn't it? Why is a record being sent in such conditions in the first place?

Erecting Fences and Guardposts

Whether or not this is the cause of the bug, perhaps `Sub SearchForRecord ()` should be modified so that a record isn't written to the file unless there's some substance to that record. Here's the procedure following modification:

```
Sub SearchForRecord (id$)
If ProductTitle.Text <> "" Then
    Put Products, Current(Products, Instance), Listing(Instance)
End If
ReloadArrays
qsort PrID$(), PrLoc(), Total(Products)
spot% = bsearch(PrID$(), PrLoc(), Total(Products), id$, False)
Current(Products, Instance) = spot%
ShowRecord
End Sub
```

The other potential problem relates to my earlier assumption that the contents of `IDField.Text` must not be assigned to the record variable `Listing(Instance)` unless the user is making a legitimate entry. The first text field in the entry sequence is the product number field, so the user always enters contents there first while the other fields are empty. The assumption that the first entry is not legitimate if the other fields are empty is, therefore, incorrect. I must therefore correct myself with the following procedure:

```
Sub IDField_LostFocus ()
Listing(Products).ProductNo = LTrim$(IDField.Text)
If ProductTitle.Text = "" Then
    If Total(Products) > 1 Then
        id$ = RTrim$(IDField.Text)
        SearchForRecord id$
    End If
End If
End Sub
```

Now the contents of IDField.Text are assigned to the record variable at all times, not conditionally. It appears I've fixed the problem somewhat. Actually, I haven't yet; there's still a bug somewhere feeding the search procedure a false field and causing it to hang. Sub RecordShown_Change () now places a field in the file unconditionally. Perhaps it needs the same type of change as applied to the previous two procedures.

```
Sub RecordShown_Change ()
If IDField.Text <> "" And ProductTitle.Text <> "" Then
    Put Products, Current(Products, Instance), Listing(Instance)
End If
Register.Caption = "Record #" + Str$(RecordShown.Value)
Current(Products, Instance) = RecordShown.Value
ShowRecord
End Sub
```

Notice, I deleted the products file with each change, so that blank record—wherever it comes from—won't be hanging on to life if I've actually found the cure for it. At this point, the program isn't hanging, but on the other hand, it isn't even executing. I placed a breakpoint at the final instruction of Sub bsearch () in the INVCTRL1.BAS module, and the interpreter never reaches it. When I manually break, the current instruction hazy line is someplace in the middle of Sub bsearch (). For whatever reason, the binary search procedure is hanging the application.

A situation such as this often requires the programmer to change or adjust the process model somewhat. My program is causing a blank record to be saved to the file. To explain my somewhat esoteric theory, the scroll bar RecordShown can always scroll down one record more than the actual number of records in the file. This is deliberate—so that the user always has room to add one record to the end of the file. The form module counts the final record in memory, in whatever state of completion, as an open slot. This incomplete record in memory becomes a formal record only when you click the Add button.

Backing down and altering your process model.

Once again, here is the Sub Form_Load () procedure. This time, look for the two points where the maximum value of RecordShown exceeds the number of records in a new file.

```
Sub Form_Load ()
tl = Total(Products)
ReDim Preserve PrID$(tl), PrNam$(tl), PrX(tl), PrLoc(tl)
Instance = ActiveInstance(Products)
If tl > 0 Then
    RecordShown.Max = tl + 1
Else
    RecordShown.Max = 1
    Register.Caption = "New File"
    Exit Sub
End If
ShowRecord
End Sub
```

In the conditional clause, if the total number of records exceeds zero (if the file is evidently not new) RecordShown.Max is deliberately set to the total number of records *plus one*. If the total number of records is zero, however, RecordShown.Max is set to 1, which is still one more than the actual number (zero) if this false side of the clause is executed.

Is it possible the form module is saving the incomplete record in memory as a real record at some point? It wouldn't hurt to build some fail-safe features into the program that prevent this from happening. The objective now is to give the incomplete record a special status as the "New Record" rather than as a numbered record. The first procedure where this distinction should be made, in my opinion, is the procedure that changes the value of the scroll bar:

```
Sub RecordShown_Change ()
DoEvents
If RecordShown.Value <= Total(Products) Then
    If IDField.Text <> "" And ProductTitle.Text <> "" Then
        Put Products, Current(Products, Instance),
➥   Listing(Instance)
    End If
    Register.Caption = "Record #" + Str$(RecordShown.Value)
    Add.Caption = "Edit New"
Else
    Register.Caption = "New Record"
    Add.Caption = "Add"
End If
Current(Products, Instance) = RecordShown.Value
ShowRecord
End Sub
```

Using
DoEvents to
reorganize the
procedural
order.

This is now a far more complex procedure than its prototype. Notice, this procedure starts to change the role of the Add button. Now, its caption only reads "Add" when the value of the scroll bar is at its end, which is one unit beyond the value of Total(Products), the object of the initial comparison. When the scroll bar does reach its maximum, it registers its classic caption. The DoEvents instruction is added to the top because the interpreter tends to process the _Change event procedures before it executes the _LostFocus procedures. Also, the _LostFocus procedures are necessary to save a field being edited if it's losing the focus to the scroll bar; otherwise, the field's new contents are lost.

> **Technique Note:** You can use the DoEvents statement at the beginning of an event procedure, to instruct the interpreter to process now those events normally recognized after the End Sub of this event procedure. The statement doesn't really alter the order of events, only the procedures associated with them.

The next step is to split the purpose of the Add button in its native event procedure:

```
Sub Add_Click ()
If Add.Caption = "Add" Then
```

```
        tl = Total(Products) + 1
        ReDim Preserve PrID$(tl), PrNam$(tl), PrX(tl), PrLoc(tl)
        Put Products, Current(Products, Instance), Listing(Instance)
        Current(Products, Instance) = tl
        Total(Products) = tl
        RecordShown.Max = RecordShown.Max + 1
        RecordShown.Value = RecordShown.Max
Else
        RecordShown.Value = RecordShown.Max
        Current(Products, Instance) = RecordShown.Max
        ShowRecord
End If
ClearForm
End Sub
```

I've split this procedure into two parts. If the caption does not read "Add" now, the button acts only as a navigational tool, moving the scroll bar to its end and setting the current record pointer to one beyond the length of the actual record. Remember, the value of Current(Products, Instance) is set to where the next record goes during the Put # operation. It's not necessary to place the instruction Add.Caption = "Add" here, because the change in RecordShown.Value triggers the event procedure Sub RecordShown_Change (), and the instruction already appears there once.

Next, Sub ShowRecord () needs to be amended slightly, near the end of the procedure:

```
Sub ShowRecord ()
If LOF(Products) >= Len(Listing(Instance)) Then
        Get Products, Current(Products, Instance), Listing(Instance)
        IDField.Text = RTrim$(Listing(Instance).ProductNo)
        ProductTitle.Text = RTrim$(Listing(Instance).Title)
        ProductCategory.Text = RTrim$(Listing(Instance).Category)
        PubName.Text = RTrim$(Listing(Instance).Publisher)
        PrPriceBreak.Text = Str$(Listing(Instance).PriceBreak)
        NumInStock.Text = Str$(Listing(Instance).InStock)
        NumOnOrder.Text = Str$(Listing(Instance).OnOrder)
        NumBackOrder.Text = Str$(Listing(Instance).BackOrder)
        NumReOrder.Text = Str$(Listing(Instance).ReOrderQuan)
        ListPrice.Text = Str$(Listing(Instance).RetailPrice)
        OurPrice.Text = Str$(Listing(Instance).StdShelfPrice)
        PrComments.Text = RTrim$(Listing(Instance).Comments)
```

```
    If Listing(Instance).ReOrderPrd > 0 Then
        ReOrderWhen(Listing(Instance).ReOrderPrd).Value = True
    Else
        For w = 1 To 3
            ReOrderWhen(w).Value = False
        Next w
    End If
    RecordShown.Value = Current(Products, Instance)
    If RecordShown.Value < RecordShown.Max Then
        Register.Caption = "Record #" + Str$(Current(Products,
➡  Instance))
    End If
End If
End Sub
```

The new conditional clause near the end has the form display the "Record #" caption in the Register only if the current RecordShown.Value is below its maximum. Next, I make a simple change to Sub ClearForm ():

```
Sub Clear_Click ()
ClearForm
Register.Caption = "New Record"
RecordShown.Value = RecordShown.Max
End Sub
```

With these changes implemented, I again deleted the PRODUCTS.I1 data file and started the products module. Wonder of wonders, it is no longer generating false records. The apparent solution to the false record problem is to make record addition contingent on two conditions—that record must be the last one that can be pointed to in memory, and it must have legitimate contents.

Clue #6

The every-other-one bug and how to track it down.

Unfortunately, my tests show the search procedure is still hanging, but now it isn't hanging every time. In a test with two records, the module cross-referenced the first record perfectly, but hung when I gave it the product number for the second record. In a three-record test, the even-numbered records hang the application, whereas the odd-numbered records cross-reference perfectly.

This odd/even pattern is a dead ringer for a particular type of bug—a mathematical problem. Apparently, the real bug is in the search procedure. Odd/

even problems historically occur during divisions by two, and that is exactly what the search algorithm does to its internal array, several times. Variable 1 represents the leftmost boundary of the portion of the array being searched, and r represents the rightmost boundary. My formula for finding the halfway point was taking the rightmost boundary element number, subtracting from it the leftmost element number, dividing the remainder by two, and using Int() to make the result an integer.

Using the Debug Window CLI as a tool, I can make two immediate statements for this test of my formula. I can write 1 = 1 and r = 2, representing a two-record array. I then ask the CLI ?int((r-1)/2). The result is 0. This is definitely a problem, whether or not this is the cause of the bug. There is no record number 0 in my model. If the search procedure is counting "record zero" as a real record, possibly it hasn't been counting the last record in the array, or the second record in a two-record test. To keep the result of the expression non-zero, I add + 1 to the end of the two formulas in the algorithm. It now appears as follows:

```
Function bsearch (dta() As String, locat() As Integer,
➥   arraylength As Integer, s As String, over1 As Integer)
➥   As Integer
i = Int(arraylength / 2)
l = 1
r = arraylength
Do While t <> s
    t = RTrim$(dta(i))
    Select Case True
        Case t = s
            Exit Do
        Case t < s
            l = i
            i = i + Int((r - l) / 2) + 1
        Case t > s
            r = i
            i = i - Int((r - l) / 2) + 1
    End Select
Loop
If over1 = True Then
    n = 1
    For d = -1 To 1 Step 2
        m = i
        Do
```

```
              m = m + d
              If dta(m) = dta(i) Then
                  n = n + 1
                  If d = -1 Then
                      i = i - 1
                  End If
              Else
                  Exit Do
              End If
        Loop
    Next d
    over1 = n
End If
bsearch = locat(i)
End Function
```

In my tests, using both the `Sub IDField_LostFocus ()` and `Sub Add_Click ()` methods and after entering two records in a fresh file, no false fields were generated, and both even- and odd-numbered fields were found. The bug was in my original, supposedly bulletproof, algorithm. The search algorithm does work, of course, but only with arrays and sets of records whose first element starts with zero, not one.

If It's Not One Thing, It's Another

The solution to this bug—as is often the case with solutions to the many bugs you might encounter—is actually the cause of another anomaly somewhere else in the module; another possibility is that an existing anomaly comes to light. In any event, at one time the system was capable of handling a three-record file, and it isn't capable of that now. When trying to enter the third record, a "Subscript out of range" error is generated.

Efficiently debugging algorithms.

Using the Debug Window, I learned that during the search routine, adding 1 to the value of i when the search area—the distance between 1 and r—becomes one unit causes the algorithm to search the array at one unit *beyond* the value of r. This means if the file is two records long (and granted, few files that a real store generates are only two records long), the algorithm tries to search dta(3), which is one beyond the redimensioned upper boundary of the array.

Originally, I added the incrementer of + 1 to the region-splitting formula so the operation's result could not yield a zero value. Although this solves one problem, it creates another. Now, the search unit i, which is supposed to fall directly between l and r, can miss its target altogether if there really is no difference between them.

I could add a conditional clause to this algorithm, but I'd rather not. A well-crafted algorithm should be capable of executing the same primary formula time after time, and have its results be the proper value each time. If I imposed stipulations on the formula, by stating it should be executed only if it's "safe" to do so, the existence of the executional condition is an indicator that the formula isn't that well crafted.

The QuickSort algorithm is an exception to this rule. The algorithm conceivably could split the sorting subdivisions indefinitely and successfully sort the array even if it didn't send small subdivisions to a BubbleSort routine or subroutine. QuickSort, however, doesn't know when to stop. It keeps a running tally k for the subdivisions it's created; the BubbleSort portion decrements k each time it successfully sorts a small subdivision.

I'd prefer not to impose a conditional clause on the binary search routine, the secondary reason being that other successful binary searches have been written without such a device. I tried changing the addition of + 1 to + .5 and placed that incrementer within the parentheses so the formula read i = i + Int((r - l) / 2 + .5). As a result, the original bug—the one I spent the first several pages of this chapter hunting down—returned. Evidently, this isn't the solution.

In his book, *Programming Pearls,* Jon Bentley of AT&T Bell Laboratories says he's amazed how few professional programmers are capable of successfully crafting a binary search algorithm. Bentley wrote a solution in old BASIC that utilized a function CINT(); I honestly thought it performed a different function in Visual Basic. I was under the impression that Visual Basic's CInt() function only converted another data type to type Integer; however, the old function purpose is also there.

Borrowing ideas from the best.

Revelation: The CInt() function rounds the expression within the parentheses to the next closest integer. Unlike Int(), it can round *down* to the nearest even integer. This function works in Visual Basic

> in much the same way it did in old BASIC, although the documented
> purpose of the function in VB is to convert data types to straight
> integers.

I can use the `CInt()` function in place of `Int()` with an incrementer. Also,
Bentley's implementation gave me an idea I didn't see at first: placing new left
boundaries immediately after the location of search element `i` and new right
boundaries immediately before `i`. So I borrowed from a guy at Bell Labs; at
least I know the right people to borrow from. Here's the search procedure after
my transformations:

```
Function bsearch (dta() As String, locat() As Integer,
➥    arraylength As Integer, s As String, over1 As Integer)
➥    As Integer
ReDim Preserve dta(arraylength), locat(arraylength)
Dim i As Integer, l As Integer, t As String, r As Integer
i = CInt(arraylength / 2)
l = 1
r = arraylength
Do While t <> s
    t = dta(i)
    Select Case True
        Case t = s
            Exit Do
        Case t < s
            l = i + 1
        Case t > s
            r = i - 1
    End Select
    i = CInt((r + l) / 2)
    If i < l Or i > r Then
        bsearch = 0
        Exit Function
    End If
Loop
If over1 = True Then
    n = 1
    For d = -1 To 1 Step 2
```

```
        m = i
        Do
            m = m + d
            If dta(m) = dta(i) Then
                n = n + 1
                If d = -1 Then
                    i = i - 1
                End If
            Else
                Exit Do
            End If
        Loop
    Next d
    over1 = n
End If
bsearch = locat(i)
End Function
```

This is a far more efficient search procedure than its counterpart, thanks largely to Mr. Bentley. The halving formula for finding left and right is now more efficient because the same formula works for both cases, whether the target value or contents is before or after the searched element i. I took the halving formulas out of the Case subclauses and put their single replacement outside the Select Case clause. The formula isn't executed in Case t = s anyway. I also added a conditional clause for what happens if the algorithm doesn't find the target anywhere in the array. Bentley was right about his assessment of professional programmers' prowess.

A Simple Case of Neglected Padding

I encountered one problem without realizing it: the tail ends of a fixed length record written to disk are padded with ASCII zero characters. If you'll allow me for a moment to represent an ASCII zero with ~, then if the record number being searched for is taken from the graphics object IDField just after being typed, the contents of IDField.Text will not be padded with zeros. The search algorithm might then try to find record number 01234 in a file that recorded number 01234~. I declared, after all, the ProductNo field to be a String * 6, which means the string is always six characters long and padded with ASCII zeros if the contents are actually shorter.

Fixing string
lengths at
declaration.

One solution I implemented was to have the PRODUCT.FRM form module place the declaration `Dim id As String * 6`. The procedures section then uses the `id` string variable as the courier between the form module and the global sort and search routines in the INVCTRL1.BAS general module. This way, the string being searched for is always six characters long, even if the contents of `IDField.Text` are shorter and the instruction `id = IDField.Text` is executed.

> **Technique Note:** The `String * n` syntax for declaring a string for a fixed length of n characters works as well *outside* the `Type` declaration clause. Most documentation on the subject shows the syntax declaring only fixed lengths for fields in record variables.

Undoing
corrections that
are no longer
corrections.

Earlier, as a possible solution to a bug, I placed conditions on the `Sub SearchForRecord ()` procedure's ability to write a record to a data file using `Put #`. It just turns out that, with the same failsafes implemented on all the other procedures, this procedure doesn't have to write a record to the file in the first place. Corrected, it now reads as follows:

```
Sub SearchForRecord (id$)
ReloadArrays
qsort PrID$(), PrLoc(), Total(Products)
spot% = bsearch(PrID$(), PrLoc(), Total(Products), id$, False)
If spot% > 0 Then
    Current(Products, Instance) = spot%
    ShowRecord
End If
End Sub
```

Notice I added a conditional clause that responds to the case in which no matching record is found by doing nothing whatsoever. It doesn't sound any sirens or whistles; it just allows the user to continue to enter the rest of the record. If the entered ID number is unique, it probably belongs to a new record anyway.

One of the failsafes I added appears in procedure `Sub Add_Click ()`. It's the same one I added to `Sub RecordShown_Change ()` earlier:

```
Sub Add_Click ()
If Add.Caption = "Add" Then
    tl = Total(Products) + 1
    ReDim Preserve PrID$(tl), PrNam$(tl), PrX(tl), PrLoc(tl)
    If IDField.Text <> "" And ProductTitle.Text <> "" Then
        Put Products, Current(Products, Instance),
➡   Listing(Instance)
    End If
    Current(Products, Instance) = tl
    Total(Products) = tl
    RecordShown.Max = RecordShown.Max + 1
    RecordShown.Value = RecordShown.Max
Else
    RecordShown.Value = RecordShown.Max
    Current(Products, Instance) = RecordShown.Max
    ShowRecord
End If
ClearForm
End Sub
```

The failsafe is the conditional clause enclosing the Put # instruction, so the procedure won't save any record to disk unless there is some substance to it.

What Did I Do Wrong?

The chief psychological assumption you must discard as a practicing programmer is that errors and bugs are mistakes. They are not. They are merely anomalies. This is not an effort at politically correct phraseology. It is advice to those of you conditioned to believe flaws in your work along the way make you a lesser person.

At the risk of sounding like Ross Perot, when I come across an anomaly, I admit it. As an artist, when I draw a person's portrait, I start by drawing faint geometric lines connecting the spaces in that person's face—for example, from the edge of the mouth to the outmost extent of the cheekbone to the top of the ear. This line won't be visible in the final product, but it's there during the drawing process. When I begin to enter the shading and the features start to stand out, I might notice at some time the fact that the eyes aren't aligned. If the eyes don't align, the face isn't right; it's a person's face, but not one belonging to the person I'm drawing.

I may go on drawing for minutes, wondering why the face seems a little squat or unpleasant or confused. I might redraw little guidelines here and there, adjust the line between the earlobe and the nostril, and perform all sorts of minor adjustments; the main problem inevitably is the eyes aren't aligned. When I fix the eyes, suddenly everything falls into place.

You earlier witnessed a rather ordinary few hours of bug-hunting on an average programming day on my 486DX2/50. The problem started when, all of a sudden, tabbing to the second field on the form caused the entire application to hang. A small anomaly was the first indicator of what might be wrong with the program—an empty field was being loaded in the sort array, re-sorting to the beginning, and offsetting all fields by one. I tried to fight the bug by employing failsafes—"guardrails," if you will—that would keep empty fields from proceeding to a `Put #` instruction and being written to a file. The guardrails eventually worked. In fact, because I put up more of them than I needed, I can retract a few after the `Put #` instructions are made safe.

Still, something was wrong, and the application was hanging. When I added the conditional clause to the search procedure that allowed it to exit if it didn't find anything, the procedure would exit even if what it was looking for appeared to be there. I adjusted the `id` string to fix its length at six characters just like the `RecordNo` field. This made the interpreter place as much zero-character padding on the tail end of the search string as is given to the `RecordNo` fields stored to disk. The zero-character padding was the problem all along.

Now, suppose I were clairvoyant enough to have predicted at the beginning that the zero-character problem was the underlying cause of the hang. In that case, I could have applied the string-padding solution right away, but look what that causes the program as a whole to miss. The sort algorithm would not be nearly as efficient—my tweaks, inspired by *Programming Pearls*, improved it somewhat. The failsafes are necessary and welcome additions. I might have installed them later, anyway, when anomalies cropped up due to their absence. Because something embarrassing was wrong with the program, I cleaned house early.

It's arguable that I have a better application now because of the original bug. Granted, I do not apply the same philosophy to writing books as I do to writing programs; if I misinform you here, my career is justifiably on the line. What you read here is a final product, the result of a long, creative process and countless hours of brainstorming. Certainly, I wrote twice as many pages for this book than are in it now. This doesn't mean I'm an inefficient writer, and having initial bugs in a program doesn't make me an incapable programmer, nor will it you.

Your mission is to use the debugging process to your advantage, by letting it guide you in the task of housecleaning. You should put your best ideas in your code as soon as you can. The performance of these ideas in the interpreter's environment will be the determinant of their success or failure.

It's Like, an Operator

Now, you have a working model for a binary search operation. To use it further, copy it and adjust it for a new purpose. Visual Basic 2 adds a new alphanumeric comparison function to its vocabulary, borrowed from popular database management system languages that already use it extensively.

Technique Capsule: Wildcard String Comparisons

Definition: At the DOS prompt, when you search for files that match a specific textual pattern, you can define that pattern using wildcard characters—for instance, the asterisk * stands for any number of characters and the question mark ? stands for any single character. Visual Basic 2 has added a string comparison function `Like` to the vocabulary that you can use in place of the equality operator = to compare a string or string variable to a pattern containing these or other wildcard characters.

Execution: The syntax of an expression utilizing `Like` is as follows:

```
string Like pattern
```

The expression tests true (–1) when the arrangement of the characters in string matches the mixture of characters in pattern.

Example: Imagine you have a list of automobile models you're testing to determine which ones are Chevrolets. The first characters in the title might be "Chevrolet," though they might also be "Chevy." If your search algorithm encounters the title strings "Chevrolet Corvette," "Chevy Nova," or "Chevy Chase," the expression `title$ Like "Chev*"` evaluates true. By contrast, if you encounter the string "Che Guevara," the expression tests false.

Example: Suppose you need to test a string to see if it contains a standardly formatted dollar amount. In a conditional clause, you can use as the test expression test$ = "$*.##". This expression tests true for all cases where the string starts with a dollar sign, is followed by any number of dollars, and is terminated by a decimal point and two digits. The # character in a test pattern stands in place of a digit.

To use this operator, I devised a function procedure similar to the IDField search procedure. It is identical to Function bsearch () except for the inclusion of the Like operator and the addition of an extra instruction. My objective is to make the form module capable of extracting a record from the file based on the contents of the Title field in the form, whether those contents are complete or partial. This enables the user to search for records with titles that *begin* with certain characters.

```
Function blikesearch (dta() As String, locat() As Integer,
➥   arraylength As Integer, s As String, over1 As Integer)
➥   As Integer
ReDim Preserve dta(arraylength), locat(arraylength)
Dim i As Integer, l As Integer, t As String, r As Integer
i = CInt(arraylength / 2)
l = 1
r = arraylength
s = s + "*"
Do While t Like s = False
    t = dta(i)
    Select Case True
        Case t Like s
            Exit Do
        Case t < s
            l = i + 1
        Case t > s
            r = i - 1
    End Select
    i = CInt((r + l) / 2)
    If i < l Or i > r Then
        blikesearch = 0
        Exit Function
    End If
Loop
If over1 = True Then
```

```
    n = 1
    For d = -1 To 1 Step 2
        m = i
        Do
            m = m + d
            If dta(m) Like dta(i) Then
                n = n + 1
                If d = -1 Then
                    i = i - 1
                End If
            Else
                Exit Do
            End If
        Loop
    Next d
    over1 = n
End If
blikesearch = locat(i)
End Function
```

This function procedure still receives the s parameter as a string like its progenitor, but this time an instruction s = s + "*" is added to place a wildcard character at the end. The sorted array now compares the search string against the pattern contained in string variable s.

This works in the Product Display form much the way the equality search works for the IDField. The self-triggering procedure pattern is borrowed from Sub IDField_LostFocus () to produce the following:

```
Sub ProductTitle_LostFocus ()
Listing(Instance).Title = ProductTitle.Text
If IDField.Text = "" Then
    If Total(Products) > 1 Then
        lik$ = ProductTitle.Text
        SearchLikeRecord lik$
    End If
End If
End Sub
```

String variable lik$ does not need to be specially declared because its length for this comparison is not important. Assuming all the conditions are met, this procedure branches to another parallel procedure:

```
Sub SearchLikeRecord (lik$)
ReloadArrays
qsort PrNam$(), PrLoc(), Total(Products)
spot% = blikesearch(PrNam$(), PrLoc(), Total(Products), lik$,
➡  False)
If spot% > 0 Then
    Current(Products, Instance) = spot%
    ShowRecord
End If
End Sub
```

The other procedure that branches to this point is `Sub Find_Click ()`. Although this procedure was previously considered complete, it now needs to be modified. Notice the procedure needs to know whether the user means to search for an ID number or a title.

```
Sub Find_Click ()
If IDField.Text <> "" And ProductTitle.Text = "" Then
    id = IDField.Text
    If Total(Products) > 1 Then
        SearchForRecord id
    End If
ElseIf ProductTitle.Text <> "" And IDField.Text = "" Then
    lik$ = ProductTitle.Text
    If Total(Products) > 1 Then
        SearchLikeRecord lik$
    End If
End If
End Sub
```

The two-part conditional clause tests to see which field is empty—the ID field or the title field—and which one is full. If the ID field is full, the user must be searching for the title field. I could have left `Else` on a line by itself, but what if both fields are full or both empty? The procedure doesn't know what the user is searching for. Rather than alert the user with a dialog box saying, "What are you doing??? You haven't told me what your compare field is!!!" the procedure does nothing.

One problem caused by the Find button occurs when a partial string has been set up for a search field. When the user clicks Find, this partial string is saved as part of a record. The only way to prevent this natural course of events from happening is to keep the Find button disabled unless the scroll bar is at

the "New Record" setting. To accomplish this, I added the instruction
`Find.Enabled = False` to the `Sub Form_Load ()` procedure and modified the
`Sub RecordShown_Change ()` procedure to reenable the Find button when the
scroll bar moves all the way to the bottom:

```
Sub RecordShown_Change ()
DoEvents
If IDField.Text <> "" And ProductTitle.Text <> "" Then
    Put Products, Current(Products, Instance), Listing(Instance)
End If
If RecordShown.Value <= Total(Products) Then
    Register.Caption = "Record #" + Str$(RecordShown.Value)
    Add.Caption = "Edit New"
    Find.Enabled = False
Else
    Register.Caption = "New Record"
    Add.Caption = "Add"
    Find.Enabled = True
End If
Current(Products, Instance) = RecordShown.Value
ShowRecord
End Sub
```

Now that the Product Display module is, for the most part, perfected, you
can copy the model for this module—literally with the Windows system clipboard—and reedit it within the boundaries of form module SHLFITEM.FRM
(defined in Listing 6.1). So you can build a fair likeness of the form, here's
another shot of it in Figure 6.1.

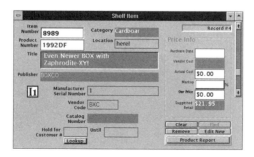

Figure 6.1. The item entry form for INVENT1.

Listing 6.1. SHLFITEM.FRM Property Settings.

```
Form ShelfItemID
    BorderStyle     =   1  'Fixed Single
    Caption         =   "Shelf Item"
    Height          =   4932
    Left            =   600
    MDIChild        =   -1  'True
    Top             =   948
    Width           =   8340

    SSPanel Panel3D5
        AutoSize        =   3   'AutoSize Child To Panel
        BevelWidth      =   2
        BorderWidth     =   2
        Height          =   228
        Left            =   1800
        ShadowColor     =   1  'Black
        Top             =   4080
        Width           =   840

    CommandButton Lookup
        Caption         =   "Lookup"
        FontName        =   "Lucida Sans"
        FontSize        =   7.8
        Height          =   180
        Left            =   24
        Top             =   24
        Width           =   792

    MaskEdBox HoldCustDate
        FontName        =   "Lucida Sans"
        FontSize        =   9.6
        Format          =   "dd-mmm-yy"
        Height          =   336
        Left            =   3240
        TabIndex        =   11
        Top             =   3720
        Width           =   1212
```

```
TextBox HoldCustNo
   FontName        =    "Lucida Sans"
   FontSize        =    9.6
   Height          =    324
   Left            =    1800
   TabIndex        =    10
   Top             =    3720
   Width           =    852

TextBox VenCode
   FontName        =    "Lucida Sans"
   FontSize        =    9.6
   Height          =    324
   Left            =    2640
   TabIndex        =    4
   Top             =    2760
   Width           =    1092

SSPanel Panel3D7
   AutoSize        =    3    'AutoSize Child To Panel
   BevelOuter      =    1    'Inset
   BevelWidth      =    2
   Height          =    252
   Left            =    6600
   Top             =    3480
   Width           =    1212

   CommandButton Find
      Caption      =    "Find"
      FontName     =    "Lucida Sans"
      FontSize     =    7.8
      Height       =    204
      Left         =    24
      Top          =    24
      Width        =    1164

SSPanel Register
   Alignment       =    4    'Right Justify - MIDDLE
   AutoSize        =    3    'AutoSize Child To Panel
   BevelOuter      =    1    'Inset
   BevelWidth      =    3
```

continues

Listing 6.1. continued

```
        Caption          =    "Record #"
        Font3D           =    1    'Raised w/light shading
        FontName         =    "Lucida Sans"
        FontSize         =    7.8
        Height           =    252
        Left             =    6000
        Top              =    120
        Width            =    1812

    SSPanel Panel3D8
        Alignment        =    4    'Right Justify - MIDDLE
        AutoSize         =    3    'AutoSize Child To Panel
        BevelWidth       =    3
        Height           =    2652
        Left             =    7920
        Top              =    0
        Width            =    252

        VScrollBar RecordShown
            Height           =    2580
            LargeChange      =    10
            Left             =    36
            Max              =    1
            Min              =    1
            Top              =    36
            Value            =    1
            Width            =    180

    TextBox IDField
        FontName         =    "Lucida Sans"
        FontSize         =    10.8
        Height           =    372
        Left             =    960
        TabIndex         =    1
        Top              =    672
        Width            =    1548

    SSPanel Panel3D6
        AutoSize         =    3    'AutoSize Child To Panel
        BevelOuter       =    1    'Inset
```

```
      BevelWidth        =    2
      Height            =    252
      Left              =    5400
      Top               =    3720
      Width             =    1212

      CommandButton Remove
         Caption        =    "Remove"
         FontName       =    "Lucida Sans"
         FontSize       =    7.8
         Height         =    204
         Left           =    24
         Top            =    24
         Width          =    1164

   SSPanel Panel3D4
      AutoSize          =    3    'AutoSize Child To Panel
      BevelOuter        =    1    'Inset
      BevelWidth        =    2
      Height            =    252
      Left              =    6600
      Top               =    3720
      Width             =    1212

      CommandButton Add
         Caption        =    "Add"
         FontName       =    "Lucida Sans"
         FontSize       =    7.8
         Height         =    204
         Left           =    24
         Top            =    24
         Width          =    1164

   SSPanel Panel3D2
      AutoSize          =    3    'AutoSize Child To Panel
      BevelOuter        =    1    'Inset
      BevelWidth        =    2
      Height            =    252
      Left              =    5400
      Top               =    3480
      Width             =    1212
```

continues

Listing 6.1. continued

```
CommandButton Clear
    Caption         =    "Clear"
    FontName        =    "Lucida Sans"
    FontSize        =    7.8
    Height          =    204
    Left            =    24
    Top             =    24
    Width           =    1164

TextBox LocatItem
    FontName        =    "Lucida Sans"
    FontSize        =    9.6
    Height          =    324
    Left            =    3600
    TabIndex        =    2
    Top             =    640
    Width           =    1572

SSPanel Panel3D3
    AutoSize        =    3    'AutoSize Child To Panel
    BevelInner      =    2    'Raised
    BevelWidth      =    2
    BorderWidth     =    2
    Height          =    372
    Left            =    5400
    Top             =    3960
    Width           =    2412

CommandButton ProductReport
    Caption         =    "Product Report"
    FontName        =    "Lucida Sans"
    FontSize        =    7.8
    Height          =    228
    Left            =    72
    Top             =    72
    Width           =    2268

TextBox CategItem
    BorderStyle     =    0    'None
    FontName        =    "Lucida Sans"
```

```
        FontSize        =    9.6
        Height          =    324
        Left            =    3600
        TabIndex        =    12
        TabStop         =    0    'False
        Top             =    240
        Width           =    1572


SSPanel Panel3D1
        BevelOuter      =    1    'Inset
        BevelWidth      =    2
        Height          =    612
        Left            =    960
        ShadowColor     =    1    'Black
        Top             =    1080
        Width           =    4212

        TextBox ProductTitle
            BorderStyle     =    0    'None
            FontName        =    "Lucida Sans"
            FontSize        =    10.8
            Height          =    564
            Left            =    120
            MultiLine       =    -1   'True
            TabIndex        =    47
            TabStop         =    0    'False
            Top             =    24
            Width           =    3972

    TextBox ManSerialNo
        FontName        =    "Lucida Sans"
        FontSize        =    9.6
        Height          =    324
        Left            =    2640
        TabIndex        =    3
        Top             =    2280
        Width           =    2532

SSPanel SSPanel1
        AutoSize        =    3    'AutoSize Child To Panel
        BevelOuter      =    1    'Inset
```

continues

Listing 6.1. continued

```
        BevelWidth        =    2
        Height            =    396
        Left              =    960
        Top               =    240
        Width             =    1548

        TextBox ItemID
            FontName      =    "Lucida Sans"
            FontSize      =    10.8
            Height        =    348
            Left          =    24
            TabIndex      =    0
            Top           =    24
            Width         =    1500

    SSFrame SSFrame1
        Caption           =    "Price Info"
        FontName          =    "Lucida Sans"
        FontSize          =    10.8
        Height            =    2892
        Left              =    5400
        Top               =    480
        Width             =    2412

        SSPanel Panel3D9
            AutoSize      =    3    'AutoSize Child To Panel
            BevelWidth    =    2
            BorderWidth   =    2
            Height        =    336
            Left          =    1080
            ShadowColor   =    1    'Black
            Top           =    1560
            Width         =    1068

            TextBox Markup
                FontName  =    "Lucida Sans Typewriter"
                FontSize  =    9.6
                Height    =    288
                Left      =    24
```

```
            TabIndex        =   54
            Top             =   24
            Width           =   1020

    MaskEdBox ListPrice
        BorderStyle         =   0   'None
        FontName            =   "Lucida Sans Typewriter"
        FontSize            =   9.6
        Format              =   "$#,##0.00;($#,##0.00)"
        Height              =   336
        Left                =   1080
        TabIndex            =   46
        TabStop             =   0   'False
        Top                 =   2280
        Width               =   1068

    MaskEdBox ShelfPrice
        FontName            =   "Lucida Sans Typewriter"
        FontSize            =   9.6
        Format              =   "$#,##0.00;($#,##0.00)"
        Height              =   336
        Left                =   1080
        TabIndex            =   9
        Top                 =   1920
        Width               =   1068

    MaskEdBox ActualCost
        FontName            =   "Lucida Sans Typewriter"
        FontSize            =   9.6
        FontStrikethru      =   0   'False
        FontUnderline       =   0   'False
        Format              =   "$#,##0.00;($#,##0.00)"
        Height              =   336
        Left                =   1080
        TabIndex            =   8
        Top                 =   1200
        Width               =   1068

    MaskEdBox VendorCost
        BorderStyle         =   0   'None
        FontName            =   "Lucida Sans Typewriter"
```

continues

Listing 6.1. continued

```
            FontSize        =    9.6
            Format          =    "$#,##0.00;($#,##0.00)"
            Height          =    336
            Left            =    1080
            TabIndex        =    7
            TabStop         =    0    'False
            Top             =    840
            Width           =    1068

        MaskEdBox VendorDate
            FontName        =    "Lucida Sans Typewriter"
            FontSize        =    7.8
            Format          =    "dd-mmm-yy"
            Height          =    336
            Left            =    1080
            TabIndex        =    6
            Top             =    480
            Width           =    1068

        Label Label11
            Alignment       =    1    'Right Justify
            Caption         =    "Purchase Date"
            FontBold        =    0    'False

        Label Label7
            Caption         =    "%"

        Label Label12
            Alignment       =    1    'Right Justify
            Caption         =    "Markup"

        Label Label6
            Alignment       =    1    'Right Justify
            Caption         =    "Vendor Cost"

        Label Label8
            Alignment       =    1    'Right Justify
            Caption         =    "Actual Cost"
```

```
    Label Label9
       Alignment        =   1  'Right Justify
       Caption          =   "Suggested Retail"

    Label Label10
       Alignment        =   1  'Right Justify
       Caption          =   "Our Price"

TextBox PubName
   BorderStyle          =   0  'None
   FontName             =   "Lucida Sans"
   FontSize             =   9.6
   Height               =   324
   Left                 =   960
   TabIndex             =   13
   TabStop              =   0    'False
   Top                  =   1800
   Width                =   4212

TextBox VendCatNo
   BorderStyle          =   0  'None
   FontName             =   "Lucida Sans"
   FontSize             =   9.6
   Height               =   324
   Left                 =   2640
   TabIndex             =   5
   TabStop              =   0    'False
   Top                  =   3240
   Width                =   1812

PictureBox Picture1
   Height               =   408
   Left                 =   480
   Picture              =   I1.ICO
   Top                  =   2280
   Width                =   408

Label Label14
   Alignment            =   1  'Right Justify
   Caption              =   "Until"
```

continues

Listing 6.1. continued

```
Label Label13
    Alignment        =    1  'Right Justify
    Caption          =    "Hold for Customer #"

Label Label4
    Alignment        =    1  'Right Justify
    Caption          =    "Vendor Code"

Label Label18
    Alignment        =    1  'Right Justify
    Caption          =    "Item Number"

Label Label15
    Alignment        =    1  'Right Justify
    Caption          =    "Location"

Label Label16
    Alignment        =    1  'Right Justify
    Caption          =    "Category"

Label Label17
    Alignment        =    1  'Right Justify
    Caption          =    "Manufacturer Serial Number"

Label Label1
    Alignment        =    1  'Right Justify
    Caption          =    "Product Number"

Label Label2
    Alignment        =    1  'Right Justify
    Caption          =    "Title"

Label Label3
    Alignment        =    1  'Right Justify
    Caption          =    "Publisher"

Label Label5
    Alignment        =    1  'Right Justify
    Caption          =    "Catalog Number"
```

Programming Through Parallelism

The major difference between the Item Entry form and the Product Display form is that the former borrows data from the file belonging to the latter, in order to compose its visible record. Because of this, you see both variable type Product and ShelfItem referred to in the general declarations for the ShelfItemID form:

```
Dim Instance As Integer
Dim Loader As ShelfItem
Dim PrLoader As Product
Dim id As String * 6
Dim iid As String * 8
```

Notice the addition of the declaration for string variable iid for eight characters, the fixed length set for component variable ItemNo in the Type declaration for ShelfItem.

The Sub Form_Load () procedure requires only the type of changes brought about by the find-and-replace function of the editor:

```
Sub Form_Load ()
tl = Total(Packages)
ReDim Preserve PaID$(tl), PaNam$(tl), PaX(tl), PaLoc(tl)
Instance = ActiveInstance(Packages)
If tl > 0 Then
    RecordShown.Max = tl + 1
Else
    RecordShown.Max = 1
    Register.Caption = "New File"
    Exit Sub
End If
ShowRecord
Find.Enabled = False
End Sub
```

Sub ClearForm (), Sub Add_Click (), and Sub RecordShown_Click () procedures also only require minor changes—for instance, changing references of Products to Packages. The split comes at Sub ShowRecord (), where the initial call is placed to the new procedures that call the Products file to help fill in the blanks:

```
Sub ShowRecord ()
If LOF(Packages) >= Len(Package(Packages)) Then
    Get Packages, Current(Packages, Instance), Package(Packages)
    IDField.Text = RTrim$(Package(Packages).ProductNo)
    ItemID.Text = RTrim$(Package(Packages).ItemNo)
    LocatItem.Text = RTrim$(Package(Packages).Location)
    ManSerialNo.Text = RTrim$(Package(Packages).SerialNo)
    VenCode.Text = RTrim$(Package(Packages).VendorCode)
    VendorDate.Text = RTrim$(Package(Packages).VenPurchDate)
    ActualCost.Text = Str$(Package(Packages).UnitCost)
    ShelfPrice.Text = Str$(Package(Packages).UnitPrice)
    RecordShown.Value = Current(Packages, Instance)
    If RecordShown.Value < RecordShown.Max Then
        Register.Caption = "Record #" + Str$(Current(Packages,
➥ Instance))
    End If
    If IDField.Text <> "" Then
        id = IDField.Text
        SearchForProduct id
    End If
End If
End Sub
```

The main addition to the structure here is the conditional clause. It checks to see if there's any entry in the product number field. If there isn't, a branch is made to procedure Sub SearchForProduct ().

```
Sub SearchForProduct (id$)
For arr = 1 To Total(Products)
    Get Products, arr, PrLoader
    PrID$(arr) = PrLoader.ProductNo
    PrNam$(arr) = PrLoader.Title
    PrLoc(arr) = arr
Next arr
qsort PrID$(), PrLoc(), Total(Products)
spot% = bsearch(PrID$(), PrLoc(), Total(Products), id$, False)
Get Products, spot%, PrLoader
ProductTitle.Text = PrLoader.Title
CategItem.Text = PrLoader.Category
PubName.Text = PrLoader.Publisher
ListPrice.Text = PrLoader.RetailPrice
End Sub
```

This procedure contains a sampling of the best from the Product Display form. The procedure reloads the arrays native to the Products data file and then calls the sort and search procedures. After acquiring the target record in utility record variable PrLoader, four fields on the Item Entry form are filled with data from the Products file. For the record, the Sub SearchForRecord () procedure exists in this module too, only with a minor bit of tailoring:

```
Sub SearchForRecord (id$)
ReloadArrays
qsort PaID$(), PaLoc(), Total(Packages)
spot% = bsearch(PaID$(), PaLoc(), Total(Packages), id$, False)
If spot% > 0 Then
    Current(Packages, Instance) = spot%
    ShowRecord
End If
End Sub
```

Notice the Item Entry form's native sorting array PaID$() is referred to here rather than PrID$(). Besides a few characters of correction, however, this procedure has an identical structure to its counterpart in the Product Display form. Also notice, the same procedures are called for sorting and searching as the Product Display form calls. Thus the objective of making the utility algorithms accessible to multiple outside modules in different contexts has been achieved.

The Watch System In Depth

One of the debugging features programmers greatly appreciate in Microsoft's "professional" programming environments is the inclusion of *watch expressions*. These are mathematical expressions that you can phrase as complex as a hierarchical Boolean comparison, or as simple as a single variable. The current status of these watch expressions are displayed within the Watch panel, which is the upper portion of the Debug window (you may not have seen it up to now, because it requires the existence of watch expressions to make it visible).

How to employ Visual Basic 2's idea of "watchpoints" in debugging.

Technique Capsule: Implementing the Watch Variable System

Definition: The purpose of the Visual Basic 2 watch system is to allow the programmer to monitor the status of variables and expressions regarding those variables. With the new system, you can have the interpreter break the program's execution whenever a certain mathematical condition evaluates true or when it becomes false. This condition is written as an expression of comparison, just as though it were appearing beside If in an If-Then clause; you don't have to include the If, however. The break expression is never "seen" by your VB application, so it never knows it's being watched. The interpreter evaluates all watch expressions separately; they never affect the execution of the application, except perhaps to slow it down—the degree of speed reduction is hardly noticeable on faster computers. Watch expressions may be phrased simply as variables unto themselves; remember, the VB interpreter evaluates single variables as whole expressions.

Execution: When you break a VB application manually by pressing Ctrl-Break, selecting **R**un/Brea**k**, or pressing the break button in the toolbar, the interpreter switches into its watch display mode and reevaluates those watch expressions you've told it to monitor for you. The status and result of those expressions is then displayed within the Watch panel, which is the upper portion of the Debug window.

Example: You can have the interpreter break the application for you conditionally, at any time during run time. Suppose someplace in your VB application, you use some sort of a "progressive value"; for instance, a loop that counts from 1 to 1000, or an axis coordinate value for a control being dragged over the form. You want to stop the program at a specific point in the progression and poll the Immediate Panel for the contents of specific variables. To do this, you can place an expression in the watchpoint list, stating the mathematical condition that must exist in order for the program to break.

There are two ways to enter a watchpoint into your current VB application. Here is the conventional method:

1. From the control window **D**ebug menu, select **A**dd Watch. A dialog panel will appear.

2. Within this dialog is a text line marked "Expression" within which you may enter a Visual Basic expression, using the standard VB syntax for expressions. This is the expression that triggers execution to be suspended. You don't have to write If before the expression; just the

variable, a mathematical operator, and something to compare it to. If you want the interpreter simply to watch the value or contents of a variable for you, you may state this variable on the text line by itself. Otherwise, you could also state any rationally interpretable and logically reducible VB expression, containing any number of mathematical and Boolean operators, as well as parentheses.

3. Within the frame marked "Context" are two drop-down lists, which currently register the names of the module and the procedure whose code editing window is currently active in the VB interpreter workspace. Because local variables across multiple procedures may share names with one another, designating the context of the watch expression here is necessary to prevent the interpreter from becoming confused.

4. Within the frame marked "Watch Type" is a list of three conditions inside an options set. The first item, marked "Watch Expression," is the default setting; the interpreter doesn't break the application, regardless of the outcome of the evaluation. For the other two options, the interpreter will break if the expression proves true for the second option or false for the third. In both of these cases, it's advisable that the entry into the watch line be an actual expression, complete with operator, because the interpreter will break when the evaluation results in −1 or 0.

5. Click OK. The watch expression will be entered into the Debug window.

Alternately, while the interpreter is in break mode, you may highlight an expression within the source code and select **D**ebug / **I**nstant Watch. The expression you highlighted will appear within a dialog panel. Click the Add Watch button, and the familiar dialog panel will appear. The Expression line will already be filled in for you, though you may choose to edit it at this point to read something else. Click OK, and the expression will be added to the Watch panel of the Debug window. This process lets you enter a line into the Watch panel that already appears in the source code, without you having to type it over again.

A watch expression entered into the Debug window is marked with a "pair of eyeglasses" icon, followed by a line of information with the following syntax:

```
[MODULE[:Procedure]] watch: {status¦<Not In Context>}
```

The context of the *watch* variable or expression appears at the beginning of this line, while the current *status* of the evaluation appears at the end of the line, unless the variable doesn't officially "exist" at the point of execution. Even in break mode, the interpreter won't let you accidentally enter into the watch line an expression containing a variable that doesn't exist.

This completes Part I, which focuses on the processes of programming in depth. In Part II, I change the pace of things a bit, by introducing more isolated cases and situations.

PART TWO

From Concept to Ingenuity

CONTEXTS, SCOPES, AND RELATIONSHIPS

In this chapter, I begin examining in detail the individual pieces of the overall programming process. With Situation #1, the inventory control application introduced in Part I, I introduced context planning, a type of planning and process routing that is not flowcharting. I might have given you the impression that planning your application is a matter of drawing a bunch of boxes and arrows on infinite sheets of paper; however, about 95 percent of the programming process is spent debugging.

7

Flowcharts for modern programming are obsolete. With the event-driven model of the windowed application, there is no way for the programmer to predict exactly which route the user might take to achieve her objectives. Besides, flowcharting is generally "busy work." It makes other people think you're busy with something important. Save the drawing for your artwork. Whenever possible, take time before you start writing source code to think about the division and delegation of duties in an application. This prepares you to know how your data can be routed and distributed. It facilitates the job of conceiving data formats and dimensioning variables in memory.

What happens, though, when the application you're writing is far more experimental and undefined than a business task such as inventory or accounting? When the job is being invented—or, more to the point, when you're inventing it—it's not as easy to sit down and start drawing boxes where contexts belong; it is more difficult to let the contexts define themselves. When you get new ideas along the way and discover you probably should have planned ahead for such possibilities (in other words, if you were clairvoyant), what can you do to rechannel the course of the river you've already constructed?

As the example application for this chapter, I've concocted an idea inspired by the need to do something unique, not by the ever changing global economy. Microsoft Windows has been praised for its graphic capability, but to paraphrase a country song, I was graphic when graphic wasn't cool. I learned to program on Ataris and Apples and Commodores, so I come from the extreme left wing of the body politic of programmers. I was a left-winger and I moderated, and sometimes I miss the old ways. I miss sprites and player/missile graphics. I miss the POKE statement. I've wanted a utility application that might give back to computing some of the old graphical flare, as well as some of the spirit of ingenuity.

Haul Out the Pegs and Twine

I admit to never having been asked to write a program that generates rotational clip art, nor having ever met anyone who has been given such a request. Having worked part-time in a software store, however, I remember having been asked for a program that performed the job of a drawing template, especially to draw furniture layouts for an office or for an interior decorator. I've also had an inkling from time to time to write a tactical space battle game that utilized ship designs drawn by the user.

What led me to decide to write something as odd as a rotational clip-art generator was a need for an unusual, complex, graphical program that utilized several procedures and passed many parameters between them. Unlike the Inventory Control application, this is a situation in which reality, to some extent, invents itself. I originally devised the graphical mechanism of this application for the Atari 800; my inspiration at that time was the possibility of building a space game.

Situation #3: The Rotational Clip-Art Generator

Suppose a client is using a Windows drawing application to plot a street layout for a metropolitan business district. This client needs automobile symbols for the streets in his drawings; however, if those streets are curved, such as Picadilly Circus, four clip-art images of a car pointed north, east, west, and south copied into the drawing might look like a formal plan for rush-hour traffic. The test application for Situation #3 stores to disk a vectored image that is created as though it were "string art," and whose final product can be pointed in any direction to a tenth of a degree. The bitmap it generates then can be cut to the Windows clipboard, and pasted to the graphics application. It also can be saved to disk as a .BMP file and used in another program at a later date. I call this program the Graphic Repositionable Unit Utility Module. Figure 7.1 shows the GRUUM main form with an object drawn in its main display.

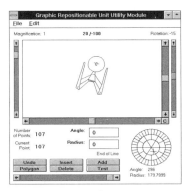

Figure 7.1. An extremely high-strung program.

Distinguishing
between
Cartesian and
angular
coordinate
systems.

Here's how GRUUM works: The objective of the program is to create a vectored graphics unit that can be magnified and rotated. The term "graphics unit" refers to these creations not only because it forms a nice acronym, but because the category of what can be plotted to the GRUUM display has not been defined. The graphics unit is formed on the screen by the placement of a virtual pen in a designated plotting area. The pen is moved between points represented by pairs of geometric coordinates—not Cartesian coordinates, but angles and coefficients. Because the graphics unit will be resizable and shiftable as well as rotatable, the angle/coefficient pair method of representation is more efficient because Cartesian coordinates are based on a fixed-grid geometric model. These angle/coefficient coordinate pairs act also as the command structure for how the pen operates, and a specific set of coordinates causes the pen to be lifted from the virtual page and reset.

As far as practical uses for this program are concerned, the user is free to be symbological, practical, or artistic. The image formed by the unit plotted in the plot area can be cut and pasted to another graphics application. The arrays in memory that describe the unit can be saved to disk and used in Visual Basic applications you program in the future. This is an example of the use of data in memory where the length of a "record" is variable and, furthermore, unpredictable.

To create the graphics units, the pen-plotting model I devised has the user place a crosshair down into the plotting area, which acts as a sort of "peg," denoting the point where a line ends and another may potentially begin. The plotting area where the pegs are poked down behaves like a turntable platform. The "z" axis this turntable rotates around is depicted by the "absolute center," which is the point represented by the coordinates 0/0 (no angle, no distance). The system of representation for each coordinate pair is depicted in Figure 7.2.

In the display area, each peg forms the end vertex of a line between it and the "absolute center" of the plotting area. This is not the visible line that the program actually plots. Instead, this invisible line is used to determine the distance measurement for the second array, which contains the second parameter for each pair. The angle formed by this invisible line against the "origin line"— which extends from the center to the right of the screen—is the first parameter, belonging to the first array. The GRUUM application remembers the vertices of the plotted lines, not the lines themselves. When the user rotates the plotting area, the angle of each peg is reoriented with respect to the origin line; therefore, the line segments joining the pegs are rotated automatically.

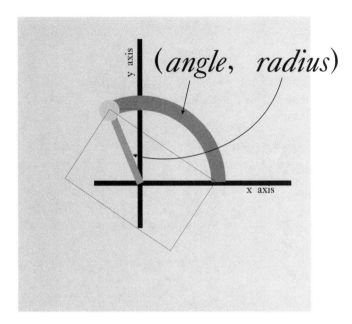

Figure 7.2. The point-by-point plan in detail.

To make the pen "rise" from the plotting area and be reset, a point with a radius of 0 from the absolute center of the turntable is entered into the array. As a result, the only point where you can't plot a peg is at the absolute center. The next point in the array then starts a new string. The final point in the array is automatically an end-of-line point.

The largest slice of this application fits in a single form module. As a result, the context divisions don't require their own general modules. Listing 7.1 shows the property settings for the GRUUM central form.

Listing 7.1. GRUUM.FRM Property Settings.

```
AutoRedraw          True
BackColor           &HFFFFFF
BorderStyle         1 - Fixed Single
Caption             Graphic Repositionable Unit Utility
                        Module
```

continues

Listing 7.1. continued

```
FormName          GRUUM
Icon              (Icon)
LinkTopic         Form2

Active Form Event Procedures
  Form_Load

Control Type: PictureBox
    Control Name: Compass
    AutoRedraw        True
    BorderStyle       0 - None
    CtlName           Compass
    DrawMode          7 - Xor Pen
    MousePointer      2 - Cross
    Picture           (Bitmap)
    TabIndex          1

    Active Control Event Procedures
      Compass_Click Compass_MouseMove

    Control Name: PlotArea
    AutoRedraw        True
    BackColor         &HFFFFFF
    CtlName           PlotArea
    ForeColor         &H0
    MousePointer      2 - Cross

    Active Control Event Procedures
      PlotArea_MouseDown

Control Type: Label
    Control Name: AngleNow
    Caption
    CtlName           AngleNow
    FontBold          False
    FontName          Helv
    FontSize          7.78125
    TabIndex          11
```

```
Control Name: CenterMark
Alignment               2 - Center
Caption                 0 / 0
CtlName                 CenterMark
TabIndex                29

Control Name: CurPoint
Caption
CtlName                 CurPoint
FontName                Helv
FontSize                9.5625
TabIndex                10

Control Name: EndLine
Alignment               1 - Right Justify
BackColor               &HFFFFFF
Caption
CtlName                 EndLine
FontBold                False
FontName                Helv
FontSize                7.78125
ForeColor               &HFF0000
TabIndex                14

Control Name: Label1
Alignment               1 - Right Justify
Caption                 Number of Points:
CtlName                 Label1
FontBold                False
FontName                Helv
FontSize                7.78125
TabIndex                5

Control Name: Label2
Alignment               1 - Right Justify
Caption                 Angle:
CtlName                 Label2
TabIndex                6
```

continues

Listing 7.1. continued

```
Control Name: Label3
Alignment               1 - Right Justify
Caption                 Radius:
CtlName                 Label3
TabIndex                7

Control Name: Label4
Alignment               1 - Right Justify
Caption                 Current Point:
CtlName                 Label4
FontBold                False
FontName                Helv
FontSize                7.78125
TabIndex                9

Control Name: Label5
Caption                 Angle:
CtlName                 Label5
FontBold                False
FontName                Helv
FontSize                7.78125
TabIndex                20

Control Name: Label6
Caption                 Radius:
CtlName                 Label6
FontBold                False
FontName                Helv
FontSize                7.78125
TabIndex                21

Control Name: Magnific
Caption                 Magnification: 1
CtlName                 Magnific
FontBold                False
FontName                Helv
FontSize                7.78125
TabIndex                18
```

```
    Control Name: NumPoints
    Caption
    CtlName              NumPoints
    FontName             Helv
    FontSize             9.5625
    TabIndex             8

    Control Name: RadiusNow
    Caption
    CtlName              RadiusNow
    FontBold             False
    FontName             Helv
    FontSize             7.78125
    TabIndex             12

    Control Name: Rotate
    Alignment            1 - Right Justify
    Caption              Rotation:  0
    CtlName              Rotate
    FontBold             False
    FontName             Helv
    FontSize             7.78125
    TabIndex             19

Control Type: TextBox
    Control Name: CurAngle
    CtlName              CurAngle
    FontName             Helv
    FontSize             9.5625

    Control Name: CurRadius
    CtlName              CurRadius
    FontName             Helv
    FontSize             9.5625
    TabIndex             3

    Active Control Event Procedures
     CurRadius_LostFocus
```

continues

Listing 7.1. continued

```
Control Type: Command Button
      Control Name: Add
      Caption          Add
      CtlName          Add
      TabIndex         13

      Active Control Event Procedures
       Add_Click

      Control Name: Center
      Caption          C
      CtlName          Center
      TabIndex         28

      Active Control Event Procedures
       Center_Click

      Control Name: Delete
      Caption          Delete
      CtlName          Delete
      TabIndex         23

      Active Control Event Procedures
       Delete_Click

      Control Name: Insert
      Caption          Insert
      CtlName          Insert
      TabIndex         22

      Active Control Event Procedures
       Insert_Click

      Control Name: Polygon
      Caption          Polygon
      CtlName          Polygon
      TabIndex         24

      Active Control Event Procedures
       Polygon_Click
```

```
    Control Name: Test
    Caption          Test
    CtlName          Test
    TabIndex         16

    Active Control Event Procedures
     Test_Click

    Control Name: Undo
    Caption          Undo
    CtlName          Undo
    TabIndex         25

    Active Control Event Procedures
     Undo_Click

Control Type: H-Scroll
    Control Name: PointFind
    CtlName          PointFind
    LargeChange      10
    Max              1
    Min              1
    TabIndex         4
    Value            1

    Active Control Event Procedures
     PointFind_Change

    Control Name: XSlide
    CtlName          XSlide
    LargeChange      100
    Max              10000
    Min              -10000
    SmallChange      10
    TabIndex         26

    Active Control Event Procedures
     XSlide_Change
```

continues

Listing 7.1. continued

```
Control Type: V-Scroll
    Control Name: Magnification
    CtlName            Magnification
    LargeChange        10
    Max                100
    Min                1
    TabIndex           17
    Value              10

    Active Control Event Procedures
     Magnification_Change

    Control Name: Rotation
    CtlName            Rotation
    LargeChange        10
    Max                1800
    Min                -1800
    TabIndex           15

    Active Control Event Procedures
     Rotation_Change

    Control Name: YSlide
    CtlName            YSlide
    LargeChange        100
    Max                10000
    Min                -10000
    SmallChange        10
    TabIndex           27

    Active Control Event Procedures
     YSlide_Change

Control Type: Menus
    Control Name: Edit
    Caption            &Edit

    Control Name: EditCopy
    Caption            &Copy
```

```
Active Control Event Procedures
 EditCopy_Click

Control Name: File
Caption             &File

Control Name: FileExit
Caption             E&xit

Active Control Event Procedures
 FileExit_Click

Control Name: FileMerge
Caption             &Merge At End...

Active Control Event Procedures
 FileMerge_Click

Control Name: FileNew
Caption             &New

Active Control Event Procedures
 FileNew_Click

Control Name: FileOpen
Caption             &Open...

Active Control Event Procedures
 FileOpen_Click

Control Name: FileSave
Caption             &Save...

Active Control Event Procedures
 FileSave_Click

Control Name: FileSaveImage
Caption             Save &Image as...

Active Control Event Procedures
 FileSaveImage_Click
```

continues

Listing 7.1. continued

```
Control Name: hyphen1
Caption          -


Control Type: Common Dialog
    Control Name: Selector
```

Employing Redundant Controls

Dividing the usage model for redundant control.

In an application that requires graphical, mathematical, or geometric precision, the easiest way to operate the program isn't necessarily the most precise. With that in mind, I integrated three ways the user can place "pegs" into the usage model for the plotting area (see Figure 7.3a):

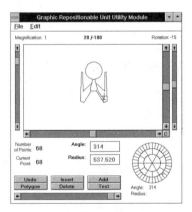

Figure 7.3a. Usage mode 1.

1. Move the mouse pointer into the plotting area and click the index button of the mouse. A red crosshatch appears in the plotting area, indicating the area where the next peg may appear (see Figure 7.3b). To plot the peg at this point, click the Add button.

Angle: 313
Radius: 237.7393

Figure 7.3b. Usage mode 2.

2. Move the mouse pointer into the area of the "compass" in the lower-right corner of the form. A red crosshatch follows the mouse pointer, indicating the angle and radius currently under consideration. To place a test crosshatch at the location within the plotting area indicated by the compass, click the index button while the pointer is within the compass area (Figure 7.3c). A red crosshatch appears in the plotting area. If this crosshatch is not at the right point, click the index button on the compass again. If it is at the correct point, click the Add button.

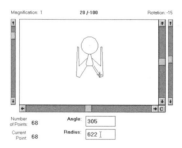

Magnification: 1   20 /-100   Rotation: -15

Number of Points: 68   Angle: 305
Current Point: 68   Radius: 622

Figure 7.3c. Usage mode 3.

3. Type the angle and radius values into their respective text boxes. If you're confident about the coordinates you've entered, you can click Add now; otherwise, you can click Test to see a red crosshatch that designates where in the plotting area a peg would appear. Click Add if this is the correct position; the red crosshatch should disappear.

In an event-driven application, the use of multiple input methods to achieve the same ends is called redundant control. The concept probably was born in several programming laboratories simultaneously, although it was popularized by the application model put forth by Apple Computer for its Lisa (later

Macintosh) developers' guidelines. Redundant control works well in computing because it enables the user to choose her own way to work and not rely specifically on one method professed by one manual written by one programmer. The application is more adaptive to the user's personal tastes.

The process model for this application is shaping up as depicted in Figure 7.4, and it can be described as follows: The classic division between user communication and data processing forms the main fork in this road. The data processing division has a section for loading the geometric arrays into memory and assimilating them, and another section for plotting the graphics unit. The user communication division has three sections for the three usage models described earlier.

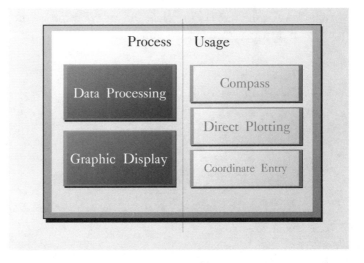

Figure 7.4. The apparent process model for GRUUM.

Accumulating Primary Contexts as You Go

When I started programming this application, I had a rough idea of the process model, but I discarded it piece-by-piece as I began entering procedures. You pick up the action with the global module in Listing 7.2.

Listing 7.2. GRUUM.GBL Global Module.

```
Global angle() As Single, radius() As Single
Global backangle() As Single, backradius() As Single
Global npoints As Integer, cpoint As Integer, backpoints
➥   As Integer
Global offset As Single, magnify As Single

'File Open/Save Dialog Flags
Global Const OFN_OVERWRITEPROMPT = &H2&
Global Const OFN_HIDEREADONLY = &H4&
Global Const OFN_PATHMUSTEXIST = &H800&
Global Const OFN_FILEMUSTEXIST = &H1000&
```

The array variables that contain the main body of data are declared on the first instruction line. The second set of arrays is a backup array; this set is necessary for an Undo procedure. The number of points—or vertexes—in the array is kept in variable npoint; the point number currently under scrutiny is assigned to variable cpoint. The Global Const declarations are utilized later by the common dialog box system, which you will be seeing in action later in this chapter.

Listing 7.3. GRUUM.FRM General Declarations.

```
Dim pokedown As Integer
Dim testx As Integer, testy As Integer
Dim oldx As Single, oldy As Single
Dim curx As Single, cury As Single
Dim otx As Single, oty As Single
Dim savestatus As Integer, clearstatus As Integer
Dim TestOn As Integer
```

As I added necessary features to the user communication sections, I found myself declaring new form-level variables on the fly. I like to profess that the main body of the data in memory should be defined by the programmer beforehand; but in this particular case, because many of my ideas came to mind in mid-stream, much of my advance planning was discarded in favor of better ways to interpret the problem at hand.

Calling a Twip a Twip

One of the problems with the presence of varying resolutions of Windows screens is addressed by the conditional clause at the beginning of Sub Form_Load ():

```
Sub Form_Load ()
If Screen.Height <= 7000 Then
    Compass.Picture = LoadPicture("d:\vbasic\dfs\compass.bmp")
Else
    Compass.Picture = LoadPicture("d:\vbasic\dfs\compassb.bmp")
End If
GRUUM.Show
cpoint = 1
npoints = 1
magnify = 1
DispStat
End Sub
```

Logical screen inches versus real inches.

I created two bitmaps that act as backdrops for the compass control you see in the lower-right corner of the GRUUM form in Figure 7.1. Both bitmaps have different sizes; if you intend to use a bitmap as the background for a graphic control on your form for all possible Windows resolutions, you need at least two editions of this bitmap. The .Height property of the VB universal object Screen. yields what Windows documentation describes as the entire Windows display in *twips*.

A twip is defined by Microsoft as a square unit approximate to 1/1440 of an inch. On most Windows screens, this is close to correct; however, when a screen is printed, the correlation between twips and inches is not always balanced because there is an abundance of screen and printer drivers for Windows. Although both kinds of drivers are written to work well with Windows, it's nearly impossible to predict how well they will work with one another. Let me warn you now about the conditional clause in Sub Form_Load () above: When entering this program into your computer, you might need to change the 7000 to a number that results in the loading of the proper compass backdrop for your screen graphics system.

> **Technique Note:** Use the Screen. object to find out specific information about the graphic environment of your copy of Windows. Don't use Screen., however, to make assumptions about the screen/printer/reality correlation for units of measurement. Despite all documentation to the contrary, my personal tests show the correlation can be variable.

Borrowing Windows-Supplied Dialogs

The GRUUM form begins its life in the Windows workspace without a graphics unit to plot; to load an existing graphics unit, the procedure must have a filename.

Listing 7.4. GRUUM.FRM General Procedures.

```
Sub FileOpen_Click ()
On Error GoTo cancl
Selector.DefaultExt = "*.grm"
Selector.DialogTitle = "Open Graphic Unit File"
flt$ = "GRUUM Files (*.grm)¦*.grm¦All Files (*.*)¦*.*"
Selector.Filter = flt$
Selector.FilterIndex = 1
Selector.Flags = OFN_FILEMUSTEXIST Or OFN_HIDEREADONLY
➡   Or OFN_PATHMUSTEXIST
Selector.Action = 1
On Error GoTo 0
Open Selector.Filename For Input As #1
Input #1, npoints
ReDim angle(npoints), radius(npoints)
For np = 1 To npoints
    Input #1, angle(np), radius(np)
Next np
Close #1
cpoint = npoints
```

Listing 7.4. continued

```
PointFind.Max = npoints
PointFind.Value = cpoint
offset = 0
magnify = 1
ClearCompass
DispStat
DrawUnit
Exit Sub
cancl:
On Error GoTo 0
MsgBox "No file is opened.", 48
Resume downhere
downhere:
End Sub
```

This procedure invokes a special feature of the common dialog custom control, provided with Microsoft's Professional Edition of Visual Basic 2. With this control, your application can access the standard, good-looking dialog boxes Microsoft provides to all Windows applications by way of internal DLLs.

Technique Capsule: Common Dialog Access

Definition: In the native dynamic link libraries of Microsoft Windows are programs for displaying oft-requested dialog boxes in a standardized format. As soon as new users learn how to operate these standard dialogs for one application, they know how to use the same dialogs by default for several other applications. These same Windows dialog boxes now can be attached easily to a Visual Basic form by adding the file CMDIALOG.VBX to the Visual Basic project.

Execution: To employ the common dialog system, place the common dialog symbol in the form the same way you attach the timer control symbol. The contents of the Windows dialogs then can be passed to the Windows DLL by way of Visual Basic property settings. The recipient of these settings is the object name that is the .Name property of the common dialog control. Many of these property settings are easier to enter if you use constant declarations in the startup module of the application. You can copy these declarations to the global or general applications section by loading into the Windows Notepad the CONSTANT.TXT file supplied with Visual Basic, copying the necessary constants into the clipboard (they are appropriately marked) and pasting them directly into the module.

Once the necessary properties are set, the common dialog can be loaded into the workspace by a statement of expression with the syntax `CMDialogName.Action = type`, where `type` is a numeral between 1 and 6 denoting which dialog to show. Type 6 actually brings up the WINHELP.EXE application and feeds it a compiled help file of your choice. A file selector box is shown with a type setting of 1, and the RGB color selector is available by supplying a type setting of 3.

The common dialog box brought into the workspace by `Sub FileOpen_Click ()` is shown in Figure 7.5.

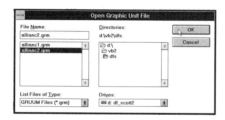

Figure 7.5. A familiar face joins Visual Basic.

To implement this common dialog within the GRUUM application, I took several steps. I wanted the default file extension *.grm for graphic unit files saved to disk. The `.DefaultExt` property was assigned this extension pattern. The general instructions, "Open Graphics Unit File," were supplied to the title bar of the common dialog through the `.DialogTitle` property setting. At the lower-left corner of the standard Windows dialog box is a drop-down list box that enables you to select a standard file extension pattern; for this application, there only need to be two available patterns. A string describing these choices and the patterns to which they apply was assigned to variable `flt$`, which was passed in turn to `Selector.Filter`. The default entry from this list box is entry number 1, which is passed to `Selector.FilterIndex`.

Back in the global module, I copied some constant declarations from the CONSTANT.TXT file pertinent to the common dialogs. These overly-long constant terms refer to bitwise patterns denoting yes/no binary states. These states describe the appearance, contents, and handling of the dialog box. The

Sending parameters for Windows dialogs through properties.

three flags shown here tell Windows that the file and path selected by the user must exist before attempting to load the file, and to hide the "Read Only" check box because it isn't required here. With the flags, filter pattern, and list box contents set, the instruction Selector.Action = 1 is invoked, bringing up the dialog. If the dialog returns an error code, the error-handling routine brings up an exclamation-point dialog that states no file was loaded.

Note the similarity between the Sub FileLoad_Click () and Sub SaveFile () procedures; the latter is listed next.

```
Sub SaveFile ()
On Error GoTo cancl2
Selector.DefaultExt = "*.grm"
Selector.DialogTitle = "Save Graphic Unit File"
flt$ = "GRUUM Files (*.grm)¦*.grm¦All Files (*.*)¦*.*"
Selector.Filter = flt$
Selector.FilterIndex = 1
Selector.Flags = OFN_CREATEPROMPT Or OFN_OVERWRITEPROMPT
➥  Or OFN_PATHMUSTEXIST
Selector.Action = 2
On Error GoTo 0
Open Selector.Filename For Output As #1
If cancl = True Then Exit Sub
Print #1, npoints
For np = 1 To npoints
    Print #1, angle(np), radius(np)
Next np
Close #1
savestatus = True
Exit Sub
cancl2:
On Error GoTo 0
Resume downhere2
downhere2:
End Sub
```

This is really the Sub FileLoad_Click () procedure, only copied into this new procedure frame and adjusted to suit the purposes of saving. The former procedure performs the same job as the latter, only in the opposite direction. Some notable adjustments are the addition of the OFN_OVERWRITEPROMPT flag to Selector.Flags, which has the selector box quiz the user—if he chooses a filename that already exists—whether he means to save over an existing file.

This subdialog is supplied to the application by Windows. Also, the `.Action` setting for the common dialog is now 2, bringing up the File Save dialog. Frankly, there are few differences between the File Open and the File Save dialog; you could bring up dialog 1 with the "Read Only" check box hidden and it would still supply you with a save filename.

The reason `Sub SaveFile ()` was placed in the general procedures section was because there will be two commands in the menu that can evoke a save process—File / Save and File / Exit. Only one set of saving instructions is necessary in the long run, but you have been employing a flag variable, `savestatus`, to keep track of whether the file has been saved in its current form. Any time something new is added to the form, `savestatus` is set to `False`. This way, if the user invokes File / Exit without saving the file first, a dialog box pops up asking whether the user wants to save the file first. Here's the day-saving procedure:

```
Sub FileExit_Click ()
If savestatus = TRUE Then
    m$ = "Are you sure you wish to exit?"
    r% = MsgBox(m$, 36)
    If r% = 7 Then
        Exit Sub
    Else
        GRUUM.Hide
        End
    End If
Else
    m$ = "Are you sure you wish to exit without saving first?"
    r% = MsgBox(m$, 35)
    Select Case r%
        Case 2
            Exit Sub
        Case 7
            SaveFile
            GRUUM.Hide
            End
        Case 6
            GRUUM.Hide
            End
    End Select
End If
End Sub
```

Notice that if the user complies with the option to save the file first—`Case 7` for the sake of the `MsgBox` dialog—a branch is made to `Sub SaveFile ()`. The event procedure for clicking the Save button, on the other hand, is not nearly as complex:

```
Sub FileSave_Click ()
SaveFile
-End Sub
```

The Mechanics of Variable-Length Records

The way GRUUM works, both array variables are manipulated in memory at all times, not on disk. Many databases are stored and manipulated on disk, with only the fields or records being manipulated in memory. For this particular application, this is not the case. Therefore you can use the simplest method available for storage and retrieval—the sequential-access method. The first item read from disk is the value of npoints; this way, the loop clause to follow knows how many values to read into the two arrays. Values then are input from the disk into the arrays all at once, and they are saved by way of the `Print #` statement all at once.

Fenceposts in a variable-length record scheme.

Notice, however, that in an unobvious way, the data files used by GRUUM contain, in effect, variable-length records. In the INVENT1 application, all the data files were of fixed length, as declared in its global module. It's relatively easy for the interpreter to store and retrieve a set of fixed-length records. Because the structure of the record is already outlined, the interpreter can predict where a record begins and ends, and where the fields begin and end within that record.

With the data file used for GRUUM, a "record" is a chain of coordinate pairs that form a meandering line when plotted to the display. The end of one record and the beginning of the next are determined by using "fenceposts"— here, the zero-value radii. The random-access model won't work for this application because the data-loading procedure finds the boundaries of the variable-length record by starting at the beginning of the data file and counting the fenceposts until it finds the number of the fencepost it's looking for. Not only is this method inefficient, it isn't truly *random*.

The data-processing procedures for the GRUUM application were delegated to the general procedures area. The two procedures, whose general form I borrowed from an Atari 800 program I wrote several years earlier, were the one that loaded the array into memory and the one that draws the graphic unit. For the most part, the changes I made to these procedures were cosmetic.

```
Sub DrawUnit ()
PlotArea.Cls
PlotArea.DrawMode = 13
For B = 1 To npoints
    An = ((angle(B) + 90 + offset) Mod 360) * (pi / 180)
    Rad = radius(B) * magnify
    If Rad = 0 Then
        E = 1
        GoTo backdown
    End If
    If B = 1 Or E = 1 Then
        PlotArea.PSet (Rad * Sin(An) + 2500 + XSlide.Value,
    Rad * Cos(An) + 1500 + YSlide.Value), RGB(0, 0, 0)
        E = 0
    Else
        PlotArea.Line -(Rad * Sin(An) + 2500 + XSlide.Value,
    Rad * Cos(An) + 1500 + YSlide.Value), RGB(0, 0, 0)
    End If
backdown:
Next B
clearstatus = TRUE
End Sub
```

Here is the most crucial procedure of the entire application. Because it is so crucial, here it is translated into pseudocode:

```
Procedure for drawing the graphic unit:
Clear the plotting area.
Set the drawing mode for the plotting area to the default mode;
  don't apply any Boolean logic to the drawing process.
Start counting from 1 to the number of points in the unit.
The plotting angle is equal to the angle stored in the array,
  rotated 90 degrees to the left, and rotated again by the
  number of degrees in the current offset value.
The hypotenuse value is equal to the radius stored in the array,
  multiplied by the current plotting area magnification factor.
```

```
If the radius appears to be zero, then
    This must mean the line ends here.
    Forget drawing the line any further; skip this
      point.
End of condition.
If plotting the very first point in the array, or the
  last point was an end-of-line point, then
    Set a black point at the x/y coordinate point in
      the plotting area, relative to the origin point
      (2500, 1500).
    Reset the end-of-line indicator; starting a new
      line.
Otherwise,
    Extend the black line to the current x/y coordinate
      point.
End of condition.
Here's the point to skip to if you skipped plotting a point.
Count the next point in the array.
End of procedure.
```

Here's how I arrived at the trigonometry formulas for translating angle/radius format to x/y coordinate format. Figure 7.6 shows an example of the Cartesian coordinate system in action.

Assume that point (0, 0) in Figure 7.6 is in the middle of the PlotArea. viewport, and the first point in the array is at (50, 75). With respect to GRUUM's definition of angles and radii, the angle for this point is between line x and line r. Assume you know the angle and radius, and you need to know the x/y coordinates—you don't know they're (50, 75) yet. The sine of the angle for this or any other right triangle is equal to the length of side x divided by the length of r. You know the length of r already—that's the radius—and because you know the sine of the angle (x/r), all you have to do is multiply that by r to arrive at x. Likewise, you can find the length of y by taking the cosine of the angle (y/r) and multiplying that by r to arrive at y.

Now assume the opposite; say you know about (50, 75) but need to know the angle and radii for the array variables. The length of x is 50, and the length of y is 75. The tangent of your right triangle is the length of the adjacent angle divided that of the opposite angle (x/y); therefore, it follows that the arctangent of that same division is the measurement of your angle. You then can use the Pythagorean Theorem to determine the length of the radius; it is the square root of the length of one adjacent side, squared, plus the length of the other adjacent side, squared. With the aid of a bit of Greek philosophy, you have a graphics unit.

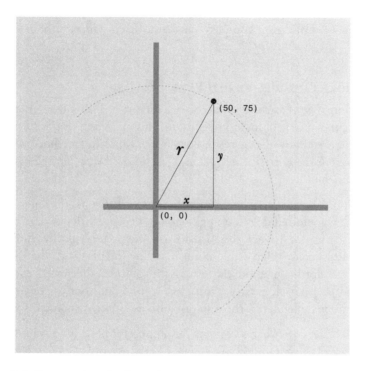

Figure 7.6. Some points in Cartesian space.

Creating an Erasable Whiteboard

At the center of the GRUUM form is a display area that acts as the operating table for the graphic unit under construction. The picture sent to this Visual Basic graphic object is continually erased and replotted. Now, the .Cls method is available for wiping the slate clean and starting over, but using .Cls and re-plotting, and using .Cls again and replotting, results in a display that looks like a 1920s silent film.

Many programmers aren't aware that a Visual Basic draw operation to a picture box is the result of a logical comparison between the color value of the twip, point, or pixel to be drawn and the color value of the twip, point, or pixel beneath it. As a result, a particular setting of the picture box's .DrawMode property enables the programmer to draw the same image twice and have the second instance of the image completely erase the first instance, without any screen flicker.

Technique Capsule: Virtual Plane Plotting

Definition: The .DrawMode property for a picture box is set to an integer value that describes a type of logical operation. This operation relates to the Visual Basic interpreter how the current color value of a drawing method is combined logically with the current color value of each pixel being plotted over within the picture box.

Execution: Normally, in the default state of a picture box, the color of a pixel or twip being plotted does not appear to be affected by the color of the point "beneath" the plot. In fact, the Visual Basic interpreter logically combines the current RGB color value of the point receiving the plot with the RGB color value of the plotting method; the result is the color that the newly-plotted point will assume. This logically produced color is neither an optical nor a pigmentational blend, but the result of a Boolean bitwise comparison.

Example: The .DrawMode setting of 7 is important here; it's always the Boolean inverse of the combined color values. In other words, if a red line of mode 7 is plotted over another red line of mode 7, the second line makes the first disappear. The background behind the first mode 7 line is then restored to its original appearance.

For plotting a crosshatch that can appear and disappear, the .DrawMode settings 7 and 13 are used interchangeably throughout the GRUUM form. The user can plot this crosshatch to estimate where a line ends if it is added to the end of the current graphics unit. Mode 13 is the default mode of all drawing; it directs the interpreter to place the new pixel on top of the old pixel, eliminating the old pixel. Believe it or not, this is the mode to which you've already grown accustomed.

> **Technique Note:** Visual Basic considers angular measurements in radians rather than ordinary degrees. To convert angular measurements from degrees to radians, the degree values are multiplied by (Pi / 180). Conversely, to convert from radians to degrees, the radian values are multiplied by (180 / Pi). When the position of a point is described as a line extending Rad units away from a center coordinate point, positioned at an angle of An degrees from the origin line, the x coordinate point can be obtained by multiplying the cosine of the angle An by the length of Rad. Likewise, the y coordinate point can be obtained by multiplying the sine of the angle An by the length of Rad.

Engineering the Compass

My intention for the compass control is for it to be extremely versatile and practically self-operating, such as a real compass in that regard. Finding a test angle and distance into the compass is not a point-and-click operation; it's a point operation. The _MouseMove event for the compass takes over whenever the pointer is above it. Here's the listing of the Sub Compass_MouseMove () event procedure for GRUUM.FRM, which shows this process in action:

```
Sub Compass_MouseMove (Button As Integer, Shift As Integer,
➥  x As Single, y As Single)
If pokedown = True Then Exit Sub
dist = Sqr(((750 - x) ^ 2) + (750 - y) ^ 2)
If dist > 700 Then
    ClearCompass
    Exit Sub
End If
RadiusNow.Caption = Str$(dist)
If oldx <> 0 And oldy <> 0 Then
    Compass.Line (oldx - 100, oldy)-(oldx + 100, oldy),
➥  RGB(0, 255, 255)
    Compass.Line (oldx, oldy - 100)-(oldx, oldy + 100),
➥  RGB(0, 255, 255)
```

```
End If
posx = x - 750
posy = y - 750
If y <> 750 Then
    angl = Atn(posx / posy) * (180 / pi)
Else
    angl = Atn(posx) * (180 / pi)
End If
If posy <= 0 Then
    angl = (angl + 90) Mod 360
Else
    angl = (angl + 270) Mod 360
End If
AngleNow.Caption = Str$(angl)
Compass.Line (x - 100, y)-(x + 100, y), RGB(0, 255, 255)
Compass.Line (x, y - 100)-(x, y + 100), RGB(0, 255, 255)
oldx = x
oldy = y
End Sub
```

The form-level variable pokedown is used as a determinant of whether the index button has been pressed while the pointer was in the compass area. If it has (pokedown = True), the entire procedure is exited. The rest of the procedure deals with the red crosshatch following the pointer, and the angle and radius values registering themselves below the compass.

Visual Basic recognizes certain events that are triggered whenever the mouse pointer enters a rectangular region. As long as the pointer is already in the rectangular region of the picture box called Compass, this _MouseMove event procedure is executed; however, this particular procedure determines for itself whether the pointer has entered a geometrically-defined circular region within the rectangular one. Here the two-dimensional distance-finding formula is used to determine the distance between the variable mouse pointer position (x, y) and the fixed center of the compass (750, 750). In other words, the distance formula returns the length of the radius of a circle. If that radius is greater than the radius of the compass itself (If dist > 700...), the pointer must fall outside the boundaries of your control and, again, the procedure is exited.

The variables oldx and oldy are used here to record the previous position of the red crosshatch within the compass. The .DrawMode property of the compass is set at design time to 7. This way, if a procedure plots a line or shape on top of a background image, and then a procedure plots the identical line or shape over exactly the same points, the shape disappears and the background pattern (in this particular case, plain white) reemerges. The red crosshatch now will not interfere with the appearance of the compass. All procedure `Sub Compass_MouseMove ()` has to do now is remember to replot the crosshatch on top of itself before it replots it at its new position later, to avoid a shadow or comet-tail effect. The first two instructions that use the `Compass.Line` method will plot over the old crosshatch; however, these instructions will be skipped if the variables containing the old pointer position are both 0—meaning most likely that the pointer has never entered the compass area before.

In coordinate geometry, the origin point (0, 0) of a graph appears at the center of the graph. In Visual Basic, the origin point (`0`, `0`) of a form or picture box appears at its upper-left corner. As a result, the VB programmer constantly has to offset the coordinate values of the point currently being operated on, by the coordinate values of the true origin point, which in geometry is at the absolute center. This offset is the purpose of the two instructions `posx = x - 750` and `posy = y - 750`. These two variables are used to find the angle measurement for a point whose coordinates are (`posx`, `posy`). This measurement is placed beside the "Angle:" label below the compass.

Cartesian and Visual Basic geometries compared.

Next, two more `Compass.Line` instructions are used to plot a new red crosshatch at the current mouse pointer location automatically returned as (`x`, `y`). Notice the `RGB()` function is loaded with the color bright cyan rather than red—this is optically the opposite color of red. Since the `.DrawMode` for the compass is set at 7, the logical `Xor` (Boolean exclusive-or) combination of a white point (`255`, `255`, `255`) and a bright cyan point (`0`, `255`, `255`) results in the survival of only those bits that do not appear in both values. The second and third pair of `255`s thus cancel each other out, leaving the first `255` followed by two zeros. A color with the RGB mix of (`255`, `0`, `0`) remains; the result is a bright red.

Finally, the current crosshatch coordinates (`x`, `y`) are stored as (`oldx`, `oldy`). Next time the procedure is executed, these form-level variables will have "aged"; that is, their contents will be considered old and ready to be overwritten.

The procedure `Sub Compass_MouseMove ()` was not conceived from top to bottom as it appears now. Rather, it was conceived and developed a portion at a time, then tested to see whether one process worked before adding another process on top of it. First, the instructions were written for having a crosshatch follow the pointer wherever it went in the picture box. Next, code was attached for preventing the rest of the procedure from being executed until the pointer entered the circle, or in other words was 700 twips away in any direction from the center of the compass (750, 750). After that, the process for overplotting the old crosshatch was developed; setting Compass.DrawMode to 7 at design time proved to be convenient here. Finally, the mathematics that determines the angle formed by the pointer was added to top off the procedure.

Each component process in the procedure was developed and tested before the next was added. It would be a bit too bold of me to state that each process worked the first time exactly as I conceived it; however, by layering processes on top of each other in this way, I easily can remove a new process from the top layer of development if it fails to work as I had conceived—or more to the point, if *I* failed to work as Visual Basic has conceived.

In the Visual Basic repertoire of events, the _MouseDown event is recognized before the _Click event for any given graphic object. It can therefore be concluded ergonomically that a click is a more deliberate act than a press of the index button because a click involves two motions—a downward motion and a rebounding upward motion. Here is the procedure for the Compass_Click event:

```
Sub Compass_Click ()
If pokedown = False Then
    pokedown = True
    CurAngle.ForeColor = RGB(255, 0, 0)
    CurRadius.ForeColor = RGB(255, 0, 0)
    CurAngle.Text = AngleNow.Caption
    CurRadius.Text = RadiusNow.Caption
    If CurRadius.Text = "0" Or CurRadius.Text = " 0" Then
        EndLine.Caption = "End of Line"
    Else
        EndLine.Caption = ""
    End If
    UnTestPlot
    TestPlot
Else
    UnTestPlot
    ClearCompass
    CurAngle.ForeColor = RGB(0, 0, 0)
    CurRadius.ForeColor = RGB(0, 0, 0)
    CurAngle.Text = "0"
```

```
    CurRadius.Text = "0"
    EndLine.Caption = "End of Line"
End If
End Sub
```

The _Click event occurs when the index button (having been pressed) pops back up—not when it goes down. When a pop-back-up happens in the area of the compass, then If pokedown = True, you can assume the crosshatch should be "poked down." Thus pokedown is set to True (–1), and the angle and radius currently registered by the compass are sent to the two text boxes and displayed in red type rather than the usual black. The variable pokedown is one of those flag variables that I use often in this category of applications. You'll notice the "End of Line" indicator EndLine which displays itself as a reminder to the user whenever the value under the "Radius:" text box is set to 0.

When is a _Click clicked?

If the crosshatch is registered as already having been poked down, the _Click event must be assumed to be a directive to release the crosshatch and let it float free again. Variable pokedown is reset to False (0), and the numbers in the angle and radius text boxes are both cleared and reset to black. With pokedown = False, the principal instructions in Sub Compass_MouseMove () now are permitted to be executed.

When the user adds a point to the object by clicking Add, the crosshatch shown in the Compass control disappears as a result of the following procedure:

```
Sub ClearCompass ()
    AngleNow.Caption = ""
    RadiusNow.Caption = ""
    If oldx <> 0 And oldy <> 0 Then
        Compass.Line (oldx - 100, oldy)-(oldx + 100, oldy),
➡ RGB(0, 255, 255)
        Compass.Line (oldx, oldy - 100)-(oldx, oldy + 100),
➡ RGB(0, 255, 255)
    End If
    pokedown = False
    oldx = 0
    oldy = 0
End Sub
```

This is actually the compass-clearing portion of `Sub Compass_MouseMove` (), copied and pasted to this procedure. Variable `pokedown` is set to `False` so the "echo crosshatch" can be free to follow the mouse pointer again.

The final instruction in the preceding procedure is a call to the procedure `Sub TestPlot ()`. Its purpose is to place a red crosshatch in the plotting area at the same point as the one the user chose with the compass. This process enables the user to preview where a point might appear if it were added to the graphics unit.

```
Sub TestPlot ()
PlotArea.DrawMode = 7
xs = XSlide.Value
ys = YSlide.Value
If testx > 0 And testy > 0 Then
    PlotArea.Line (testx - 100 + xs, testy + ys)-
      (testx + 100 + xs, testy + ys), RGB(0, 255, 255)
    PlotArea.Line (testx + xs, testy - 100 + ys)-
      (testx + xs, testy + 100 + ys), RGB(0, 255, 255)
End If
An = Val(AngleNow.Caption)
Rad = Val(RadiusNow.Caption) * magnify
testx = Rad * Sin(((An + 90 + offset) Mod 360) * (pi / 180))
➥  + 2500
testy = Rad * Cos(((An + 90 + offset) Mod 360) * (pi / 180))
➥  + 1500
PlotArea.Line (testx - 100 + xs, testy + ys)-
  (testx + 100 + xs, testy + ys), RGB(0, 255, 255)
PlotArea.Line (testx + xs, testy - 100 + ys)-
  (testx + xs, testy + 100 + ys), RGB(0, 255, 255)
PlotArea.DrawMode = 13
TestOn = True
End Sub
```

At design time, the `.DrawMode` property for the `PlotArea` object was left at the default value 13. As a result, any plotting takes place "on top of" the old contents of the picture box. For an overwritable red crosshatch to appear in the plotting area, the `.DrawMode` for that area must be set temporarily to 7. The coordinates (`testx`, `testy`) are retained within form-level variables; if this procedure has been executed before, `testx` and `testy` must not equal zero. This is the reason for the initial conditional clause; if there are values in `testx` and `testy`, there must be a crosshatch in `PlotArea`, so it must be cleared to make room for the new one.

After the old crosshatch location has been plotted over, the angle and radius registered by the compass are retrieved and assigned to variables An and Rad. To reorient the point with respect to the plotting area, the point is rotated 90 degrees counterclockwise, then the rotation value offset is added to the degree count. Trigonometry is used to retrieve the new coordinates (testx, testy) from the angle and radius values, and the red crosshatch is plotted to the form at those coordinates.

Notice the offsets here in Sub TestPlot (); variables xs and ys represent the "thumb" locations of the two slider bars, which determine which portion of the PlotArea the user is currently observing. If the viewport is slid to one side, at least one of these variables is nonzero. The amount of the offset is taken directly from the .Value properties of the two slider bars at the beginning of the procedure, then added directly to the plot coordinates for the crosshatch. This shows how simple it is to implement scrolling in a picture box. Notice also the variable magnify; its value is set by setting the Magnification slider bar on the far right side of the form. The size of the plotted object is plotted by the factor magnify; this shows how easy it is to zoom in and out of an image, as long as you use trigonometry to do it.

Finally, the .DrawMode property is set back to 13 (normal), and a flag variable TestOn is set to True to indicate to other procedures in the form module that a red crosshatch does appear in PlotArea. Notice that form-level flag variables (rather than a huge set of parameters) are used here as a communication tool between procedures.

What's potentially confusing about procedure Sub TestPlot () is the way in which the offsets have been handled for the scroll bar values. Assume the user has typed the bearing and distance for an experimental point location into the AngleNow and RadiusNow text boxes. The angle and radius of this location are not calculated with respect to the center of PlotArea because that center can be changed from place to place with the scroll bars; on the other hand, the user is calculating in her mind with respect to absolute center, regardless of where she's looking through the viewport at the moment. So for the portion of the procedure where the Cartesian coordinate pairs for the absolute bearing are calculated, I concluded while writing this procedure I should not add relative offsets for the position of the viewport scroll bars; I should only add those offsets when I intend to plot a point. I use the relative coordinate system when I'm plotting a point to PlotArea; I use the absolute system when I intend to store the coordinates to the angle() and radius() arrays.

Later in this program's development, I discovered there would be situations where the test plotting system has to remove the red crosshatch and not replot it. Thus the following reversal of fortune:

```
Sub UnTestPlot ()
PlotArea.DrawMode = 7
xs = XSlide.Value
ys = YSlide.Value
If testx <> 0 And testy <> 0 Then
    PlotArea.Line (testx - 100 + xs, testy + ys)-
      (testx + 100 + xs, testy + ys), RGB(0, 255, 255)
    PlotArea.Line (testx + xs, testy - 100 + ys)-
      (testx + xs, testy + 100 + ys), RGB(0, 255, 255)
End If
PlotArea.DrawMode = 13
TestOn = FALSE
End Sub
```

Obviously, this is a scaled-down version of `Sub TestPlot ()`, with the final flag-setting instruction set now to `False`. This procedure is called, for instance, when the entire object is being redrawn.

A separate slider bar on the bottom of GRUUM.FRM is used to set the current point in case the user wants to replace the coordinates for that point or delete that point. When this `PointFind` slider bar is moved and a real point—not a (0, 0) end-of-line point—is indicated, a blue crosshatch is drawn within `PlotArea` at the location of the "current" peg—in other words, the point within the array currently registered in the form as the "Current Point."

```
Sub PointNow ()
PlotArea.DrawMode = 7
xs = XSlide.Value
ys = YSlide.Value
An = Val(CurAngle.Text)
Rad = Val(CurRadius.Text) * magnify
If clearstatus = False And Rad > 0 Then
    PlotArea.Line (curx - 100 + xs, cury + ys)-
      (curx + 100 + xs, cury + ys), RGB(255, 255, 0)
    PlotArea.Line (curx + xs, cury - 100 + ys)-
      (curx + xs, cury + 100 + ys), RGB(255, 255, 0)
End If
```

```
If Rad > 0 Then
    curx = Rad * Sin(((An + 90 + offset) Mod 360) * (pi / 180)) + 2500
    cury = Rad * Cos(((An + 90 + offset) Mod 360) * (pi / 180)) + 1500
    PlotArea.Line (curx - 100 + xs, cury + ys)-
      (curx + 100 + xs, cury + ys), RGB(255, 255, 0)
    PlotArea.Line (curx + xs, cury - 100 + ys)-
      (curx + xs, cury + 100 + ys), RGB(255, 255, 0)
End If
PlotArea.DrawMode = 13
End Sub
```

By now, the structure of this procedure should look somewhat familiar. Sub PointNow () was actually written by copying the source code of Sub TestPlot () to the system clipboard, and pasting it into the preceding procedure. The variables were changed, to paraphrase Jack Webb, to protect them from interfering with the other form-level variable values—in this procedure, the current blue crosshatch coordinates are (curx, cury). The procedure will only plot the blue crosshatch if the radius value is greater than zero—in other words, if the point is not an end-of-line register—and if another flag variable clearstatus shows there is already a blue crosshatch in PlotArea (If clearstatus = False). If both conditions fail, the Else portion of the conditional clause is executed, and the old crosshatch coordinates are cleared.

A fairly simple procedure is used to update the current values appearing on the form:

```
Sub DispStat ()
numpoints.Caption = Str$(npoints)
CurPoint.Caption = Str$(cpoint)
CurAngle.ForeColor = RGB(0, 0, 0)
CurRadius.ForeColor = RGB(0, 0, 0)
CurAngle.Text = Str$(angle(cpoint))
CurRadius.Text = Str$(radius(cpoint))
If radius(cpoint) = 0 Then
    EndLine.Caption = "End of Line"
Else
    EndLine.Caption = ""
End If
End Sub
```

Again, the variable npoints contains the number of points held in the array, whereas cpoint represents the current point. The color of the angle and radius text boxes is set to black before displaying the current values.

Back to some of the event procedures now: Generally, a red test crosshatch is placed within the plotting area to display where the next peg might appear—before that spot is officially selected. The easiest way for the user to place this crosshatch within the plotting area is to click within the plotting area itself. Unfortunately, it is not the easiest procedure to implement, as its size implies:

```
Sub PlotArea_MouseDown (Button As Integer, Shift As Integer,
➥  x As Single, y As Single)
UnTestPlot
xs = XSlide.Value
ys = YSlide.Value
pntx = x - 2500 - xs
pnty = y - 1500 - ys
PlotArea.DrawMode = 7
If otx <> 0 And oty <> 0 Then
    PlotArea.Line (otx - 100 + xs, oty + ys)-
➥  (otx + 100 + xs, oty + ys), RGB(0, 255, 255)
    PlotArea.Line (otx + xs, oty - 100 + ys)-
➥  (otx + xs, oty + 100 + ys), RGB(0, 255, 255)
End If
otx = x - xs
oty = y - ys
PlotArea.Line (x - 100, y)-(x + 100, y), RGB(0, 255, 255)
PlotArea.Line (x, y - 100)-(x, y + 100), RGB(0, 255, 255)
PlotArea.DrawMode = 13
rdius = Sqr(pntx ^ 2 + pnty ^ 2) / magnify
If y <> 1500 Then
    angl = (Atn(pntx / pnty) * (180 / pi) + 180)
Else
    angl = (Atn(pntx) * (180 / pi) + 180)
End If
If pnty <= 0 Then
    angl = (angl - 90) Mod 360
Else
    angl = (angl + 90) Mod 360
End If
ClearCompass
AngleNow.Caption = Str$(angl)
RadiusNow.Caption = Str$(rdius)
```

```
posx = (750 + pntx) / magnify
posy = (750 + pnty) / magnify
Compass.Line (posx - 100, posy)-(posx + 100, posy),
➡  RGB(0, 255, 255)
Compass.Line (posx, posy - 100)-(posx, posy + 100),
➡  RGB(0, 255, 255)
oldx = posx
oldy = posy
pokedown = True
CurAngle.ForeColor = RGB(255, 0, 0)
CurRadius.ForeColor = RGB(255, 0, 0)
CurAngle.Text = AngleNow.Caption
CurRadius.Text = RadiusNow.Caption
If CurRadius.Text = "0" Or CurRadius.Text = " 0" Then
    EndLine.Caption = "End of Line"
Else
    EndLine.Caption = ""
End If
End Sub
```

First, the current viewport offsets are acquired and assigned to variables. Again, xs and ys will represent the values of the scroll bars. In trigonometry the center point is generally in the center of the graph, whereas in Visual Basic it's in the upper-left corner by default. Variables pntx and pnty will hold the absolute coordinates of the point being plotted; this way, when the user moves the image, the points can move with it because they all have absolute coordinates (absolute coordinates can be shifted in any one axis direction). With the relative coordinate system, the center of PlotArea. can be made the center of the graph by subtracting from each axis a value that's half the length of the x axis and half the width of the y axis, respectively. This is where the negative offsets of 2500 and 1500 are derived, since the .Width and .Height of PlotArea. are 5000 and 3000.

Next, using the relative coordinate system (coordinates x and y as the VB interpreter sees them), the old red crosshatch (if there is one) in the drawing area is cleared, and a new one is drawn. The old crosshatch coordinates are then updated. Next, the angle and radius formed by this new point are derived trigonometrically, and their values are placed in the compass. After that, the old compass red crosshatch is cleared, and a new one is added at the point corresponding to the angle and radius derived from the plotting area. The compass is officially "poked down," and the text boxes are updated to reflect the angle and radius values under consideration—which means they're displayed in red type.

Notice the same types of processes are reused by many of these procedures without having had to write them from scratch—for instance, clearing and replotting crosshatches, and determining coordinate values from angles and radii. Although each process in every nearly-identical procedure is essentially the same, in actuality there are minute specifics that make each procedure functionally unique. You therefore cannot have one generic general procedure called by name by several procedures, and let that generic procedure discern the specifics for itself. Each process modeled within the procedures you've seen listed is just different enough to mandate that its routine source code must be copied into a new procedural framework each time, then altered to suit the specific purposes of the procedures in which the routine appears.

The way I've designed GRUUM, when the user places a point onto the PlotArea, a point is not yet added to the graphics unit. By clicking the Add button, the user directs the program to add the point currently indicated by the red crosshatch to the array. If there's a blue crosshatch in the PlotArea, however, the Add button's .Caption property is altered so that the button reads Replace.

```
Sub Add_Click ()
BackupArray
ClearCompass
CurAngle.ForeColor = RGB(0, 0, 0)
CurRadius.ForeColor = RGB(0, 0, 0)
angle(cpoint) = Val(CurAngle.Text)
radius(cpoint) = Val(CurRadius.Text)
If Add.Caption = "Add" Then
    cpoint = cpoint + 1
    npoints = npoints + 1
    ReDim Preserve angle(npoints), radius(npoints)
    PointFind.Max = cpoint
    PointFind.Value = cpoint
End If
otx = 0
oty = 0
End Sub
```

The current values of the last point in both arrays are substituted with the values displayed in the text boxes, which now have turned black to indicate their acceptance into the arrays. If and only if the button reads Add (not Replace), 1 is added to the current point value, a space is added to the slider bar that enables the user to choose the current point value, and all four general procedures are executed in turn.

The .Caption contents of the button whose .Name is Add are changed whenever the .Value of the PointFind scroll bar is changed to some nonzero point before the end of the array.

```
Sub PointFind_Change ()
cpoint = PointFind.Value
If PointFind.Value = npoints Then
    Add.Caption = "Add"
Else
    Add.Caption = "Replace"
End If
clearstatus = False
ClearCompass
DrawUnit
DispStat
PointNow
End Sub
```

This procedure belongs to the horizontal scroll bar which sets the point whose blue crosshatch currently appears in the PlotArea. When the number of the point along the array is less than the total number of points in the graphics unit—and when the blue crosshatch represents a point that has already been entered into the array—the caption of the Add button is changed to read Replace. It is set again to Add once the point being viewed is the same as the total number of points. The status registers on the form are updated, and the blue crosshatch is added to the plot area indicating which point you're discussing.

The other way for the user to place a red test crosshatch into the plotting area is to find a position for that crosshatch using the compass or by typing one in directly, and clicking the Test button. The event procedure for that button follows:

```
Sub Test_Click ()
angl = (360 - Val(CurAngle.Text)) * (pi / 180)
rdius = Val(CurRadius.Text)
crsx = 750 + Cos(angl) * rdius
crsy = 750 + Sin(angl) * rdius
If oldx = 0 And oldy = 0 Then GoTo overcome
Compass.Line (oldx - 100, oldy)-(oldx + 100, oldy),
➥  RGB(0, 255, 255)
Compass.Line (oldx, oldy - 100)-(oldx, oldy + 100),
➥  RGB(0, 255, 255)
overcome:
```

```
Compass.Line (crsx - 100, crsy)-(crsx + 100, crsy),
➥ RGB(0, 255, 255)
Compass.Line (crsx, crsy - 100)-(crsx, crsy + 100),
➥ RGB(0, 255, 255)
oldx = crsx
oldy = crsy
AngleNow.Caption - CurAngle.Text
RadiusNow.Caption = Str$(rdius)
TestPlot
End Sub
```

Here the angle and radius values currently under consideration are extracted from their text boxes, and the coordinate values (`crsx`, `crsy`) are extracted trigonometrically from them. The old compass crosshatch is plotted over, and the new one is added. A call is then placed to procedure `Sub TestPlot ()`, whose listing appeared earlier. This procedure places the test red crosshatch within the plotting area.

In generating some test graphics units to see whether my program "felt" right, I came across a few situations where I wanted to break a line into two, so I could have an extra point between them. With this in mind, I added the Insert and Delete buttons.

```
Sub Insert_Click ()
BackupArray
If npoints = 1 Then Exit Sub
An = angle(cpoint - 1)
Rad = radius(cpoint - 1) * magnify
onex = Rad * Sin(((An + 90 + offset) Mod 360) * (pi / 180))
➥ + 2500
oney = Rad * Cos(((An + 90 + offset) Mod 360) * (pi / 180))
➥ + 1500
An = angle(cpoint)
Rad = radius(cpoint) * magnify
twox = Rad * Sin(((An + 90 + offset) Mod 360) * (pi / 180))
➥ + 2500
twoy = Rad * Cos(((An + 90 + offset) Mod 360) * (pi / 180))
➥ + 1500
midx = (onex + twox) / 2
midy = (oney + twoy) / 2
rdius = Sqr((2500 - midx) ^ 2 + (1500 - midy) ^ 2) / magnify
```

```
If midy <> 1500 Then
    angl = (Atn(midx / midy) * (180 / pi) + 180)
Else
    angl = (Atn(midx) * (180 / pi) + 180)
End If
For Shift = npoints + 1 To cpoint + 1 Step -1
    angle(Shift) = angle(Shift - 1)
    radius(Shift) = radius(Shift - 1)
Next Shift
angle(cpoint) = angl
radius(cpoint) = rdius
CurAngle.ForeColor = RGB(0, 0, 0)
CurRadius.ForeColor = RGB(0, 0, 0)
CurAngle.Text = Str$(angle(cpoint))
CurRadius.Text = Str$(radius(cpoint))
PointFind.Max = PointFind.Max + 1
npoints = npoints + 1
DispStat
PointNow
TestPlot
DrawUnit
End Sub
```

The objective of this procedure is not only to break a line into two pieces, but to make it appear broken on the screen. The effect is a bent line where there was a straight one. Imagine the array in your mind: The "current" point—the one represented in the viewport by a blue crosshatch—is somewhere in the middle of the array. When you click Insert, the current point and all points to the right of it are moved one to the right, and a point between the former current point and the point just before it is generated for the current array location. The array-regulative variables are incremented to show that there's now one more point.

To place the new point somewhere between the other two, trigonometry is employed once again. The now familiar sine and cosine formulas are used to find the coordinates of the current point and those of the point before it. These coordinates are added together and divided by two to arrive at a reasonable pair of coordinates. This pair is somewhere between the two once-adjacent points, without actually resting on the line between them. The user may then select a new location for this point and click Replace.

```
Sub Delete_Click ()
If npoints < 2 Then Exit Sub
BackupArray
For Shift = cpoint To npoints
    angle(Shift) = angle(Shift + 1)
    radius(Shift) = radius(Shift + 1)
Next Shift
CurAngle.ForeColor = RGB(0, 0, 0)
CurRadius.ForeColor = RGB(0, 0, 0)
CurAngle.Text = Str$(angle(cpoint))
CurRadius.Text = Str$(radius(cpoint))
PointFind.Max = PointFind.Max - 1
npoints = npoints - 1
ReDim Preserve angle(npoints), radius(npoints)
DispStat
PointNow
TestPlot
DrawUnit
End Sub
```

Naturally, if you can Insert a point, you should have the capability to Delete it. This procedure takes all points in the two arrays to the right of the current one, then shifts them one element to the left of their prior position. In so doing, the current point's location is "covered over."

One of the last items I added to the program was an Undo button that would allow the user to restore the previous state of the object before the last drawing event. I found this system was extremely simple to implement:

```
Sub BackupArray ()
Dim count As Integer
ReDim backangle(npoints), backradius(npoints)
For count = 1 To npoints
    backangle(count) = angle(count)
    backradius(count) = radius(count)
Next count
backpoints = npoints
End Sub
```

This procedure makes a backup copy of the current array and the current number of points in a second set of array variables. Every time a draw operation takes place (as you've probably noticed), a simple BackupArray call branches to this procedure and backs up the current array just before it's changed, and a

new point is added to it later. When the user clicks Undo, the following procedure reloads the arrays in the opposite direction:

```
Sub UndoArray ()
Dim count As Integer, Max As Integer
If backpoints > npoints Then
    Max = backpoints
Else
    Max = npoints
End If
ReDim Preserve angle(Max), radius(Max)
For count = 1 To Max
    angle(count) = backangle(count)
    radius(count) = backradius(count)
Next count
npoints = backpoints
cpoint = npoints
PointFind.Max = backpoints
PointFind.Value = cpoint
backpoints = npoints
DispStat
DrawUnit
End Sub
```

The procedure that takes execution here is a single instruction:

```
Sub Undo_Click ()
If npoints > 0 Then UndoArray
End Sub
```

To some degree, the remaining event procedures are academic:

```
Sub CurRadius_LostFocus ()
If CurRadius.Text = "0" Or CurRadius.Text = " 0" Then
    EndLine.Caption = "End of Line"
Else
    EndLine.Caption = ""
End If
End Sub
```

The _LostFocus event procedure for a text box is generally executed whenever the user presses Tab, signalling that text entry is completed. The focus then
shifts to the next graphic object in the cycle for that form. In this case, the End
of Line indicator is set whenever the interpreter finds that the user purposefully entered a zero into the radius text box.

```
Sub Magnification_Change ()
magnify = Magnification.Value / 10
Magnific.Caption = "Magnification: " + Str$(magnify)
DrawUnit
End Sub

Sub Rotation_Change ()
offset = Rotation.Value / 10
rotate.Caption = "Rotation: " + Str$(offset)
DrawUnit
End Sub
```

These procedures are executed when the user moves the magnification and rotation vertical scroll bar values. The scale of a scroll bar in Visual Basic is always integral; the value of a scroll bar cannot be changed by .1 or .001. To make a scroll bar work for fractional values, the value it represents must be set at an order of 10 lower than the value scale for that scroll bar. To make `Magnification` register values of one tenth, therefore, the value indicated by the scroll bar is divided by 10.

Now, after all this plotting and crosshatching takes place, the user can still dump it all with a click of the New button.

```
Sub FileNew_Click ()
msg$ = "Is it OK to clear the array?"
answer = MsgBox(msg$, 36, "G.R.U.U.M.")
If answer = 7 Then Exit Sub
For clr = 1 To npoints
    angle(clr) = 0
    radius(clr) = 0
Next clr
npoints = 1
ReDim angle(npoints), radius(npoints)
cpoint = 1
PointFind.Value = 1
PointFind.Max = 1
offset = 0
magnify = 1
ClearCompass
YSlide.Value = 0
XSlide.Value = 0
```

```
DispStat
DrawUnit
savestatus = False
End Sub
```

The second parameter in the `MsgBox()` function, the number 36, is a sum of two bitwise values, 32 and 4. The 32 tells the interpreter to display the warning query icon with the dialog box; the 4 tells the interpreter to include only Yes and No buttons. An answer of 7 tells the interpreter the user clicked No; any other response allows the procedure to continue. As you can see, the initial values of the important variables are reset, and every point in the array thus far is zeroed.

Perhaps the single feature that makes this application usable is the capability to take an object, rotate that to any degree, and save the image of that object as a bitmap (.BMP) file. The procedure that performs the saving of the image should look strangely familiar to the careful reader:

```
Sub FileSaveImage_Click ()
On Error GoTo cancl3
Selector.DefaultExt = "*.bmp"
Selector.DialogTitle = "Save Bitmap"
flt$ = "Bitmap Files (*.bmp)¦*.bmp¦All Files (*.*)¦*.*"
Selector.Filter = flt$
Selector.FilterIndex = 1
Selector.Flags = OFN_OVERWRITEPROMPT Or OFN_PATHMUSTEXIST
Selector.Action = 2
On Error GoTo 0
SavePicture PlotArea.Image, Selector.Filename
Exit Sub
cancl3:
On Error GoTo 0
Resume downhere3
downhere3:
End Sub
```

The `.Image` property for a graphic object, when saved to disk, is quite luckily a .BMP file. All this procedure has to do is use the `Selector` form to determine the save filename for the image; the VB interpreter takes it from there.

Better Functionality Through Polygons

Now, for the *pièce de résistance*: Late in the development of this program, I considered adding routines for drawing rectangles and circles. It then hit me that most programs draw circles in the form of multisided polygons; there are so many sides that at lower resolutions the shape might appear to be a circle. I decided instead to have a polygon-drawing feature and let the user choose the number of sides to be drawn. Here are the parameters for the form:

Listing 7.5. GRPOLYGN.FRM Property Settings.

```
General Procedures:
    <None>

        BorderStyle          3 - Fixed Double
        Caption              Polygon Control
        FormName             GetPolygon
        LinkTopic            Form1
        MaxButton            False
        MinButton            False

Control Type: Label
    Control Name: Label1
        Alignment            1 - Right Justify
        Caption              Initial Offset
        CtlName              Label1
        FontBold             False
        FontName             Helv
        FontSize             7.78125
        TabIndex             5

    Control Name: Label7
        Alignment            1 - Right Justify
        Caption              Vertices
        CtlName              Label7
        FontBold             False
        FontName             Helv
        FontSize             7.78125
        TabIndex             2
```

```
    Control Name: Label8
    Alignment          1 - Right Justify
    Caption            Radius
    CtlName            Label8
    FontBold           False
    FontName           Helv
    FontSize           7.78125
    TabIndex           3

Control Type: TextBox
    Control Name: DegOffset
    CtlName            DegOffset
    FontBold           False
    FontName           Helv
    FontSize           9.5625
    TabIndex           4

    Control Name: PolyRadius
    CtlName            PolyRadius
    FontBold           False
    FontName           Helv
    FontSize           9.5625
    TabIndex           1

    Control Name: Vertices
    CtlName            Vertices
    FontBold           False
    FontName           Helv
    FontSize           9.5625
    TabIndex           0

Control Type: Command Button
    Control Name: Cancel
    Cancel             True
    Caption            Cancel
    CtlName            Cancel
    TabIndex           7

    Active Control Event Procedures
     Cancel_Click
```

continues

Listing 7.5. continued

```
Control Name: Draw
Caption           Draw
CtlName           Draw
Default           True
TabIndex          6

Active Control Event Procedures
  Draw_Click
```

There are only two procedures in this form; the smallest (which appears next) is minimal, and the largest is gargantuan.

```
Sub Cancel_Click ()
GetPolygon.Hide
End Sub
```

Now here's a large procedure for plotting a multisided, closed polygon around any central point on the plotting area, without appearing to disturb the rest of the graphics unit:

```
Sub Draw_Click ()
Static atend As Integer
If Vertices.Text = "" Or PolyRadius.Text = "" Then Exit Sub
If DegOffset.Text = "" Then
    vertangl = 0
Else
    vertangl = Val(DegOffset.Text)
End If
polyrad = Val(PolyRadius.Text)
If radius(cpoint) <> 0 Then
    An1 = angle(cpoint + 1)
    An2 = angle(cpoint + 2)
    Rad1 = radius(cpoint + 1)
    Rad2 = radius(cpoint + 2)
    cpoint = cpoint + 1
    angle(cpoint) = 0
    radius(cpoint) = 0
    atend = 1
Else
    atend = 0
```

```
End If
points = Val(Vertices.Text)
cpoint = cpoint + 1
If cpoints < npoints Then xend = 1
ipoints = points + atend + xend
toend = npoints - cpoint + atend
If cpoint < npoints Then
    For shift = toend To 0 Step -1
        angle(cpoint + shift + ipoints) = angle(cpoint + shift
    - 2)
        radius(cpoint + shift + ipoints) = radius(cpoint + shift
    - 2)
    Next shift
    angle(cpoint + ipoints + 1) = An1
    angle(cpoint + ipoints + 2) = An2
    radius(cpoint + ipoints + 1) = Rad1
    radius(cpoint + ipoints + 2) = Rad2
End If
CenterAn = Val(GRUUM.CurAngle.Text)
CenterRad = Val(GRUUM.CurRadius.Text)
centx = CenterRad * Sin(((CenterAn + 90) Mod 360) * (pi / 180))
centy = CenterRad * Cos(((CenterAn + 90) Mod 360) * (pi / 180))
ainterval = 360 / points
For vertex = 1 To points
    vertx = polyrad * Sin(((vertangl + 90) Mod 360)
    * (pi / 180))
    verty = polyrad * Cos(((vertangl + 90) Mod 360)
    * (pi / 180))
    pntx = centx + vertx
    pnty = centy + verty
    Rad = Sqr(pntx ^ 2 + pnty ^ 2)
        If pnty <> 0 Then
        Angl = (Atn(pntx / pnty) * (180 / pi) + 180)
    Else
        Angl = (Atn(pntx) * (180 / pi) + 180)
    End If
    If pnty <= 0 Then
        Angl = (Angl - 90) Mod 360
    Else
        Angl = (Angl + 90) Mod 360
    End If
```

```
      curx = Rad * Sin(((Angl + 90 + offset) Mod 360) *
➥ (pi / 180))
      cury = Rad * Cos(((Angl + 90 + offset) Mod 360) *
➥ (pi / 180))
      If vertex = 1 Then
          initx = curx
          inity = cury
          initangl = Angl
          initrad = Rad
      End If
      vertangl = vertangl + ainterval
      angle(cpoint) = Angl
      radius(cpoint) = Rad
      cpoint = cpoint + 1
Next vertex
angle(cpoint) = initangl
radius(cpoint) = initrad
If atend = 1 Then
    cpoint = cpoint + 1
    angle(cpoint) = 0
    radius(cpoint) = 0
End If
cpoint = cpoint + 1
npoints = npoints + ipoints + 1 + atend
For zeroshave = npoints - 1 To 1 Step -1
    If radius(zeroshave) = 0 Then
        If cpoint = npoints Then
            cpoint = cpoint - 1
        End If
        npoints = npoints - 1
    Else
        Exit For
    End If
Next zeroshave
GRUUM.PointFind.Max = npoints
GRUUM.PointFind.Value = cpoint
GRUUM.PlotArea.Refresh
GetPolygon.Hide
End Sub
```

To describe this procedure briefly, but in sequence: A variable `atend` is dimensioned `Static`; it will act as a flag denoting whether an end-of-line indicator was placed at the end of the current or the previously plotted polygon. Next, the procedure checks to see whether there was any vital user input in the text boxes; if there isn't any, the procedure is exited. If the input is present, it is converted from text to values by using the `Val()` function.

The first conditional clause tests to see whether the center point of the polygon is indeed the center point of the entire object. If it is not, then obviously the polygon has to be plotted in the middle of the existing array; `atend` will be set to 1. This is important because it means that the part of the array that falls after the polygon will have to be shifted to the right for the number of points in the polygon, plus one, plus any number of points denoting an end-of-line at both ends of the polygon, plus one if an existing line is to pick up where it left off. It's important here that the procedure keep track of the first two sets of angles and radii after the current point because the shifting procedure will result in a hole where these points should appear after the polygon is plotted. Next, if the point is to be plotted in the middle of the array, the procedure writes an end-of-line at the current point—it will pick up this point later, after the polygon is printed.

Variable `cpoint` (the current point) is shifted one to the right again. As long as you haven't reached the far right side of the array (`If cpoints < npoints`), another flag, `xend`, is set to 1 to indicate this fact. Notice you aren't using `True` and `False` like you usually do because these flag variables `atend` and `xend` will be used as increments in determining the length of the array after the polygon is plotted.

The shifting part begins to make room for the polygon. The number of points necessary to plot the polygon is calculated as `ipoints`. The number of points, then, from the current point to the end is calculated as `toend`. As long as you haven't reached the end, the shift process can start, counting backward from the end of the `toend` interval to 0. Counting backward from the tail end of the new array toward the end of the polygon, the point values are shifted to the end. Those two variable pairs taken account of earlier are then used to fill the strange hole at the end of the polygon reserved area.

The center of this polygon will appear at whatever point is registered in the text boxes on the panel, even if these numbers are red and are being used as a test—that is, even if they're not part of the array. This way, you can have a polygon plotted around a point that is not part of the array. From these text boxes, the *x/y* coordinates of the center of the polygon are determined. The angle interval `ainterval` will equal the angle formed by each side of the polygon opposite the center; this is determined, sensibly enough, by dividing 360 by the number of sides in the polygon.

The loop clause starts, which places each vertex of the polygon into the array. Trigonometrically, the coordinates of each vertex are determined relative to the center of the polygon. These coordinates are added to those of the center, to arrive at the coordinates of each vertex relative to absolute center. The radius and angle of this vertex are determined using the arctangent formula.

To plot a five-sided polygon, the routine needs to plot six points in order to close the polygon. The last point in the polygon is plotted over the first point. For this reason, the coordinates of the first point in the polygon are retained. Next, the angle interval is added for the sake of the next vertex, and the angle and radius just determined are added to the array. The current point is then shifted one to the right, and the loop clause closes. At the end of the loop clause, the bearings of the first point in the polygon are added to the array to close the polygon, then an end-of-line indicator is added.

The number of points the polygon actually consumed are added to the tally `npoints`. Because of another strange anomaly, I added a "cheat clause" that looks for any extra trailing zeroes at the end of the array and hacks them off. The scroll bar values are then refreshed, the `PlotArea` is cleaned up, and the `GetPolygon` window gets out of the way. Whew.

The Point-by-Point Summary

Here are some of the programming principles demonstrated: First of all, decide which variables are most important to your application and declare them first. Nonetheless, be ready to add new variables to those declarations as you go because you are likely to come up with new ideas along the way. As you start conserving source code, more of your instructions become re-executable and callable from various sources. As a result, rather than having parameters passed, you might find it more convenient to declare all your variables as form-level or global. Notice not a single procedure in this application was passed variables by way of procedure declaration; all shared variables were declared at the form level. Oftentimes, broader-level variables are preferable to parameter-passing, especially if the values are shared among nearly all the procedures.

Second, if you can, determine which procedures are most crucial to your application's execution and program those first, preferably in the general procedures area of a form or in a general module. If an event procedure needs to execute this code, it can place a call to this general procedure.

Third, perhaps the best way to program a procedure is to add routines— short sequences of instructions—to that procedure one routine at a time and make adjustments to that routine so that it works properly before adding the next routine. You will rarely find yourself programming a procedure in sequence from the first instruction line to the last; you'll generally be adding processes and routines throughout, like a *papier-mâché* sculpture.

Fourth, you might find yourself reusing the same types of processes several times within a VB application, though not necessarily in exactly the same way. In such cases, the cut and paste functions of the VB editor prove to be quite convenient.

COMMUNICATION WITH THE USER

8

I'd like to begin this chapter by awakening the skeptic in everyone. Have icons really revolutionized computing? Do we as programmers seriously believe we're capable of representing all the major functions of computing graphically, pictorially, or symbolically? Quick—think of an icon that represents the concept "Assign index to data table."

When I wrote for an all-computers-considered magazine in the late 1980s (back when there was such a publication), the Macintosh-oriented software reviews covering the first great graphical applications for the Macintosh would speak of how programmers were just beginning to break the mold. They were finding their own way and charting new territory by making applications graphical and, where they could, symbological. (Note my use of the term *symbological,* which refers more to the direct representation and correlation between concept and symbol.) Mac programmers, in the early days of that computer, were the renegades.

The question of usage model standardization.

When it was decided that what made the Apple Macintosh such a usable computer was its unique "look-and-feel," Apple sought to define just what it was that constituted the Mac's uniqueness. Apple then began publishing the standards that resulted from those efforts as something it called the *Macintosh interface.* Before long, magazine reviewers used the Mac guidelines as the official litmus test for a program's overall quality. Eventually, a program didn't earn a "passing grade" by the publishers' new numerical scale of overall quality until that program followed the Mac interface.

Suddenly, the system that broke the mold became the mold. No matter how skillful a programmer became at layout and organization of ideas, even if the program concept was ingenious, if the usage model didn't conform to a preconceived specification of adequacy, out the door it went. The philosophy was that to educate users about the mechanics of a particular computing platform, the different programs sharing the platform must appear to be components of an integrated computing concept. If a user understands Macintosh, therefore, he should already know enough to operate the basics of any Mac program with a fair degree of skill.

As much as I hate to admit it, this theory makes quite a bit of sense. Today, every major computing environment includes some form of true multitasking. If the usage models of several applications inhabiting the same system differ too radically, cooperation between them in a multitasking environment where these applications are joined together is nearly impossible. The user would be faced with numerous mind-set shifts in mid-job.

Uniformness in multitasking operations' appearance.

So a degree of uniformity in the construction of applications' usage models is preferable. A user feels comfortable with a new program when some of its tools seem even slightly familiar to him. But just what is it that the user feels familiar with? Would a user be so terribly shocked if a dialog box was suddenly placed on a background other than white, or if the buttons were suddenly not gray?

People are legitimately asking such questions. When Microsoft premiered its Version 4 of Excel at developer conferences nationwide, a programmer and registered Microsoft developer asked Excel's product manager in Dallas why Excel's dialog boxes were placed on a gray background. It wasn't the standard dialog box provided by the Windows DLLs, the programmer noticed. Since Microsoft continues to complain about its outside developers not following the standard, the developer asked, why should Microsoft be the first to break its own rules?

The question was rhetorical in this context, or at least should have been; this product manager bore no responsibility for Excel's new dialog box design. From my point of view, the gray dialogs were a nice change of pace. When, however, does the level of whiteness or grayness of a dialog box adhere to or violate a published, sacrosanct standard? If a dialog box were suddenly multi-colored, would there be a feeling of discomfort or revolt?

What Makes a Dialog Box?

In the standard Visual Basic vocabulary, there is a hybrid statement/function MsgBox that displays the ordinary dialog box on the screen. For the standard dialog where the user has about three standard choices—such as Yes, No, and Cancel—the usual Windows dialog box is adequate.

I've often written, though, that where there's standardization, there follows mediocrity. A Windows application might appear stylish to the user who has become accustomed to the DOS application, which has all the style and liveliness of plain yogurt. To that person, being asked politely by a dialog box whether he really wants the program to do what he appears to have asked it to do is quite impressive.

If you have to stare at Windows for hours at a time daily, however, you might enjoy a flash of something with just enough flare and originality to break the monotony. One of my complaints about the standard dialog box is that it contains too much white space for its small buttons. The Visual Basic MsgBox() function gives you only limited access to the Windows standard dialog anyway and does not enable you to set the specific text within the buttons.

The Converser Project

My main objective for the Converser was to offer the Visual Basic programmer a more versatile dialog box, but also to provide the user with a radically different appearance coupled with a far more effective utilization of space. Figure 8.1 shows the Converser, my replacement dialog box form.

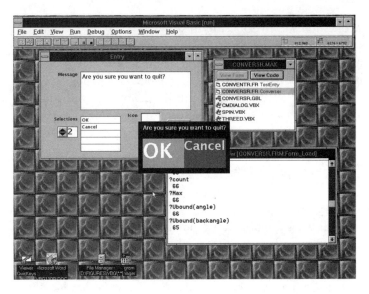

Figure 8.1. The Converser doing an ordinary job.

Figure 8.2 shows the Converser in a more unconventional role.

What makes the Converser dialog box unique is that its included graphics objects are self-shaping. The width of the dialog is stretched automatically to fit the width of the textual message, plus an icon if there happens to be one. This width then is divided evenly among however many buttons appear in the form at the time. Rather than button controls, I've used picture boxes because they, too, have _Click events associated with them.

The property settings for the graphic objects in this particular form have, if you can believe it, no real bearing on their final appearance when the Converser.Show method is executed. Their importance instead is as an "opening position" of sorts, so you can create these controls in an out-of-the-way location. Here are the initial property settings:

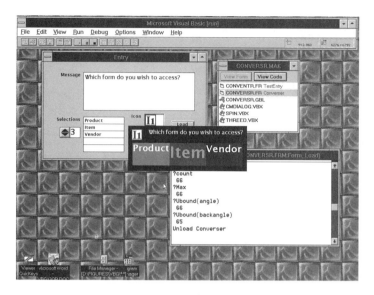

Figure 8.2. The Converser doing an extraordinary job.

CONVERSR.FRM Property Settings

```
Form Converser
   BackColor       =    &H00000000&
   BorderStyle     =    0    'None
   Caption         =    "Converser"
   ForeColor       =    &H00000000&
   Height          =    4104
   Left            =    3288
   LinkTopic       =    "Form2"
   MaxButton       =    0    'False
   MinButton       =    0    'False
   ScaleHeight     =    3636
   ScaleWidth      =    6264
   Top             =    4584
   Width           =    6408

   PictureBox Feedback
      AutoRedraw   =    -1   'True
      BackColor    =    &H00404080&
      BorderStyle  =    0    'None
```

```
    FontBold        =   -1   'True
    FontItalic      =   0    'False
    FontName        =   "Lucida Sans"
    FontSize        =   7.8
    FontStrikethru  =   0    'False
    FontUnderline   =   0    'False
    ForeColor       =   &H000080FF&
    Height          =   972
    Index           =   4
    Left            =   4920
    ScaleHeight     =   972
    ScaleWidth      =   1212
    TabIndex        =   5
    Top             =   2520
    Width           =   1212

PictureBox Feedback
    AutoRedraw      =   -1   'True
    BackColor       =   &H00400040&
    BorderStyle     =   0    'None
    FontBold        =   -1   'True
    FontItalic      =   0    'False
    FontName        =   "Lucida Sans"
    FontSize        =   7.8
    FontStrikethru  =   0    'False
    FontUnderline   =   0    'False
    ForeColor       =   &H00C000C0&
    Height          =   972
    Index           =   3
    Left            =   3720
    ScaleHeight     =   972
    ScaleWidth      =   1212
    TabIndex        =   4
    Top             =   2520
    Width           =   1212

PictureBox Message
    AutoRedraw      =   -1   'True
    BackColor       =   &H00000000&
    FontBold        =   -1   'True
    FontItalic      =   0    'False
    FontName        =   "Lucida Sans"
    FontSize        =   9.6
```

```
       FontStrikethru   =   0    'False
       FontUnderline    =   0    'False
       ForeColor        =   &H00FFFFFF&
       Height           =   492
       Left             =   720
       ScaleHeight      =   468
       ScaleWidth       =   5388
       TabIndex         =   3
       Top              =   120
       Width            =   5412

   PictureBox Feedback
       AutoRedraw       =   -1   'True
       BackColor        =   &H00400000&
       BorderStyle      =   0    'None
       FontBold         =   -1   'True
       FontItalic       =   0    'False
       FontName         =   "Lucida Sans"
       FontSize         =   7.8
       FontStrikethru   =   0    'False
       FontUnderline    =   0    'False
       ForeColor        =   &H00FFFF80&
       Height           =   972
       Index            =   2
       Left             =   2520
       ScaleHeight      =   972
       ScaleWidth       =   1212
       TabIndex         =   2
       Top              =   2520
       Width            =   1212

   PictureBox Feedback
       AutoRedraw       =   -1   'True
       BackColor        =   &H00004000&
       BorderStyle      =   0    'None
       FontBold         =   -1   'True
       FontItalic       =   0    'False
       FontName         =   "Lucida Sans"
       FontSize         =   7.8
       FontStrikethru   =   0    'False
       FontUnderline    =   0    'False
       ForeColor        =   &H0000C000&
```

```
        Height        =   972
        Index         =   0
        Left          =   120
        ScaleHeight   =   972
        ScaleWidth    =   1212
        TabIndex      =   1
        Top           =   2520
        Width         =   1212

    PictureBox Feedback
        AutoRedraw    =   -1   'True
        BackColor     =   &H00000040&
        BorderStyle   =   0    'None
        FontBold      =   -1   'True
        FontItalic    =   0    'False
        FontName      =   "Lucida Sans"
        FontSize      =   7.8
        FontStrikethru =  0    'False
        FontUnderline =   0    'False
        ForeColor     =   &H000000FF&
        Height        =   972
        Index         =   1
        Left          =   1320
        ScaleHeight   =   972
        ScaleWidth    =   1212
        TabIndex      =   0
        Top           =   2520
        Width         =   1212

    Image ConvIcon
        Height        =   492
        Left          =   120
        Top           =   120
        Width         =   492
```

Implementing the Source Code

Function procedures cannot contain forms.

It would be nice if I could declare the Converser a `Function`, so it could be utilized like the `MsgBox()` function. The problem is, in order for this dialog to be included within another VB project by just adding the file, the main body of the Converser source code must appear within the form module. Procedures in a form module have a context native only to that form. Therefore, you couldn't declare a Function procedure in the general procedures area of the Converser form, pass parameters to it, and have it render a response result through an equation. You could, however, make a Function procedure edition of the Converser engine and import it into a general module, if your application actually has one. To do so, however, you would have to amend the instructions referring to the Converser form so Converser would be referred to specifically.

In any event, here are the global parameter declarations to enter into the global or general start-up module of your application:

```
Global msg$, Button$(4)
Global IcFN As String
Global ConvResponse As Integer, NumButtons As Integer
```

The message displayed in the upper region of the Converser dialog will be contained in msg$. The contents of the five buttons are set in advance in the Button$() array. Remember, a declaration of 4 means the array has five elements, counting element #0. The icon filename will be set in variable IcFN. The user's response to the Converser dialog will be represented by an integer variable ConvResponse, reflecting the button that was pressed. This would be the returned response if the engine were to be rewritten as a Function procedure. The actual number of buttons that will appear in the Converser is set within the form module through the integer NumButtons.

When you draw the Converser main form in the design mode of the interpreter, all you need to do is create a control array of five picture boxes and place them, literally, anywhere on the form. Next, place an image control with enough room for an icon in the upper-left corner. Also, place a black picture box control along the upper portion of the form, just to the right of the icon, with its .FontSize set to about 10 points and its .FontColor set to white. Black is a shade nearly forgotten in the era of graphical applications. I suppose designers had become fed up with white-on-black in the era of the TRS-80 and DOS 1, so much so that black is rarely to be found as a background in windowing environments. I set the form's .BorderStyle color to 0 - None, to remove all semblance of this being a Windows window.

Here's the Converser engine in its sole executing procedure:

```
Sub Form_Load ()
If IcFN = "" Then
    Message.Left = 150
```

```
        mwid = Message.TextWidth(msg$)
Else
    Message.Left = 720
    ConvIcon.Picture = LoadPicture(IcFN)
    mwid = Message.TextWidth(msg$) + 570
End If
Message.Width = mwid
Converser.Width = mwid + 300
Message.Top = 100
wdb = Int(mwid / NumButtons)
bcount = 150
For setb = 0 To NumButtons - 1
    Feedback(setb).Width = wdb
    Feedback(setb).Left = bcount
    Feedback(setb).Top = 600
    bcount = bcount + wdb
Next setb
If NumButtons < 5 Then
    For rest = setb To 5
        Feedback(setb).Visible = False
        Feedback(setb).Enabled = False
    Next rest
End If
For btn = 0 To NumButtons - 1
    For fnt = 36 To 4 Step -1
        Feedback(btn).FontSize = fnt
        wid = Feedback(btn).TextWidth(button$(btn))
        If wid <= Feedback(btn).Width Then Exit For
    Next fnt
    mm = Feedback(btn).TextHeight(button$(btn))
    If mm > mht Then
        mht = mm
    End If
Next btn
For btn = 0 To NumButtons - 1
    Feedback(btn).Height = Int(mht * 1.25)
Next btn
Converser.Height = Message.Height + Feedback(0).Height + 300
sh = Screen.Height
sw = Screen.Width
ft = Int((sh / 2) - (Converser.Height / 2))
fl = Int((sw / 2) - (Converser.Width / 2))
Converser.Top = ft
```

```
Converser.Left = fl
Message.Print msg$
For btn = 0 To NumButtons - 1
    Feedback(btn).Print button$(btn)
Next btn
Converser.Show
End Sub
```

Size-to-Fit Text

Each control in the Converser moves and resizes itself, so it only takes up as much space as it needs. At the same time, however, it consumes all the space it possibly can. The engine decides how much space is required for a control with the `.TextWidth()` function. In a strange twist toward nonstandardization of phraseology, Microsoft expressed `.TextWidth()` like a property, even though the reference between the parentheses is to a string variable and not a control index, and even though the width of text at any given point size is fixed and cannot be set like a property.

The point size for the `Message` control—the black picture box along the upper border of the Converser—was set in advance to about 10 points. This point size will stay fixed. The first conditional clause in the previous procedure checks whether there will be an icon in the upper-left corner by testing for the presence of a filename in `IcFN`. If there's no filename, the `Message` control is scooted up against the left side; otherwise, it leaves room along the left for a standard-sized icon. The width of the entire message area then is set to the textual width of the message when it becomes displayed within the `Message` picture box. The `.TextWidth()` function only works within picture boxes and the backgrounds of forms. This is why text for this form is conceived and sized in advance and sent to the control using the `.Print` method. After the width of the message area is obtained, the planned width for the Converser form (which is not yet visible) is set to just beyond the combined message and icon boundaries to give 150 twips of room on both sides for margin.

This message width `mwid` is then divided by the number of buttons to appear in the dialog `NumButtons` to determine the width for each button assigned to variable `wdb`. A tally variable `bcount` is used to set the origin point for the next button in the sequence. Each time one button's location is placed and given a `.Width` of `wdb`, the tally is spaced `wdb` twips to the right to arrive at the origin of the next button.

Distinguishing
between a
picture box
and an image
box.

Again, these aren't really buttons by the Visual Basic definition, but cooler looking picture boxes bearing `_Click` properties that work the same way. The native toolbox of Visual Basic 2 now includes an image control. However, keep in mind that the image box is meant only to act as a backdrop, not to receive text—thus, a nomenclatural distinction between *picture* and *image* that a child of four can point out in a heartbeat.

The next conditional clause disables and makes invisible any remaining buttons, just in case a piece of one, wherever you placed it in the form, slips into the display area of the Converser after it finally becomes displayed.

The purposes of the loop clause counting for `btn` are to place text in each button and to give the buttons an adequate height. All this functionality is purely for the sake of show. I wanted buttons with a simplistic but artistic appearance. With TrueType fonts, the size of characters can be rendered in decimal points, and the font display system obliges faithfully. I wanted the text within the buttons to take up as much width as they could. If there were only a few characters in the button text—for instance, "No"—I wanted those characters to expand to fill the space. I didn't mind if the point sizes for the text in the various buttons differed from one another; in fact, I would enjoy the break in the monotony.

Sizing Text to Fit

The way the text sizes for each picture box "button" are determined is as follows: First, a second-tier loop clause sets the picture box for a 36-point font size. If the `.TextWidth()` for the picture box is too large, the point size is reduced by one and reset. When the point size is precisely right, the loop is exited. At that point, the `.TextHeight()` of the button is tested. The ideal minimum ratio of text to background is 1.25 to 1, with the text resting against the upper edge rather than centered. A conditional clause measures the `.TextHeight()` it sees. If the result is the highest amount tested thus far, it's assigned to a tally variable `mht`. After all the buttons have been tested, `mht` will contain the point size of the tallest characters. Generally these characters belong to the buttons with the least characters, because they'll be made larger to fit the space. This tallest size is then multiplied by 1.25 and assigned to all the active buttons in sequence.

Now that the height of the message and feedback (upper and lower) sections of the form have been determined, the height of the dialog form can be estimated as the sections' combined heights plus 300 twips margin. That figure is assigned to the .Height property of the Converser form. Next, because the resolution of a Windows screen is always variable, the .Height and .Width of the user's screen are obtained. Using an old formula borrowed from typing, the center point of the screen is obtained by dividing the .Height and .Width by two; the .Height and .Width of the current incarnation of the Converser are also halved. Half the height of the form is subtracted from the middle latitude of the screen, and half its width is subtracted from the middle longitude of the screen. The results are the .Top and .Left properties for the new dialog. At long last, the text can be loaded into the picture boxes with the .Print method, and the dialog box can now show itself. A numeral 1 may be added to the end of the .Show method to make this dialog *modal*—that is, to have it take command of the screen and not let go until the user submits his response.

Each button within the Converser panel belongs to a control array Message() and shares a common _Click event procedure that records the user response.

```
Sub Feedback_Click (Index As Integer)
ConvResponse = Index
Unload Converser
End Sub
```

Now, so you can play around with possibilities for the Converser, I've constructed a supplementary form that enables you to set the message and button contents manually, as depicted in Figure 8.3. Here are the necessary property settings for this supplementary form:

Listing 8.1. CONVENTR.FRM Property Settings.

```
Form TestEntry
   BackColor        =    &H00C0C0C0&
   Caption          =    "Entry"
   ForeColor        =    &H00C0C0C0&
   Height           =    3840
   Width            =    5952

   SSPanel Panel3D3
      AutoSize         =    3    'AutoSize Child To Panel
      BevelOuter       =    1    'Inset
```

continues

Listing 8.1. continued

```
BevelWidth       =   2
Caption          =   "Panel3D3"
Height           =   732
Left             =   3600
Top              =   1800
Width            =   732

PictureBox IconShow
   Height        =   684
   Left          =   24
   ScaleHeight   =   660
   ScaleWidth    =   660
   Top           =   24
   Width         =   684

CommonDialog Selector
   Left          =   5640
   Top           =   3000

SpinButton ButtonsSpin
   Height        =   372
   Left          =   600
   TdThickness   =   3
   Top           =   2280
   Width         =   372

SSPanel Panel3D2
   AutoSize      =   3   'AutoSize Child To Panel
   BevelWidth    =   2
   Height        =   252
   Left          =   4560
   Top           =   2040
   Width         =   852

CommandButton ShowIcon
      Caption       =   "Load"
      FontName      =   "Lucida Sans"
      FontSize      =   7.8
      Height        =   204
      Left          =   24
```

```
        Top             =    24
        Width           =    804

SSPanel Panel3D1
    AutoSize            =    3   'AutoSize Child To Panel
    BevelWidth          =    2
    Height              =    372
    Left                =    3600
    Top                 =    2760
    Width               =    1812

  CommandButton Activator
        Caption         =    "Activate"
        FontName        =    "Lucida Sans"
        FontSize        =    7.8
        Height          =    324
        Left            =    24
        Top             =    24
        Width           =    1764

TextBox Selection
    FontName            =    "Lucida Sans"
    FontSize            =    7.8
    Height              =    264
    Index               =    0
    Left                =    1440
    TabIndex            =    2
    Top                 =    1920
    Width               =    1452

TextBox Selection
    Index               =    1
    Top                 =    2160

TextBox Selection
    Index               =    2
    Top                 =    2400

TextBox Selection
    Index               =    3
    Top                 =    2640
```

continues

Listing 8.1. continued

```
TextBox Selection
    Index          =    4
    Top            =    2880

TextBox Message
    FontName       =    "Lucida Sans"
    FontSize       =    9.6
    Height         =    1332
    Left           =    1440
    MultiLine      =    -1   'True
    TabIndex       =    0
    Top            =    360
    Width          =    3972

Label Buttons
    BorderStyle    =    1   'Fixed Single
    FontName       =    "Lucida Sans"
    FontSize       =    13.8
    Height         =    372
    Left           =    960
    TabIndex       =    13
    Top            =    2280
    Width          =    372

Label Label2
    Alignment      =    1   'Right Justify
    Caption        =    "Icon"
    FontName       =    "Lucida Sans"
    FontSize       =    7.8

Label Label3
    Caption        =    "Selections"

Label Label1
    Caption        =    "Message"
```

The Sub Form_Load () procedure handles the initial settings for a three-button dialog:

```
Sub Form_Load ()
NumButtons = 3
Buttons.Caption = "3"
End Sub
```

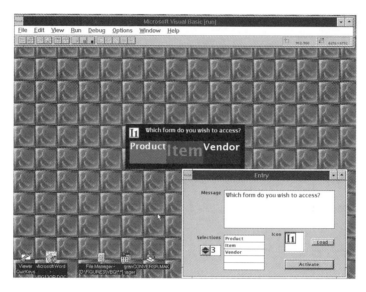

Figure 8.3. Pre-seeding the conversation.

The Load button once again employs the common dialog control for loading a picture in any of the formats handled by the LoadPicture() statement (yet another strange permutation of a supposedly standardized language syntax).

```
Sub ShowIcon_Click ()
On Error GoTo cancl
Selector.DefaultExt = "*.bmp"
Selector.DialogTitle = "Open Icon/Bitmap"
flt$ = "Icon files (*.ico)¦*.ico¦Bitmap files (*.bmp)¦*.ico¦
➥   Metafiles (*.wmf)¦*.wmf"
Selector.Filter = flt$
Selector.FilterIndex = 1
Selector.Flags = OFN_FILEMUSTEXIST Or OFN_HIDEREADONLY
➥   Or OFN_PATHMUSTEXIST
```

```
Selector.Action = 1
On Error GoTo 0
IcFN = Selector.Filename
IconShow.Picture = LoadPicture(IcFN)
Exit Sub
cancl:
On Error GoTo 0
MsgBox "No file is opened.", 48
Resume downhere
downhere:
End Sub
```

By now, you're probably familiar with the set-up pattern of instructions for invoking a standard Windows file selector box. In this instance, the three constants joined together with the logical Or for the Selector.Flags setting are declared within the global module, as follows:

```
Global Const OFN_HIDEREADONLY = &H4&
Global Const OFN_FILEMUSTEXIST = &H1000&
Global Const OFN_PATHMUSTEXIST = &H800&
```

The procedures for the _SpinUp and _SpinDown events are actually quite simple:

```
Sub ButtonsSpin_SpinDown ()
If NumButtons > 1 Then
    NumButtons = NumButtons - 1
End If
Buttons.Caption = LTrim$(Str$(NumButtons))
End Sub

Sub ButtonsSpin_SpinUp ()
If NumButtons < 5 Then
    NumButtons = NumButtons + 1
End If
Buttons.Caption = LTrim$(Str$(NumButtons))
End Sub
```

The message for the dialog box sets itself as it's being typed, with a single instruction:

```
Sub Message_Change ()
msg$ = Message.Text
End Sub
```

Finally, here's the procedure that initiates the dialog box:

```
Sub Activator_Click ()
Converser.Show
End Sub
```

From Dialog Box to Input Box in Minutes

Now, if the purpose of the dialog box is also to elicit a bit of text from the user, it isn't too difficult to attach a text line at the bottom of the Converser dialog box. There isn't a `.TextWidth()` function for finding the proper point size for a text box, so I had to devise proper proportions for the text box size and thus contained `.FontSize` through trial-and-error. The resulting modified "engine" procedure follows:

```
Sub Form_Load ()
If IcFN = "" Then
    Message.Left = 150
    mwid = Message.TextWidth(msg$)
Else
    Message.Left = 720
    ConvIcon.Picture = LoadPicture(IcFN)
    mwid = Message.TextWidth(msg$) + 570
End If
Message.Width = mwid
Converser.Width = mwid + 300
Message.Top = 100
Response.Left = 150
Response.Width = mwid
rht = Int(mwid / 14)
Response.Height = Int(rht / 1.8)
Response.FontSize = Int(rht / 10)
wdb = Int(mwid / NumButtons)
bcount = 150
For setb = 0 To NumButtons - 1
    Feedback(setb).Width = wdb
    Feedback(setb).Left = bcount
    Feedback(setb).Top = 600
    bcount = bcount + wdb
```

```
Next setb
If NumButtons < 5 Then
    For rest = setb To 5
        Feedback(setb).Visible = False
        Feedback(setb).Enabled = False
    Next rest
End If
For btn = 0 To NumButtons - 1
    For fnt = 36 To 4 Step -1
        Feedback(btn).FontSize = fnt
        wid = Feedback(btn).TextWidth(button$(btn))
        If wid <= Feedback(btn).Width Then Exit For
    Next fnt
    mm = Feedback(btn).TextHeight(button$(btn))
    If mm > mht Then
        mht = mm
    End If
Next btn
For btn = 0 To NumButtons - 1
    Feedback(btn).Height = Int(mht * 1.25)
Next btn
Response.Top = 600 + Int(mht * 1.25)
Converser.Height = Message.Height + rht + Feedback(0).Height
➥   + Response.Height
sh = Screen.Height
sw = Screen.Width
ft = Int((sh / 2) - (Converser.Height / 2))
fl = Int((sw / 2) - (Converser.Width / 2))
Converser.Top = ft
Converser.Left = fl
Message.Print msg$
For btn = 0 To NumButtons - 1
    Feedback(btn).Print button$(btn)
Next btn
Converser.Show
Response.SetFocus
End Sub
```

The text box is called Response, and at the beginning, it is set flush with the left margin 150 twips from the left edge of the form. It extends the full length of the form. The font point size "weights" were determined by testing values, redisplaying the dialog, and making adjustments on the fly. After the button regions are set, the .Top of the response box is set just beneath the buttons. An example of a Converser II dialog appears in Figure 8.4.

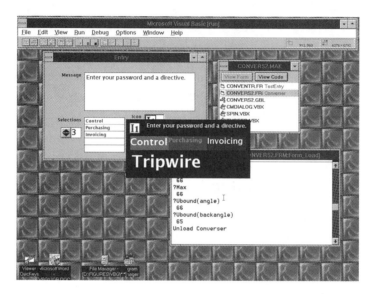

Figure 8.4. One step closer to becoming conversational.

The contents of Response.Text, after one of the Feedback() buttons is clicked, are assigned to the global variable ConvRWord.

Although the appearance of the Converser dialog forms are radically different in their execution, the basis for their structure is essentially a dialog box. What makes a dialog familiar to users is the presence of OK and Cancel and other such staples. Perhaps if the general arrangement of the dialog is maintained, the user will be able to readily discern its purpose when it appears, without saying "Huh?" The objective of the Converser is to add a little "Ah!" to the usage model of Visual Basic applications.

The Front Ends of Utility Programs

Originally, I intended to make the Expressor a programmable calculator, to the extent that it would not only memorize the sequence of keys necessary to solve a formula, but also the textual descriptions of the parameters in their slots. The resulting memorized "program" would be one step above a macro and one step below a symbolic language. Many programmable calculators I've used feature conditional execution functions. To accomplish that, however, the various "steps" of the program have to be numbered so the program might know where to branch, and spending too much time symbolizing "steps" would be too taxing for a calculator whose main job is to solve formulas.

Situation #2: The Expressor Mark III Calculator

Figure 8.5 depicts the Expressor after its face-lift for the Mark III edition, and next to it is the Mark II counterpart. Obviously, I went all out—nearly overboard—with Sheridan's 3D Panel control. Before its advent, I had been experimenting with placing command buttons within modified picture boxes in an attempt to give them some extra life.

What makes a utility program such as the Expressor structurally unique is that its usage model demands nearly all the program's functionality be made available to the user up front. There is no backing in and out of modules, because this is supposed to be a calculator. The graph and chart modules are exceptions, but mostly because they require so much screen space to work properly.

Forgive me if I ask you to check the enclosed disk to see in detail how the various graphics objects and properties were set for this form. I generated a textual listing of the form's contents using Visual Basic 2's new text-based form generator, and the property settings alone would consume 65 pages in this book, by my estimation—a few less, perhaps, when edited down and when the layout department decides to use five-point text, although nonetheless gargantuan. I figured it would be the most boring reading since the Hite Report, so I left it out.

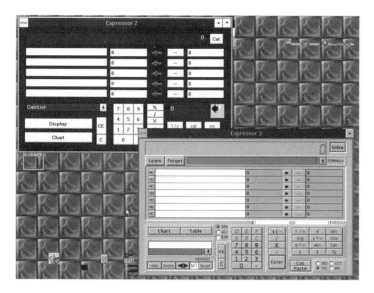

Figure 8.5. The Sams' Visual Basic make-over.

Allow me instead to describe for you in summary how I approached the task of revamping the appearance of this application. The new numeric readout uses an Adobe Type 1 font called Liquid Crystal. If someone else were to install Expressor Mark III on her system , and she did not have the Liquid Crystal font in Adobe or TrueType formats, the font displayed should default back to MS Sans Serif, which is quite legible and, to some degree, still attractive. The readout is really a label control whose .BackStyle property set to 0 - Transparent. This is so another label could inhabit the same general region as the readout without one label overwriting a portion of another.

I moved what was the Apply Formula button just to the right of the readout; it is now the Solve button. Expressor II had the Cut button at this location. I concluded this was really not the place for it after all, because it would be used, in my estimation, far less often than the Apply Formula/Solve button, and the upper-right corner is a far more visible location. The appearance of a deep-set ridge or "moat" around the Solve button was achieved by setting it within another 3D panel whose .BevelOuter property is set to 1 - Inset and whose .BevelWidth property is 3. Drawing the button within the frame is quite simple, because the frame's .AutoSize property was set in advance to 3 - AutoSize Child to Parent. The button drawn within the frame expands to fit the space.

There are now seven slots in the parameter input bay rather than the original five—for some financial formulas I had been itching to try, five was simply too few. Adjusting the control array indexes in the source code was no problem; where there had been loops that searched through elements `0 To 4`, they now search from `0` to `6`. All of these controls rest within a large 3D panel whose `.BevelOuter` property is set to `1 - Inset` and whose `.BevelWidth` is 3. Recall, the 3D panel works like a standard Visual Basic frame control: controls drawn in the panel's perimeter "belong" to it. When you move the panel, you move its contents. For this reason, to make the existing slot controls fit within the parameter bay (notice what I'm calling it now, rather than "slot area" or something else that sounds like it was devised by the Defense Department). I had to select each one with the mouse and, using the VB main window, select Edit/Cut. For selecting multiple controls, the VB2 environment makes available a "lasso" that the VB1 environment did not have; thus, I can draw a rectangle around them all in one motion. The controls disappear after the cut; then I select the 3D panel and, with its indicator nodes showing, select Edit/Paste. The cut controls appeared in the 3D frame boundary, pushed against its upper-left corner, so I repositioned them manually. I then cloned two more rows of input controls.

I had to duplicate this cut-and-paste procedure for the other sets of buttons in the lower part of the form. The "staircase" effect for the lower sections was achieved for each panel by setting both its `.BevelInner` and `.BevelOuter` properties to `2 - Raised`, its `.BevelWidth` property to 1, and its `.BorderWidth` to 3. The digit and function keys are all standard VB command buttons, though in order to give them a more cubic, less rounded look, I set these buttons' `.BackColor` properties to a dark blue. Normally, the command buttons aren't affected by color property settings even though they have color property settings; but believe it or not, the individual pixels along the four corners of a VB command button are susceptible to color settings (for what they're worth). I replaced the picture boxes for the `StoreBank()` control array with buttons whose text is set using the Lucida Arrows font. The Lucida series of fonts, by the way, is included with Microsoft's first TrueType Fonts collection package.

Astute observers will easily identify a Macintosh application by its use of the "Chicago" font; in my opinion, Lucida should become the identifying font set for Windows. It offers a simple, understated appearance without sacrificing prestige. Its implementation as a TrueType font makes it a screen font that maintains its well weighted structure and clarity even at the smallest sizes.

The Paste button in the Expressor Mark III panel now joins the Cut button at the bottom, just to the left of the new option settings for the numeric base. The bevel settings here are 1 - Inset, primarily to help the dimensional effect. The newest and perhaps most interesting control is the labeled memory device at the lower-left corner. This device remembers not only values but also an element of text that describes these values; so not only does it remember values arrived at through calculation, but also the constants so important to scientific calculations, from the value of pi to Planck's Constant. The user can either type a figure directly into the memory field—the white text box atop the list box—or press the Add button. Removing a value from the memory list is done with the Delete button. The Recall button places the value from the list into the display.

Sending a memory value into one of the parameters in the bay is accomplished by selecting the bay number with the new spin control. This spinner is a custom control supplied to the VB application by way of the file SPIN.VBX. The text field next to the spinner will read from "M1" to "M7," denoting the slots which are now numbered in the parameter bay. The spinner only sets the slot destination for the memory constant; clicking the text field sends the constant currently displayed in the memory box into the parameter bay.

The spin control was one of the missing elements of the original Visual Basic interpreter environment, quickly filled by the Professional Toolkit and extended into the Professional Edition of Visual Basic 2.

Technique Capsule: The Spinner Control

Definition: Many standard Windows dialogs and application windows contain a spinner device that enables the user to set a numeric value contained in a text box without reaching for the keyboard. The spinner implies the presence of a *range* of values that is represented by the text field attached to the spinner.

The spin control is supplied to Visual Basic 2 Professional Edition by way of the custom control file SPIN.VBX . On its own, the control changes no numeric values and represents no value of its own as does a scroll bar. The spin control does not have a text box attached to it; the programmer is trusted to supply one for it, if the spinner is to be used in the conventional fashion.

Execution: The spin control is really a command button divided into two halves. By default, these are an upper and a lower half. However, by setting the control's .SpinOrientation property to 1 - Horizontal, the button may be divided into a left and a right half. The button is drawn into the VB form like a standard command button. By default, the spinner has no beveling whatsoever; it may be given a variable amount of beveling by setting its .TdThickness property. A setting of 2 gives the control an apparently even status with standard Visual Basic command buttons.

There are only four events attributed to the spin control. The _SpinUp and _SpinDown events replace the _Click event for a command button. When the .SpinOrientation is horizontal, "up" is left and "down" is right. The control also recognizes the standard _DragOver and _DragDrop events. If the spinner is to manipulate a text box, the instructions governing the contents of that text box must be supplied manually within the spinner's event procedures.

Example: A spin control is being used to set a saturation percentage. The spinner is given a .Name of SaturChange, and a text box placed just to the right is given a .Name of Saturation. For registering a change in the saturation whenever the spinner is moved up, the following event procedure would be needed:

```
Sub Saturation_SpinUp ()
    satur% = satur% + 1
    Saturation.Text = Val(satur%)
End Sub
```

The _SpinDown event procedure would read the same, except the + in the second line would be a - instead.

Cautions: No _GotFocus or _LostFocus events are maintained for the spin control; so if operating the spinner is supposed to have an echo effect on some element in the active form other than a text box, the instructions for that echo will need to be described in both the _SpinUp and _SpinDown procedures in an identical fashion. Also, the spinner maintains no .Value property of its own as does a slider bar. The spinner is therefore a less versatile control, mechanically speaking, than the slider bar, although the spinner does fit into tighter spaces.

When "Easy" and "Self-Evident" Differ

I doubt, with the number of features the Expressor is capable of performing now, that a new user is going to be able to sit down to this panel and make sense of it immediately. In large part, I've violated many of the rules of ease-of-use in conceiving a process model for this utility.

Recall, however, the first time you held a Texas Instruments or Hewlett-Packard programmable calculator: were you able to glean the major points of its operation just from looking at it? Picture in your mind the buttons with labels on their faces, as well as two different colors of labels printed just above each one. Picture such old standbys as the 8 key labeled twice, even three times. Remember the 1970s model HPs that stored their programs on magnetic tape cards that were read into the calculator like a credit card validator? Did you know how to use those things when you first saw them? When you finally prepared the program for the A key, the B key, and the C key, were you able to remember which letter key stood for what program?

Granted, the fact that programmable calculators are, by nature, difficult to use is no excuse to make their simulated counterparts in computing just as difficult. Yet for certain utility programs, there comes a point in time when constantly focusing on being easily graspable to the first-time user should be tabled for the nonce, in favor of establishing a usage model that may eventually become familiar to the user. Familiarity breeds comfort, and with comfort comes, eventually, ease-of-use.

The newcomer will probably not instantly grasp the concepts of operating Expressor III's parameter bay. In fact, I'd accept it if someone told me it was confusing. This utility, however, is an example of a program in which familiarity is the key to efficient operation. It's difficult for me to understand some people's explanations through the years about why WordPerfect for DOS is such an easy program for them to use. From my perspective, memorizing five or six different purposes for 12 function keys whose numbers have no logical, numerological, syntactic, symbological, or superficial relationship to the functions which they're assigned to represent is a waste of human activity. From many user's perspectives, however, WordPerfect for DOS has become a familiar program. They like it because they *know* it. They refuse to upgrade to even WordPerfect for Windows merely because it looks different.

The Front Page

What makes graphical applications amiable for those users who have taken the plunge, is partly that geometry and symbology play such a great role in the applications' presentation. People remember where things are located in a picture easier, on the whole, than they remember words or, more complicated yet, abbreviations.

Layout has become as important a principle to computing as it is to publishing. The layout of newspapers such as *The Wall Street Journal* and *USA Today,* and of newsmagazines such as *Time,* have undergone alterations throughout their history, but they have managed to remain well regulated. Issue after issue, you know your way around the publication as though it were a familiar office you stop by each day. When the decor changes, for a few issues the publication is a bit unfamiliar; but if the new layout is well designed, easy to navigate, and balanced, it becomes just as comfortable as before.

At the time of this writing, one of the major complaints among programmers of graphical applications is that icons have become such a tool of marketing that manufacturers will add them to their programs in abundance even if the icons clutter the screen with unnecessary functionality. As these programmers search for principles to guide them in designing usage models for their applications, a related set of principles exists and thrives today, and it is in use in the layout departments of news publishers. Although it is the job of writers to make their copy concise and easy to read, the layout department gives the copy you read something of a *voice,* if you will. It gives flavor to the text that is missing when it is not being read aloud.

Until a standard for sound is established and voice becomes an essential element in computing, we programmers must rely on a blend of artistry and conservatism in layout to give our applications a voice—some measure of inflection, rhyme, and meter. A standardized voice is about as memorable as a particular choirboy you may have heard once in a cathedral. Don't let any book of standards convince you that style is an unimportant issue in computing. Style is as important to a program as it is to this book. As an artist, I suppose, I can't easily brush the issue of style aside.

Because *ease-of-use* is defined so many ways these days, put that word out of your mind for a moment. A reader of a publication expects continuity, concise presentation, and a conservative appearance that does not bombard the eyes with loud text, screaming headers, and stupid graphical embellishments that patronize the reader, bringing back memories of alphabet primers. When considering how to present your application to the user, your best course of action may be to import these principles to computing—perhaps through a cut-and-paste.

ENGINEERING ORIGINAL DEVICES

Visual Basic deals primarily with rectangular controls, but not all real-world objects users are familiar with as control devices are necessarily rectangular. Those who study ergonomics—the way things are situated within a work environment—can attest that people want control devices that are round and streamlined. They learned people around the world had grown tired of driving square cars; so automotive manufacturers immediately began designing cars that were anything but square—regardless of whether they were functional.

9

Housing architects tried to escape the trap of squareness by setting some rooms at odd angles with respect to other rooms; still, this escape from the norm tends to be interesting only in the blueprints. From the inside, an occupant of the fully-constructed room has difficulty discerning at what angle the square box he inhabits is tipped with respect to the world; he tends only to realize he inhabits another box.

This, philosophically speaking, is the current problem plaguing the operation of modern computer programs. Programmers try to reconcile user boredom with computer operation by making what appears, from the programmers' standpoint, to be sweeping alterations to the program's architecture. These alterations might be intriguing and even beautiful from the point of view of other programmers, but in many cases, the users of these programs simply cannot be expected to recognize such admittedly esoteric changes, especially when all they're trying to do is keep their business alive.

When New Is Not Improved

Although there appears to be some recent reversal of this trend, ever since the advent of Microsoft Windows 3.0, major DOS-based software packages have been reconstructed and recompiled to run on the Windows platform. With each upgrade announcement, industry observers are reportedly thrilled that a Windows application can be made to work so much like a DOS application, giving users an assumed (or alleged) easy upgrade path into the Windows environment. As a software systems consultant (read: part-time salesman), I have conveyed the happy message to clients that their favorite brands are alive and well and living on the new platform.

Upon further reflection, I realized that making such advancements in program architecture would be similar to making CD players downwardly-compatible with 8-track tapes. As maligned as the latter format has become today, and although the statistics clearly prove that 8-track sound quality was indeed an oxymoron, you cannot ignore that the format was popular at a time in which more capable formats were simultaneously available. Certainly the compact disk has fine-tuned the sound quality of recorded music, and perhaps in so doing improved the listening capacity of the next generation of human ears. Yet since the advent of the CD, has the quality of recorded music become better as well? Or has the old music just been upgraded to the new format?

The way to improve the quality of microcomputer applications as micro-computers themselves continue to improve is to make the control mechanism of these applications more realistic and less esoteric. A new user should be able to perceive and grasp a new control as though it were an object she could hold in her hand. Visual Basic is the perfect test bed for modeling new forms of program-control devices, because it executes code relatively fast, and the code itself is relatively simple for describing the construction and use of new logical devices.

Situation #3: The Rotational Clip-Art Generator

As an example of a more realistic model control device, look at the compass device from Situation #3, the rotational graphic unit generator. The device appears to "turn on" whenever the pointer enters the area of the outermost circle—notice roundness plays an important role in this control. The red cross-hatch becomes visible, following the mouse pointer as it traverses the control. Below, the angle and radius currently depicted by the compass is registered numerically. When the user presses the mouse button, the compass is locked; the red crosshatch is frozen in place. The pointer is now free to exit the area of the compass without disturbing the current measurement.

The compass device is one example of a customized control, created strictly through the use of conventional Visual Basic tools. Visual Basic contains no provisions for drawing lines or circles within a picture or image box at design time; nonetheless, I used a VB procedure to create the appearance of the compass control. Here is the procedure that generated the compass bitmap:

Using a small VB program to create a control.

```
Sub Form_Load ()
Form1.Show
origx = 750
origy = 750
For radius = 300 To 700 Step 200
    For an = 0 To 360
        Picture1.PSet (radius * Cos(an * (pi / 180)) + origx,
        radius * Sin(an * (pi / 180)) + origy), RGB(0, 0, 0)
    Next an
Next radius
For an = 0 To 360 Step 10
```

```
    Select Case -1
        Case (an / 60 = Int(an / 60))
            rstart = 0
        Case (an / 30 = Int(an / 30))
            rstart = 300
        Case Else
            rstart = 500
        End Select
    Picture1.Line (rstart * Cos(an * (pi / 180)) + origx,
➡ rstart * Sin(an * (pi / 180)) + origy)-
➡ (700 * Cos(an * (pi / 180)) + origx, 700
➡ * Sin(an * (pi / 180)) + origy), RGB(0, 0, 0)
Next an
End Sub
```

Assume the picture box of the compass has a `.Width` of 1500 and a `.Height` of 1500. The center or origin coordinates relative to the box would be expressed as (750, 750), so those coordinates are assigned to variables `origx` and `origy`. Three circles are drawn extending from the origin point; here I used the `.PSet` method rather than the `.Circle` method to ensure the symmetry of the circle. The angle divisions in the circles must be precise; otherwise the control cannot be operated with precision. The radii of the three circles are 300, 500, and 700 twips, as defined by the first loop clause.

The `.PSet` method plots each circle point-by-point, determining the coordinate location of each point using trigonometric functions. The angles most people are accustomed to using are converted to radians for the computer, by multiplying each angle measurement by (pi / 180). In the general declarations area of this form module, the instruction `Const pi = 3.1415927` is invoked so that pi has a constant value throughout the form.

Converting Between Coordinate Representation Systems

To determine the x and y coordinate values for a point expressed in terms of angle and radius, think of x and y as lengths of sides of a right triangle whose hypotenuse is the radius value. An angle is formed extending between the triangle base line at 0 degrees, and the radius line (hypotenuse). The cosine of this angle is equivalent to the value of the length of the adjacent line of the angle, divided by the hypotenuse—in this case, x / radius. You know the value of radius already; so it therefore follows that x / radius * radius = x, or cos(an) * radius = x. The cosine of the angle is then multiplied by the radius value to determine the length of x. Likewise, because the sine of an angle is the measure of the line opposite to the angle divided by the length of the hypotenuse, sin(an) * radius = y, the length of the angle's opposite side. A point can now be plotted to (x, y).

To test whether a number divides into another evenly, you may use a conditional instruction such as If an / 60 = Int(an / 60) Then.... You also might use such comparisons in a Select Case clause, as I did in the preceding example. The hatch lines for the compass extend from a point a specified distance from the center, to a point along the outermost circle at 700 points from the center. If the angle currently being considered is a multiple of 60 degrees, the hatchline extends from the center itself (rstart = 0). If the angle is some other multiple of 30 degrees, the line extends from the first circle outward (rstart = 300); otherwise, it extends from the second circle outward (rstart = 500).

Here's how to make the file COMPASS.BMP for inclusion as the Compass.Picture property of the GRUUM application:

☐ Select New Project from the VB File menu.

☐ Within Form1, create a picture box with .Width and .Height properties set to precisely 1500.

☐ Type into a procedure window the Sub Form_Load () procedure listed earlier.

☐ To run the procedure, click the run button in the Visual Basic toolbar.

☐ After the compass design is fully plotted, click the break button. The Debug Window appears.

☐ Type into the CLI the following line:

```
SavePicture Picture1.Image, "C:\WINDOWS\VBASIC\COMPASS.BMP"
```

You can substitute a more suitable pathname for your computer. You now have a compass control image for the GRUUM application, or for any other program which requires you to click within a round area, regulated by degrees.

Distributing programs for users with variable screen resolutions.

> **Advisory Note:** One of the problems with distributing Visual Basic applications to others is that bitmapped images large enough to fit a picture box on a VGA 640x480 system are too small to fit the same picture box in VGA 1024x768 resolution. This often results in large right and lower margins in picture boxes for higher-resolution machines. If your graphical control relies on a bitmap, you might want to write similar programs that generate proportional bitmaps for differing resolutions, or otherwise draw at least two separate copies of the backdrop. The proportion for standard 640x480 bitmaps to standard 800x600 and 1024x768 bitmaps is 3:4.

The previous procedure solves this problem as far as the GRUUM compass is concerned; within any VGA system, it generates a compass large enough to fit the picture box at that particular resolution. After I had a conditional clause load the new, larger bitmap for higher resolutions, though, I found I had to reprogram the compass control handler itself for the new proportions. The center of the circle had actually moved down and to the right. Determining the angle/ coefficient parameters for the current position of the mouse pointer at any time relied entirely on the location of the center of the circle.

The original distance determination in `Sub Compass_MouseMove ()`, for example, looked like this:

```
dist = Sqr(((600 - x) ^ 2) + (600 - y) ^ 2)
```

The height and width of the original bitmap I generated were both 1200 twips because I used to work in 640x480 resolution before moving to 1024x768. The bitmap for the high-resolution version of the form, COMPASS2.BMP, has a height and width of 1500 twips; so I modified the formula to read:

```
dist = Sqr(((750 - x) ^ 2) + (750 - y) ^ 2)
```

I made similar adjustments throughout the application, though I admittedly had not gotten around to implementing a system for having the program adjust these figures itself. Conceivably, I could declare a global variable `Proportion`, and set a value for it in the crucial conditional clause in `Sub Form_Load ()`:

```
If Screen.Height <= 7000 Then
    Compass.Picture = LoadPicture("d:\vbasic\dfs\compass.bmp")
    Proportion = 600
```

```
Else
    Compass.Picture = LoadPicture("d:\vbasic\dfs\compassb.bmp")
    Proportion = 750
End If
```

I could then adjust the distance-finding formula to read:

```
dist = Sqr(((Proportion - x) ^ 2) + (Proportion - y) ^ 2)
```

Hard-Wiring a Button Bank

The set of buttons for a calculator might not appear to the user to be a very original device. Beneath the surface, however, when the duties performed by the buttons have to be shared, the procedures for these buttons must coalesce. In effect, you don't have a set of individuated graphic objects, but rather one large object divided into touch-sensitive segments.

Situation #2: The Expressor Mark III Calculator

From the beginning of the project, it was my intention to make the Expressor a programmable calculator. For this to work, the application must maintain some system for memorizing which buttons were pressed in sequence. The first problem I faced was the fact that nearly every button on the calculator panel, with the exception of the positive digit buttons, had its own _Click event procedure with independent contexts. If I were to invent an instruction that placed some sort of button-identifying tag into an array in memory, I would need to invoke that instruction in each _Click event procedure.

Here is my original plan for how the utility would memorize its own programs:

☐ A global array is established that gives an arbitrary value to each button that can be programmable.

☐ A second global array is established to hold the program being learned by the Expressor, as well as the program being executed.

☐ Each button's _Click procedure loads into the program a value equivalent to the pattern established in the first global array. The program is then saved to disk as a sequential-access data file with its own unique filename.

☐ When executing a memorized program, dialing the program from the formula selector calls the unique data file name from disk.

☐ Clicking the Solve button makes the `Sub Solve_Click ()` procedure the nerve center for the calculator's internal program execution. Using a large `Select Case` clause, each value in the sequential access file is evaluated, and for each `Case` of its value, the `_Click` event procedure that normally is executed on pressing a panel button, is executed now.

This particular usage model would not be too difficult for me as a programmer to implement, provided I enjoyed the job of cutting-and-pasting the button-value assignment instruction between all the `_Click` event procedures. One of the problems with working in Visual Basic, in comparison with working in earlier editions of BASIC, is that the narrowing of a programmer's perspective for a module to one procedure at a time shields the programmer from possibly seeing the redundancies in the program. Writing an old BASIC program is a process of assembling one large module where absolutely every element is combined into a single body. This may make it more difficult for the programmer to define primary and peripheral contexts, but it at least helps the programmer notice when he's becoming too repetitious. If I copied the same numeral-assignment instructions to all the vital `_Click` procedures in the Expressor application, I would be routing the exact same physical process through any one of several possible directions, which would be unthinkable for a programmer of old BASIC.

Tightening the usage model through the use of a control array.

In the original usage model I had planned for Mark III of the Expressor, each button in the calculator panel would retain its own `_Click` event procedure, as it had in Mark II. Each native procedure would then place a call to a general procedure that would record the event as an entry into the calculator program. In the usage model I later opted for, each programmable button in the calculator panel became enrolled within a collective control array `Button()`, to which a single event procedure is attributed. Notice the reduction in overall bulk; the newer model performs the same overall job with a lesser investment in source code. Here is how the Expressor's programmability works now:

☐ A `Type` structure is declared in the general module describing the sequence of buttons necessary to execute the program (as many as 100), along with the seven parameters and their descriptions.

☐ Every button on the panel that can be part of the calculator program is redrawn as part of a control array, affectionately entitled Button(). One procedure is used rather than close to 38 for enlisting the button pressed into the roll of the program. The identifier for each button is, naturally, its .Index in the control array.

☐ A set of Select Case clauses is used, following the memorization of the button just pressed, to route the process to the unique handling routines for each button. In effect, all the programmable buttons check in for inspection at Sub Button_Click () before moving on to their assigned duties.

The division of responsibilities in the application has been modified only slightly. The majority of the calculation features still are allocated to EXPRSOR3.FRM, the module for the Panel form. The previously existing set of Function procedures for solving general formulas created for EXPRSOR2.BAS remain in EXPRSOR3.BAS, the single general module which also contains the global declarations along with the Type clause explaining the variable structure for memorized programs. The form module can place calls to the procedures in the general module, but not vice versa. Procedures that address the visible contents of more than one form have been entered into the general module, however, with the object name references extended so that when an instruction addresses a graphic object, the interpreter knows which form is its source. A new form module has been added for displaying data tables in the manner of a spreadsheet; that module is examined later.

So you don't find yourself flipping back through pages earlier in the book, here's another view of the Expressor III form in its completed state, with important elements pointed out.

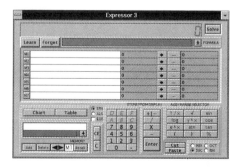

Figure 9.1. The anatomy of Expressor III.

Concentrating now on the modifications to the form module in the order in which they were made, here are the current global and form-level variable declarations for Expressor III:

Listing 9.1. EXPRSOR3.BAS General Declarations.

```
'
'¦ Expressor Mark III                                          ¦
'¦    by D. F. Scott for Sams' Visual Basic Developers' Guide ¦
'¦_____¦
'
Global xmin As Single, xmax As Single
Global ymin As Single, ymax As Single
Global xslot As Integer, yslot As Integer
Global norows As Integer, nocolumns As Integer
Global p(7) As Double
Global frmula As Integer
Global maxlen(500) As Integer
Global noconsts As Integer
Global convBase As Integer, convValue As Double
Global title$, xaxis$, yaxis$
Global learnmode As Integer, formulanow As Integer, formulaplace
➥ As Integer
Global partition As Integer, nofms As Integer

Type Memory
    Constant As Double
    title As String
End Type
Type Formula
    title As String * 128           '128
    length As Integer              '  2
    setting As Integer             '  2
    Pattern(100) As Integer        '200
    Variable(6) As Double          ' 56
    VariableName(6) As String * 128 '896
    VariableAxis(6) As Integer     ' 14
    VariableTo(6) As Double        ' 56
End Type
    'add                             2
    'record length is..................1356
Global mem(1000) As Memory
Global fn(1000) As Formula
```

```
Global Const PI = 3.1415927
Global Const GRAV = .000000000066732     'gravitational constant
Global Const gracc = 9.80665       'acceleration of free fall
                                   ' in m/s^-2

Dim xi(50) As Single, yi(50) As Single, xln(50) As Single,
➥  yln(50) As Single
Dim charty(1000)

'File Open/Save Dialog Flags
Global Const OFN_OVERWRITEPROMPT = &H2&
Global Const OFN_HIDEREADONLY = &H4&
Global Const OFN_PATHMUSTEXIST = &H800&
Global Const OFN_FILEMUSTEXIST = &H1000&
```

The new table display module solves for two different axis ranges, between xmin and xmax (the same variables used for the chart module) and ymin and ymax for the y axis of the table. The variables that point to the range slots in the parameter bay, for both the chart and table form modules, are xslot and yslot. Assume, for instance, the user wants to see solutions for a formula describing the amount of energy needed for a ballistic missile to escape the earth's atmosphere. The entry parameters in the bay are the the deadweight tonnage of the missile, the amount of propellant expended in cubic centimeters per second, and the initial trajectory of the missile from the launch point. Using the x/y chart, the user can see a plot depicting the variance in solutions for a range of values along the x axis only. The charting mechanism, you may remember, automatically determines the minimum and maximum values for the chart. So the user chooses an x-slot that represents the x axis—say, the variance in solution values for the formula for all possible initial trajectories ranging between the value in the left bank and the value in the right bank.

Using the table form, however, the user can see a scrollable listing of solutions for all possible trajectories ranging from the left bank to the right bank value for the x axis of the table, as well as solutions for several different tonnages ranging between a value in the left bank and a value in the right, for the y axis of the table. The global variables norows and nocolumns keep track of the cell dimensions of the table.

The p() array is one of the earliest in the project's existence; it still holds the values of variables in the left bank of the parameter bay. The values are used to solve for one value only with a solution in the standard readout. The variable `frmula` still contains the index number for the formula currently registered in the formula selector. The `maxlen()` array, as you'll see soon, helps determine the column width for values appearing in the table form.

For the new listable memory system, the variable `noconsts` contains the number of elements currently in memory. The memory file is saved to disk continually, so whenever the Expressor is started up again, its main body of constants and vital values is still remembered. The variables `convBase` and `convValue` are reserved for the numeric base conversion formulas, so the user can convert among decimal, hexadecimal, octal, and binary values.

The `title$`, `xaxis$`, and `yaxis$` contents consist of labels taken from the panel parameter bay and transferred to the chart and table modules. The variable `learnmode` is a flag denoting whether the calculator is memorizing the buttons being pressed, whereas `formulanow` maintains the number of the formula being learned and `formulaplace` maintains the index number of the button being memorized. The variable `partition` contains the first formula number in the list that is actually an Expressor program; those in the list before it are the old hard-coded formulas. Finally, `nofms` contains the total number of memorized (not hard-coded) formulas currently memorized.

As for the `Type` structure for elements of memory, all that needs to be considered is the `title` for each constant and its value. For the formula structure, each memorized formula is given a title, a total `length` of buttons memorized, and a setting for whether the calculator is in Reverse Polish or algebraic (T.I.) notation. The buttons are stored in the `pattern()` array, dimensioned for as many as 100 units. The parameters memorized from the bay are stored in `Variable()`, with each parameter title in `VariableName()`, the settings for range values in `VariableAxis()`, and the range (right bank) parameters in `VariableTo()`. As many as 1,000 constants can be memorized in `mem()`, and 1,000 formulas in `fn()`.

The final portion of the declarations section for EXPRSOR3.BAS contains non-global `Dim` declarations for values pertaining to charting and an array `charty()` used by the chart module for the returned values of formulas along the x axis.

Just when you thought you'd seen enough variables, Listing 9.2 contains the form-level declarations for the Panel.

Listing 9.2. EXPRSOR3.FRM General Declarations.

```
Dim label$(1000, 6)
Dim point_lock As Integer, function_on As Integer
Dim readout_value As Double, combine_value As Double
Dim ready As Integer
Dim solution As Single
Dim oldbase As Integer
Dim cformat$
Dim rpnalg As Integer, lastbutton As Integer, execbutton
➥ As Integer
Dim ParenHold(100) As Double, FunctionPrior(100) As Integer,
➥ ParenPlace As Integer
Dim memspin As Integer
Dim learnfmla(100) As Integer
```

At the form level, the label$() array contains the textual descriptions for all formulas, whether they are hard-coded or memorized. You might remember the point_lock flag variable from the very first Mark I edition of the program; its new counterpart, function_on, is somewhat similar; it holds the true/false state of an ongoing multibutton function. If it takes more than one button to register a function, and just the first few have been entered, function_on registers True.

The variable ready denotes the active state of digits in the calculator readout, whereas solution contains the individual answer to one formula in the readout, in the standard calculator mode. In converting a value in the readout from one numeric base to another, oldbase keeps track of what numeric base the number was originally entered in, or last converted. The semi-constant cformat$ contains a format descriptor depicting how the total should appear in the readout, in case the user is figuring in dollars and cents and does not wish to see the zero in "80 cents" dropped off.

The new Mark III version of the Expressor will be able to operate in both Reverse Polish and algebraic notation. Adaptation to the latter format requires the calculator engine to remember which function was entered previous to the one being entered now. You may remember, the calculation engine needs to be able to think one step behind itself in order for the user to be able to enter functions in the order in which they would appear on paper. When you enter 2 × 3 + 6 = in algebraic notation, the multiplication operation does not take place

Implementing two systems of calculator notation.

when the user presses ×, but instead when she presses +—the calculator recalls the previous function entered. In Reverse Polish notation, the same formula would be entered as 2 [Enter] 3 × 6 [Enter] (the [Enter] button doubles as a plus button). The user of the calculator has to think a little backwards, but the calculator performs the functions at the time they're entered; so the notation isn't reverse from the machine's point of view.

On the lower part of the calculator panel is a pair of option dots for setting the notation for the calculator's operation. The current state of this setting is held in the variable rpnalg. When algebraic notation is turned on, lastbutton contains the index number of the previous function, so that its native _Click event procedure is executed whenever the next function button is pressed, and execbutton holds the index number of the current function button—the one pressed following lastbutton. One of the side benefits of using a collective button-handling procedure is that only one set of instructions is needed to re-member and recall the previous function button setting.

Implementing parenthetical function processing.

The next three variables pertain to a system that took me about three days of hard work to fully debug. The parentheses buttons are used to create subformulas within the current formula, and are necessary in financial equa-tions where fractions are raised to powers. When the user presses the left pa-renthesis, the status of the current formula is saved. The ParenHold() array holds the subtotal value in the readout at the time the left parenthesis was pressed. If algebraic notation is active, the FunctionPrior() array holds the last function button pressed, so that it can activate that function during the next function button following the right parenthesis. The variable ParenPlace keeps track of how many parenthetical formulas are currently active.

The variable memspin holds the name of the parameter that receives the current contents of the memory list. Finally, the variable learnfmla() contains the program currently being learned. I realized I needed this array late in the program's development, when it occurred to me that writing the formula to disk required each element to be written to the composite variable all at once. The complete array describing the program had to be in place in order for the learning process to work efficiently.

At long last, you've reached the Sub Form_Load () procedure. Since you've already seen the initial loading of the hard-wired formula parameters from Expressor II, I've placed ellipses in place of the two long lists. What's impor-tant here is the setup process toward the end of the procedure:

```
Sub Form_Load ()
On Error GoTo NoFile1
Load Chart
Load Table
CalcList.AddItem "Surface Area of RC Cylinder"
    .
    .
    .
label$(0, 0) = "Radius of right circular cylinder"
label$(0, 1) = "Height of cylinder"
    .
    .
    .
formulanow = 12
partition = formulanow
'***** A reminder to the programmer:  If any new formulas are
'   to be added to the source code rather than to the learned
'   formula list, the value of variable _formulanow_ above
'   should be incremented with each function added.   -DFS
xslot = -1
yslot = -1
oldbase = 10
lastbutton = -1
memspin = 1
MemSlot.Caption = "M" + LTrim$(Str$(memspin))
cformat$ = "###################.00"
Panel.Show
Button(17).SetFocus
Open "exprcnst.dat" For Input As #1
Input #1, noconsts
For loadlist = 0 To noconsts - 1
    Input #1, mem(loadlist).Constant
    Input #1, mem(loadlist).Title
Next loadlist
Close #1
GoTo errorskip1
NoFile1:
mem(0).Constant = 3.1415927
mem(0).Title = "Pi"
mem(1).Constant = .000000000066732
mem(1).Title = "Gravitational constant"
```

```
mem(2).Constant = 9.80665
mem(2).Title = "Acceleration of free fall"
noconsts = 3
Open "exprcnst.dat" For Output As #1
Print #1, noconsts
For savelist = 0 To 2
    Print #1, mem(savelist).Constant
    Print #1, mem(savelist).Title
Next savelist
Close #1
On Error GoTo 0
Resume errorskip1
errorskip1:
For dump = 0 To noconsts - 1
    Memory.AddItem mem(dump).Title
Next dump
On Error GoTo nodata
Open "exprfmla.dat" For Random As #2 Len = 1356
Get #2, 1, nofms
If nofms = 0 Then GoTo errorskip2
For acquire = 1 To nofms
    Get #2, acquire + 1, fn(acquire)
    CalcList.AddItem fn(acquire).Title
    For layin = 0 To 6
        label$(acquire + partition, layin) =
        fn(acquire).VariableName$(layin)
    Next layin
Next acquire
formulanow = formulanow + nofms
Close #2
Exit Sub
nodata:
nada% = 0
Put #2, 1, nada%
Resume errorskip2:
errorskip2:
Close #2
End Sub
```

I'll pick up the action following the second ellipsis. Variable formulanow, the index number in the formula list where the next learned formula is placed, is set initially to 12. The partition is placed here, because the first 12 (0 to 11) formulas are hard-coded. Several values are then initialized as -1; this is not a substitute value for True in this case, but a value meaning "non-active" because the first indexes for both the left and right parameter banks, and of the first programmable button in the panel, are numbered 0. Because zero is the default value of a formally declared variable, a zero might be interpreted as a realistic value.

Later, the program loads into memory the saved memory values from the EXPRCNST.DAT sequential access file. Notice the error-trap routine marked NoFile1:. Should the constant file not exist on the user's system yet, the first three constants are created and saved to disk. Notice also what appears to be an error in routing the branches; at the end of the error trap is the instruction Resume errorskip1, when the mark errorskip1: is immediately below the Resume statement. This is a necessary (although unproductive) state of affairs. The interpreter will still think it's correcting errors if it does not encounter a Resume statement.

The memory constants are stored to disk using the sequential-access scheme, while the formula file is stored using random access. In both files, the first entry contains the number of records in the file; a loop clause counts from 1 to this number. In the case of the fn() structure, declared earlier as having composite type Formula, the loop clause that loads each record into memory also assigns certain elements of that record to the two-dimensional label$ array, so that when the user dials the formula, the labels for the parameter bay can be retrieved instantaneously and displayed. The formulas aren't memorized here, mind you, just the necessary labels. Notice the second error-trap routine in case the formula file EXPRFMLA.DAT does not yet exist; it creates the file for future use, but it saves a zero to the file indicating there are no records in it yet.

You're past the setup stage. At this point, the application is waiting for the user to press a button. As I stated earlier, I reworked the usage model so that all the buttons that are memorizable as part of the calculator program share a single event procedure:

```
Sub Button_Click (Index As Integer)
Button(17).SetFocus
FormulaHistory.Caption = FormulaHistory.Caption +
➥   Button(Index).Tag
If learnmode = True Then
    learnfmla(formulaplace) = Index
    formulaplace = formulaplace + 1
```

```
End If
Select Case True
    Case Index > 34
        MemRecall Index - 35
        Exit Sub
    Case Index > 0 And Index < 10
        ButtonPos Index
        Exit Sub
    Case Index > 9 And Index < 16
        ButtonHex Index
        Exit Sub
    Case Index = 0
        Button0
        Exit Sub
    Case Index = 16
        ButtonPoint
        Exit Sub
End Select
function_on = True
Select Case Index
    Case 22
        PosNeg
    Case 23
        Reciprocal
    Case 24
        Root
    Case 25
        Sine
    Case 26
        Logarithm
    Case 27
        PowerRaise
    Case 28
        Cosine
    Case 29
        NaturalLog
    Case 30
        Arctangent
    Case 31
        Tangent
    Case 32
        ParenLeft
```

```
    Case 33
        ParenRight
    Case 34
        Percent
End Select
If rpnalg = 0 Then
    execbutton = Index
Else
    If Index > 16 And Index < 22 Then
        execbutton = lastbutton
        lastbutton = Index
    Else
        execbutton = Index
    End If
End If
Select Case True
    Case execbutton = 17 And rpnalg = 0
        EnterPlus
    Case execbutton = 18 And rpnalg = 1
        EnterPlus
End Select
Select Case execbutton
    Case -1
        EnterPlus
    Case 19
        Minus
    Case 20
        Times
    Case 21
        DividedBy
End Select
If Index = 17 And rpnalg = 1 Then
    Equals
End If
End Sub
```

For Figure 9.2, I used Sheridan Software's VBAssist program to place the index for each control in the panel form belonging to the Button() array, in the corner of that control.

Notice all the procedures in the Select Case clauses in the previous code. All the _Click event procedures that used to pertain to these buttons in the Button() array have been moved to the general procedures area. This doesn't change their efficiency in any way; it just enables Sub Button_Click () to act as the switchboard for the programmable buttons in the panel.

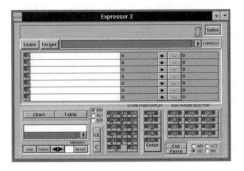

Figure 9.2. The control index map for the Button() array.

The Sub Button_Click () procedure works for all the controls marked on this map. The first ten controls in the array, numbered 0–9, are the 0–9 buttons; the next six are the hexadecimal entry buttons for digits A–F. The first conditional clause in the procedure checks to see whether the button pressed was a digit button, or if one of the new memory recall buttons was pressed. If the index of the button survived the Select Case clause, the button must be a function, and the flag function_on is set to True. At that point, the special mathematical functions are checked. If the index survives that Select Case clause, the button must be a simple arithmetic function.

Here's where the Reverse Polish/algebraic notation detectors kick in. Variable rpnalg represents which notation is in use at the time; if it's set to zero, the procedure assumes you're using RPN. The remainder of the procedure tests a value called execbutton; if RPN is active, its value is set to Index. If the calculator is in algebraic mode, the value of the previous function executed—represented by lastbutton—is given to execbutton, and Index is handed over to lastbutton for when the next arithmetic button is pressed. The algebraic system remembers the last function, and "plays" it when the next one is pressed.

When the Enter button is showing, it is actually covering a plus button. When the user dials algebraic notation, the .Width of the Enter button is halved, and the plus button is revealed. A single procedure Sub EnterPlus () handles the addition process for both notations. A new procedure, Sub Equals (), handles the equals button when algebraic notation is turned on:

```
Sub Equals ()
assess_readout
FormulaHistory.Caption = FormulaHistory.Caption + Readout.Caption
ready = 0
lastbutton = -1
execbutton = -1
point_lock = False
function_on = False
tally
readout_value = 0
combine_value = 0
End Sub
```

As far as arithmetic is concerned, the Sub Equals () procedure does absolutely nothing. It performs the necessary equations for resetting the calculator, making it ready for the next equation. The function that would have been performed has been executed already by the time Sub Equals () starts.

You might be wondering if I ever made use of Sub assess_readout (), the "open hook" procedure I created in Expressor Mark I for when future capabilities might be able to take advantage of it. True to form, I have made use of this procedure. It now handles the process of converting the arithmetic values to and from base 10:

```
Sub assess_readout ()
If function_on = True Then
    Select Case NumBase(1).Value
        Case False
            Select Case True
                Case NumBase(0) = True
                    convBase = 16
                Case NumBase(1) = True
                    convBase = 10
                Case NumBase(2) = True
                    convBase = 8
                Case NumBase(3) = True
                    convBase = 2
            End Select
            send$ = Readout.Caption
            readout_value = ConvertTo10(send$, convBase)
        Case True
            readout_value = Val(Readout.Caption)
```

```
            If CurRound.Value = True Then
                Readout.Caption = Format$(readout_value,
➡            cformat$)
            Else
                Readout.Caption = LTrim$(Str$(readout_value))
            End If
    End Select
End If
End Sub
```

Any values not written in base 10 that will be receiving arithmetic functions are sent to the procedure Function ConvertTo10 () in case the option dot in the numeric base frame is set to False (non-base 10). If the value is base 10, its characters are trimmed in case there are any left spaces in it, and the value is formatted for currency display if the user has checked the box marked "$.00". From time to time, a procedure Sub Tally () is called to reformat the readout value:

```
Sub tally ()
If CurRound.Value = True Then
    Readout.Caption = Format$(readout_value, cformat$)
Else
    Readout.Caption = Str$(readout_value)
End If
End Sub
```

Like all related option dots, the option dots for setting the numeric base are part of a control array.

```
Sub NumBase_Click (Index As Integer, Value As Integer)
display$ = Readout.Caption
Select Case Index
    Case 0
        convBase = 16
        For ndx = 2 To 15
            Button(ndx).Enabled = True
        Next ndx
    Case 1
        convBase = 10
        For ndx = 2 To 9
            Button(ndx).Enabled = True
        Next ndx
        For ndx = 10 To 15
```

```
                Button(ndx).Enabled = False
            Next ndx
        Case 2
            convBase = 8
            For ndx = 2 To 7
                Button(ndx).Enabled = True
            Next ndx
            For ndx = 8 To 15
                Button(ndx).Enabled = False
            Next ndx
        Case 3
            convBase = 2
            For ndx = 2 To 15
                Button(ndx).Enabled = False
            Next ndx
End Select
Select Case True
    Case oldbase = 1 And Index <> 1
        Readout.Caption = ConvertFrom10$(display$, convBase)
    Case oldbase <> 1 And Index = 1
        newvalue = ConvertTo10(display$, oldbase)
        Readout.Caption = Str$(newvalue)
    Case oldbase <> 1 And Index <> 1
        newvalue = ConvertTo10(display$, oldbase)
        send$ = Str$(newvalue)
        Readout.Caption = ConvertFrom10$(send$, convBase)
End Select
oldbase = convBase
Button(17).SetFocus
End Sub
```

The first Select Case clause in Sub NumBase_Click () disables all the digit buttons that do not pertain to the current numerical base. The final Select Case clause compares the previous base oldbase to the current one indicated by the Index of the control array. If the old base was 10 and the current one is not, a call is placed to Function ConvertFrom10$(). If the old base was not 10 and the current one is, a call is placed to Function ConvertTo10 (). Notice the From function procedure returns a string because the result can contain characters A–F, which the interpreter does not recognize as digits even though the calculator is simulating hexadecimal arithmetic. Finally, if the previous base is not 10, and the current base is not 10, the result value of the calculation is first converted to base 10, and then converted once again into its new base since the function procedure that produces a non-base 10 value requires a base 10 input. If the old base is 10 and the current base is 10, no conversion is needed.

Programming the Keyboard to Double for Command Buttons

Assigning
alias keys to
command
buttons.

At long last, I made Expressor III capable of accepting input from the keyboard. In Visual Basic, this process is not as easy as you might think; there is no property that assigns an "alias key" to a command button. A keypress is considered an event; one of the graphic objects in the `Panel` form must be assigned the role of "receiver" of the event. The `Panel` form is itself a graphic object, and would seem like the most likely candidate; except in the Visual Basic scheme of things, a form object can not be the receiver of a `_KeyPress` event.

As a result, one of the buttons in the panel must be assigned the role of receiver, but the Visual Basic system again hampers this process. For a button to receive a keypress event, it must have the focus—in other words, the black halo must be over that particular button at the time of the keypress. When the mouse is used to click a command button, the focus is passed by nature to that button; if one button was assigned the focus, a mouse click on any other button will grab the focus from it.

What the user input procedures must do is grab the focus back and place it where it belongs—which is what the instruction `Button(17).SetFocus` does. Conceivably, because the "receiver" of the `_KeyPress` event could be set to any of the `Button()` buttons, I could just pick one button from this array arbitrarily; the problem that might arise from this has to do with the "default button" status. The Enter key is a legitimate key on the numeric keypad, which will be used prominently if you let the user operate the keyboard for the calculator. If the focus is allowed to shift about the `Button()` array, the purpose for the Enter key could be to activate any of these buttons because the last button pressed is the one that has the focus, the one that has the focus becomes the default button, and the default button is the one that can be operated by pressing Enter.

So it only makes sense that the Enter button in the panel (which is the same as the equals button when the Expressor is in algebraic notation) be forced to act as receiver of the key press; it should be the duty of the Enter key to press the Enter button anyway. Here's the procedure which handles the _KeyPress event for button #17:

```
Sub Button_KeyPress (Index As Integer, KeyAscii As Integer)
Dim ndx As Integer
Select Case True
    Case KeyAscii > 47 And KeyAscii < 58
        ndx = KeyAscii - 48
    Case KeyAscii = 46
        ndx = 16
    Case (KeyAscii > 64 And KeyAscii < 71) And NumBase(0) = True
        ndx = 75 - KeyAscii
    Case KeyAscii = 45
        ndx = 19
    Case KeyAscii = 42
        ndx = 20
    Case KeyAscii = 47
        ndx = 21
    Case KeyAscii = 43 And rpnalg = 1
        ndx = 18
    Case KeyAscii = 13 And rpnalg = 1
        ndx = 18
    Case KeyAscii = 13 And rpnalg = 0
        ndx = 17
End Select
Button_Click ndx
End Sub
```

This is the switchboard procedure that leads to the switchboard procedure. After the procedure determines which key was pressed by its ASCII value, it assigns the index number of the corresponding alias button to the variable ndx, and execution proceeds to Sub Button_Click (), with ndx mimicking the index of the button that would be clicked if this were a mouse-driven operation.

The Program Learning Process

Here's how the programmability portion of this program works: The user sets the parameters by typing descriptions into the parameter bay—the textual descriptions are now within standard text boxes, so they're editable. The title for the new formula is entered into the formula list, which is now an editable combo box. Constant values are entered into the slots, along with range values. Next, the user clicks the Learn button and operates the Expressor as he would normally. Each important button he presses is memorized, until he presses the button again, which now reads "Save." Here's what happens:

```
Sub Learn_Click ()
If learnmode = False Then
    learnmode = True
    formulanow = formulanow + 1
    formulaplace = 1
    Learn.Caption = "Save"
    Forget.Caption = "Abort"
Else
    Learn.Caption = "Learn"
    rec = formulanow - partition
    fn(rec).Title = CalcList.Text
    fn(rec).Length = formulaplace
    fn(rec).Setting = rpnalg
    CalcList.AddItem CalcList.Text
    For sv = 0 To 6
        fn(rec).Variable(sv) = Val(Param(sv).Text)
        fn(rec).VariableName(sv) = ParamText(sv).Text
        Select Case AxisSelect(sv).Caption
            Case "x >>"
                fn(rec).VariableAxis(sv) = 1
            Case "y >>"
                fn(rec).VariableAxis(sv) = 2
        End Select
        fn(rec).VariableTo(sv) = Val(ParamTo(sv).Text)
    Next sv
    For sv = 0 To formulaplace
        fn(rec).Pattern(sv) = learnfmla(sv)
    Next sv
    Open "exprfmla.dat" For Random As #2 Len = 1356
    Put #2, rec + 1, fn(rec)
    Close #2
End If
Button(17).SetFocus
End Sub
```

The Learn button—or more to the point, the button that reads "Learn" by default—performs both functions, learning and saving the learned formula.

Setting up the learn operation is no problem; an extra place is made for the formula in the `formulanow` variable and the button being remembered, `formulaplace`, is set to 1. With the flag variable `learnmode` set to `True`, Sub `Button_Click ()` takes care of placing each new index received in the learn array and incrementing `formulaplace`. When the button is in its "Save" mode, the procedure loads the current `fn()` composite variable with the formula's title, length, notation setting, axis settings, and finally the formula itself.

Executing a learned formula is a simple matter. The Solve button replaced the Apply Formula button; here's its `_Click` event procedure:

```
Sub Solve_Click ()
frmula = CalcList.ListIndex + 1
If frmula <= partition Then
    For in = 0 To 6
        p(in) = Val(Param(in).Text)
    Next in
    solution = calculate(frmula)
Else
    solution = recite(frmula)
End If
Readout.Caption = Str$(solution)
ready = 0
Button(17).SetFocus
End Sub
```

Remember, the `partition` variable divides the list into the hard-wired portion and the learned portion. Now, if the formula selected is one of the learned formulas, execution proceeds to a new procedure, Sub `recite ()`:

```
Function recite (frmula) As Double
Open "exprfmla.dat" For Random As #2 Len = 1356
num% = frmula - partition
Get #2, num% + 1, fn(num%)
ln% = fn(num%).Length
rpnalg = fn(num%).Setting
Notation(rpnalg).Value = True
For rec% = 1 To ln%
    Button_Click fn(num%).Pattern(rec%)
Next rec%
recite = Val(Readout.Caption)
Close #2
End Function
```

The selected formula is retrieved from the random-access EXPRFMLA.DAT file; subtracting partition from the index of the selected formula yields one less than the record number for retrieval; that's why there's a + 1 in the Get #2 statement. The calculator settings are made, and the program runs in a one-instruction loop just as if it were recorded on a spool. The loop retrieves the next button in the program sequence and sends that index to Sub Button_Click (), with the index being mimicked. The solution to the Function procedure is whatever the readout currently states it is.

The procedure for the Forget button has a similar pattern:

```
Sub Forget_Click ()
If learnmode = False Then
    If CalcList.ListIndex + 1 < partition Then
        MsgBox "This particular formula is hard-coded into the
➥       program and cannot be deleted", 48, "Expressor 3
➥       Message"
        Exit Sub
    Else
        resp% = MsgBox("Are you sure you wish to delete this
➥       formula?", 36, "Expressor 3 Message")
        If resp% = 7 Then Exit Sub
        For shift = formulanow + 1 To nofms
            fn(shift - 1).Title = fn(shift).Title
            fn(shift - 1).Setting = fn(shift).Setting
            fn(shift - 1).Length = fn(shift).Length
            For pat% = 0 To 100
                fn(shift - 1).Pattern(pat%) =
➥           fn(shift).Pattern(pat%)
            Next pat%
            For slot% = 0 To 6
                fn(shift - 1).Variable(slot%) =
➥           fn(shift).Variable(slot%)
                fn(shift - 1).VariableName(slot%) =
➥           fn(shift).VariableName$(slot%)
                fn(shift - 1).VariableAxis(slot%) =
➥           fn(shift).Variable(slot%)
                fn(shift - 1).VariableTo(slot%) =
➥           fn(shift).VariableTo(slot%)
                label$(shift - 1, slot%) = label$(shift, slot%)
            Next slot%
        Next shift
        nofms = nofms - 1
```

```
        Open "exprfmla.dat" For Random As #2 Len = 1356
        Put #2, 1, nofms
        For deposit = 1 To nofms
            Put #2, deposit + 1, fn(deposit)
        Next deposit
        Close #2
    End If
Else
    formulanow = formulanow - 1
    formulaplace = 0
    Learn.Caption = "Learn"
    Forget.Caption = "Forget"
    learnmode = False
End If
End Sub
```

The process of making an array "forget" one of its entries is generally the same; it's a pattern you begin to memorize over time. A loop counts from the element being deleted to the end of the array—in this case, the loop variable is `shift`. The array entries for the element just behind `shift` are made equivalent to the entries in `shift`, and that duplication and shifting continues until the end of the array. The number of formulas is reduced by one, and the entire data file from the point of deletion until the end is rewritten to disk.

Preparing for Dual-Axis Range Calculations

You may remember from the previous directions for operating Expressor II, to indicate which parameter slot is to act as the range setting for the chart, the user presses a button on the panel beside the right parameter bank. This button's caption changes to "x>>", meaning the x-axis maximum value now appears in the right bank.

For two-axis systems such as the table form, the same button bank needs to be able to show "y>>" as well, for indicating which range represents the y-axis values. Here's the modified event procedure for this particular control array:

```
Sub AxisSelect_Click (Index As Integer)
If ParamTo(Index).Text = "0" Or ParamTo(Index).Text = "" Then
    ParamTo(Index).Text = Readout.Caption
```

```
End If
ready = 0
Select Case AxisSelect(Index).Caption
Case "---"
    If xslot <> Index Then
        AxisSelect(Index).Caption = "x >>"
        xslot = Index
        For correct = 0 To 6
            If correct <> Index And AxisSelect(correct).Caption
            = "x >>" Then
                AxisSelect(correct).Caption = "---"
            End If
        Next correct
        Exit Sub
    End If
    If xslot = Index Then
        AxisSelect(Index).Caption = "y >>"
        yslot = Index
        xslot = -1
        For correct = 0 To 6
            If correct <> Index And AxisSelect(correct).Caption
            = "y >>" Then
                AxisSelect(correct).Caption = "---"
            End If
        Next correct
        Exit Sub
    End If
Case "x >>"
    If yslot <> Index Then
        AxisSelect(Index).Caption = "y >>"
        yslot = Index
        xslot = -1
        For correct = 0 To 6
            If correct <> Index And AxisSelect(correct).Caption
            = "y >>" Then
                AxisSelect(correct).Caption = "x >>"
                For corr2 = 0 To 6
                    If corr2 <> correct And
                    AxisSelect(corr2).Caption = "x >>" Then
                        AxisSelect(corr2).Caption = "---"
                    End If
                Next corr2
```

```
                xslot = correct
            End If
        Next correct
        Exit Sub
    End If
Case "y >>"
    If yslot = Index Then
        AxisSelect(Index).Caption = "--"
        yslot = -1
    End If
End Select
End Sub
```

The description of this procedure sounds something like the old shell game. If the user clicks a button marked "- - -", this button becomes marked "x>>", and any other button currently marked "x>>" becomes marked "- - -". If the user clicks a button marked "x>>", it becomes marked "y>>", and if any other button is marked "y>>" and any other button marked "y>>" becomes marked "x>>", if another button marked "x>>" exists, it becomes marked "- - -." Still with me? If the user then clicks a button marked "y>>", it becomes marked "- - -." There won't be a quiz on this later. In any event, this switching ensures there will only be one x-axis row and one y-axis row at any one time, and that there won't be a y-axis row unless an x-axis row also exists.

Finally, I'd like to show you how I implemented the table form. I would have been writing this part of the program forever and might not have completed this book on time, were it not for the advent of the GRID.VBX custom control. Figure 9.3 shows the table form in action.

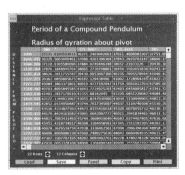

Figure 9.3. Solving for both x and y axes.

The style of this form is taken in large part from its chart form counterpart.

Listing 9.3. EXPTABLE.FRM Property Settings.

```
BackColor       =   &H00400000&
Caption         =   "Expressor Table"
Height          =   6804
Left            =   900
LinkTopic       =   "Form1"
MaxButton       =   0   'False
MinButton       =   0   'False
ScaleHeight     =   6336
ScaleWidth      =   7452
Top             =   840
Width           =   7596


CommonDialog Selector
   Left         =   0
   Top          =   5520


SpinButton ColumnSpin
   Height       =   264
   Left         =   3120
   Top          =   5640
   Width        =   252


SpinButton RowSpin
   Height       =   264
   Left         =   1560
   Top          =   5640
   Width        =   252


PictureBox TableTitle
   AutoRedraw   =   -1  'True
   BackColor    =   &H00400000&
   BorderStyle  =   0   'None
   FontBold     =   -1  'True
   FontItalic   =   0   'False
   FontName     =   "Lucida Sans"
   FontSize     =   7.8
```

```
    ForeColor       =   &H0000FFFF&
    Height          =   492
    Left            =   960
    Top             =   120
    Width           =   5532

PictureBox YAxisName
    AutoRedraw      =   -1   'True
    BackColor       =   &H00400000&
    BorderStyle     =   0    'None
    FontBold        =   -1   'True
    FontItalic      =   0    'False
    FontName        =   "Lucida Sans"
    FontSize        =   7.8
    ForeColor       =   &H0000FFFF&
    Height          =   4212
    Left            =   120
    Top             =   1320
    Width           =   252

PictureBox XAxisName
    AutoRedraw      =   -1   'True
    BackColor       =   &H00400000&
    BorderStyle     =   0    'None
    FontBold        =   -1   'True
    FontItalic      =   0    'False
    FontName        =   "Lucida Sans"
    FontSize        =   7.8
    ForeColor       =   &H0000FFFF&
    Height          =   300
    Left            =   960
    Top             =   720
    Width           =   5292

Grid WriteArea
    BackColor       =   &H00400000&
    BorderStyle     =   0    'None
    Cols            =   13
    FontBold        =   -1   'True
    FontItalic      =   0    'False
    FontName        =   "Lucida Sans Typewriter"
```

continues

Listing 9.3. continued

```
        FontSize        =   7.8
        ForeColor       =   &H00FFFFFF&
        Height          =   4500
        Left            =   480
        Rows            =   21
        Top             =   1080
        Width           =   6732

Label NoCols
        Alignment       =   1   'Right Justify
        Caption         =   "Columns"
        FontName        =   "Lucida Sans"
        FontSize        =   7.8
        ForeColor       =   &H0000FFFF&
        Height          =   204
        Left            =   1920
        Top             =   5660
        Width           =   1092

Label NoRos
        Caption         =   "Rows"
        FontName        =   "Lucida Sans"
        FontSize        =   7.8

Label Prnt
        Caption         =   "Print"
        FontName        =   "Lucida Sans"
        FontSize        =   9

Label Cutter
        Caption         =   "Copy"

Label FlipPanel
        Caption         =   "Panel"

Label TableSave
        Caption         =   "Save"

Label TableLoad
        Caption         =   "Load"
```

The star of this form is the grid control, a custom control shipped with both Visual Basic 2 Standard and Professional Edition.

Technique Capsule: Spreadsheet-Style Tables

Definition: The grid control is supplied to the Visual Basic toolbox by including the GRID.VBX file in the current project. This symbol for the grid control then appears in the toolbox:

The grid control provides a form with a scrollable mechanism for displaying tabular figures and textual labels, and the potential for endowing cells with graphics. Although it has the appearance of a spreadsheet, the grid control is only a value-display system; so formulas per se may not be assigned to a cell.

Execution: The default state of an initialized grid control gives it a total of two columns and two rows. The labeling cells for columns and rows—the specially shaded cells along the top and left sides of the grid—are called fixed cells. These are counted as belonging to legitimate rows and columns; so a two-by-two grid in effect starts life with one, not four, tabular display cells. A table of one item is somewhat pointless, so it's necessary to set the total number of rows and columns in a grid.

Example: A grid named `Loan` is used to display the monthly payments for a 36-month prorated loan, given ten different potential annual interest rates. Only one fixed row and one fixed column is necessary for labeling, so counting fixed cells, the grid needs 37 columns and 11 rows. The `.Cols` and `.Rows` properties of the grid control sets these parameters as follows:

```
Loan.Cols = 37
Loan.Rows = 11
```

Each cell is treated as an individual text box; it is expecting string contents, not a numeral value. The grid control maintains pointers to the cell that currently is receiving text, in the form of the `.Col` and `.Row` properties. Notice the lack of an `-s` at the end of these properties; be careful to distinguish between the `.Cols` and `.Col` properties. The first column and row in a grid are numbered 0, so the cell at location (0, 0) might not require any contents. Notice that cells in the grid are not referred to like cells in a spreadsheet; so the upper left cell is not called "A1."

The first order of business is to set the labels in the first row, row #0. Resetting the row pointer is accomplished with this instruction:

```
Loan.Row = 0
```

A loop clause then loads the label row for the x-axis of the table with reference labels for the month number in the payment schedule, starting with the second column, numbered 1:

```
For xlab% = 1 To 36
    Loan.Col = xlab%
    Loan.Text = Str$(xlab%)
Next xlab%
```

Assigning text to the current cell is done in the same manner as setting the contents of a text box, through an expression of assignment to the `.Text` property of the entire grid. This statement is in no way augmented with the coordinates of the cell receiving the text; that is set in advance with assignments to the `.Row` and `.Col` properties. The labels for the y-axis are set with a similar loop.

Assuming the results of all the calculations have been pre-loaded into a two-dimensional array `payment()`, here's how a two-tier loop clause assigns the contents of the body of the table:

```
For ycell% = 1 To 10
    Loan.Row = ycell%
    For xcell% = 1 To 36
        Loan.Col = xcell%
        Loan.Text = payment(xcell%, ycell%)
    Next xcell%
Next ycell%
```

If the width of the column requires expansion to fit the text assigned to it, the `.ColWidth()` property for that column can be set as follows:

```
Loan.ColWidth(xcell%) = newwidth
```

Similarly, the `.RowHeight()` property can be adjusted for larger `.FontSize` settings. Finally, the number of fixed columns and rows in a grid may be reset using the `.FixedCols` and `.FixedRows` properties. These rows remain set in the upper and left sides of the grid, even when scroll bars are used to navigate through the table contents.

EXPRSOR3.BAS

The procedure that manages Expressor III's table is structured much like its charting counterpart, only with a second loop clause enclosing the first, counting for the y axis. I break this procedure into parts so you can see what's going on:

Listing 9.4. Part 1.

```
Sub CreateTable (xmin As Single, xmax As Single, ymin As Single,
➥   ymax As Single, xslot As Integer, yslot As Integer)
Table.Show
nocolumns = 12
norows = 22
Table.NoCols.Caption = LTrim$(Str$(nocolumns)) + " Columns"
Table.NoRos.Caption = LTrim$(Str$(norows)) + " Rows"
For dm = 0 To nocolumns
    maxlen(dm) = 600
Next dm
Table.WriteArea.Cols = nocolumns + 1
Table.WriteArea.Rows = norows + 1
```

The `.Cols` and `.Rows` properties for the grid control are determined here. The array `maxlen()` keeps the widest contents read thus far for each column, so the procedure may later set the maximum width of that column to the width of its widest entry. Because this procedure appears outside of `Table`'s native form module, the table name is mentioned specifically when setting properties.

Listing 9.5. Part 2.

```
title$ = Panel.CalcList.Text
Table.TableTitle.FontSize = 20
Try2:
If Table.TableTitle.TextWidth(title$) > Table.TableTitle.Width
➥   Then
    Table.TableTitle.FontSize = Table.TableTitle.FontSize - 1
    GoTo Try2
End If
```

continues

Listing 9.5. continued

```
Table.TableTitle.Print title$
xaxis$ = Panel.ParamText(xslot).Text
Table.XAxisName.FontSize = 16
Try3:
If Table.XAxisName.TextWidth(xaxis$) > Table.XAxisName.Width
➥   Then
    Table.XAxisName.FontSize = Table.XAxisName.FontSize - 1
    GoTo Try3
End If
Table.XAxisName.Print xaxis$
yaxis$ = UCase$(Panel.ParamText(yslot).Text)
For prnty = 1 To Len(yaxis$)
    pn$ = Mid$(yaxis$, prnty, 1)
    Table.YAxisName.Print pn$
Next prnty
```

This is the section that prints the table title and axis names. If you've read this book from front to back, you're probably familiar with the process for setting the font size for a picture box and testing the text that might be going into that box with the `.TextWidth()` function to see whether it fits. If not, the loop clause reduces the point size by one, and the picture box is retested. This process is done for the table label and the x-axis label. The y-axis label isn't tested in this way; individual characters of the y-axis label are printed one after the other, so that the label can fit along a narrow vertical strip along the left side of the grid. Visual Basic does not have any functions for printing text along a variable-degree baseline, so you can't yet print sideways text with the Visual Basic standard vocabulary. There are Windows API functions that allow for sideways text, but for now, this process is adequate.

Listing 9.6. Part 3.

```
frmula = Panel.CalcList.ListIndex + 1
intrvalx = (xmax - xmin) / nocolumns
intrvaly = (ymax - ymin) / norows
For in = 0 To 6
    p(in) = Val(Panel.Param(in).Text)
Next in
```

```
If xmin = xmax Or ymin = ymax Then
    Panel.Show
    Exit Sub
End If
Table.WriteArea.Row = 0
xl = xmin
For xaxlabl = 1 To nocolumns
    Table.WriteArea.Col = xaxlabl
    s$ = Str$(xl)
    If Len(s$) * 100 > maxlen(xaxlabl) Then
        maxlen(xaxlabl) = Len(s$) * 100
        Table.WriteArea.ColWidth(xaxlabl) = maxlen(xaxlabl)
    End If
    Table.WriteArea.Text = s$
    xl = xl + intrvalx
Next xaxlabl
Table.WriteArea.Col = 0
yl = ymin
For yaxlabl = 1 To norows
    Table.WriteArea.Row = yaxlabl
    s$ = Str$(yl)
    If Len(s$) * 100 > maxlen(0) Then
        maxlen(0) = Len(s$) * 100
        Table.WriteArea.ColWidth(0) = maxlen(0)
    End If
    Table.WriteArea.Text = s$
    yl = yl + intrvaly
Next yaxlabl
```

Each column contains result values for the formula for input values increasing (or decreasing) in equal increments from the value in the left parameter bank to the one in the right. The two equal intervals are figured by taking the difference between the two banks' values and dividing them by the current number of columns and rows. Unlike the charting module, the number of rows and columns can be adjusted by the user on the fly. The loop clauses for xaxlabl and yaxlabl check to see whether the current cell widths for the label rows are large enough to fit the text. Because the textual contents of cells in a grid control are treated like text in a text box, there is no .TextWidth() function for determining the absolute twip length; a general formula of length_of_character * 100 is used instead.

Listing 9.7. Part 4.

```
Table.WriteArea.Row = 0
Table.WriteArea.Col = 1
For cvaly = ymin To ymax Step intrvaly
    p(yslot) = cvaly
    If Table.WriteArea.Row < Table.WriteArea.Rows - 1 Then
        Table.WriteArea.Row = Table.WriteArea.Row + 1
    End If
    For cvalx = xmin To xmax Step intrvalx
        p(xslot) = cvalx
        s$ = LTrim$(Str$(calculate(frmula)))
        If Len(s$) * 100 > maxlen(Table.WriteArea.Col) Then
            maxlen(Table.WriteArea.Col) = Len(s$) * 100
            Table.WriteArea.ColWidth(Table.WriteArea.Col) =
➡           maxlen(Table.WriteArea.Col)
        End If
        Table.WriteArea.Text = s$
        If Table.WriteArea.Col < Table.WriteArea.Cols - 1 Then
            Table.WriteArea.Col = Table.WriteArea.Col + 1
        End If
    Next cvalx
Table.WriteArea.Col = 1
Next cvaly
End Sub
```

The final section contains a two-tier loop that begins the formula-solving process for each cell, counting for the first cell in a row and proceeding until the last before moving to the next row down. Remember that the `.Row` and `.Rows`, and the `.Col` and `.Cols` properties have different purposes from one another. The non-plural form refers to the current cell receiving text, whereas the plural form refers to the total number of rows or columns in the grid. What might be confusing to the reader is that text is assigned to the grid in the manner one assigns text to a text box, by setting its `.Text` property. Yet nowhere in the `.Text` property-setting instruction is there any reference to what cell is receiving the text. The receiver cell is located by setting the `.Row` and `.Col` (non-plural) properties of the grid. Granted, the text-assignment instruction is a slight violation of object-oriented syntax, but because Visual Basic isn't really an object-oriented language, I doubt the Object Police will be imposing any penalties.

The final two-tier loop clause performs no formula calculation on its own; in fact, if you weren't looking carefully, you'd probably gloss over the instruction that passes control to the calculation section, `s$ = LTrim$(Str$(calculate(frmula))`. The deeply embedded term `calculate` passes control to `Function calculate ()`, the results of which are made into a string, stripped of any leading space characters and assigned to `s$`. The rough length of `s$` is tested to see whether the string will fit in the cell given its current column width. Resetting the `.ColWidth` adjusts the column width.

Objects As Variables

In Visual Basic, as in everyday life, some general graphic object-related tasks are best performed—more to the point, they are more *efficiently* performed— when these objects are not being referred to specifically. Say, for instance, you want to make all your text fields line up against the left margin of a form, regardless of where they were placed at design time. To create a process model for such a procedure that works for most any form containing a set of text fields, it's good to have a single object variable referring to each text field indirectly, in turn. Object variables are good excuses for having your VB procedures "daydream" on the job.

Technique Capsule: Object Variables

Definition: With the new edition of Visual Basic 2, it is now possible to declare variables that refer to a graphic object, and whose components are addressed like the properties of that object. Such variables may be declared to address any specific object, and may be used in turn to address several different objects. One major purpose of object variables is to make it possible for generic procedures to perform graphical operations upon types of objects or upon certain objects, without having to be programmed to refer to a specific form.

Execution: Here is the syntax of the statement used to declare object variables:

```
Dim objectvar1[([minobject1 To ]maxobject1)] As [New]
{controlname¦controltype}[, objectvar2[([minobject2
To ]maxobject2)] As [New] {controlname¦controltype}. . .
objectvar60[([minobject60 To ]maxobject60) As [New]
{controlname¦controltype}]
```

The Dim statement may be used with this new syntax to declare the existence of one or more graphic objects. The object referred to by *controlname* may be a control addressed generically, or a new instance of an existing control. The object is given an exclusive object variable name *objectvar*. The new control represented by the declared object variable will exist in its *virtual state,* so it will not be officially loaded into the Windows workspace until a specific instruction is invoked for that purpose.

If the Properties Window was used during design time to create the style and layout of the control declared with the Dim statement, then declaring its object variable As New *controlname* will give those style properties to the new control. Without the New qualifier, the new control's properties will be set to their default conditions. These property settings may be changed with instructions before the new control is displayed.

Once an object variable has been declared, *objectvar* will be the term used for any further reference to the object, especially within the Set, Load, and .Show instructions.

To bring into the form a new control that has not been designed in advance, its declared object variable is given a *controltype*. For the standard lot of Visual Basic controls, these control types are written as any of the following:

CheckBox	ComboBox	CommandButton	DirListBox
DriveListBox	FileListBox	Frame	Grid
HScrollBar	Image	Label	Line
ListBox	Menu	OptionButton	PictureBox
Shape	TextBox	Timer	VScrollBar

Custom or extension controls may use their own *controltype* terms. The New qualifier is unnecessary for declaring an object variable for a generic *controltype*, because the term always refers to a generic and undesigned control.

When an object variable for a form is declared and the form to which it refers is in its virtual state, it may be brought to the screen with *objectvar*.Show. Likewise, a declared control may be brought to the screen using the Set statement, making sure to designate the form to which the new object shall belong.

If Dim is invoked using Syntax 3 within a procedure, then upon the interpreter processing End Sub, any of Dim's declared objects brought into their running state using the As New qualifier will be removed, from memory as well as the screen. If Dim is invoked in the general declarations section of a form module, then objects declared by Dim and brought to the screen are, naturally, lost.

> **Note:** The Global statement may be used to declare object variables with global scope; that is to say, objects that may not be taken out of their running state without the program invoking a specific instruction to do so. Also, the Static statement may be used to declare object variables with scope local to a procedure, though which operate in a state of suspension while the interpreter is executing instructions outside of the object variable's native procedure.

If an object variable has been declared without the aid of the New qualifier, then to give that object variable some identity requires invoking the Set statement. This statement may be phrased using either of the two following syntaxes:

```
Set objectvar = [parentref!]objectref
Set objectvar = New objectname
```

The Set statement, using the first syntax listed here, attributes the object variable *objectvar* to the stated existent graphic object *objectref*. The reference *objectref* to this existent object may be placed by way of the .Name property for that object, or by way of yet another object variable. Once invoked, any reference to *objectvar* applies to the same graphic object as does *objectref*. The object variable *objectvar* may be set later to refer to some other graphic object, or disengaged altogther by setting its reference to Nothing. Any object variable referred to by the Set statement must first have been formally declared using the Dim, Global, or Static statements.

If the parent object of *objectref* is not currently active (if it doesn't have the focus on the form level), then to attribute the reference for the graphic object to the particular parent object to which it belongs, that parent's object reference *parentref* must be stated first, followed by the child control reference *objectref*. The two references are separated from one another with an exclamation mark.

Using its second syntax, the Set statement attributes the object variable *objectvar* to a new instance of a pre-designed object whose .Name property was set to *objectname* at design time. Invoking this syntax of the Set statement brings this New instance of the graphic object into existence. The parent of *objectname* must be currently active, or have the focus on the form level.

> **Note:** At the time of this writing, Syntax 2 of the `Set` statement worked successfully only in cases of declaring new instances of forms, but not new constituent controls. It is apparently Microsoft's intent to declare new instances of controls within a form using Syntax 2.

Example: Follow along with me for a page or two as I present this step-by-step demonstration of object variables in play. Somewhere along the way, you just might say to yourself, "Aha!" Start by initializing a new project. Place a text box within `Form1` of this project—it doesn't matter where. Currently this graphic object has a `.Name` of `Text1` as well as a `.Text` property set to `Text1`. Next, add the following line to the general declarations area of Form1:

```
Dim TextCopy As Control
```

Now run the program; all we need it to do is dimension the object variable `TextCopy` as a generic `Control` variable. Next, break it—don't stop it, but press the break button in the toolbar or select **Run/Break**. For this demonstration to work, you'll need the services of the Debug window, which contains a command-line interpreter capable of responding to your direct commands. Type into the Debug window the following command:

```
Set TextCopy = Form1!Text1
```

If everything's going well thus far, the VB interpreter should not respond to this command at all—no news is good news. Now, you know full well that the `.Name` of this text box is `Text1`. Type the following command, however, and you'll see that there are now other ways to refer to this control:

```
TextCopy.Text = "Wow! It works!"
```

Your message between the quotation marks should immediately appear within the text box `Text1`, even though the name itself appears nowhere in the preceding command. Congratulations; you've just successfully invoked an object variable.

Now, to experiment further with this concept, change the only line in the entire VB application to read as follows:

```
Dim TextCopy As TextBox
```

Next, repeat the remainder of the steps. You should notice absolutely no difference in what happens.

Example: So what's the difference between declaration as a text box and as a control? Specifying the text box type seems to be more specific as far as the source code is concerned, but it doesn't appear to add any efficiency to the code. This extension to the demonstration should answer some of these questions. Someplace on `Form1`, add a vertical scroll bar. Next, edit the general declarations section to read as follows:

```
Dim Whapjaw As Control
Dim TextCopy As TextBox
Dim ScrollCopy As VScrollBar
```

There are two specific object variable references here, and one generic one. When you run the application now, break it, and type into the Debug window `Set Whapjaw = Text1`, you get no response—so far, success. When you enter into the Debug window `Whapjaw.Text = "When in the course..."` you should see an echo in the text box `Text1`.

Now, try typing this in the Debug window: `Set Whapjaw = VScroll1`. Follow it with the following two instructions:

```
Whapjaw.Max = 50
Whapjaw.Value = 25
```

The `.Min` minimum value for the scroll bar should already be 0; so the scroll box should now appear in the middle of the bar. Notice what's been accomplished; in the course of five instructions, the same object variable refers to two totally different types of controls. Notice, though, you've been using the one object variable that was declared `As Control`. Try the same succession of steps in the Debug window with either `TextCopy` or `ScrollCopy` and at some time, you'll find the VB interpreter responds with a "Type mismatch error" panel. The restriction placed on the other two object variables allows them to refer to only one type of graphic object.

Example: Finally, just as the value of a unit variable may be set to the value of another unit variable, as in `valence = v1`, the components of an object variable may be assigned to another object variable. The following instructions typed into the Debug window prove this:

```
Set TextCopy = Form1!Text1
Set Whapjaw = TextCopy
```

It's the second instruction that is key here; it sets the object reference as being equivalent to another object reference. You may now address the `.Text` property of `Whapjaw` (not the `.Max` property, mind you).

You might be able in your mind to apply this demonstration to broader tasks. Suppose you have a set of general modules containing procedures that generate results regardless of what form the inputs or outputs may be contained in. You may use the `Global` statement within general procedures to declare object variable names; the results of these general procedures may be assigned to the properties of these object variables. Within the `Sub Form_Load ()` procedures of your form modules, then, you can place `Set` statements equating the object variables referred to in the general procedures, to the `.Name` properties of the real controls in your form modules. This enables you to create fully-functional *libraries* that you can employ in your applications with extraordinary ease.

> **Note:** To disengage an object variable reference and release the memory apportioned to it, use the `Set` statement with the syntax `Set objectvar = Nothing`. The `Nothing` keyword will release the object variable back to the state it was in before the initial `Set` statement was invoked.

The two examples of original control design I've shown you in this chapter have differing purposes. The first, the compass control from Situation #3, was designed to be a new device for addressing the specific requirements of an application. It is a unique device that bears some resemblance to something you'd find in reality, though admittedly not a lot. The second, the programmable control bank from Expressor III, was designed to have a considerable degree of similarity to something you'd find in reality. In both cases, the usage models for the controls were unconventional in that there was never a one-to-one-to-one correlation—one control, one purpose, one procedure.

One of the primary criticisms of BASIC is that throughout its evolution, it creates new programming structures, and every innovation programmers make in utilizing those structures comes from breaking them. Unfortunately, these criticisms do have some basis in fact; in Visual Basic, innovations come through unconventional means. C provides the necessary tools for innovation without breaking established structure, although C as a language is really a switchboard mechanism for innovative libraries. C has a handful of keywords, whereas

Visual Basic's entire language structure is defined in its primary keyword vernacular. When Visual Basic 2 was released, that vernacular was augmented with even more keywords, especially relating to functions for which programmers had been turning to the Windows API for help.

The chief way to make Visual Basic more productive is to break the mold. The next chapter introduces some more ways in which this can be done.

THE WINDOWS ENVIRONMENT

If you have read that the revolutionizing principle in the business of computing has been the invention of overlapping rectangles and documents that can appear on top of other documents, think again. Overlapping rectangles probably cannot revolutionize computing any more than overlapping stacks of paper on your desk has ever revolutionized paperwork. The principle that made this industry suddenly flourish is far more substantial, though far more esoteric:

10

it has led, inadvertently, to overlapping rectangles, but American business seems to be quite adept at overlapping these days.

Open Architecture

The principle of openness in computing is this: Every working element of a computer is part of its overall program, but each part unto itself is said to provide a service. This service can benefit either the computer or the user. The party of the computing "conversation" most benefitted by this service is determined in degrees or levels. Each part of the computer thus forms an interlocking chain from user to computer and back, like townspeople carrying pails of water from the well to the fire.

Once you've determined where each part belongs, you can easily substitute one part in the chain for another similar part without disrupting the chain. This is the key to both successful and marketable computing. An operating system is but one part in the chain; it can be replaced or upgraded while the rest of the system goes about its business. Without this idea of openness, there would be no modern software industry; user applications are yet another element in the chain. Computing is an industry today because you have some choice, some say-so regarding the software you run. You don't just turn on the machine, and que será, será. Because of openness, you choose the set of instructions that best fits your business and even your life-style.

Figure 10.1 depicts those elements in the computing chain with which this book is concerned; there are others which have to do with networking services, but for now, the figure assumes a single-user environment. Those elements that best serve the computer are arranged toward the bottom of the heap, with those that serve the user toward the top. At the bottom is the most logical element, the Central Processing Unit (CPU) (this part of the chain can be shared with coprocessors). The CPU is the logical switchboard for the entire computing operation—the "receiving end," if you will, of the conversation.

The hierarchy of service providers in a computer.

The Basic Input/Output System (BIOS) is the nerve center of the system. Its purpose is to be sensitive to every form of input you can give the computer at any one time (keyboard, mouse, pen, iron boot) and to respond quickly with individual characters or pixels sent over the wire like a very fast Morse code.

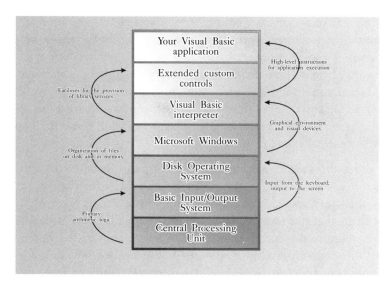

Figure 10.1. The division of resources in your computing system.

The Disk Operating System is responsible for bundling those characters into files, both on disk and in memory. Those files are provided to Microsoft Windows, which acts as an environment for the display and manipulation of these files. With Windows, you begin to see the human element coming into play. Streams of bits and disjointed files now become tangible devices you can move and command.

The next layer up from Windows is generally the user application. There, you expect the chain would reverse directions and head down, but because Visual Basic has been added, the chain proceeds upward. Visual Basic takes the fundamental resources brought to it from the bottom of the chain and gives them names and terms so you might address them more directly and fashion complex instructions with your own choice of phraseology.

Built into the Visual Basic structure is the next layer, Visual Basic extensions. It is their purpose to give you greater access to the existing resources provided from the very bottom of the chain. A database link, a common dialog box control, an animated button, and a BIOS status analyzer routine are all examples of open-ended resource providers. Because of openness, you can add these providers to your personal computing system randomly without disruption.

At the end of the chain, of course, is the Visual Basic application for which you are the programmer. Notice that with each step in the chain, more and more room is provided for aesthetic enhancement, for freedom of personal expression. There isn't much that's aesthetically pleasing about the logic of the CPU; but as you go more toward Windows, there are files, forms, graphic objects. As you enter the realm of Visual Basic, you have instructions and tangible, programmable devices. By the time you reach your Visual Basic application, you practically have choreography.

The resources shared among the elements in this chain are the same from the bottom to the top, though as they proceed upward and onward, their "packaging" improves. A character of input data, for instance, is a resource. Moving up the chain, that character becomes part of a data field or a command. A character is a resource provided by the BIOS. A button, however—the little gray beveled thing you click with the mouse—is a resource whose origin is Windows, further up the chain. Peel the wrapping off the button, though, and you'll see it's actually a graphical method to provide a command option to the screen. A command consists primarily of characters, which brings you right back to the original resource provided by the BIOS further down the chain.

Placing a Call to Your Local API

The Windows Applications Program Interface (API) is a series of routines which give applications direct access to the operational, interactive, and graphical functions and processes of Microsoft Windows. The API constitutes the link in the chain of communiation between Windows and those elements further up; it provides resources to applications, as well as to application environments such as Visual Basic. The API is supplied in the form of Dynamic Link Libraries (DLLs). Contained within each .DLL file can be a series of graphical resources—for instance, icons or window contents. Most often, though, you find small program files that can connect to your application like prefabricated building components.

Comparing definitions of "libraries" in computing systems.

Programmers in C are familiar with the concept of libraries. The C programming language contains no instructions for user interaction or graphical display of data. Instead, C utilizes libraries of functions integrated into the program by a preprocessor. Standard input/output functions, for example, are provided by a library called "stdio.h" that contains preassembled or compiled routines. The syntax for each routine is the same for all computers or C compilers; only the processes differ among brands of compilers. What's important is that the C programmer need not retrain himself about standard I/O functions whenever he switches from one compiler to another.

The Windows API libraries operate under a similar premise. For each successive maintenance release of Windows, the library routines either change or become susceptible to change. What's important is that Windows provides—or at least offers—standardized access to these routines for each programming language or system in the Windows environment. If you understand the API, you are assured that the routine that changes the blink rate of the cursor is accessed in much the same way when programming in Borland C++ as it is accessed in the Word for Windows background "macro" language, as it is in Visual Basic.

What is different about using API routines with Visual Basic, however, is that each routine becomes accessible like a keyword. If you include the proper declaratives in the global module of your application, you can accentuate the operative vocabulary of your own personal Visual Basic environment with keywords that call those resources intrinsic to the operation of Windows.

Here is a list of the key DLLs accessible by Visual Basic:

Kernel   A set of routines representing key operations of Windows as it connects to and exchanges information with the operating system of the computer.

Keyboard   Routines for processing keyboard input.

User   A set of routines provided generously by Microsoft granting users (programmers) extra access to the functions of the Windows environment, including composite functions that represent multiple interconnected Windows processes.

GDI   Routines which provide direct access to the Windows Graphics Device Interface (GDI), giving the user access to more direct methods of drawing shapes, handling graphic objects, and processing animation.

The statement in the global module that declares a DLL routine as part of the Visual Basic application is, naturally, called `Declare`. Here are two ways to phrase the statement:

```
Declare Sub process$ Lib library$ [Alias secondname$]
➡ ([[ByVal] argument1 As type$1, [ByVal] argument2
➡ As type$2. . . [ByVal] argumentn As type$n])

Declare Function process$ Lib library$ [Alias secondname$]
➡ ([[ByVal] argument1 As type$1, [ByVal] argument2
➡ As type$2. . . [ByVal] argumentn As type$n])
➡ As functype$
```

Once declared, a DLL process has a name or "handle" which links it to the Visual Basic program. If the DLL process is expected to return a value to the Visual Basic program, the process is declared as a Function; otherwise, it is declared as a Sub procedure.

In the previous syntax examples for the Declare statement, the string *process$* refers to the name of the process or routine as it is addressed in the DLL. This is the name which will be used later in the Visual Basic application to refer to that process. Alternately, you may attribute a *secondname$* to this process by means of the Alias optional term. The naming of *secondname$* is your choice, though it does not override the possible use of *process$* anywhere else in the application.

The string *library$* beside the term Lib may be set either to the filename of the dynamic link library where the declared process is located, or to the name of the library assumed by the Visual Basic interpreter to be a part of the Windows API system—for instance, Kernel, Keyboard, User, or GDI. This string must be stated in quotation marks. Once a Visual Basic extension library is installed, its filename is referred to by the Lib term in the declaration statement for each extension DLL routine used in the Visual Basic application.

Qualifiers to Library Declaration

Passing values through variables, though not by reference.

If the ByVal term appears before a declared variable, only the value of that term is passed to the DLL process, not its reference or identity as a Visual Basic variable. Because DLL processes do not recognize Visual Basic variable names, those processes during their execution cannot change the values of the variables which the processes received as parameters. It follows, therefore, that most values will be passed to the process by way of ByVal declarations, because you cannot expect the values or contents of the parameters to either change or be changed by the process.

It's vitally important that the variable types for each argument to be passed to the DLL routine be mentioned someplace within the `Declare` statement that declares the routine. The most common variable types Visual Basic supports are `Integer`, `Long` (integer), `Single`, `Double`, `String`, and `Currency` (you won't need to worry about `Currency` types when addressing the API). There will be some instances in which you may be using composite variable types; in such cases, these types must be declared earlier in the global module using the `Type` declarative. There also will be cases when the particular input variable for a process might not be of any particular type whatsoever; for these cases, Visual Basic supports a special declarative type `As Any`. An element of data returned from a database by a DLL routine to a data field, for instance, may be a person's name (`String`), a dollar amount (`Currency`), or a value (`3.1415927`). In such cases, you cannot predict ahead of time what the variable type will be, but you can at least inform the Visual Basic interpreter of this uncertainty in advance. The `Any` type is not supported for any other Visual Basic statement except `Declare`.

The Windows environment contains hundreds of DLL routines, so it would be a waste of your good time to declare each routine manually every time you write a Visual Basic application. It also would be a waste of my good time to recite within these pages each and every listing in the API library. Microsoft provides two text files with every copy of Visual Basic. The file `WIN31API.TXT` is a set of declarations for inclusion in your global or general start-up module, for accessing routines in the Windows API library. The file CONSTANT.TXT includes constant declarations for numerals used by API and VB routines with standardized terms. Another book on the subject of Visual Basic presents a listing of WIN31API.TXT as one of its appendixes (and as a way to fill space); Microsoft, on the other hand, gives you the same file for free. To borrow constant declarations from this file, use the Windows Notepad application to load this file into memory. Indicate the declarations your application will actually need (there are thousands of them, so you won't want to use them all), cut them into the Windows clipboard, and paste them into the general declarations section of your Visual Basic application.

Predeclaration text files.

Graphics Device Contexts

In the Visual Basic vocabulary, the graphic object that receives the text being output is generally a text box or a label, and on occasion the printer. In the realm of the GDI, each graphics device is an element for the output or display of some form of data. All devices accessible by GDI are referred to uniformly. Generally, processes that output to some device—whatever that might be—have been given standardized names and syntax fashioned like English verbs, so not to confuse the programmer. The GDI knows to distinguish between output to a window, output to the screen in general, output to the printer, and output to an LCD color projector that may currently be connected.

Some computing terms have more than one meaning, and "context" is certainly a good example. The Windows GDI maintains independent contexts for all graphic devices accessible by Windows. Realize that a screen and a window are two separate devices; it might not seem that way to you in the real world, but in the realm of Windows, distinctions like these are frequently drawn, and for good reason. This is why those contexts are maintained in the first place.

Defining
device
contexts.

> **Definition:** A device context is a combination of a structured segment of data in memory, along with encoded instructions that define its purpose and operation in the graphic environment.

Sometimes the study of computing can easily give one the feeling there are too few words in the English language. (One wonders whom to blame: the Norman conquerors? King James? the Pentagon?) The term "device context" refers to something quite different from the term "context" as you've seen it used in previous chapters: Each potential recipient of graphical output, be it a window or a plotter, is given a device context by the Windows GDI. At any one time, this context is referred to by its "handle"; in this case, the abbreviation for "handle to the device context" is hDC—notice the lowercase h. Although the device and its contents stay constant, this handle number may change over time as its priority is constantly changed and its representative location in memory is swapped. For this reason, Visual Basic graphic objects that qualify as virtual terminals have the following property associated with them.

Technique Capsule: Windows Context Handles

Definition: The .hDC property for a graphic object that acts as a virtual terminal is set automatically to the number the Microsoft Windows GDI gives the object, as the handle to the device context. This property is used to refer to the antecedent graphic object, within calls to a DLL process whose region of output will be that object. The value of this property should not be passed to a DLL process by way of a variable, because between the time the variable is assigned the value and the call is placed, the hDC for the graphic object may have changed. This property may not be set by the programmer at any time.

Similarly, the GDI maintains a separate window identification number for each window during the time it appears on the screen. This number is considered the handle for that window, and Visual Basic maintains a property that refers to this handle. The .hWnd property for a form is set automatically to the window identification handle for the form's window. The window receives this handle from the Microsoft Windows GDI upon its creation. The value of this property should not be passed to a DLL process by way of a variable, because between the time the variable is assigned the value and the call is placed, the hDC for the graphic object might change. This property may not be set by the programmer at any time.

Example: A routine for plotting an ellipse to a window is in the Windows GDI library. The declaration for that routine in the global module would appear as follows:

```
Declare Function Ellipse Lib "GDI" (ByVal hDC As
➥   Integer, ByVal X1 As Integer, ByVal Y1 As Integer,
➥   ByVal X2 As Integer, ByVal Y2 As Integer) As Integer
```

The GDI routine is a function because it returns an integer value. This value is declared integral at the end of the Declare instruction. The title of the function follows the word Function. It takes five parameters, starting with the handle to the logical context hDC. This handle tells the GDI which window in the Windows workspace will contain the ellipse. The remaining parameters comprise two pairs of coordinates representing the upper-left and lower-right corners of an invisible rectangle whose borders contain the ellipse—that is, the sides of the rectangle are tangential to the ellipse.

With this function declared, it is possible for a procedure to issue the following instruction:

```
c = Ellipse(Form1.hDC, 50, 50, 100, 100)
```

Because the device context handle is subject to change at any moment, it would be unsafe to render its hDC value to a variable and pass that variable as the first parameter. In this example, therefore, the .hDC property of Form1 must be passed directly. Two pixel coordinate pairs (50, 50) and (100, 100) are then passed as the upper-left and lower-right "corners" of the ellipse, so to speak. The value of this function is returned in variable c. GDI graphics functions return unsigned true/false integer values signalling whether the function succeeded in its task; thus if the ellipse were drawn correctly, c = 1.

Example: Here's a function from the User library you might find useful:

```
Declare Function IsWindowVisible Lib "User" (ByVal hWnd
➡  As Integer) As Integer
```

If you had a form whose control .Name was Stars, and you wanted to make your procedure more efficient by having it refuse to print anything to Stars if you can't see the form anyway, you could invoke the following function:

```
vis% = IsWindowVisible(Stars.hWnd)
```

You could then have a procedure be executed based on the result value of vis%. However, it might be more elegant—because the functional result of IsWindowVisible() is going to be 1 or 0 anyway—to make this routine name the conditional expression for a clause, as follows:

```
If -IsWindowVisible(Stars,hWnd) Then
    .
    .
    .
End If
```

No mathematical operators need to be included in the comparison. If the window is not visible, the function returns 0, and the clause does not execute. However, if the window is visible, the function returns the unsigned true value 1, which is negated by the minus sign before the DLL function to derive the logical true value from Visual Basic's viewpoint (–1).

Example: Next, suppose your Visual Basic application must install a set of files to Windows, or must access your WIN.INI file (the text file that describes the standard operating characteristics of your copy of Windows). Not everyone stores their copy of Windows in a directory with the same name. For instance, because I may be using other editions of Windows , I store my Windows 3.1 in the directory C:\WIN31. The default directory for Windows file storage is C:\WINDOWS.

Two routines that obtain the location of the currently running edition of Windows on its particular computer are found within the Kernel library. These routines may be declared within the global module as follows:

```
Declare Function GetWindowsDirectory Lib "Kernel"
➥ (ByVal lpBuffer As String, ByVal nSize As Integer)
➥ As Integer
Declare Function GetSystemDirectory Lib "Kernel" (ByVal
➥ lpBuffer As String, ByVal nSize As Integer) As
➥ Integer
```

The next order of business is to create two strings whose contents will be passed to the two API functions just declared. These strings will act as buffer areas; because the API cannot create variables on behalf of Visual Basic, you as programmer must perform the job yourself. By creating two blank variables, you allow room for the products of these functions in advance. Here are the preparatory instructions:

```
wd$ = String$(255, " ")
sd$ = String$(255, " ")
```

These instructions create two string variable areas 255 spaces long; spaces in this case are represented by " ". The maximum length of an alphanumeric string returned by a DLL function is 255 characters. Now the routines themselves may be called:

```
s1% = GetWindowsDirectory(wd$, Len(wd$))
s2% = GetSystemDirectory(sd$, Len(sd$))
```

The first parameter of each DLL function is the blank string, and the second parameter is the length of that string (currently 255). Because this length can be a variable and the DLL function is operating blind—remember, DLL functions aren't aware of Visual Basic—you must manually inform a DLL routine of how much space it has to work with. On my machine, the contents of wd$ are now C:\WIN31, and those of sd$ are C:\WIN31\SYSTEM.

> **Note:** The Windows Graphics Device Interface considers the graphics coordinate system for all device contexts as *consisting of pixels*, not twips. If you intend to use standard VB methods along with API routines for plotting graphics to the same VB graphic object, you will need to either use an equation to convert twip coordinate values to pixel values for the sake of the API function calls or change the .ScaleMode property setting for the graphic object to 3 - Pixel at design time.

Why Bother with the API?

At this point, you might be asking yourself why you would *want* to program using the Windows API, when the VB vocabulary is so rich and rewarding. Here are some possible answers to your quandary: First, the API is addressed in much the same manner whether you program in Visual Basic or in some brand of C++. Whenever you choose to switch high-level languages, you have the opportunity to port that knowledge of the API vocabulary into your new environment.

Second, the API has more functions and routines than Visual Basic. One GDI function structurally related to the ellipse-drawing routine is called RoundRect. This function draws a rounded rectangle to the specified device context. Within the Kernel library, you have access to the lowest-level processes of Windows. As you communicate with a Windows program as its *user*, each motion you make triggers a standard series of events. When you engage a scroll bar, you indirectly send a message to one part of the system stating you want a logical value change, and a message to another part stating you want the positioning of a certain gray box on the screen shifted, and a message to another part stating you want the contents of the window associated with the scroll bar updated. These are but three messages among many that may have been triggered by that one motion, depending upon the current conditions of your Windows environment at the time.

Within the standard confines of the Visual Basic environment, you as *programmer* of the API are able to establish multiple instances of this standard sequence of events and perhaps alter this sequence should you prefer your application window to behave differently. The scroll bar could, for instance, change colors while the user moves the scroll box. Better yet, it could send a message to a certain sound library loaded into memory as a Windows DLL, in order to give the scroll bar its own noise. Using the API, you are not bound by the restrictions of a programming language meant for—to borrow a misunderstood phrase—beginners.

A third reason it's beneficial to program with the Windows API is that other applications access the API by means of their own background languages. You can access the same Windows API functions, for example, from Microsoft Word for Windows and Excel. The API can act as the proverbial tie that binds several Windows applications and your Visual Basic application so they share the workload of your primary office tasks. This is the purpose of the meta-application: joining several programs to handle one job.

ByVal or Not ByVal?

This is your official confusion warning for the paragraphs to follow. Normally when writing a Sub or Function procedure declaration, if you specify within the parentheses the ByVal term before a parameter, this generally means the variable delivering the value or string contents to this procedure should not be changed or altered by the procedure. In other words, stating ByVal x As Integer means variable x can have the value of the integer that passed it, but not its identity. Normally, if q passed a value to a procedure that used x to receive it, changing the value of x changes q; stating ByVal turns this off—normally.

The exception involves the use of ByVal to pass a value to DLL routines, especially those declared as Function procedures. This is done because a DLL wouldn't know the identity or reference of a Visual Basic variable if it saw one. (It can, however, recognize certain composite structures, as you'll see later.) The point of invoking DLL routines, however, is to change the value or contents of variables in a way that Visual Basic alone cannot. Therefore, even though values often are passed to DLL routines solely by value, the Declare statement ensures the necessary variables that perform the passing—such as the previous buffer strings—are changed by the results of the DLL routines.

When ByVal does affect the calling variable's value.

ByVal is used mostly to distinguish which data elements are being passed to the Function routine as *input*. Any other variables not carrying ByVal on their shoulders are used as *output* variables for the Function routine, except for the variable result value of the Function itself, declared outside the parentheses.

Appointing a Ruler

Here's a sample Visual Basic application using declaratives to the Windows API. Visual Basic alone has no functions that determine the characteristics of the computer in which it currently resides, such as the current ratio of pixels to the inch. Suppose you want to place a ruler in your form, but you want the ruler to display true inches—that is, as true as Windows is capable of estimating. You can use the commonly stated ratio of 1,440 twips to the "logical inch," but that might not be too accurate, especially because Visual Basic doesn't know the size of your monitor. You might also use the new .TwipsPerPixelX and .TwipsPerPixelY properties to determine the current approximate conversion scale, but the settings for those properties are integral, and as a result not necessarily precise. Windows is much more likely to know the relative sizes of devices installed within its own system than is Visual Basic, because it's currently handling the drivers for the screen and other devices. Suppose you bypass this "logical inch" business and have Windows determine the current ratio of pixels to the inch. You must set the .ScaleMode for the objects in your form to 3 - Pixel, but that's no problem.

For each graphic output device installed in Windows, whether it is the screen, a window on the screen, or the printer, the GDI maintains a list of that device's capabilities in memory. These capabilities can be retrieved by means of an API function. The most convenient way to implement this function requires several lines of preprogramming in the global module:

```
Global Const DRIVERVERSION = 0        '  Device driver version
Global Const TECHNOLOGY = 2           '  Device classification
Global Const HORZSIZE = 4             '  Horiz. size in millimeters
Global Const VERTSIZE = 6             '  Vert. size in millimeters
Global Const HORZRES = 8              '  Horiz. width in pixels
Global Const VERTRES = 10             '  Vert. width in rasters
Global Const BITSPIXEL = 12           '  Number of bits per pixel
Global Const PLANES = 14              '  Number of planes
Global Const NUMBRUSHES = 16          '  Number of brushes
Global Const NUMPENS = 18             '  Number of pens
Global Const NUMMARKERS = 20          '  Number of markers
Global Const NUMFONTS = 22            '  Number of fonts
Global Const NUMCOLORS = 24           '  Number of colors
                                      '     supported
Global Const PDEVICESIZE = 26         '  Size required for
                                      '     device descriptor
Global Const CURVECAPS = 28           '  Curve capabilities
Global Const LINECAPS = 30            '  Line capabilities
Global Const POLYGONALCAPS = 32       '  Polygonal capabilities
Global Const TEXTCAPS = 34            '  Text capabilities
Global Const CLIPCAPS = 36            '  Clipping capabilities
Global Const RASTERCAPS = 38          '  Bitblt capabilities
Global Const ASPECTX = 40             '  Relative pixel width
Global Const ASPECTY = 42             '  Relative raster height
Global Const ASPECTXY = 44            '  Relative pixel diagonal
Global Const LOGPIXELSX = 88          '  Horizontal pixels/inch
Global Const LOGPIXELSY = 90          '  Vertical rasters/inch
Global Const SIZEPALETTE = 104        '  Number of entries in
                                      '     physical palette
```

```
Global Const NUMRESERVED = 106     '  Number of reserved
                                   '    entries in palette
Global Const COLORRES = 108        '  Actual color resolution
```

Here I left the remarks beside each declaration to help identify its purpose. You might recall, `Const` is a declarative statement placed within the global module that sets an arbitrary term as equivalent to a fixed value for the duration of the program. Each item in this GDI routine's capabilities list is numbered, though not consecutively. Because it's easier to remember a term than a number, you can declare these terms as constants in the global module. You could just as easily declare other terms, especially if you speak a language other than English, but the terms shown above have been suggested by Microsoft and are used by its in-house programmers.

Later in the global module, this declaration is placed to the GDI routine that will return an entry from the capabilities list:

```
Declare Function GetDeviceCaps Lib "GDI" (ByVal hDC
➡   As Integer, ByVal nIndex As Integer) As Integer
```

The first parameter of this function—as is common for GDI device-related functions—is a handle to a device context. The second parameter `nIndex` is an index number for the entries in the capabilities list. The value for this number can be replaced by its corresponding `Const` name from that rather large list.

Assume now you have named all the capabilities list items and declared the function that calls an item from the list. Suppose you have a long picture box called `RulerX` along the upper edge of the form `DrawForm`. The `.Height` of `RulerX` is about 70 pixels. This shall be your horizontal ruler, as shown in Figure 10.2.

A routine that displays this ruler appears within the `Sub Form_Load ()` procedure:

```
Sub Form_Load ()
DrawForm.Show
inch = GetDeviceCaps(DrawForm.hDC, LOGPIXELSX)
For hack = 0 To RulerX.Width Step (inch / 8)
    Select Case True
    Case countmark / 8 = Int(countmark / 8)
        extent = 40
        inchmark = 1
    Case countmark / 4 = Int(countmark / 4)
        extent = 30
    Case Else
```

```
        extent = 15
    End Select
    RulerX.Line (hack, 72)-(hack, 72 - extent), QBColor(1)
    If inchmark = 1 Then
        RulerX.CurrentX = RulerX.CurrentX - 7
        RulerX.CurrentY = RulerX.CurrentY - 15
        If inches > 0 Then RulerX.Print inches;
        inches = inches + 1
    End If
    countmark = countmark + 1
    inchmark = 0
Next hack
End Sub
```

To give you a better idea of what's going on, here is the previous procedure in pseudocode:

```
Procedure for loading the form:
Show the form now.
Find out how many pixels there are in an inch by
  looking up that value in the device capabilities
  list.
Start counting by eighths of an inch.
    Compare the following cases for truth:
    If the eighths-of-an-inch are multiples of 8,
        Make the inch line high.
        Call this line an inch interval.
    If the eighths-of-an-inch are some other
      multiple of 4,
        Make the inch line medium-size.
    In all other cases,
        Make the inch line small.
    End of cases.
    Draw the line from the bottom up, however long
      as designated in the case structure
      and make it blue.
    If this line is an inch interval then,
        Place the current X point 7 pixels to the left.
        Place the current Y point 15 pixels up.
        If the inch count is above zero then
          print the current inch number.
        Increment the inch count.
    End of condition.
```

```
    Increment the eighths-of-an-inch count.
    Call the next line a non-inch interval.
Count the next interval.
End of procedure.
```

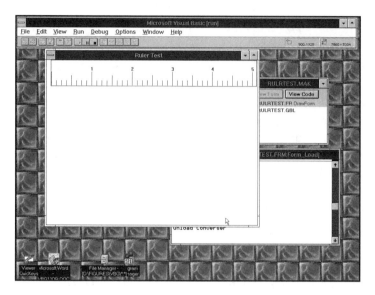

Figure 10.2. The horizontal ruler, inch by inch.

Marching to the Blit of a Different Drum

In the normal course of Visual Basic programming, you've been able to move "icons" about the screen—or rather, small bitmaps of a fixed size whose general purpose is to depict some type of control operation. The Visual Basic vocabulary does provide a primitive means for animation, by way of the .Move method, but this method is unquestionably slow in its operation. What you need—or perhaps, selfishly speaking, what *I* need—are some commands that perform bit-plane movement, in the way the older BASIC interpreters for the Atari 400/800 and Commodore 64 handled "playfields."

The trouble with implementing such a system in the Windows environment is that from the view of Windows, the screen is a mesh of multiple logical devices, and not just one. You can't tell Windows to move objects about *the screen* because certain parts of Windows are, on the whole, unconvinced of the fact that there's only one screen. A logical context, from the point of view of the GDI, is like a screen unto itself with stretchable boundaries.

> **Definition:** A *logical context* is a programmatic structure that simulates an electronic device for any routine that directs data to it for output.

Every process in the GDI library refers either to the number or handle of a logical context, or to an alternate window number. Conceivably, the device number for "the screen" (as the GDI sees it; and remember, there can be more than one such "screen") can be passed to any of these processes as an argument, though perhaps for safety's sake, the `.hDC` (handle to the Device Context) property is not obtainable for the `Screen.` object. The Visual Basic interpreter does recognize this property for forms, picture boxes, and the `Printer.` object.

The graphical contents of each device context in Windows are represented point-by-point someplace in memory at all times. This representation cannot be considered a direct result of each device's graphical contents; changing the contents of those regions of memory reserved for the device in turn changes the appearance of the contents of that device. Every pattern of bits or pixels you see on the screen is a representation of the contents of memory. It therefore follows that moving patterns about the screen to animate them is a memory-related operation.

Distinguishing between device and logical contexts.

A device context is a logical structure that represents the area of memory where these patterns appear. Imagine, if you will, two semitransparent sheets of graph paper. On both sheets are charts plotting mathematical functions. You can slide these sheets about your desk, at times laying one chart partially on top the other. In so doing, your mind may join elements of both charts to form a collective image. As you plot the functions of those charts, however, you probably ignore the coordinate system of the other chart momentarily when drawing a line on one chart to a coordinate position (40, 15). The coordinate system you recognize for each chart is an independent logical context. The coordinate system by which data is plotted to that chart pertains only to its particular piece of paper.

Now, suppose you take these charts and place them both onto the face of a photocopy machine; you might choose to make the charts overlap so their copies fit on the same page. On this photocopy page, you make some notes and draw arrows referring to the interesting parts of both charts. The notes you've written are positioned with respect to the arrangement of elements on the photocopy page. Your mind has just created an independent logical context for the photocopy page. Yet if you were to add a point or line here and there to the *image* of one of the original charts shown on the photocopy page, your mind would first recall the coordinate system you developed for that chart. Your logical frame of reference shifts depending on the portion of the image to which you presently refer.

A device context describes for Windows the coordinate system—the frame of reference—for the object that either contains or will contain the data. Your screen is an image of each logical device—a "copy," to borrow a term from the last paragraph—which may display the contents of each device and may, in the process, obstruct portions of it. The full contents of every device context, obstructed or not, are mapped out someplace in memory. It is therefore possible to move a rectangular portion of an image displayed in a form or picture box—which are themselves classified by device contexts—to another area of the object or to some other object, by way of a process whose true intent is to move the contents of memory from place to place. This process is the block memory transfer, also known as a *blit*. Short for "block transfer" (somehow), a blit is an instantaneous relocation of a grouping of memory contents from one region to another.

The Windows API contains a single, powerful process for the blit. It's declared in a Visual Basic global module as follows:

```
Declare Function BitBlt Lib "GDI" (ByVal hDestDC As
➡   Integer, ByVal X As Integer, ByVal Y As Integer,
➡   ByVal nWidth As Integer, ByVal nHeight As Integer,
➡   ByVal hSrcDC As Integer, ByVal XSrc As Integer,
➡   ByVal YSrc As Integer, ByVal dwRop As Long) As
➡   Integer
```

I stated earlier that API functions were deceptively simple; declarative statements such as this are largely responsible for this deception. The function takes nine parameters and returns a single integer, an unsigned true/false value designating whether the process was successful.

The variables in the previous declaration are to a great extent merely symbolic; you don't have to use these particular variable references in the course of your program. These references hold open space for integral values to be passed to the BitBlt process in a specific order.

The purpose of the BitBlt process is to copy a rectangular region or block of memory most likely represented as graphics, from its current address in the device context hSrcDC (handle to the Source Device Context) to hDestDC (handle to the Destination Device Context). Keep in mind that the destination address is always listed first in this process. X and Y denote the pixel coordinates of the new origin point of the block after it is moved, at the upper-left corner. The region then is stated to extend nWidth points to the right and nHeight elements down from that origin. These coordinates are supplied in the destination side of the declaration, because the process will first be reserving space for the blitted region (you'll just have to get used to this new verb). The origin point of the block to be moved is at coordinates XSrc, YSrc.

The final parameter dwRop is short for "double-word Raster operation." Using Boolean arithmetic, the blit operation compares each bit being moved to the bit that currently resides at the location where it's being moved. The bit comparison process is similar to the one addressed by the .DrawMode property discussed earlier. Because colors are combinations of multiple bits, the resulting image after each bit is compared may be a combination of the existing and moved images, or a "wash" of one image on top of another. Windows API programmers like to use terms rather than numbers to represent states being sent to a process or messages being received from it. These terms can be designated in a Visual Basic application by Const declarations, like those for the BitBlt and related processes:

```
'  Ternary raster operations
Global Const SRCCOPY = &HCC0020
                              ' dest = source
Global Const SRCPAINT = &HEE0086
                              ' dest = source OR dest
Global Const SRCAND = &H8800C6
                              ' dest = source AND dest
Global Const SRCINVERT = &H660046
                              ' dest = source XOR dest
Global Const SRCERASE = &H440328
                              ' dest = source AND (NOT dest )
Global Const NOTSRCCOPY = &H330008
                              ' dest = (NOT source)
Global Const NOTSRCERASE = &H1100A6
                              ' dest = (NOT src) AND (NOT dest)
Global Const MERGECOPY = &HC000CA
                              ' dest = (source AND pattern)
```

```
Global Const MERGEPAINT = &HBB0226
                            ' dest = (NOT source) OR dest
Global Const PATCOPY = &HF00021
                            ' dest = pattern
Global Const PATPAINT = &HFB0A09
                            ' dest = DPSnoo
Global Const PATINVERT = &H5A0049
                            ' dest = pattern XOR dest
Global Const DSTINVERT = &H550009
                            ' dest = (NOT dest)
Global Const BLACKNESS = &H42&
                            ' dest = BLACK
Global Const WHITENESS = &HFF0062
                            ' dest = WHITE
```

With these constant declarations in place, it's now possible to pass a bit-blit directive to the GDI library such as the following:

```
c% = BitBlt(Form2.Picture1.hDC, startx, starty,
➡  deltax, deltay, Form1.Picture1.hDC, grabx, graby,
➡  SRCCOPY)
```

Don't be put off by the size of this function call. By the time you've thoroughly comprehended what the function is moving and where, you'll have memorized the order of the parameters in this function. The function call first reserves a space in the Picture1 box on Form2, starting at coordinates (startx, starty) at the upper-left corner of the reserved area and extending deltax points to the right and deltay points below. The image that will inhabit this region is taken from the Picture1 box on Form2, starting at its upper-left corner coordinates (grabx, graby). You don't have to specify deltax and deltay again; a region with that width and height, respectively, already exists in Form2.Picture1.

The term SRCCOPY is one of those constants defined earlier within the global module. When an image is blitted from one region to another, a Boolean operation compares the contents that inhabit that region with the contents being blitted to that region. The result is a new color pattern for that region. This pattern could be a negative—photographically and logically—of the blitted image; or the negative points in the blitted image might show only nonblack points in the destination region; or a negative of the destination region's current points might show through any nonblack points of the blitted image. When Boolean bitwise operations take place among the points that form an image, some pixels survive, some are logically altered, and some are cancelled—much depends on the effect you want. SRCCOPY is a common pattern because it tells the Windows API to compare the blitted image to the existing one and then to ignore those points in the existing image. The upshot of this is that the old image is totally overwritten—thus the name of the constant, which is short for "source copy."

To see the 16 possible results of such Boolean comparisons, you can write a quick Visual Basic project. Create a long, tall Form1 on your screen with .Width and .Height property settings of about 3300 and 6700, respectively. You don't need any graphic objects in this form. Type the DLL process declaration for BitBlt() as shown previously into your global module. Below that declaration, enter the constant declarations listed earlier for ternary raster operations. Next, enter the following code into the event procedures section of your main form module:

```
Sub Form_Load ()
Static dwROP(15) As Long
dwROP(1) = BLACKNESS
dwROP(2) = NOTSRCERASE
dwROP(3) = NOTSRCCOPY
dwROP(4) = SRCERASE
dwROP(5) = DSTINVERT
dwROP(6) = PATINVERT
dwROP(7) = SRCINVERT
dwROP(8) = SRCAND
dwROP(9) = MERGEPAINT
dwROP(10) = MERGECOPY
dwROP(11) = SRCCOPY
dwROP(12) = SRCPAINT
dwROP(13) = PATCOPY
dwROP(14) = PATPAINT
dwROP(15) = WHITENESS
Form1.Show
Line (30, 30)-(80, 50), RGB(255, 0, 0), BF
For bluebox = 0 To 15
    Line (150, 30 + (bluebox * 30))-(200, 50 + (bluebox
 * 30)), RGB(0, 0, 255), BF
    CurrentX = CurrentX - 45
    CurrentY = CurrentY - 20
    Print bluebox
Next bluebox
```

```
For blitbox = 0 To 15
    c% = BitBlt(hDC, 125, 25 + (blitbox * 30), 50, 20,
➡  hDC, 30, 30, dwROP(blitbox))
Next blitbox
End Sub
```

I declared the array variable to be Static in order to fit this program neatly into one procedure. The contents of the 16 array subscripts are hexadecimal values (preceded in Visual Basic by &H) which refer to specific double-word raster operations in the Windows API. The value for each subscript in this dwROP array corresponds to the same number for the visual effect produced by the .DrawMode property settings. (If the VB vocabulary provided access to the old BASIC DATA command, you could condense these 16 array-loading statements into one. However, Visual Basic has no equivalent for the old DATA command.)

Following the array loading statements, Form1 is shown within the workspace so that the plotting process won't go unseen. The first .Line method plots a solid red rectangle at roughly the upper-left corner of the form. This is the rectangle that will be blitted 16 times during the demonstration.

The first loop clause, counting for bluebox, plots equal-sized blue rectangles down the right side of the form. The .ForeColor for Form1 is set at design time to pure green so that there will be examples of R, G, and B in the same form. Green numerals will be printed within each blue rectangle. They, along with part of the blue rectangle itself, will be overwritten partially by each blitted red rectangle. After each blue rectangle is drawn, the .CurrentX and .CurrentY properties point to the lower-right corner of the rectangle. Both are scooted up a bit so the numerals will be printed inside the rectangles. Notice the absence of references to the Form1 object for each property and method in this procedure, basically because the blit process takes place entirely within Form1 anyway.

The second loop clause, counting for blitbox, reserves a destination area above and just to the left of each blue rectangle. The BitBlt() call has the red rectangle blitted partly atop each blue one in sequence; however, each time it does, the raster operation for the current count is called by invoking the array variable dwROP(blitbox). Every time blitbox is incremented, the raster operation to be performed changes. The result of this procedure appears in Figure 10.3.

Figure 10.3. Raster blit operations compared.

If you've drawn images before using raster graphics applications, you've probably cut a block from the middle of an image and scooted it to a new location with the mouse pointer. For such applications to determine the current location of the region you're cutting—while keeping a resemblance of the image "beneath" the region—they use Boolean operators to blend the bits from both portions of the image. The result is often not a pigment blend of the colors of both image portions, but the appearance or outline of both their contents overlaid upon each other. This is one reason you have so many Boolean copy patterns available for the BitBlt() process.

Blitting in the Space Age

The next test of the blit routines involves a simple cutting operation. To set the stage, the Visual Basic workspace should be furnished with the following items: Two forms will be created, one large enough to fit a screen-size bitmapped image (or at least a portion of one if you operate in 640 x 480 resolution) within a picture box, and another smaller form which will house the extracted region of that image, as though that form were the clipboard viewer. The workspace for this demonstration program appears in Figure 10.4.

Listing 10.1. CUTBOX.GBL Global Module.

```
Global Const SRCCOPY = &HCC0020
Declare Function PatBlt Lib "GDI" (ByVal hDC As Integer,
➥ ByVal X As Integer, ByVal Y As Integer, ByVal nWidth
```

```
➡ As Integer, ByVal nHeight As Integer, ByVal dwRop As
➡ Long) As Integer
Declare Function BitBlt Lib "GDI" (ByVal hDestDC As
➡ Integer, ByVal X As Integer, ByVal Y As Integer, ByVal
➡ nWidth As Integer, ByVal nHeight As Integer, ByVal
➡ hSrcDC As Integer, ByVal XSrc As Integer, ByVal YSrc
➡ As Integer, ByVal dwRop As Long) As Integer
Declare Function StretchBlt% Lib "GDI" (ByVal hDC%,
➡ ByVal X%, ByVal Y%, ByVal nWidth%, ByVal nHeight%,
➡ ByVal hSrcDC%, ByVal XSrc%, ByVal YSrc%, ByVal
➡ nSrcWidth%, ByVal nSrcHeight%, ByVal dwRop&)
Type Rectangle
    origx As Integer
    origy As Integer
    deltax As Integer
    deltay As Integer
End Type
Global downx As Integer, downy As Integer
Global BlitSnip As Rectangle
Global ROP2(15) As Long
```

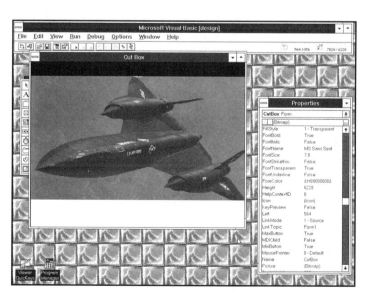

Figure 10.4. The most capable antique aircraft ever built.

Because you'll be performing only the straight copy raster operation in this application, only the SRCCOPY constant is being declared from the "ternary raster operations" section, and the rest are left out. The three Declare statements are undoubtedly a mess to type. You might find it easier to copy and paste declarations from the WIN31API.TXT file to the global module using a text editor such as the Windows Notepad. (This is what I did, and that is perhaps why you are reading this book today and I'm not still writing it.) The final declaration for the StretchBlt% function could logically have been arranged like the other two before it, with variables explicitly declared As Integer, rather than symbolized with %. However, the Visual Basic interpreter cannot handle an instruction line that large. The break in protocol is necessary to fit the entire declaration on one instruction line.

A Type clause is included here in order to represent the coordinates of the region being cut as composite variable type Rectangle. The variable object BlitSnip will be used to carry the composite elements between procedures in different form modules. The variables downx and downy will refer to the coordinates where the mouse pointer currently is held over the image being cut. The act of cutting the image will involve clicking and dragging the rectangle in the region—some call this lassoing.

The array variable ROP2() contains a set of raster operation codes for the PatBlt() process, which performs the Boolean operation on a region without having to move it. You'll see that process in progress shortly.

Listing 10.2. CUTBOX.FRM Property Settings.

```
Form CutBox
    BorderStyle     =    1   'Fixed Single
    Caption         =        "Cut Box"
    DrawMode        =    7   'Xor Pen
    Height          =    6228
    ScaleMode       =    2   'Point
    Width           =    7824

    PictureBox CutPict
        AutoRedraw  =    -1  'True
        DrawMode    =    7   'Xor Pen
        Height      =    6012
        Left        =    0
```

```
Picture        =   CUTBOX.FRX:0000
ScaleMode      =   3   'Pixel
TabIndex       =   0
Top            =   0
Width          =   8568
```

The names for these two forms are CutBox—which contains the image being hacked to bits—and ExtractBox—which contains the image that was cut. By setting the .Picture property of CutBox at design time, you can load any bitmap (.BMP) file on your system into the picture control. I set this property to point to a picture of an SR-71 downloaded from the Hobby Shop SIG on the Delphi telecom network. The .DrawMode of CutBox is set to 7 - Xor Pen. This way, a representative rectangle can be plotted around the portion of the image being cut. The procedure can give the rectangle the appearance of movement by plotting another rectangle atop the old one—thus restoring the pixels beneath it to their previous state—and by plotting another rectangle at the new position.

```
Sub CutPict_MouseDown (Button As Integer, Shift As
➡   Integer, X As Single, Y As Single)
CutPict.Refresh
downx = X
downy = Y
CutPict.Line (downx - 1, downy - 1)-(X + 1, Y + 1),
➡   RGB(255, 255, 255), B
oldx = X
oldy = Y
End Sub
```

Here's how the lasso routine works: When CutBox processes the _MouseDown event, it assigns values to downx and downy that record the upper-left corner position of the lasso while the index button is held down. Naturally, X and Y hold the coordinates of the mouse pointer when the event is processed. To enable overplotting the old rectangle later, when the mouse moves again, the values of X and Y are retained in the variables oldx and oldy. If the old rectangle is left as it is, fuzzy white boxes will eventually clutter the form.

```
Sub CutPict_MouseMove (Button As Integer, Shift As
  Integer, X As Single, Y As Single)
Static oldx, oldy
If Button = 1 Then
    CutPict.Line (downx, downy)-(oldx, oldy),
```

```
➡        RGB(255, 255, 255), B
      CutPict.Line (downx, downy)-(X, Y), RGB(255,
➡         255, 255), B
      oldx = X
      oldy = Y
End If
End Sub
```

This routine is executed whenever the mouse pointer moves, but the main body of the routine is processed only If Button = 1—if the index button is still being held down. Because the .DrawMode property for CutPict was set to 7 - Xor Pen at design time, overplotting a white rectangle with a white rectangle creates a black rectangle (see the logic in that?). The current rectangle's lower-right corner at (X, Y) now is recorded as the old rectangle corner (oldx, oldy).

```
Sub CutPict_MouseUp (Button As Integer, Shift As
➡   Integer, X As Single, Y As Single)
CutPict.Line (downx, downy)-(oldx, oldy), RGB(255,
➡   255, 255), B
ExtractBox.Show
ExtractBox.ExtractPict.Cls
c% = BitBlt(ExtractBox.ExtractPict.hDC, 0, 0,
➡   X - downx, Y - downy, CutPict.hDC, downx, downy,
➡   SRCCOPY)
BlitSnip.origx = downx
BlitSnip.origy = downy
BlitSnip.deltax = X - downx
BlitSnip.deltay = Y - downy
End Sub
```

The _MouseUp event is recognized when the button is released. At this point, the old rectangle is covered up for the last time, and the second form ExtractBox is given orders to show itself. Its Sub Form_Load () procedure is executed here, sharing execution time with Sub CutPict_MouseUp (). The picture box within ExtractBox is told to clear itself.

Following that instruction is, at long last, the first instance of the BitBlt() process. As seems to be customary with GDI routines, the destination point of the move or copy is listed first. The handle to the device context for ExtractPict is related to ExtractBox directly because the procedure that contains this handle, Sub CutPict_MouseUp (), actually belongs to the CutBox form.

It's now time to refer to the cut region as though it's an object. The upper-left corner or origin of this region is represented by the coordinates (downx, downy), and the width and height or delta coordinates are (X - downx, Y - downy). These two coordinate pairs are classified by the final four instructions of this procedure as belonging to the object composite variable BlitSnip (bless you). You don't have to pass BlitSnip as a parameter because the image of the cut region is, in essence, "force-fed" to the destination form rather than passed. This is another functional distinction between the mechanisms of Visual Basic functions and API processes. Because API routines specify the destination of their data packages first as handles to the device context, they tend to do more giving than receiving.

Listing 10.3. CUTBOX2.FRM Property Settings.

```
Form ExtractBox
   BorderStyle     =   1   'Fixed Single
   Caption         =   "Extract Box"
   Height          =   4188
   ScaleMode       =   3   'Pixel
   Width           =   6276

   VScrollBar Pattern
      Height       =   3372
      Left         =   0
      Max          =   16
      TabIndex     =   1
      Top          =   0
      Value        =   16
      Width        =   252

   PictureBox ExtractPict
      Height       =   3372
      Left         =   240
      ScaleMode    =   3   'Pixel
      TabIndex     =   0
      Top          =   0
      Width        =   5628
```

continues

Listing 10.3. continued

```
VScrollBar Magnification
      Height        =    3372
      LargeChange   =    10
      Left          =    5880
      Max           =    500
      TabIndex      =    2
      Top           =    0
      Value         =    100
      Width         =    252

Label PatLabel
      Caption       =    "Pattern: None"
      Height        =    252
      Left          =    0
      TabIndex      =    4
      Top           =    3360
      Width         =    2532

Label MagLabel
      Alignment     =    1    'Right Justify
      Caption       =    "Magnification:    "
      Height        =    252
      Left          =    3960
      TabIndex      =    3
      Top           =    3360
      Width         =    2172
```

Note that the `.ScaleMode` for all forms and picture boxes in this project have been changed to `3 - Pixel`, from their default of `1 - Twip`. Windows API routines recognize pixels as their native coordinate system, although they will also recognize coordinate systems expressed for objects whose `.ScaleMode` is `2 - Point`. A point, in Visual Basic as well as in common measurement standards, is 1/72 inch. Microsoft approximates this size assuming the screen is a 14-inch diagonal monitor.

```
ROP2(0) = &H42
ROP2(1) = &H500A9
ROP2(2) = &HA0329
ROP2(3) = &HF0001
```

```
ROP2(4) = &H500325
ROP2(5) = &H550009
ROP2(6) = &H5A0049
ROP2(7) = &H5F00E9
ROP2(8) = &HA000C9
ROP2(9) = &HA50065
ROP2(10) = &HAA0029
ROP2(11) = &HAF0229
ROP2(12) = &HF00021
ROP2(13) = &HF50225
ROP2(14) = &HFA0089
ROP2(15) = &HFF0062
End Sub
```

Here's another instance where a veteran BASIC programmer wishes he had access to the old DATA command. The hexadecimal codes for the 15 types of raster operations reserved for the PatBlt() process are assigned to the ROP2() array.

```
Sub Magnification_Change ()
magnify BlitSnip
End Sub

Sub Pattern_Change ()
crunch BlitSnip
End Sub
```

One of the strange quirks about event procedures is that they attempt to process elements of composite variables at the moment runtime begins. Even if the procedure makes perfect sense logically, the Visual Basic interpreter might display an error message saying an element of the composite variable is undefined, regardless of what the global module says. Because of this, you must pass this object in full to other procedures in the general area for processing.

```
Sub magnify (object As Rectangle)
destx = object.deltax * (Magnification.Value / 100)
desty = object.deltay * (Magnification.Value / 100)
ExtractPict.Cls
c% = StretchBlt%(ExtractPict.hDC, 0, 0, destx, desty,
➡   CutBox.CutPict.hDC, downx, downy, object.deltax,
➡   object.deltay, SRCCOPY)
If Pattern.Value > 0 Then
```

```
    c% = PatBlt(ExtractPict.hDC, 0, 0, destx, desty,
➥       ROP2(Pattern.Value))
End If
MagLabel.Caption = "Magnification:   " + Str$
➥   (Magnification.Value)
End Sub
```

The value of the scroll bar `Magnification` represents the percentage factor by which the cut image is magnified. The `StretchBlt%()` process does the honors, literally taking the cut image and making it smaller or larger without you doing much mathematics. An example of increased magnification appears in Figure 10.5.

Figure 10.5. Who's responsible for this brilliant piece of ingenuity, anyway?

The current width and height of the cut image are magnified by the percentage factor to obtain variables `destx` and `desty`. After the picture box is cleared of excess or leftover pieces of image following the image size reduction, the `StretchBlt%()` process is invoked. Again, the destination is listed first, extending from coordinates (`0`, `0`) to the stretched (or shrunken) lower-right corner coordinates (`destx`, `desty`). The source coordinates are listed next, extending from the point where the user originally positioned the mouse (`downx`, `downy`) to the original width and height passed from the composite variable `BlitSnip`.

Notice, the width and height of the *source* image are among the
StretchBlt%() parameters. This is because this process' sole purpose is to make
the color image from one region snugly fit the rectangle of another region,
despite the differences between the two regions. The image from a tall, thin
rectangle could be stretched and squashed to fit a small, squat rectangle with
StretchBlt%(). This particular procedure Sub magnify () will stretch and shrink
the cut image to scale.

The conditional clause checks whether the user has dialed up a Boolean
blit pattern for the image with the left scroll bar. If such a pattern is set, it is
applied here again using the PatBlt() process. The process is demonstrated best
in the following procedure:

```
Sub crunch (object As Rectangle)
ExtractPict.Cls
destx = object.deltax * (Magnification.Value / 100)
desty = object.deltay * (Magnification.Value / 100)
c% = StretchBlt%(ExtractPict.hDC, 0, 0, destx, desty,
➡   CutBox.CutPict.hDC, downx, downy, object.deltax,
➡   object.deltay, SRCCOPY)
If Pattern.Value = 16 Then
    PatLabel.Caption = "Pattern:  None"
Else
    c% = PatBlt(ExtractPict.hDC, 0, 0, destx, desty,
➡   ROP2(Pattern.Value))
    PatLabel.Caption = "Pattern:   " +
➡   Hex$(ROP2(Pattern.Value))
End If
End Sub
```

After the picture box is cleared, the magnification factor is figured again.
The StretchBlt%() process then moves the original cut image back to
ExtractBox, even if the magnification factor is 100 percent and no stretches
take place. The comparison pattern specified for StretchBlt%() is SRCCOPY, which
stands for a direct copy pattern.

If the scroll bar is at the bottom (its default state), no Boolean comparison
is made; otherwise the PatBlt() process is invoked for the image in the
ExtractBox display. The value of the Pattern scroll bar (below 15) dials up a
Boolean comparison pattern. This is passed to the PatBlt() process through
the ROP2() array seeded earlier. The seventh pattern in this sequence makes the
cut image a negative—that is, it inverts the image as shown in Figure 10.6.

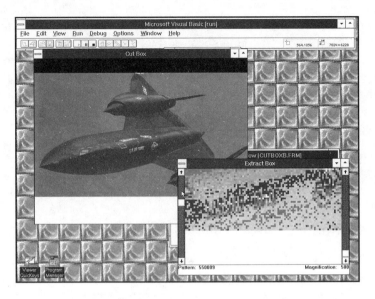

Figure 10.6. Logical inversion, or a negative as a Soviet spy may have captured it.

The Highs and Lows of Programming

As a guest of the Microsoft Windows GDI, you've just taken a peek into the vast and interesting world of image manipulation. What's unique about Visual Basic is that it is perhaps the highest-level *interpreted* programming language produced capable of handling such low-level processes.

When I make references to "high-level" and "low-level" languages, what I'm really referring to is the degree to which the processes of the operating system are represented as linguistic. Visual Basic is considered a high-level programming language because it borrows its syntax partly from mathematics and partly from English. Lower-level processes are not as linguistic; they can best be stated with terms that are more logical from the computer's perspective. As a result, low-level processes are generally more capable from a computer's standpoint, as evidenced by the blit processes introduced in this chapter.

As shown by the blit functions of the Windows GDI library, API functions concentrate largely upon the location in memory or the device context *to* which data is sent; whereas Visual Basic functions focus more upon the locations *from* which data may be acquired. These syntactic distinctions become clear when you attempt to integrate the two languages into one program. Still, Visual Basic provides adequate facilities for blending such languages—so necessary API functions can be accessed efficiently, the same way a person speaking English who's trying to sound intelligent often invokes a phrase from French.

Programming in the Express Lane

If you can imagine the structure of programs running in the Windows environment as though it were an interstate highway system, you might consider a library to be something of a turnpike between points. A turnpike is a major component of the overall system; but in order for a car to enter a turnpike, its driver must supply the proper token of exchange at the turnpike gate.

The roadmap of Windows' network of libraries.

Each routine catalogued within a Dynamic Link Library is a portion of some larger overall program. It's one road in a much larger network. By itself, it's pointless; although it's a complete program, it generally performs only one function and then quits. In Windows, however, a DLL routine is like a procedure in Visual Basic or a subprogram in earlier editions of BASIC; that is, it is re-entrant. The program currently running—what I often call the "calling body"—passes control to the DLL routine by declaring its address. In interpreted source code such as Visual Basic, this address is an abbreviated name that gives the programmer some clue about its function. A program may place as many such calls to DLL routines as is necessary at virtually any time.

When program control is passed to a DLL routine, the calling body gives the routine a handful of data as a sort of token. At the beginning of the routine's runtime, this data is acquired from a mutual access point in memory—for this analogy, a toll gate. Usually, the gatekeeper accepts only exact change. The data can be any values or string contents, though the order in which the data elements are presented, and the form and "denomination" in which they are presented, must conform to the types specified by the header at the beginning of the DLL file. In this case, Visual Basic variables may be compared to coins of various denominations. The different standard type structures form a system of tokens for passing values or contents down the pike to the Windows DLLs.

One use for
declaring
variables
`As Any`.

Technique Note: Because the types of variable values being passed to a DLL are always fixed, it generally is best not to use an implicitly declared variable or one declared to be a `Variant`, as a carrier of values to a DLL routine. By all means, the `Currency` type should not be used.

For the sake of simplicity, the Visual Basic interpreter considers all values stored in variables as *signed*—these variables can contain positive or negative values. In the C programming language, among others, variables can be declared as unsigned—these contain absolute values, and the bit (binary digit) that normally stores the sign of the value can be used as only one more power of two; thus doubling the value's positive range. Visual Basic doesn't have as many variable types as C. Therefore, if the API does not understand the variable type of the token at the gate, the variable often is declared in the Visual Basic application's global module `As Any`—meaning a nonspecific variable type.

In exchange for the bundle of small change handed it by the Visual Basic application, the DLL routine it calls often hands back to it a single value—in a sense, a receipt. This is generally an integer containing a true/false (positive 1 / 0) flag value—showing whether the routine's mission was successful. Depending on the routine's structure, however, it also might be a floating-point value of some importance to the program, such as the hexadecimal color address of a particular pixel on the screen. The variable container for this "receipt" value is declared in the Visual Basic application's global module, along with the DLL routine name. Sometimes, the point of running the DLL routine is to see what the value of this result variable will be; for instance, you might run a routine that checks your hard disk to see whether a particular file is located there. The true/false (1 / 0) result system works well for such purposes. Other times, you might want a DLL to draw a Windows metafile or complex graphical object to the screen; in this case, the true/false result passed to your program tells you whether the object was drawn successfully.

Windows' network of toll booths is referred to collectively as the Applications Program Interface (API). Visual Basic already adequately communicates with the core of Windows and with the API; though as you know now, the address of each library routine belonging to the API may be added to the working vocabulary of Visual Basic by means of the `Declare` statement. Thus, for

many programmers whose abilities have evolved beyond the proper use of the
.PSet method, programming in Visual Basic becomes programming in Windows—which has collected well over a thousand DLL routines in its API.

Slow—Pay Toll Ahead

Here's an example of the toll booth analogy in action. One Windows API routine acts as a communications station for currently active windows in the environment. A message in this instance is usually an integer previously declared as a constant using Dim Const or Global Const; each integer has its own particular meaning and its own term associated with it. For this example, you work with the message EM_GETSEL, which is a signal to the API to fetch the current character coordinates of a block of text indicated in a paragraph shown in a window.

First the setup. Two preparatory instructions are placed within the global module of the application. The first attaches the API call term to the Visual Basic vocabulary:

```
Declare Function SendMessage Lib "User" (ByVal hWnd As Integer,
➡   ByVal wMsg As Integer, ByVal wParam As Integer,
➡   lParam As Any) As Long
```

Here you see the "fee" for entering the SendMessage() routine: three integers and an Any. Here variable lParam is actually a long integer value that is by default set to zero, though it requires all four bytes to represent that zero, thus holding open a place in memory even when the value of lParam really is zero. Visual Basic doesn't understand "long zeros"; it sees no reason to use four bytes to represent a value that could be represented with only two (being zero, it should be represented by no bytes, but that's beside the point). Therefore lParam is declared here As Any in order to override VB's ordinary, though otherwise sensible, method of operation. Notice, the rest of the variables declared in the function are passed to the routine ByVal (by value), in a sense denoting these are input variables to the routine rather than output variables from it.

Elsewhere in the global module—either before or after the previous declaration—is this instruction:

```
Global Const EM_GETSEL = &H400
```

The numeral value for the message EM_GETSEL ("Please let me know where the indicated text in this window begins and ends") is 400 in hexadecimal (base 16). This message will act as your "traveling papers" in order to get it past the gate.

Later in the application, Visual Basic dispatches this message to the API:

```
received = SendMessage(TextWin.hWnd, EM_GETSEL, 0, 0)
```

Where Visual Basic functions and Windows API functions differ.

Here TextWin is the arbitrary name for an active Visual Basic form. Earlier in this chapter, you saw the .hWnd property of a form window in Visual Basic. In the entire Windows environment, the same term *hWnd* is an abbreviation for "handle to an active window." After this routine is executed, the variable received will be arranged so that it contains two *bytewise* values in the four-byte Long integer: the first in the extreme lower two bytes, representing the starting location of the indicated block; and the second in the extreme upper two bytes, representing the ending location of the block.

The question you might reasonably be asking at this point is, why go to this much trouble to find the location of indicated text, when Visual Basic provides the .SelStart and .SelEnd properties of a text box for precisely this purpose? The answer lies in the variety of styles you can apply to the window being addressed by the first parameter. Because you are dealing with a Windows API routine, there is no law in Visual Basic that states you must use the routine to address a Visual Basic window. Thus, if you know the hWnd handle of some other window—for example, a dialog box belonging to Word for Windows—you can use the same function to determine the indicated text location there. It is up to the Visual Basic application's programmer, however, to make sense of the result.

The overall point is this: Once you begin to program using DLLs, you gain direct access to the huge, amalgamated program that is Windows. So regardless of the language you're using at the time, you're now programming *in Windows*. Furthermore, every Windows application links to some extent to the Windows API; if it doesn't, it must be a DOS application. It follows that you as a Visual Basic programmer using Windows DLLs have a direct link to whatever other processes are running in Windows. Adding a library to the queue of running executable files augments the power of Windows, not unlike adding pages to a road atlas.

Building onto the Core

Table 10.1 lists the core libraries of the Windows environment, along with their general purposes:

Table 10.1. Key Windows component libraries.

Library	Description
KERNEL.EXE	Contains environmental management functions, as well as links to DOS.
SYSTEM.EXE	Contains a set of routines that affect how Windows interacts with the CPU, especially in cases where 386 protected mode is in use.
GDI.EXE	Contains GDI routines for handling windows, managing their contents, and displaying any form of graphics.
USER.EXE	Contains those routines related to user input through any and all devices.
COMM.DRV	Contains a rudimentary set of data exchange routines used in conjunction with the hardware ports.
SOUND.DRV	Contains a set of routines for generating sounds through the standard ISA sound system.
MOUSE.DRV	Contains a small set of routines for polling the specific hardware registers of the mouse, without regard to pointer location or appearance.
KEYBOARD.DRV	Contains a set of routines for polling the state of specific hardware registers of the keyboard, without regard to how keys pressed affect a window or running application.

Notice how executable files that contain libraries must not necessarily have filenames that end with the .DLL extension. A library is distinguished from a regular DOS-style executable program, from the viewpoint of Windows, by the presence of a header attached to the executable file. This acts as a table of contents for each re-entrant routine in the file; non–re-entrant routines need not be listed here. Users can't interpret this header file because it's compiled in object code. Therefore, as a Visual Basic programmer, your access to a library is determined, practically speaking, by whether its authors publish the names and addresses of the routines in the library.

Most extension products published exclusively for Visual Basic are, therefore, not too different, from a programmer's perspective, from any standard Windows application, except for these general distinctions:

▢ Visual Basic extension DLLs don't necessarily provide a front end package like an application's control panel or main window, though they can. Instead, Visual Basic extension DLLs often provide features and tools for you to embellish your own front-end panels.

▢ The purpose of the individual routines in a Visual Basic extension DLL package can vary greatly, rather than be focused as they are in a standard application. For instance, MicroHelp's *Muscle* contains routines for, among hundreds of other things, polling the active state of the NumLock key, returning the lowest value in a specified array variable, and displaying a listbox that contains a tree-form directory listing for a given device.

Can DLLs from other applications be called from Visual Basic?

▢ Many Windows applications comprised mainly of DLLs still are joined by a small .EXE file, often called "the main." This file is provided so the application as a whole can be given an icon and installed into a Program Manager group. Visual Basic extension DLL packages are not installable applications and, therefore, need no .EXE file.

Theoretically, the DLL routines from any Windows application can be declared as part of a Visual Basic project. In practice, however, if you want to make part of Lotus 1-2-3 for Windows an integral portion of your Visual Basic project, you must know the addresses and parameters of Lotus' associated DLLs—which is not likely because Lotus appropriately considers this private information. Most files comprising Asymetrix' ToolBook programming language are DLLs, though only a selected few have had their addresses made available by Asymetrix to the general public.

The Shape of Visual Basic Libraries

When programming in Microsoft Visual Basic for DOS, re-entrant object (compiled) code is attached to the main body of the program at the beginning of the source code, by means of the "metacommand" $INCLUDE. In plain DOS, a library is not an independent entity running within an environment, but a segment of precompiled code attached to the final object file by a linker. Microsoft currently calls these precompiled segments Quick Libraries because they were originated to work with QuickBasic.

The details about .VBX files.

Special dynamic link libraries have been designed exclusively for Visual Basic; their files are given the filename extension .VBX. Because Visual Basic's development environment does not include a preprocessor for $INCLUDE metacommands, as does QuickBasic and PDS, the programmer adds VBX files to the current project in much the same way she would include an existing form file or a BAS code file.

VBX files are dynamic link libraries, though depending on the package, there can be certain rules and exceptions:

☐ VBX files are designed to be included as files belonging to the project currently being edited.

☐ The contents of a VBX file can augment or extend the capabilities of a Visual Basic application without you including DLL routines specifically with the Declare statement.

☐ VBX files often include custom controls and graphic objects that are automatically added to the selections offered by the Visual Basic toolbox. These controls have their own button symbols, their own properties and default settings, and their own behavior patterns.

The Dead Giveaway

Visual Basic source code does not compile to true executable object code, so included files don't become part of the finished Visual Basic application. There's a good side to this: You don't have to concern yourself with possibly exploding the size of your program file when you want to access a library. On the other hand, the libraries included in a Visual Basic project file must remain separate files. This means if the Visual Basic application makes any declarations for DLL routines outside the core Windows API, you must provide the library files with these routines separately along with the .FRM and .BAS files related to the project.

Also, because the .VBX files supplied with Visual Basic 2 Professional Edition are DLLs with bigger handles, for "compiled" Visual Basic applications to work on other people's systems, these applications must have access to the .VBX files called by the source code and included in the forms.

This makes Visual Basic extended applications more difficult to give away... legally, that is. In some cases, extension programmers have made available defeated versions of their libraries—versions accessible by the project but inaccessible from the Visual Basic editor program. In some packages, you'll find two sets of DLLs, one that you as the Visual Basic application programmer can give away or perhaps sell with your project, as long as you remember to change the filename extension. Microsoft, at the time of this writing, has granted programmers the right to distribute the fully-operational .VBX files shipped with VB2 Professional Edition, along with any Visual Basic application you wish to distribute.

Are there runtime custom controls for other people to use?

COMMUNICATION BETWEEN APPLICATIONS

Software marketers tend to draw distinctions between MS-DOS computers and Windows computers. Certainly if you survived the long process of learning how Windows is designed and constructed, you know the operating environment is not really an operating *system*—at least not yet—but rather a resource layer atop MS-DOS, as described in the previous chapter. When you use Windows, you are using DOS; if you're continuing to experience the frustrations characteristic of DOS, you already know this well.

11

What Data {Is | Are}

If you've been using an MS-DOS computer for several years, you probably have grown accustomed to the idea that the data you generate with a computer program belongs to that program. When purchasing new applications for your office, you probably check the boxes for their data import/export paths and formats. You imagine yourself having to "get data out" of one application for it to be "put into" another. Modern software marketing and its many manifestations have given the concept of data a characteristic of inherent seclusion, of being withdrawn into its own small world. Perhaps once or twice (or several thousand times) you've thought it would be nice if two applications running simultaneously recognized the same single element of data. In other words, if you can type text into a document, why can't you draw a floor plan in that same document without making two documents with two different programs and somehow merging the documents together?

Truly defining multitasking.

The idea of true multitasking addressed by such questions has taken years to implement on MS-DOS computers; in truth, this concept is far from reality today. The first two editions of Microsoft Windows were officially called multitasking systems; however, some software engineers and technical authors (myself included) argued that true multitasking required, above all, independence of data from the application that generated it, disqualifying Windows 1 and 2. If the application generating the data contains the only method available for decoding the meaning of that data, then that data becomes restricted to that application. Since no other application can make use of it, the point of multitasking is entirely lost. Most software producers now agree that only Windows 3.1 qualifies as a true multitasking environment.

Many professional computing circles define the term "multitasking" differently. The major coalitions of engineers and programmers accept a definition that historically has been far different from the definitions imposed on newcomers to the industry. I tend to use the professional definition because it's less ambiguous. Multitasking is the planned or scheduled cooperation of multiple programs in a single computer system, with the capability for single elements of data to be recognized by those multiple programs during the same session.

Dynamic Data Exchange is Microsoft's name for a method of making elements of data accessible by multiple applications running simultaneously. In its System 7, Apple utilizes a method with similar construction called Inter-Application Communication (IAC). The term "dynamic" in DDE is not another marketing catchphrase; it technically means that such exchanges of data, once the channel is engaged, can take place at any time within the environment, instigated by events occurring within the computer rather than by direct commands from the user. As I mentioned in the previous chapter, Microsoft Windows recognizes standardized data formats, one of which is reserved for dynamic links.

A dynamic link is an established channel of communication between two or more Windows applications. In a dynamic link, all applications joined by the link recognize the same element of data, and any change to that data made by one application is recognized immediately by all other applications sharing the link. Through DDE, Windows makes it possible for another application outside of Visual Basic to peer into the Visual Basic form, look at a graphic object residing in that form, recognize the data currently within it, retrieve that data from it and place it within its own document, or replace that data with some of its own. With some Windows applications, a VB application might also send a command to another application, which can be translated into something as simple as a reminder to save your document or as complex as a spreadsheet macro.

> The official definition of a dynamic link.

Object Soup

In Windows 3.1, Microsoft advanced the development of its system for making data elements in memory recognizable by multiple applications at any one time. The philosophy of making data accessible by all programs is called objectification, and Microsoft's implementation is called *Object Linking and Embedding* (OLE). Before Microsoft's repeated use of three-letter abbreviations have you thinking Franklin Roosevelt has a seat on its board of directors, here's a bit of explanation:

In earlier chapters when you saw data files and formats under construction, you might have noticed how in saving some data files to disk, I preceded the saving of the records with some basic characteristics of the data file—most noticeably, how many records there are, and others at times, such as to what division of the program it might pertain, or what the settings are for the module using this data. On a much larger scale, this is what data objectification is

> Objectification of data as compared to object-oriented programs.

about. Each objectified data file is provided with resource data in its header (something Macintosh data files had from day one) that describes the characteristics of that data. Another program might be able to at least display this data, or even make sense of it if the program can translate these characteristics. This, however, requires some form of standardization of the characteristics, and Microsoft has provided its associated software authors with specifications for that standard.

The term "object," like the term "interface," has different definitions depending on what you're referring to. Object-oriented programming is a related concept to data objectification, though the two are different concepts. Keep this in mind and try to believe it because you will read otherwise in other books and especially in magazines. Object-oriented programming deals with the relationship of data to the programming language, whereas objectified data deals with the structure of data as it is interpreted by one or more running applications. In a sense, objectified data is probably more important to the user, although object-oriented programming is a topic for another book entirely (may I suggest *The Tao of Objects* by my colleague, Gary Entsminger).

You will read that Visual Basic is an object-oriented language; this is incorrect. You will read that Microsoft's Open DataBase Connectivity project—a prototype of which was shipped with your copy of the VB interpreter—deals with object-oriented data; technically, this is incorrect. If you've ever programmed in C++ or Modula-3, you're familiar with invoking *class libraries*. You've become accustomed to classifying and categorizing data, not only with respect to the context of your program, but also to the concepts you are trying to model and represent. Object-orientation implies that you can create and program *methods* along with your data that define how that data will be addressed and utilized. This process has *nothing* to do with the way Visual Basic or objectified data works.

Why Does Data *Need* to Be Shared?

Before this chapter plows mindlessly through the methods and properties supported by Visual Basic for DDE, think for a minute what this communication capability really means. DDE is one of the great advances in computing on systems whose primary operating system is MS-DOS, which (if you remember) doesn't know the difference between a data file, a metafile, and a nail file. DDE has been available to the general public since 1990 and it has yet to be given serious consideration, either in the press or on the software shelves.

Many software developers dream of making it feasible for computer programs to become components of larger applications—call them meta-applications—that are assembled by the user. The definition of a microcomputer's data as you know it would change, with data becoming an independent element of the environment's desktop like a patient on an operating table. The text editor, the matrical calculator, and the object-drawing program would operate in conjunction with one another like physicians on the same team, with each of the tools in their respective repertoires uniformly accessible from a common source on the screen.

The utopian goal of the meta-application.

A user adds functionality to his computer either by purchasing more tools or by making his own—which is the purpose of such packages as Visual Basic. For the meantime, however, Windows applications tend to be excessively large, and their intent often seems to be to combine every conceivable, rational function into one collected bundle. Nonetheless, quite a few Windows applications are DDE-capable. It's therefore conceivable that if your Windows app were missing a feature that could potentially be useful for your business, you could program that feature using Visual Basic, and then use DDE to integrate it into your meta-application as though it were a regular part of the main program when it was shipped to you.

To move a little closer toward programming meta-applications, this chapter begins by opening a DDE channel of communications between Visual Basic and the world outside its front door.

Who Serves?

A Dynamic Data Exchange communication is treated like a telephone conversation taking place between two parties on a party line. For now, DDE is only a point-to-point communications method between two applications; it's possible that a future form of DDE could be established as a sort of roundtable discussion between programs. In a sense, one application becomes the "moderator," and the floor is passed in turn to the individual "panelists."

A loose interpretation of the server/client model.

All DDE discussions begin with one Windows application broadcasting a message to all others in the system in an attempt to hail a specific one. Borrowing terms from modern networking, the hailer application is called the *client* and the program receiving the call the *server*. Once the server answers the call, the client may offer a topic of conversation. This topic is generally a document by the Windows definition—the primary data product of an application as it is represented in memory.

Suppose the server application contains this document topic. In general, the client requests that an item from that document be sent over the wire, as it were, so the client may place this data within its own document. This data doesn't have to be copied before it is placed within the client document; using DDE, the client has the capacity to maintain an image within its own document of the data as it appears in the server document. Therefore, whenever the server application changes the data, the client document is changed without the client application having to be involved in the change process. Alternately, the server may notify the client if a change has been made to the shared data element, and the client may choose to respond by granting the server permission to send the updated data over the wire.

Assume that Visual Basic is the client in the conversation. The data it receives from over the wire must be associated with some graphic object on a form where this data can be placed. Now assume that VB is the server in the conversation. The data that it will be sending over the wire must come from some graphic object on a form or from the form itself. Therefore, DDE operations in Visual Basic are stated using object-oriented syntax; as a result, all operations of this nature are considered methods rather than statements.

Objectified data's definition of "document."

An object recognized by Visual Basic as a qualified "guardian" for this data may be a picture box, a text box, a label, or a simple blank form—note that a button or menu item does not qualify. Note also that you can't use a variable, such as a long string variable, as a topic of discussion because such memory items are not considered documents—the primary data product of applications. The form is, in essence, Visual Basic's document.

The proper and polite way for Visual Basic to introduce itself to another application, as well as play host, is for the VB application to choose the topic of conversation beforehand, be ready to request that certain extra-special item of data—to "pop the question," so to speak—and then open the conversation by modestly setting the tempo, if not the *temperature,* of the conversation.

Technique Capsule: Establishing Dynamic Links

Definition: True multitasking systems or environments allow for the sharing of data in some mutually recognized form between applications. Dynamic Data Exchange allows two Windows applications to share a single element of data, and it allows this data to simultaneously coexist within documents that belong to those applications. The communication between these two applications is referred to as a dynamic link.

In Visual Basic, a graphic object that acts as a container of data may be set to receive that data from another application. The Visual Basic application sharing data over a dynamic link with another Windows application can be programmed to make changes to that data in a manner exclusive to the VB application, and then echo those changes in the Windows application that generated the data.

The sender of data in a DDE conversation is called the server, and the receiver of that data is the client. These two terms are borrowed from networking configurations. The client always initiates the conversation, requesting a specific element of data from the server. The location of this data is called the topic of the conversation, and the identity of this data is simply called the item.

In Visual Basic, a DDE conversation is established by setting the `.LinkMode` property for a graphic object. This object acts as guardian of the data being transferred over the DDE channel. If the link mode is set to "hot," any change made to the data in the server application causes the server to automatically notify the client of that change. If the link mode is set to "cold," the client has to place a `.LinkRequest` for updates to the data before the server will send it over the wire.

Using the `.LinkPoke` method, a client may attempt to update the topic data within the server document. Because there is so much data, relatively speaking, within a picture or image, Visual Basic does not automatically update image data. Instead, Visual Basic has the program issue a `.LinkSend` instruction for updating picture data over the wire. The VB interpreter waits only so long for a response to a signal or message; this length of time can be set using the `.LinkTimeout` property. Any error occurring during DDE transmission is recognized as a `_LinkError` event.

For commands to be sent between a Visual Basic application and a participating Windows application, the `.LinkExecute` method is used. Conversely, the `_LinkExecute` event is recognized when a Windows application attempts to send the VB application a command string. The interpreter also recognizes `_LinkOpen` and `_LinkClose` events whenever a DDE conversation is initiated and terminated, respectively.

Execution: The `.LinkTopic` property for a graphic object that is expected to contain text is set to a string which represents some portion or the entirety of the document within the server or client application that contains the data to be shared along the DDE dynamic link. If the Visual Basic application is the client in the DDE conversation, then this string takes the following format:

application$ ¦ document$

In this example, *application$* is a special identifier for the topic file that is not necessarily its filename. This identifier recognized by the receiving application. Following the ¦ character, *document$* is a particular body of data currently being assembled by the receiving application. Together, these two compose the target of a request for a specific item of data; this topic string tells the receiving server application where the requested data should reside. The elements are separated by a ¦ character, called a "pipe" for lack of a better word.

If the VB application is to be the server in the DDE conversation, then the format of the topic string might differ slightly because not all Windows applications use the same topic string format; one has yet to be standardized. The first area of contention is which type of delimiters are used between the necessary string elements. For a Windows application to be able to initiate a DDE conversation with a VB application and request that the VB application be the server of data, the Windows application must broadcast the following information as part of its link request:

☐ The DDE application callname

☐ The Visual Basic "document" or form containing the "data item," or the graphic object that contains the data

☐ The "data item" itself, or the graphic object

These three items must be separated by whatever DDE delimiters are supported by the Windows application placing the call to Visual Basic. In some cases, the name of an uncompiled VB application might have to be preceded by the term VizBasicApp/, which concludes with a forward-slash.

The name of the object within the topic document that is the subject, so to speak, of the DDE conversation is reflected in the `.LinkItem` property setting for a graphic object on the VB form. This object should contain the data that appears within the graphic object on the VB form. `.LinkItem` is set whenever the client object is not the form itself. Windows applications use different naming conventions for graphic objects within their documents, so you might need to refer to the server application's technical manual to find the proper phraseology for its own link items.

The `.LinkMode` property for a form or graphic object is set to an integer value which specifies the current state of the DDE conversation between the VB application and another Windows application. This property may be set manually at design time so the VB application can initiate the conversation. When another application initiates the conversation, `.LinkMode` is set automatically by the VB interpreter.

Whenever the VB application acts as server, the .LinkMode property may take either of the following settings:

0   The DDE channel is currently turned off, and no interaction is taking place between the VB application and any other.

1   The DDE channel is currently active, and the VB application is currently acting as server.

Whenever the VB application acts as client, `.LinkMode` may assume any of the following settings:

0   The DDE channel is currently turned off, and no interaction is taking place between the VB application and any other.

1   The DDE channel is active and considered "hot." The contents of the antecedent control are updated whenever the data to which it is linked in the other application is changed. This update takes place automatically.

2   The DDE channel is active and considered "cold." The contents of the antecedent control are updated whenever the `.LinkRequest` method is processed by the VB interpreter. Until then, the object maintains its current contents.

Here's a closer look at what happens technically during a DDE conversation, both in the "cold" and "hot" modes (Windows supports a "warm" mode, though Visual Basic chooses not to). Figure 11.1 shows the history of a hypothetical "hot" `.LinkMode` conversation:

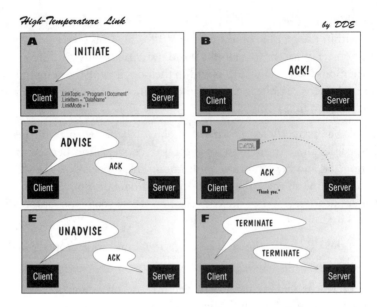

Figure 11.1. A "hot link," precisely as a New York City street vendor does not picture it.

The initiator of this conversation is the client, which seeks the server of a certain item of data. At first, it might seem more sensible for the server to start the conversation, because it is, sociologically speaking, the most important element; however, it would be inefficient for the server that is just dying to give this bit of data to some application, broadcasting a message to any application that hears it in the act of seeking potential takers.

In Panel A, the client is the Visual Basic application. It broadcasts a message in hopes that the server hears it (sounds like the movie *Tron*, doesn't it?). As the instruction block in Panel A shows, the VB application has stated its `.LinkTopic` and `.LinkItem`, and has set its `.LinkMode` property to 1 (hot). By setting this property, VB sends out the message that Windows calls the INITIATE message. This contains both the DDE callname for the application and the name of the document specified as the `.LinkTopic`. In Panel B, the called server application has responded with an acknowledgment message—or an ACK—stating not only that it is active , but also that it has access to the `.LinkTopic` document. At this point, the communication has officially begun.

The VB application believes the server has a particular item of data within the topic document. In Panel C, it sends the name of this item, in a format believed to be interpretable by the server, within the ADVISE message. Assume the link item is accessible. The server responds first with another ACK, meaning "yes." Next in Panel D, the server sends the data, in whatever form it might take—textual or graphical—in a format universally supported by Windows. The client then responds with its own ACK. Whenever the server's data changes for whatever reason, the action represented by Panel D is repeated. This sending of the data is triggered by some action performed by the user. She may have typed something in the middle of the link item, drawn on it with a paintbrush, or pasted a triangle on top of it. The server sends the data, and the client acknowledges it.

Suppose that at some time the client needs to put automatic updates on hold. It can, as shown in Panel E, send an UNADVISE message to the server; the server responds by sending an ACK message and sitting on its hands for the time being. Whenever the conversation has to be terminated—as the client should do out of respect if the application needs to be closed—the client sends a TERMINATE message, as shown in Panel F; the server responds appropriately.

With the hot link mechanism, whenever the topic document's data is changed, a message is sent to that effect to the client application, along with a copy of the changed data. By contrast, the cold link mechanism is designed for applications that desire a more terse relationship, as demonstrated below in Figure 11.2.

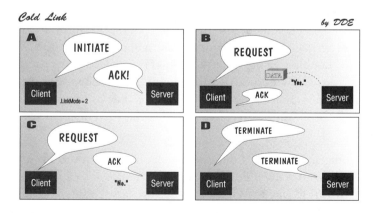

Figure 11.2. The cold link, which is more heavily dependent upon requests.

In Panel A, the client VB application sets up the same .LinkTopic and .LinkItem, but this time the .LinkMode is set to 2 (cold). The client sends the same INITIATE message as with .LinkMode 1. In Panel B, however, the client sends a REQUEST message that asks the server if the topic document's requested data item has changed. Assuming it has, the server responds with the changed data, which the client then acknowledges with an ACK. On the other hand, in Panel C, assuming the data has not been changed, the server responds to the REQUEST message with a simple ACK. Terminating the conversation is done in the same way as with a hot link, as shown in Panel D.

Manual Links

We still don't know enough about the DDE mechanism to dive headfirst into the subject of programming with it. For now, this segment will prepare a manual test that uses the Paste Link feature of both Visual Basic and Word for Windows. Feel free to follow along with me, if you have both Word for Windows and Visual Basic at your disposal. At the Visual Basic end of the communications link, I'll create a form containing a single large text box. Next, I set the form's .MultiLine property to True, its .ScrollBars property to 2 - Vertical, and its control .Name to Dynamo. This will be a test of DDE that doesn't contain any VB instructions whatsoever unto itself. Instead, I will be feeding VB instructions directly to the CLI in the Debug Window, controlling and monitoring the communications link as I go.

The manual paste-link method of establishing dynamic links.

For the first part of this test, I will copy a portion of a Word for Windows document and "paste-link" it into the text box of the VB form. I've picked a paragraph from the chapter I'm writing now and highlighted it in Word for Windows by double-clicking while the pointer is to the left of the paragraph. If you have Word for Windows, perhaps you can follow along with me using a document of your choice. From the Word for Windows menu, I select Edit/Copy, which for the time being places a copy of this paragraph onto the system clipboard.

Switching applications, I indicate the text box within the VB form, and from the VB menu, I select Edit/Paste Special. A dialog box appears, showing a list of active DDE clients. Within a list box appears the entry "Unformatted Text." After choosing this entry and clicking the Paste Link button, a copy of the indicated paragraph now appears within the text box, which is nothing unusual in and of itself. Now I return to the Word window and type something else in the middle of the paragraph I indicated earlier. These inserted characters are immediately reflected within the Visual Basic text box. If I have both applications on the screen at the same time, it's as if I'm typing into both simultaneously. Notice that the VB application is not running yet; this immediate updating of the text box is taking place as a result of DDE, not some application-related source code. Having quizzed the CLI about the status of the DDE conversation at this point, I received three responses. Here are the important DDE property settings for the `Dynamo` text box as they appear on my machine (yours may be slightly different):

Property	Setting
`Dynamo.LinkTopic`	`WinWord¦D:\BOOK\VBG\VBG110R.DOC`
`Dynamo.LinkItem`	`DDE_LINK1`
`Dynamo.LinkMode`	`1`

In response to the question about `.LinkTopic`, here you see the topic format supported by Visual Basic. `WinWord` is the DDE application callname for Word for Windows. This is separated by the filename of the open topic document with a pipe ¦ character. Had this file never been saved to disk, the topic document would be listed as a default memory name, such as "Document7." `DDE_LINK1` is the identifier tag given the currently active conversation. Finally, because the paste link took place in Visual Basic, you know the VB application is the client in this conversation because the client always requests data of the server. As a result, you know that the CLI's response of `1` to the question about `.LinkMode` shows that VB knows a hot link is still active.

Here's the process in reverse. Suppose I redraw this form and type a paragraph directly into the VB multiline text box. I want whatever is in this paragraph at any time to appear in the midst of my Word for Windows document. After assigning the text for the VB text box as the `.Text` property for that box—in design mode—I indicate that box with the mouse and select Edit/Copy from the VB main menu. For the moment, the text is on the clipboard. Switching to my Word window, I place the cursor at the point where I want the linked text to appear and select Edit/Paste Link from the Word menu. A dialog box appears showing the DDE topic name for the indicated item. This dialog box gives me the option of checking an "Auto Update" box, which is asking me whether I want the link to be "hot" or "cold." Having checked this box, I selected hot. The text now appears in the Word window. To see where this text came from, I select View/Field Codes from the Word menu. The linked paragraph is soon replaced with a Word for Windows field code, which is an element of a Word document that describes any component of that document other than standard text. The field code reads as follows:

```
{DDEAUTO Project1 Form1 Dynamo \* mergeformat}
```

Suppose the paragraph that appears in the VB text box at this time—the one now identified by a Word for Windows field code—is the same paragraph I indicated from the first test. This means if I type something in the middle of the first paragraph, thus changing the text within the VB text box, the paste-linked paragraph elsewhere in the Word document then changes as well. The second paragraph's text will always match that of the first paragraph.

This is an interesting trick, but it also raises a sticky problem: The VB text box is now client to one Word paragraph and server to another. Will the VB properties for this text box reveal which state it plays? Here's the current list:

Property	Setting
Dynamo.LinkTopic	WinWord¦D:\BOOK\VBG\VBG11OR.DOC
Dynamo.LinkItem	DDE_LINK1
Dynamo.LinkMode	1

This is the same response presented when the box was just a lowly client. It may seem odd, but the .LinkMode setting of 1 is correct whether the text box is a server, a client, or both.

Here's a strange twist to this test: Suppose I type something in the middle of the VB text box, either by running the VB application or by changing its .Caption property. The second field-coded paragraph will change in turn, but the original Word paragraph will stay as it is. Suppose I then change the original paragraph; what happens then? Does the second Word paragraph now contain both changes, to the VB text box as well as to the original paragraph? The answer is no. Believe it or not, the changes to the VB text box are scrapped, and the current form of the original Word paragraph takes over. The second Word paragraph in turn takes the form of the first. The first connections in a DDE sequence always take priority.

With the results of this experiment in hand, the conclusion may now be drawn that—programmatically speaking now—a procedure can be written for the text box Dynamo that establishes a link between it and the server WinWord, as follows:

```
Dynamo.LinkMode = 0
Dynamo.LinkTopic = "WinWord¦d:\book\vbg\vbg11or.doc"
Dynamo.LinkMode = 1
```

The .LinkMode property is first set to 0 (off) as a safety precaution because it is dangerous to tinker around with topics and data items with the link turned on—somewhat like messing with the plug of a power saw while the blade rotor is turned on.

The preceding test took place with the .LinkMode for both communications links set to 1. Had the property been set to 2, we would need to request data for the VB text box from the original WinWord server using the .LinkRequest method. This is used when the .LinkMode property for that object is set to 2, and a "cold" DDE communications link has been established between that object and some portion of a document in another Windows application.

Manually processing a DDE request.

The .LinkRequest method sends the REQUEST signal over the DDE channel. This signal asks the server application for the current image of the topic data if that image has changed since the last REQUEST. If there have been any changes, the antecedent object's contents are updated. This method works without generating an error if the .LinkMode has been set to 1; however, because hot-linked objects are automatically updated without program or user intervention, the .LinkRequest method is not necessary for that mode.

Suppose Dynamo.LinkMode is set to 2, and there is a button on the form for manual updating of the data within the text box. Here's an event procedure for that button:

```
Sub UpdateText_Click ()
Dynamo.LinkRequest
End Sub
```

The relationship between server and client in Windows is very flexible. In some cases, data can be sent from the client to the server even when the server has not requested it; actually, it is out of protocol for the server to request data of the client in the first place. Still, if a link exists between two objects, it may be possible for the VB application, acting as client, to send data back up the channel and in turn update the server. In such a case, the .LinkPoke method would be used. This term is reserved for cases in which the Visual Basic application acts as the client in a server/client DDE communication and the duty for some reason falls upon the VB application to update the data contents of the server's topic data item. `.LinkPoke` sends the contents of the antecedent object—assuming it is involved in the current link—to the server application. The server then may or may not update the contents of its own data, depending on how it is programmed to respond to backwards requests.

Making Picture Boxes Wake Up

The Visual Basic interpreter does not automatically send the updated contents of a raster-based image within a picture box to a client application, whether or not the communications link between the box and the client's recipient object is assumed to be hot. The reason for this is quite simple: It would take too long. Suppose you created a paint program that used an airbrush to paint color into the picture box. Should the interpreter send a copy of the entire picture to a client application whenever each single pixel is updated? The system simply doesn't have time for such matters.

Therefore, updates to a picture box are sent manually in all cases, by means of the `.LinkSend` method. This sends the `.Picture` property contents for a picture box through the currently open DDE channel to the client application for processing.

As is the potential case with all real-world conversations, one party might take too long to provide the other with a response. The purpose of the `.LinkTimeout` property is to determine just how long "too long" is. This property is set to a value that determines, in tenths of a second, how long the Visual Basic interpreter should wait for a response from the other party in the current DDE communications link. This property is used whether the Visual Basic application is acting as client or server. By default, `.LinkTimeout` is set to 50—approximately five seconds. A setting of –1 directs the interpreter to wait indefinitely for a response.

The VB interpreter recognizes a series of special errors as specific to Dynamic Data Exchange. These errors can be "trapped" and responded to by the `_LinkError` event. This is generated whenever a fault occurs during DDE communication with another Windows application or the attempt at communication with that application, or during an attempt by a Windows application to communicate with the Visual Basic application. In the procedure for this event, the error number is returned as variable `LinkErr`, which may take any of the following values:

1. A Windows application, acting as client, requested data of the VB application, acting as server, that was not of the type of data provided by the topic data item.

2. A request for data was placed by a Windows application without first formally initializing the DDE conversation.

3. A DDE message was passed by a Windows application without the conversation having first been initialized.

4. A Windows application requested that the topic item of the conversation be changed when no conversation has yet been established.

5. A Windows application attempted to act as server and poke data to the VB application without first initializing the conversation.

6. The Windows application, with which communication had supposedly been broken off by setting .LinkMode to 0, continued to make attempts to send messages.

7. The number of existing DDE links in the system has overflowed.

8. Only part of a string has been sent through the DDE channel because the string is excessively long.

9. The topic item requested of a Windows application client to the VB application server is invalid or does not exist.

10. A Windows application sent the VB application a DDE message for no apparent reason.

11. Not enough memory is present to continue DDE operations.

12. A Windows application designated as server has sent a REQUEST or ADVISE message, acting as if it were the client.

Remote Control

Some Windows applications, such as Word for Windows and Excel, accept and respond to actual commands remotely through a DDE channel, specified in the macro languages of those applications. Visual Basic does not automatically recognize commands through DDE, although it does accept terms that are passed to it as commands and it can interpret commands as alphanumeric strings passed to it from another application. A VB application, therefore, can take on its own command vocabulary for utilization by other Windows applications.

Giving
an actual
command to
a remote
Windows
application.

The `.LinkExecute` method sends the contents of a command string over the currently active DDE channel for the specified object. Its syntax appears as follows:

```
Object.LinkExecute command$
```

The contents of this command string *command$* might have little or nothing to do with the antecedent object; an object of some form must be specified in order to initiate a DDE conversation. The VB application may be acting as server or client during the transmission of *command$*.

Now, Microsoft Word for Windows already has a background "macro" language called WordBasic, based on (to some degree) its QuickBasic vocabulary. Many of the statements in WordBasic parallel those in Visual Basic; however, there are a few instances when it would be nice for Word to be able to utilize those features unique to Visual Basic.

For example, here's a simple procedure that acts as a timer for the active Word document. Within a VB form are two controls—a timer and a text box called `Saver`. It doesn't matter where these controls are placed on the form because you're not going to see them anyway; the form is hidden throughout the entire operation. Visual Basic is operating in "stealth mode" while it has Word for Windows save its present document every one minute. Here are the only two procedures necessary for `Form1`:

```
Sub Form_Load ()
Form1.Hide
Timer1.Interval = 60000
Saver.LinkMode = 0
Saver.LinkTimeout = 600
Saver.LinkTopic = "WinWord¦System"
Saver.LinkMode = 2
End Sub

Sub Timer1_Timer ()
c$ = "[FileSave]"
Saver.LinkExecute c$
End Sub
```

At the start of the form, the form itself is hidden (who needs it?) and the timer interval is set to 60,000 thousandths of a second (one minute). For safety, the link is unplugged and the time-out is set to 600 tenths of a second (again one minute, long enough for Word for Windows to get its file saved). The topic is set to "Winword|System"; Word for Windows recognizes the topic "System" as a reference to the program, not to a document. In other words, it now knows to expect to receive commands rather than data. The link is initiated at cold temperature; a hot link isn't necessary because there won't be any data translated.

The _Timer event procedure is triggered whenever the timer has counted to the designated interval (60,000). Once that happens, the command string [FileSave] is sent through the system using the .LinkExecute method. Word for Windows recognizes a command to its system as any instruction in its own WordBASIC language placed within square brackets. Word executes the command as if its user had selected File/Save from its main menu.

As I stated earlier, the VB application can receive a command string too; it just doesn't know what to do with it yet. In such cases, the _LinkExecute event is recognized when a DDE channel of communication attributed to a form receives from the client application an alphanumeric string, identified by Windows as a command string. The procedure for this event takes two parameters: Variable CmdStr is a string that contains the command string received. After interpretation instructions have been performed, setting variable Cancel to any nonzero value automatically tells the client application, upon the execution of End Sub, that the command was rejected.

The _LinkOpen event for a graphic object is recognized when its .LinkMode property has been set to a nonzero value, and the receiving application on the DDE channel responds to the INITIATE message with an ACK acknowledgment signal. Similarly, the _LinkClose event for a graphic object is recognized when its .LinkMode property is set to zero and when the other party responds to the TERMINATE signal with a TERMINATE message in kind.

A Real-World Idea

One of my readers from London, Arthur J. McBryan of the Huddleston Energy Consultancy, Ltd., sent me this idea for an interapplicational task: Mr. McBryan uses Word for Windows, Visual Basic, and a remote system-to-system telecommunications program called Close-Up. What McBryan would like to have is a button that can take the current Word for Windows document, save it to disk on one system, and then start a Visual Basic process that writes an automated script for the Close-Up system. The user of the VB application would select a user on a remote computer to be the recipient of this document. Once the user is selected, the VB application generates a script containing the username for the recipient computer and the filename to be sent to that computer. This script is then delivered to the Close-Up application, which in turn parses the script, dials the user mentioned in the script, and sends the document just saved over the open comm line.

Situation #4: The Interapplicational File Transmitter

A client requests that a new command be added to the menu of an existing Windows application, giving that application access to capabilities not normally considered within its purview. The new menu function will link the application to another Windows application, although along the way it will process the data it receives in the meantime, as well as acquire extra data from the user.

The solution to this problem is rather wild, but doable. For Mr. McBryan, I've written a little semi-meta-application that's part Visual Basic, part WordBasic. Once each step in this operation is completed, there is an entry in the Word for Windows File menu marked "Send Remote." Selecting this menu item starts a Visual Basic process that takes the filename of the file in the current Word window and slates that file to be sent to a particular user. This user's name is kept on a list which is maintained by a form module whose process model is similar to the one from the inventory control application INVENT1.

The project is called E-Post, with all due respect to Emily. It contains one major form shown in Figure 11.3, a global module, one instance of the common file selector dialog, and the Converser. At the time of this writing, I did not have access to Close-Up, the telecommunications program Mr. McBryan uses. He did provide me with a model script for the Close-Up program, however. At any rate, the script that E-Post generates for Close-Up is entirely in memory, and a message box will display it once it has been conceived. Another author may tack onto the end of the application whatever code is necessary to complete the operation. Those of you who also don't have Close-Up can use this VB application as a model for tight cooperation between two Windows applications.

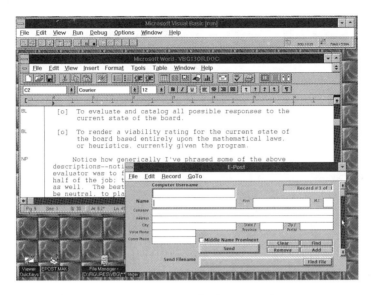

Figure 11.3. The proper etiquette is applied to e-mail.

Here are the vital property settings for the main E-Post form:

Listing 11.1. EPOST.FRM Property Settings.

```
Form EPost
   BorderStyle     =   1   'Fixed Single
   Caption         =   "E-Post"
   Height          =   3960
   Left            =   1896
   LinkMode        =   1   'Source
   LinkTopic       =   "Form1"
   MaxButton       =   0    'False
   Top             =   3180
   Width           =   8076

   CommonDialog Selector
      Left            =   120
      Top             =   2640
```

continues

Listing 11.1. continued

```
SSPanel Panel3D1
     Alignment        =    4   'Right Justify - MIDDLE
     BevelInner       =    2   'Raised
     BevelWidth       =    2
     BorderWidth      =    1
     Height           =    372
     Left             =    2640
     Top              =    2640
     Width            =    4812

     CommandButton FindFile
        Caption       =    "Find File"
        FontName      =    "Lucida Sans"
        FontSize      =    7.8
        Height        =    252
        Left          =    3720
        Top           =    60
        Width         =    1032

     Label DDETerminal
        BackStyle     =    0    'Transparent
        FontBold      =    -1   'True
        FontName      =    "Lucida Sans"
        FontSize      =    9.6
        Height        =    252
        Left          =    60
        LinkItem      =    "Topics"
        LinkTopic     =    "WinWord¦System"
        Top           =    60
        Width         =    3672

SSPanel Panel3D8
     AutoSize         =    3   'AutoSize Child To Panel
     BevelOuter       =    1   'Inset
     BevelWidth       =    2
     Height           =    252
     Left             =    6240
     Top              =    2040
     Width            =    1212
```

```
CommandButton Find
    Caption         =   "Find"
    FontName        =   "Lucida Sans"
    FontSize        =   7.8
    Height          =   204
    Left            =   24
    Top             =   24
    Width           =   1164

SSPanel Register
    Alignment       =   4   'Right Justify - MIDDLE
    AutoSize        =   3   'AutoSize Child To Panel
    BevelOuter      =   1   'Inset
    BevelWidth      =   3
    Caption         =   "Record #"
    Font3D          =   1    'Raised w/light shading
    FontBold        =   -1  'True
    FontName        =   "Lucida Sans"
    FontSize        =   7.8
    Height          =   252
    Left            =   5640
    Top             =   120
    Width           =   1812

TextBox CPhone
    FontName        =   "Lucida Sans"
    FontSize        =   7.8
    Height          =   264
    Left            =   960
    TabIndex        =   16
    Top             =   1920
    Width           =   1572

SSPanel Panel3D7
    AutoSize        =   3   'AutoSize Child To Panel
    BevelOuter      =   1   'Inset
    BevelWidth      =   3
    Height          =   372
    Left            =   960
    Top             =   240
    Width           =   3012
```

continues

Listing 11.1. continued

```
TextBox UName
    FontName        =   "Lucida Sans"
    FontSize        =   9.6
    Height          =   300
    Left            =   36
    TabIndex        =   0
    Top             =   36
    Width           =   2940

TextBox VPhone
    Height          =   264
    Left            =   960
    TabIndex        =   15
    Top             =   1680
    Width           =   1572

SSPanel Panel3D5
    AutoSize        =   3   'AutoSize Child To Panel
    BevelWidth      =   3
    Height          =   372
    Left            =   2640
    Top             =   2160
    Width           =   2172

    CommandButton Send
        Caption     =   "Send"
        FontName    =   "Lucida Sans"
        FontSize    =   7.8
        Height      =   300
        Left        =   36
        Top         =   36
        Width       =   2100

SSPanel Panel3D3
    AutoSize        =   3   'AutoSize Child To Panel
    BevelOuter      =   1   'Inset
    BevelWidth      =   2
    Height          =   252
    Left            =   5040
    Top             =   2040
    Width           =   1212
```

```
    CommandButton Clear
        Caption          =    "Clear"

SSPanel Panel3D4
    AutoSize             =    3    'AutoSize Child To Panel
    BevelOuter           =    1    'Inset
    BevelWidth           =    2
    Height               =    252
    Left                 =    6240
    Top                  =    2280
    Width                =    1212

    CommandButton Add

SSPanel Panel3D6
    AutoSize             =    3    'AutoSize Child To Panel
    BevelOuter           =    1    'Inset
    BevelWidth           =    2
    Height               =    252
    Left                 =    5040
    Top                  =    2280
    Width                =    1212

    CommandButton Remove
        Caption          =    "Remove"

SSPanel Panel3D2
    AutoSize             =    3    'AutoSize Child To Panel
    BevelWidth           =    3
    Height               =    2652
    Left                 =    7680
    Top                  =    0
    Width                =    252

    VScrollBar RecordShown
        Height           =    2580
        LargeChange      =    10
        Left             =    36
        Max              =    1
        Min              =    1
        TabIndex         =    21
```

continues

Listing 11.1. continued

```
        Top             =    36
        Value           =    1
        Width           =    180

SSCheck MidName
    Caption             =    "Middle Name Prominent"
    FontName            =    "Lucida Sans"
    FontSize            =    7.8
    Height              =    252
    Left                =    2640
    TabIndex            =    17
    Top                 =    1920
    Width               =    2292

TextBox Zip
    FontName            =    "Lucida Sans"
    FontSize            =    7.8
    Height              =    264
    Left                =    6240
    TabIndex            =    14
    Top                 =    1440
    Width               =    1212

TextBox State
    Height              =    264
    Left                =    4800
    TabIndex            =    12
    Top                 =    1440
    Width               =    852

TextBox City
    Height              =    264
    Left                =    960
    TabIndex            =    10
    Top                 =    1440
    Width               =    3012

TextBox Address
    Height              =    264
    Left                =    960
```

```
    TabIndex        =    8
    Top             =    1200
    Width           =    6492

TextBox CompanyName
    Height          =    264
    Left            =    960
    TabIndex        =    4
    Top             =    960
    Width           =    6492

TextBox MidInit
    Height          =    324
    Left            =    7080
    TabIndex        =    3
    Top             =    600
    Width           =    372

TextBox FirstName
    Height          =    324
    Left            =    4560
    TabIndex        =    2
    Top             =    600
    Width           =    2052

TextBox LastName
    Height          =    324
    Left            =    960
    TabIndex        =    1
    Top             =    600
    Width           =    3012

Label Label9
    Alignment       =    1   'Right Justify
    Caption         =    "Send Filename"
    FontName        =    "Lucida Sans"
    FontSize        =    7.8

Label Label15
    Caption         =    "Comm Phone"
```

continues

Listing 11.1. continued

```
Label Label14
    Caption              =       "Computer Username"

Label Label10
    Caption              =       "Voice Phone"

Label Label7
    Caption              =       "Zip / Postal"

Label Label6
    Caption              =       "State / Province"

Label Label5
    Caption              =       "City"

Label Label4
    Caption              =       "Address"

Label Label8
    Caption              =       "Company"

Label Label3
    Caption              =       "M.I."

Label Label2
    Caption              =       "First"

Label Label1
    Caption              =       "Name"

Menu File
    Caption              =       "&File"
    Menu FileSort
        Caption              =       "&Sort"
    Menu FileSaveMerge
        Caption              =       "Save as &Mail Merge"
    Menu FileTrim
        Caption              =       "&Trim"
Menu Edit
    Caption              =       "&Edit"
```

```
Menu EditCopy
    Caption         =    "&Copy"
Menu EditClear
    Caption         =    "&Clear"
Menu Record
    Caption      =    "&Record"
    Menu RecordInsert
        Caption     =    "&Insert"
    Menu RecordDelete
        Caption     =    "&Delete"
Menu GoToRecord
    Caption      =    "&GoTo"
```

A note about the property settings for the object DDETerminal, a transparent text box at the bottom of the form: Its .LinkTopic property is set to WinWord¦System, and its .LinkItem property is set to Topics. These settings are specified so when Word for Windows starts up the conversation and asks E-Post, "Well, E-Post, what's to chat about today?" E-Post will have an answer for it. Mind you, the system of WinWord is absolutely not what this conversation is about; but in order to prevent the possible (and with DDE, likely) occurrence of a system crash, there needs to be an active topic and item on the DDE agenda; you can't just talk about nothing even when you are talking about something. DDE-capable applications have a tendency to be shy and back out of the conversation too soon. If they get moody, they can throw tantrums and crash one or two applications.

The Word Side of the Equation

In any event, there's now a form in the Visual Basic workspace. I'd like to turn your attention away from that form for a moment and discuss what has to happen within Word for Windows. A new document template must be created. This template might mimic the normal document template NORMAL.DOT or whatever template you generally use in your office for e-mail-ready documents. The format and appearance of the new template need not be changed in any way.

With this new document template under construction, you then select Macro from Word's Tools menu and enter the new macro name SendFilename. Click the Edit button, and you soon see WordBasic's program entry screen.

Here's the macro you have to enter into the system; mind you, this is WordBasic code, *not* Visual Basic code:

```
Sub MAIN
Dim dlg As FileSummaryInfo
GetCurValues dlg
fn$ = dlg.Directory + "\" + dlg.FileName
channo = DDEInitiate("EPOST", "Form1")
If channo > 0 Then
     DDEPoke channo, "DDETerminal", fn$
Else
     MsgBox "Error in the DDE transmission."
End If
End Sub
```

Because you may be at a loss to understand a few items of WordBasic, here's what is happening: All WordBasic "macro" procedures are called Sub MAIN...all of them. The format of entries in each Word dialog box corresponds to a structure that can be applied to an object variable in the same way a Type structure in Visual Basic is applied to one of its object variables. The FileSummaryInfo dialog box structure is assigned here to an object variable dlg. The GetCurValues statement that next appears takes the current values of the summary info for the currently displayed document and assigns its contents to all the composite variables of dlg.

Two of these dialog components are .Directory and .FileName. The string contents from those components are joined together, with a backslash \ placed between the path and the filename. The next DDEInitiate() instruction starts the DDE process, giving Word the official role of client, although it will be the application doing the serving. (I told you this would be a wild solution.) In WordBasic, DDE sessions are given channel numbers, and this particular one is assigned to variable channo. As long as this number is not zero (meaning, as long as the channel is open), the DDEPoke statement sends the combined path and file names to server EPOST for topic Form1. No matter what you name your Visual Basic form, DDE topic names are always generic. The recipient of this message is declared to be DDETerminal, which is a text box in the EPost main form.

When the macro is fully entered, the Save Remote menu entry can be added to the document template's native menu through Word's Tools/Options menu. That's enough of Word for right now; shift mental parsing modes now, if you will, and skip back over into the VB application. The global module for this application looks like this:

Listing 11.2. EPOST.GBL Global Module.

```
Type NameRecord
    Username As String * 16
    LastName As String * 30
    FirstName As String * 20
    MidInit As String * 3
    CompanyName As String * 50
    Address As String * 50
    City As String * 20
    State As String * 5
    Zip As String * 10
    VoicePhone As String * 14
    CommPhone As String * 14
    MidProm As Integer
End Type
Global CurRecord As NameRecord
Global msg$, Button$(4)
Global IcH As Integer, IcW As Integer, IcFN As String
Global ConvResponse As Integer, NumButtons As Integer
Global Const OFN_HIDEREADONLY = &H4&
Global Const OFN_FILEMUSTEXIST = &H1000&
Global Const OFN_PATHMUSTEXIST = &H800&
```

Here you see the Type structure for the main form. As stated earlier, the part of the form that keeps the recipient list utilizes the same process model as a form in INVENT1; as a result, there's nothing new I have to tell you about how that works. Instead I'd like to concentrate on the DDE portion of this application.

Every Word for Windows document that uses this new template has the new menu selection Send Remote available to the user. When the user selects this item, the label field DDETerminal in the EPost form changes; Visual Basic has no control over it. In fact, the contents of this form change if you have the form in the VB interpreter workspace in design mode; nothing can stop the message from reaching its target.

With E-Post running, however, a change in the contents of the caption activates a _Change event, to which a procedure may be attached. In this case, it is the procedure that starts the send process:

```
Sub DDETerminal_Change ()
If UName.Text = "" Then
    MsgBox "Please select a user."
Else
    SendFile
End If
End Sub
```

By the way, these are the identical contents of Sub Send_Click (). When a username has successfully been entered into the UName field, the main sending procedure will be executed.

```
Sub SendFile ()
nl$ = Chr$(13) + Chr$(10)
msg$ = "Are you sending this file now or at 20:00hrs?"
Button$(0) = "Now"
Button$(1) = "20:00hrs"
NumButtons = 2
Load Converser
If ConvResponse = 1 Then
    script$ = "wait until 20:00hrs" + nl$
End If
script$ = script$ + "baud 9600" + nl$
user$ = RTrim$(UName.Text)
script$ = script$ + "dial " + user$ + nl$
script$ = script$ + "send " + RTrim$(DDETerminal.Caption) +
➥    " c:\email\" + nl$ + "hangup"
'    Dear Arthur:
'
'    Here's where the rest of your code would go
'    for sending this script to Close-Up
'    however it is this script will get there.
'                     -DFS
MsgBox script$
End Sub
```

I utilized the Converser so I can have dialog buttons with contents I can set explicitly. If the user chooses the wait option, another line is tacked to the head of the Close-Up script this procedure generates. Otherwise, the procedure takes data from the form and adds it to the "template" of a script being accumulated in *script$*. Now, I don't exactly know how Close-Up gets ahold of this script, but at least I can have one generated following the model Mr. McBryan gave me, which reads as follows:

```
wait until 20:00hrs
baud 9600
dial Mary
send c:\tmp\glycol.doc c:\email\
hangup
```

At any rate, mission accomplished. Interapplication communication over a DDE channel is obviously an extremely inexact science, and one that is bound to get you as programmer in trouble several times. Even if you've mastered the general concepts, DDE links that seem to have everything going right can suddenly crash in a brutal mess of flying bitmaps. I managed to crash Word for Windows twice, once in the form of a hang, just in the process of creating this test application. Visual Basic is even touchier, perhaps not by any fault of VB but of the DDE system itself. If you write an application that utilizes DDE, you must test it thoroughly before you decide to market it.

PART THREE

Real-World Experimental Programming

ALGORITHMIC
LOGIC

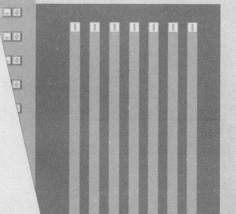

Mathematics is a creation of human beings. Like written language, mathematics represents esoteric concepts, proportions, and characteristics symbolically. This representation helps explain human concepts to human beings. Mathematics has a tendency toward repetition, recursion, and redundancy. Mathematicians define these repetitions as patterns, then apply formulas to these patterns. Recently, one of the popular trends has

12

been to make graphical patterns out of the numerical patterns, apply color to these patterns, and marvel at the beauty of precision and predictability. These patterns, declare some mathematicians, prove there is an underlying pattern to nature and that the discovery of patterning is an insight into nature itself.

Yet when these mathematicians stroll through a wooded canyon or watch the ripples formed by raindrops along the surface of a flooded prairie field, the presence of overwhelming uniqueness and unduplicable originality doesn't seem to make a fractal dent in their passion for patterns. They are on to something, or so they feel: That at last the reason for the existence of everything may be described with a unified formula, one glorious line of alphabetic symbology that may prove to the world—or rather, to other human beings—that nature is indeed a set of laws. These laws then may be taught, professed, argued about on the Sunday morning talk shows, and probably packaged as software and converted to Windows.

The real world purpose of algorithms.

Algorithmic logic puts a dent in all the theories and promises of algebraic simplification of reality by making peace with everyone and offering a compromise viewpoint. Algorithms represent real-world states with symbolic variables and simple arithmetic. The study of algorithmic logic, like the study of more scientific realms of mathematics, is concerned with the existence of underlying patterns. Yet as it is in reality, the work performed by algorithms is limited to human processes—tasks that have some bearing upon reality, not just theory. Algorithmic logic is based in the belief that for every initial state, toward every desired final state, there is an infinite number of routes. The most efficient route toward the final state is entirely reliant upon each algorithm's own definition of efficiency. Efficiency is therefore no longer a fixed state, a "given," but a characteristic of a particular situation whose bearing upon another situation is minimal at best. Efficiency—like reality itself at times—becomes a *variable*.

Is Meaning in the Eye of the Beholder, Too?

To take this discussion out of the esoteric realm and into something more concrete, consider the way you sort a row of books on your bookshelf. Would you just start with any two books that were out of order with respect to each other, swap those two, and go on from there? Would you start dividing your shelf into the sorted side and the unsorted side, accumulating books one-by-one into the sorted side?

Using what you do every day as an algorithm model.

Perhaps the most explored category of algorithms concerns sorting. In a high-level computing language, sort algorithms are implemented within database fields or memory arrays. You've seen one popular sort algorithm explored in the previous chapters. I'd like to take you on an extended tour of just how everyday sorting processes, like the one examined in the previous paragraph, are implemented in code. In algorithmic logic, there's more than one way to accomplish a goal; the efficiency of the chosen method depends on the symbology employed and the situation in which it is employed.

An Algorithmic Test of Sorts

A sort algorithm is by nature esoteric. Words can explain only to a limited degree how one works, so I invite you to experiment with this application, A Program of Sorts. It takes a series of 100 unique values ranging from 1 to 100 and randomizes their locations within the series array. Each unit in the array represents an item to be sorted, as plotted on an x/y axis. The x axis represents the value of each element, whereas the y axis represents the location of that element in the array.

The x/y axis plot starts out as a square full of a hundred points of light at randomly scattered locations, like political junkies who stayed too late at a party. To the right of the plot is your choice of sort algorithms. As the sort you choose is executed, the points are replotted to reflect each swap the algorithm makes. Notice the clear and undeniable patterns that represent the trademarks for each sort algorithm. These patterns tell you the true story of what's going on.

Figure 12.1 shows the main display for this test operation, a one-form project:

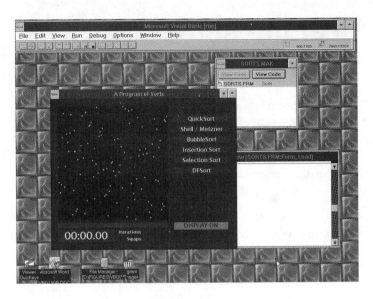

Figure 12.1. Computing's answer to the flea circus.

Here are the vital property settings for this form:

Listing 12.1. SORTS.FRM Property Settings.

```
Form Sorts
    BackColor      =   &H00400000&
    BorderStyle    =   1   'Fixed Single
    Caption        =   "A Program of Sorts"
    Height         =   5724
    Left           =   1176
    Top            =   2388
    Width          =   6828

    PictureBox SortPlot
        BackColor      =   &H00000000&
        DrawWidth      =   3
        ForeColor      =   &H00FFFF80&
        Height         =   3996
        Left           =   240
        ScaleHeight    =   3972
        ScaleWidth     =   3972
        Top            =   240
        Width          =   3996
```

```
Label DisplaySwitch
   Alignment       =    2   'Center
   BackColor       =    &H00008000&
   Caption         =    "DISPLAY ON"
   FontName        =    "Lucida Sans"
   FontSize        =    9.6
   ForeColor       =    &H00000000&
   Height          =    252
   Left            =    4440
   Top             =    4320
   Width           =    1932

Label Clock
   Alignment       =    2   'Center
   BackColor       =    &H00C00000&
   Caption         =    "00:00.00"
   FontName        =    "Lucida Bright"
   FontSize        =    18
   ForeColor       =    &H0000FFFF&
   Height          =    430
   Left            =    240
   Top             =    4560
   Width           =    2052

Label Swaps
   BackColor       =    &H00400000&
   FontName        =    "Lucida Sans"
   FontSize        =    9.6
   ForeColor       =    &H00FFFF00&
   Height          =    252
   Left            =    3360
   Top             =    4800
   Width           =    852

Label Sorted
   Alignment       =    2   'Center
   BackColor       =    &H00000040&
   Caption         =    "SORTED"
   FontName        =    "Lucida Sans"
   FontSize        =    7.8
   ForeColor       =    &H00000080&
   Height          =    180
```

continues

Listing 12.1. continued

```
        Left          =    240
        Top           =    4320
        Width         =    3972

Label Iterations
        BackColor     =    &H00400000&
        FontName      =    "Lucida Sans"
        FontSize      =    9.6
        ForeColor     =    &H00FFFF00&
        Height        =    252
        Left          =    3360
        Top           =    4560
        Width         =    852

Label Label3
        Alignment     =    1    'Right Justify
        BackColor     =    &H00400000&
        Caption       =    "Swaps"
        FontName      =    "Lucida Sans"
        FontSize      =    7.8
        ForeColor     =    &H0000FFFF&
        Height        =    252
        Left          =    2280
        Top           =    4800
        Width         =    972

Label Label2
        Alignment     =    1    'Right Justify
        BackColor     =    &H00400000&
        Caption       =    "Iterations"
        FontName      =    "Lucida Sans"
        FontSize      =    7.8
        ForeColor     =    &H0000FFFF&
        Height        =    252
        Left          =    2280
        Top           =    4560
        Width         =    972

Label SelectionSort
        Alignment     =    2    'Center
        BackColor     =    &H00800000&
```

```
Caption        =    "Selection Sort"
FontName       =    "Lucida Sans"
FontSize       =    9.6
ForeColor      =    &H0000FFFF&
Height         =    216
Left           =    4440
Top            =    2040
Width          =    2004

Label DF_Sort
  Caption      =    "DFSort"
  Top          =    2400

Label InsertionSort
  Caption      =    "Insertion Sort"
  Top          =    1680

Label BubbleSort
  Caption      =    "BubbleSort"
  Top          =    1320

Label ShellSort
  Caption      =    "Shell / Metzner"
  Top          =    960

Label QuickSort
  Caption      =    "QuickSort"
  Top          =    600
```

First, I have to discuss a bit of business about the variable declarations and how this form works. Here is the General Declarations section:

```
Dim unit(100) As Integer
Dim StartTime As Double
Dim oldx1 As Integer, oldy1 As Integer, oldx2 As Integer,
➥ oldy2 As Integer
Dim newx1 As Integer, newy1 As Integer, newx2 As Integer,
➥ newy2 As Integer
Dim Done As Integer, DisplayOn As Integer
Dim comp As Integer, swic As Integer
Dim p(100) As Integer, w(100) As Integer
```

The telltale array is stored in unit(). To keep time, the program uses the variable StartTime. For the plotting procedures, two sets of coordinate variables are declared that depict where a point is to be taken off of the plot (old-) and where it is to be replaced (new-).

Setting the
plotting scale
for a picture
box.

Now, the graphing portion of the program significantly throws off the time proportions, making QuickSort seem to be one of the slowest algorithms—although actually on its own, without any graphing, it's the fastest. For this reason, I've added a "DISPLAY ON/OFF" button (actually a label control) to the form, so the user can disable plotting momentarily for a more accurate time reading. One word of apology to the people who have extremely fast computers: Because many sorts take place in less than one second, the time figure may have an interval less than Visual Basic is capable of displaying. For a more accurate proportional time if you're testing the sort algorithms against each other, consider setting the .DrawWidth property of the SortPlot picture box to 1, resetting the .ScaleHeight and .ScaleWidth properties to 1000, and resetting the dimensions of the plotting array to 1000.

The scaling instruction may be found within the Sub Form_Load () procedure:

```
Sub Form_Load ()
Sorts.Show
Randomize
SortPlot.Scale (1, 1)-(100, 100)
Sorts.Refresh
RackEmUp
ShowPlots
DisplayOn = True
End Sub
```

When the main form is loaded into the workspace, it is immediately displayed; otherwise, the user with a slower computer might be confused, wondering why nothing seems to be happening for a minute or so. It takes a few seconds for the program to seed the plot array, and the VB interpreter treats its graphical duties as less important than its mathematical ones. As a result, the seeding of the arrays prevents the form from being shown for a little while, unless the instruction SortContest.Show is invoked first.

The coordinate scale for the plot panel is set by the .Scale method within the loop clause. Procedure Sub RackEmUp () sees the array, and Sub ShowPlots () displays its initial pattern within the three blocks.

```
Sub RackEmUp ()
For cell = 1 To 100
MakeCell:
    vl = Int(Rnd(1) * 100) + 1
    For chk = 1 To cell - 1
        If vl = unit(chk) Then GoTo MakeCell
    Next chk
    unit(cell) = vl
Next cell
End Sub
```

Each element within the array is unique, so that no two values match and the final diagonal line is perfectly straight—this way, you don't miss out on the full experience. Variable vl draws a random number between 1 and 100. This number is then checked against those previously allocated within the array to see whether the chosen value has already been allocated; if it has, the procedure jumps back to the instruction following the label MakeCell: and draws another number. This flip-flop process continues until an original number is drawn. This process is iterated 100 times until the array is full.

```
Sub ShowPlots ()
For lin = 1 To 100
    SortPlot.PSet (unit(lin), lin), QBColor(11)
Next lin
End Sub
```

This procedure displays the initial setting of the points in the plot array. Within the parentheses in the .PSet method, the unit() value acts as the *x* axis parameter, whereas the line count variable lin acts as the *y* axis parameter. If you've ever programmed in QuickBasic (chances are less likely these days that you have), a facsimile of QuickBasic's color code #11 is used for the point plots—this is a bright cyan color.

Because the *presence* of the graphing instructions slow down the sort algorithms, I've placed each algorithm belonging to the form module in two procedures. One procedure contains the plotting instructions and another leaves them out. Clicking "DISPLAY ON" ("-OFF") determines which procedure receives the branch. Here's an example procedure from one of the choice buttons:

```
Sub BubbleSort_Click ()
If Done = True Then ResetPlot
If DisplayOn = True Then
    bsort
```

```
Else
    bsort2
End If
End Sub
```

Clicking the DISPLAY ON button changes the binary status of flag variable `DisplayOn`, changes the button's color, and that's all. The preceding procedure then reads `DisplayOn` to see whether a branch is made to the procedure with the graphics display commands (the procedure name without the "2") or the procedure without them. For now, I'd like to concentrate on the plain procedures so you can get a clearer picture of what's happening. By the way, each of these procedures will be sorting element values in ascending numerical order. For each algorithm, it would be quite easy for the programmer to reverse the directions of each comparison so that the sorted array is in *descending* order instead. To start, here's how the BubbleSort algorithm looks in detail:

BubbleSort

```
Sub bsort2 ()
Dim j As Integer, k As Integer, l As Integer, t As Integer,
➡  n As Integer
StartTime = Now
n = 100
For l = 1 To n
    j = l
    For k = j + 1 To n
        If unit(k) <= unit(j) Then
            j = k
        End If
    Next k
    If l <> j Then
        t = unit(j)
        unit(j) = unit(l)
        unit(l) = t
    End If
Next l
ShowTime
Light
End Sub
```

The BubbleSort algorithm is deceptively simple, and is one of the easiest to implement. Its speed notoriously drops with larger and larger arrays, especially with comparison to QuickSort. BubbleSort starts with the first element in the array, which is currently represented by variable 1. The objective for BubbleSort now is to find the lowest possible value throughout the remainder of the array and swap that value—which will eventually be pointed to by variable j—with the one pointed to by 1. Variable k is used in a loop clause that counts from the element of the array immediately following the original value of j, to the final element n, which was set at the beginning to 100.

The loop clause counts to see whether there's any value lesser than that currently held within the unit() array at position j. If there is, j is set to the location of the least value, but the loop isn't exited yet. Instead, it continues to the end to see whether there's still a lesser value. The end result of this loop is that j has the address of the least value in the remainder of the array.

Notice how the mechanism works here: Before the For-Next begins, the value of j is set to the value of 1. Within the loop, if the conditional clause finds a lesser value in the kth unit than there in the jth unit, j is made equal to k. After the loop clause, j is tested to see whether it still equals k; in other words, j is tested to see whether the conditional clause was activated. If the two values are no longer equivalent, the conditional clause must have found a lesser value now pointed to by j. This value is swapped with the one currently pointed to by 1 so the *lowest* possible comparison address contains the *least* possible value. Variable 1 is then incremented, and all the elements behind 1 are considered *sorted*. The comparison process then continues with the new element pointed to by 1. You can say 1 acts as a zipper—which leads one to wonder why this wasn't named "ZipperSort."

After having swapped the contents of the array elements at locations 1 and j, those particular contents may not be at their final resting places, though it can definitely be concluded that element j must now contain a greater value than it did. As the sorting process continues, those values toward the end of the array that 1 hasn't touched yet become greater in value. The greater values are said to "bubble" toward the high end; this is how the sort algorithm gets its name.

Figure 12.2 depicts a plot of the array at four stages of its history, being sorted by BubbleSort.

Figure 12.2. The BubbleSort signature pattern.

So that you have an idea of what the graphing instructions do to the code structure of the algorithm, here is Sub bsort2 ()'s more graphical counterpart:

```
Sub bsort ()
Dim j As Integer, k As Integer, l As Integer, t As Integer,
➥ n As Integer
StartTime = Now
n = 100
For l = 1 To n
    j = l
    For k = j + 1 To n
        comp = comp + 1
        If unit(k) <= unit(j) Then
            j = k
        End If
    Next k
    If l <> j Then
        swic = swic + 1
        t = unit(j)
        oldx1 = unit(j)
        oldy1 = j
        unit(j) = unit(l)
        oldx2 = unit(l)
        oldy2 = l
        newx1 = unit(j)
        newy1 = j
        unit(l) = t
        newx2 = unit(l)
        newy2 = l
        ShowTime
        ShowIter
```

```
        OverPlot
        NewPlot
    End If
Next l
ShowTime
ShowIter
Light
End Sub
```

Notice the settings to the coordinate pair variables during each swap process. The call to Sub ShowTime () displays the current time elapsed, and the call to Sub ShowIter () updates the contents of the comparisons and the swaps made thus far. Notice also the variable swic is incremented each time an official value swap takes place in the array, whereas comp is incremented each time a comparison instruction is encountered. The *comparisons/swaps* figures are presented within the form as a way to measure performance rather than speed alone.

The next algorithm on the discussion list is Shell/Metzner. It is not the fastest nor the least complex, but it may be the most elegant:

ShellSort

```
Sub ssort2 ()
Dim m As Integer, j As Integer, i As Integer, t As Integer
StartTime = Now
m = 100
While m > 0
    m = m \ 2
    For i = m To 99
        For j = (i - m + 1) To 1 Step -m
            If unit(j) <= unit(j + m) Then Exit For
            t = unit(j)
            unit(j) = unit(j + m)
            unit(j + m) = t
        Next j
    Next i
Wend
ShowTime
Light
End Sub
```

Here, variable j is once again a pointer to a value being tested in this array, whereas i is a pointer to the value that the jth array value is compared to. Variable m acts as a "spanner" used to continually divide the array in half, forming smaller and smaller segments. The Shell/Metzner algorithm swaps values between these segments so that the lower-ordered segments contain the lesser values. As m is continually divided by 2 and the segment size is halved, the values in each segment are compared to those in all the segments before it. If a lower-ordered segment contains a greater value than that in the higher-ordered segment, the two values are swapped. Again, the new positions for those values might not be their final resting places once the array is entirely sorted; however, they're closer than they were before. As the segment size continues to decrease and the distance between swapped elements grows narrower, each element is nudged closer to where it eventually belongs. Once m cannot be halved any more, the array must be sorted.

Phrased more explicitly, variable i counts all the elements from the beginning of the *second* segment to the end of the array—this is the key variable of the primary For-Next loop in the preceding procedure. Variable j acts as a pointer to all elements within the array that are *n* segment-sizes (multiples of m) behind the element pointed to by i. If the former segment element pointed to by i is greater in value than the latter segment element pointed to by j—regardless of what those values actually are—the two values are swapped. Figure 12.3 shows the Shell/Metzner process at work; here you can see the effect of the variables. As the segment size variable m is continually halved, the distance between the nodes narrows like loose cotton being twisted into a string.

Figure 12.3. The incredible shrinking array.

The Insertion Sort algorithm is simpler by comparison to those others you've seen demonstrated; it is also significantly slower:

Insertion Sort

```
Sub isort2 ()
Dim i As Integer, j As Integer, v As Integer
StartTime = Now
n = 100
For j = 2 To n
    v = unit(j)
    i = j - 1
    While v < unit(i)
        unit(i + 1) = unit(i)
        i = i - 1
    Wend
    unit(i + 1) = v
Next j
ShowTime
ShowIter
Light
End Sub
```

The theory behind the Insertion sort is excessively simple; perhaps that's why it's such a slow performer. Starting with the first element, the procedure keeps track of the portion of the array that is already sorted. The array continues to be divided between the sorted and unsorted sides; periodically a new element v is extracted from the left side of the unsorted portion and inserted into its proper place in the sorted portion. The array counts back from the right edge of the sorted portion until it finds the element's proper slot. Along the way, many elements pointed to by i are shifted one unit forward to make room for v's new home. Remember early in this chapter when I asked you whether you would divide a bookshelf into its sorted and unsorted side? Having worked in a library for several years, I can report that the majority of people who use a method to sort books use their own personal Insertion sort algorithm.

Depending upon whom you consult, you might read that either the Selection sort algorithm or the Insertion sort is the easiest to implement within an application.

Selection Sort

```
Sub selsort2 ()
Dim i As Integer, j As Integer, min As Integer, t As Integer,
➥  n As Integer
```

```
n = 100
For i = 1 To n - 1
    min = i
    For j = i + 1 To n
        If unit(j) < unit(min) Then
            min = j
            t = unit(min)
            unit(min) = unit(i)
            unit(i) = t
        End If
    Next j
Next i
End Sub
```

In this particular array, there are 100 units, which is a figure reflected by the setting of the variable n. The Selection Sort algorithm starts sorting for elements starting from the left side of the array and counting toward the right, up until the next-to-the-last element in the array. The pointer for this loop is i. A second loop clause counts from one beyond the element currently pointed to by i until the end of the array n. The pointer for this loop is j. If the value of the element pointed to by j is lesser than the value of that pointed to by i, the j value belongs before the i value. The two are then swapped. This looping process continues until the broader loop i reaches its end.

The QuickSort algorithm is not quick to explain. It consists of a complex series of several processes repeated less often rather than a simple series of fewer processes repeated more often. This is a relatively difficult concept to grasp. Because the algorithm's incarnation in Visual Basic is so large, I'm presenting the listing of Sub qsort () in small segments:

QuickSort

Part 1:

```
Sub qsort ()
Dim i As Integer, j As Integer, b As Integer, l As Integer,
  ➥t As Integer, r As Integer, d As Integer
StartTime = Now
k = 1
p(k) = 1
w(k) = 100
```

```
l = 1
d = 1
r = 100
```

The array sorted by the QuickSort algorithm is continually broken into subarrays—which are like the segments in the Shell/Metzner algorithm, except that these subarrays are sorted independently from the rest of the array. The upper and lower bounds of each subarray are maintained within array variables p() and w(), respectively—these array variables don't contain the subarrays themselves, merely their start and end locations with respect to the main array. Borrowing a term from assembly language, you can say that these two array variables define the *stack*, or in this case, the ongoing list of smaller arrays to be independently bubble-sorted. The bubble sort takes place only when the subarray has been divided and subdivided until it is conveniently small.

Figure 12.4 depicts the QuickSort technique with a 25-element array. Panel A of the figure shows the algorithm starting with element 1, which for now is the extreme left element in the array. Variables l and r are placemarkers, with r pointing at the moment to the extreme right element of the array. These two placemarkers are scooted toward the middle of the array as the algorithm progresses, like the plates of a trash compactor being drawn closed. Variable d is a register depicting whether the direction of the comparison (which you learn about momentarily) is to the left (−1) or right (1).

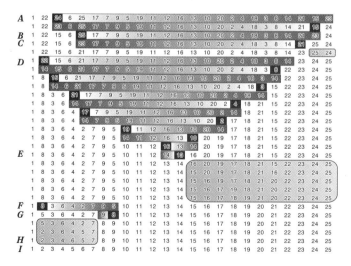

Figure 12.4. The long, drawn-out story of QuickSort.

QuickSort looks first to the right of element 1 to see whether there's any value lesser than 1. The element j is being compared to 1; Panel B shows QuickSort counting backward by one from the extreme right element r until it finds a lesser value than 1. Once it finds that value, QuickSort swaps the values of element 1 and element j, then makes variable r point to where the element that was 1 now resides. The extreme right "compactor," shall we say, has been moved toward the center. You also know for a fact that every element to the right of r is greater in value than r, so you've already made significant progress.

Panel C shows QuickSort now looking to the left of element r to see whether there's a value greater than r. The element being compared to r is i; in Panel C, you can see QuickSort is now counting forward by one from element 1, which is (for the moment) the extreme left element in the array. Once that higher value is found, QuickSort swaps that value with the value of r, then makes variable 1 point to the element that was r. The extreme left compactor is now moving toward the center, and every element that falls before element 1 is now lesser in value than 1.

At Panel D, QuickSort looks to the right of element 1 again, counting backward by one from where element r has been last positioned until it finds a value lesser than 1. This value is then swapped with 1, and r is set to point to the element that was 1. This flip-flop continues until compactors collide. This happens at Panel E. When r and 1 are next to each other, every element behind 1 is lesser in value than that of 1, and every element ahead of r is greater in value than that of r. Although the array isn't sorted yet, it's certainly closer to being sorted with only a few swaps.

Variables 1 and r now divide the sort array into two segments. The left segment may be cast aside for the moment, in order to concentrate on the right segment. At Panel F, 1 and r are set to the left and right locations of this segment, and the back-and-forth swapping process starts all over again. At Panel G, 1 and r have collided once again, dividing this subarray into two smaller segments. These segments are both small enough by QuickSort's standards that pointers 1 and r need not be repositioned for either segment; instead, the algorithm BubbleSorts both smaller subarrays. At Panel H, these subarrays are now perfectly sorted, and they may now be left peacefully alone.

At Panel I, variables 1 and r are now set to the left and right boundaries of the extreme left large segment. The QuickSort swapping procedure is reactivated until it has partitioned two small subarrays that can be easily BubbleSorted at Panel J. By Panel K, the entire 25-element array is sorted.

Now here's how this concept is implemented in Visual Basic:

Part 2:

```
Do
toploop2:
    If r - l < 9 Then GoTo bubsort2
    i = l
    j = r
    While j > i
        If unit(i) > unit(j) Then
            t = unit(j)
            unit(j) = unit(i)
            unit(i) = t
            d = -d
        End If
        If d = -1 Then
            j = j - 1
        Else
            i = i + 1
        End If
    Wend
```

The main part of this procedure is implemented in the form of a Do-Loop clause, which is exited when no more subarrays remain to be sorted. The algorithm keeps a running tally k of how many array portions have yet to be sorted; when that variable reaches zero, the loop is exited.

The first If-Then conditional statement checks to see whether the distance between the right and left boundaries r and l is lesser than 9. If it is, then execution branches to the bubble sort routine. Assuming it hasn't branched, then comparison element pointers i and j are set to the left and right boundary pointer values for the time being.

Within the Do-Loop clause is a subordinate While-Wend loop, which is only executed as long as the right element i is to the right of the left element j. The comparison clause following the While header tests to see whether the value of the left element, held within unit(i), is greater than the value of the right element within unit(j). If it is, a swap is made using t as a temporary variable as you've seen in the two earlier algorithms. (BASIC aficionados: There is no SWAP instruction in Visual Basic.)

Once the swap is made, four calls are placed to routines that update the display. Following those calls, the direction register d is negated with the instruction d = -d. This is because after the swap is completed, it's time for QuickSort to look the other direction behind the swap, as explained earlier. If d = -1 (left), then after the instruction, d = 1 (right). Following the end of the conditional clause, the directional variable d determines if the right variable j is decremented or the left variable i is incremented. The same unit(i) > unit(j) comparison may be made repetitively within the While-Wend loop; the only mechanical difference in how the algorithm is executed concerns the direction of the comparison. The addition of the d directional variable is my gift to the art of algorithm-crafting.

Part 3:

```
j = j + 1
k = k + 1
If i - l < r - j Then
    p(k) = j
    w(k) = r
    r = i
Else
    p(k) = l
    w(k) = i
    l = j
End If
d = -d
GoTo toploop2
```

After the loop clause is completed, the "compactor doors" will have collided. The job of QuickSort now is to divide the main array into a subarray, and to start the process again with new left and right boundaries. Variable j is incremented so the same comparison isn't performed twice. One is added to the tally variable k, meaning there is now one more subarray to evaluate. The comparison expression i - l < r - j determines whether the comparison should now look left (true) or right (false). The true side of the clause sets up the boundaries for right-side evaluation; the false side sets up the boundaries for left-side evaluation. The directional register d is negated again, and a direct branch is made to the label toploop2 where the While-Wend loop begins again.

Part 4:

```
bubsort2:
    If r - 1 > 0 Then
        For i = 1 To r
            b = i
            For j = b + 1 To r
                If unit(j) <= unit(b) Then b = j
            Next j
            If i <> b Then
                t = unit(b)
                unit(b) = unit(i)
                unit(i) = t
            End If
        Next i
    End If
    1 = p(k)
    r = w(k)
    k = k - 1
Loop Until k = 0
ShowTime
ShowIter
Light
End Sub
```

You should recognize the BubbleSort procedure by now. For safety's sake, the procedure is executed only if the distance between boundaries r and 1 is greater than zero. Each BubbleSort array for this particular incarnation of the QuickSort algorithm may be as many as eight elements wide; as a result, there's not much for this segment of the program to do. Toward the end of the BubbleSort section, the left and right boundaries for the next sort segment are reset to the next values from the "stack" arrays p() and w(), and one value is subtracted from the tally of subarrays to be sorted, which is variable k.

The main Do-Loop clause is exited when this tally k equals zero—in other words, when there are no more subarrays to sort. The display is updated one last time, and the procedure ends.

By the way, if you've been wondering why these procedures have a tendency to use the variables i, j, k, 1, m, and n rather than the more verbal variables to which you may be accustomed (like rightside or sluggo), here's an explanation. These six letters used for variable names are a throwback to the first edition of FORTRAN, when these six letters were the *only* ones a programmer could use to represent values. FORTRAN has grown up since then (since the mid-1960s, that is) and has recognized the rest of the alphabet; yet algorithm programmers still abide by the old rules, to a great extent. It would seem programmers are compelled to write better code when there are more rules to follow. (P.J. Plauger, are you reading this?)

A Sort of Majestic Beauty

Allow me a measure of poetic license to give you a preview of what it is you see when you run this application of sorts. After clicking the QuickSort button, the panel starts first. In your mind, scatter several grains of sand in a black, square-shaped pan. By clicking QuickSort, you've added a layer of cooking oil to this pan, making the grains float. As you watch, groups of sand grains collect themselves together in square-shaped regions. Like a splitting cell, there is one large square region dividing itself slowly into two smaller square regions side-by-side, like diamonds pulling themselves apart from each other. Once a region has become too small to bisect itself, it zips itself closed into a tight line. Remember, the perfectly tight diagonal line is an indicator that the array is completely sorted—the first pixel is at the first position, the second pixel it is at the second position, the third at the third, and so on. Perhaps QuickSort's is the panel that most resembles a biological process.

The Shell/Metzner sort, for the most part, looks like a baker folding bread dough into a roll, layer by layer. Remember, Shell/Metzner maintains a spanning variable m that helps determine the distance between each swap, and it is halved with each reexecution of the loop. You actually see m being narrowed as the roll of dough grows tighter and tighter. At last, from top to bottom this collected pastry—almost in a straight line now—is pinched together cluster by cluster as if with finger and thumb to form something of a linguini noodle.

BubbleSort might be considered by my hyphenating friends back home in Oklahoma as the no-holds-barred, down-and-dirty, let's-get-this-puppy-sorted algorithm. As stated earlier, I think you could rename this procedure "ZipperSort" because the algorithm, in one fell swoop, zips closed this diagonal line from top to bottom, like jelly leaking from a rapidly depressurized balloon.

By the way, those of you who are proofreaders at heart have probably noticed I left a button slot open for a "DFSort" algorithm. It has been my longtime wish to generate an original sort algorithm that blends speed, performance, and elegance. Regardless of how many years I worked at a library, I must admit that I don't have a wonderful original solution. When I invoke what I think is an original method—for instance, using two file pointers working in opposite directions, "funneling" the unsorted portion of the array toward the center—then I can come close to achieving a perfect sort, but not quite perfect enough. When I think I've corrected this problem, I realize later that the correction I utilized was not original—I have a tendency to borrow from one version of BubbleSort or the other.

Complex Conversions

With sorts out of the way, the focus of this chapter shifts now from sort algorithms to *conversion* algorithms. In the Expressor III application, I added a few algorithms for converting the value in the calculator display from one numeric base to another. I wanted hexadecimal functionality; although Visual Basic does contain `Hex$()` and `Oct$()` functions, they are limited in their performance.

The two algorithms I used convert values from base 10 to a string written in some other base, and from a string in some other base back to base 10. It is only the base 10 values that the calculation procedures accept for addition, even though hexadecimal mode may be active; for the sake of those procedures, the `Function ConvertTo10 ()` procedure manages to give the interpreter real values it can work with. For now, this procedure is only capable of translating the whole number portion of the value. First, here's a listing of the string function that converts from base 10:

Numeric base conversion in depth.

```
Function ConvertFrom10$ (display$, convBase)
display$ = LTrim$(display$)
whole% = Int(Val(display$))
Loop1:
comp = convBase ^ expn
If comp < whole% Then
    expn = expn + 1
    GoTo Loop1
End If
cv% = Int(whole%)
```

```
For spot = expn To 0 Step -1
    digit% = cv% \ (convBase ^ spot)
    cv% = cv% Mod (convBase ^ spot)
    If digit% < 10 Then
        cvt$ = cvt$ + LTrim$(Str$(digit%))
    Else
        cvt$ = cvt$ + Chr$(65 + (digit% - 10))
    End If
Next spot
If Left$(cvt$, 1) = "0" And Len(cvt$) > 1 Then
    cvt$ = Right$(cvt$, Len(cvt$) - 1)
End If
ConvertFrom10$ = cvt$
End Function
```

The procedure starts by trimming any leading spaces that are attached to the readout caption like leeches. Next, the whole number value and the fractional number value are separated from one another. The two remaining values, whole% and frac#, are translated separately.

Next, an implied loop starts at the point marked Loop1. This loop determines the number of digit places in the converted number, starting from the place at the far right side. Variable comp is a comparison value equal to the numeric base raised to the power of the current place. For instance, in the base 10 number 1495, the value for comp when convBase = 2 is 100 because the comparison is at the 100s place and $10_2 = 100$. As long as the comparison value comp is less than (<) the actual number being converted, places may continue to be added to the variable expn. Once comp is greater than the value being converted and the expression evaluates false, the false result is a signal that the comparison has extended beyond the boundaries of the original value, and expn has just enough digit places for the conversion number to fit snugly.

The loop that follows the comparison clause is a conventional For-Next loop, which starts with the extreme left place in the conversion number and works its way backwards (Step -1) to the right toward its ones place. The countdown is kept within the variable spot. The place value at the spot currently under consideration is represented by (convBase ^ spot), which is the base value raised to the power of spot. To determine what digit belongs in that spot, the conversion value is divided by the place value and the remainder is ignored. For instance, in the base 10 number 395, the 3 is in the hundreds (10_2) place. The value 395 divided by 100 is equal to 3 with whatever fractional remainder, so the digit 3 goes into that place in the variable cvt$. The mathematical operator \ (backslash) is used for *integer division*, where the fractional remainder is unimportant.

In the second line of the spot loop, the operator Mod is used to determine exactly what that ignored remainder was. This remainder is assigned to variable cv%, to be used as the conversion value for the next iteration of the loop. Thus the remainder from the division of cv% is assessed and then assigned to cv% itself. Next, a conditional clause checks to see whether the value of digit%, the extracted digit value, is below 10. If it's above 10, the digit sent to cvt$ has to be made into a letter ranging from digit A to digit F. Otherwise, a numeral may be assigned as the digit.

The next conditional clause is used to shave any leading "0" from the result string, should there be a leading "0." This little trick helps simplify the result, so if another procedure displays it now, the reader won't become confused.

Here is the second converter procedure:

```
Function ConvertTo10 (display$, convBase)
Dim accum As Double
display$ = LTrim$(display$)
For place = 1 To Len(display$)
    If Mid$(display$, place, 1) = "." Then
        whole$ = Left$(display$, place - 1)
        frac$ = Right$(display$, Len(display$) - place)
    End If
Next place
If whole$ = "" Then
    whole$ = display$
End If
excount% = Len(whole$) - 1
For char% = 1 To Len(whole$)
    convChar$ = Mid$(whole$, char%, 1)
    ch% = Asc(convChar$)
    If ch% < 65 Then
        valchar% = ch% - 48
    Else
        valchar% = ch% - 55
    End If
    w10% = valchar% * convBase ^ excount%
```

```
        accum = accum + w10%
        excount% = excount% - 1
Next char%
excount% = -1
If frac$ <> "" Then
    For char% = 1 To Len(frac$)
        convChar$ = Mid$(whole$, char%, 1)
        If ch% < 65 Then
            valchar% = ch% - 48
        Else
            valchar% = ch% - 55
        End If
        f10# = valchar% * convBase ^ excount%
        accum = accum + f10#
        excount% = excount% - 1
    Next char%
End If
ConvertTo10 = accum
End Function
```

The first portion of the procedure divides the whole number portion from the fractional portion. Using the string evaluation instruction Mid$(), it searches for the decimal point. If it finds one, whatever is to the right of it must be fractional. The procedure maintains a double-precision value accum that receives real number values deposited into it. The Mid$() function is then used to extract a digit from the string. This digit is converted into a place value valchar%. This is then multiplied by its place value, raised to the power excount%, to arrive at a base 10 value. This value is then added to the official basket variable accum. Once all the digits have been tested, accum is equal to the base 10 value.

A Wild Experiment in Alphanumerics

For anyone who wants to learn more about information theory and its philosophical pertinence, I recommend the book *Silicon Dreams: Information, Man, and Machine* by Dr. Robert W. Lucky, who heads AT&T Bell Labs. In one of the chapters of his book, Dr. Lucky discusses the decoding system for compact disks. CD sound can still be so clear when the disk is damaged, says Lucky, because the computer program inside the CD player maintains a continually changing list of sound probabilities. Along with its more mechanical method of reading the same sector multiple times and checking for equality each time, the player is capable of predicting when a sound falls outside the current range of sound possibilities. At any event, CD mechanisms are capable of a certain degree of error-prediction.

When the CD player thinks it's found an error, it checks to see which sounds have generally followed the sound just before the error occurred, and gives that historical sound a try. Because defects are so minimal, even if the CD player guesses wrong, the length of the incorrect sound is probably so short as to be negligible to any ear; if it guesses right, you, the listener, don't have to worry about the sound anyway. Dr. Lucky describes the code structures used to build such tables of probabilities. He goes on to say that such simple algorithms can be used on textual documents to predict which character of text is most likely to follow another character.

Predictive coding introduced.

Dr. Lucky's conclusion is that given a long enough document, a text analysis algorithm might be capable of drawing enough conclusions from the *probability* that one character follows another. After having encoded these conclusions efficiently in a probability table, then given one random initial character, the algorithm can make some startling predictions about which characters will follow the previous ones in a long list. Having analyzed extremely lengthy documents, the algorithm begins to predict the probability of silent-e falling at the end of a word. Small, frequent words such as "so," "the," and "than" begin to show up in algorithm-generated documents, complete with surrounding spaces. Given several hours' analysis of the work of a particular poet, the algorithm might even be capable of generating stanzas—meaningless ones, mind you, but perhaps with a measure of meter and even rhyme.

This type of probability theory fascinates me, so I decided to try to implement the prediction formula in a Visual Basic application. The VB application reads a standard ASCII text file and generates its own ASCII text file based on its predictions of how characters might follow other characters. The lengths of the generated file and the analyzed file are equal. Figure 12.5 shows a predictive document generator I call the Textuator. The figure is followed by a short list of the main form's primary property settings.

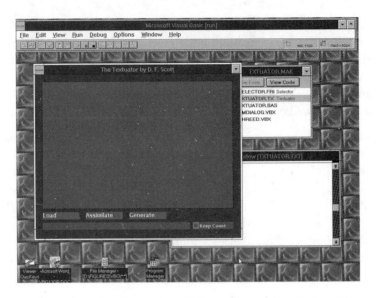

Figure 12.5. How many characters will it need to analyze before it can replace D. F. Scott?

Listing 12.2. TXTUATOR.FRM Property Settings.

```
Form Textuator
    BackColor        =   &H00400040&
    Caption          =   "The Textuator by D. F. Scott"
    ForeColor        =   &H00000000&
    Height           =   6180
    Left             =   624
    MaxButton        =   0     'False
    Top              =   1560
    Width            =   7500

    CheckBox KeepCount
        Caption      =   "Keep Count"
        FontName     =   "Lucida Sans"
        FontSize     =   7.8
        Height       =   252
        Left         =   5640
        Top          =   5160
        Width        =   1452
```

```
PictureBox Display
    BackColor       =    &H00800080&
    FontBold        =    -1   'True
    FontItalic      =    0    'False
    FontName        =    "Lucida Sans Typewriter"
    FontSize        =    7.8
    ForeColor       =    &H00FFFFFF&
    Height          =    4452
    Left            =    240
    Top             =    240
    Width           =    6852

Label Status
    BackColor       =    &H00800080&
    FontName        =    "Lucida Sans"
    FontSize        =    9.6
    ForeColor       =    &H0000FFFF&
    Height          =    252
    Left            =    240
    Top             =    5160
    Width           =    5292

Label Generate
    BackColor       =    &H00C000C0&
    Caption         =    "Generate"
    FontName        =    "Lucida Sans"
    FontSize        =    9.6
    ForeColor       =    &H00FFFFFF&
    Height          =    252
    Left            =    3360
    Top             =    4800
    Width           =    1332

Label Assimilate
    Caption         =    "Assimilate"
    Height          =    252
    Left            =    1800
    Top             =    4800
    Width           =    1332
```

continues

Listing 12.2. continued

```
Label FileLoad
    Caption        =    "Load"
    Height         =    252
    Left           =    240
    Top            =    4800
    Width          =    1332
```

When I'm programming in experimental mode, I must admit I'm not paying much attention to the process model; I'm going to avoid a great deal of discussion about the buttons and labels because it's obvious what they do. The bottom line in the form is a status line, and the check box suspends graphic updates to the form so the formula can assimilate the form faster.

Listing 12.3. TXTUATOR.BAS.

```
Global probability(255, 255) As Integer
Global strikearray() As Integer
Global byte&, char As Integer, compchar As Integer
Global poke As Long, filepos As Long
Global seedchar$
Global nl$
```

The main two-dimensional array here is probability. It keeps track of the number of times in a document that the character referred to by the second dimension falls immediately after the character referred to by the first dimension. The strikearray() is used to set up a list of all those characters that have fallen after the character currently considered.

Now, after the user clicks the File button, she enters the text file to analyze into the file selector box. This file is then loaded into memory using the binary access model, in which not records but individual characters are written into memory using the Get # instruction. You've seen what a selector box looks like, so I'll avoid that part. The three main assimilation procedures appear within the general module TXTUATOR.BAS. Here's the first, which assimilates the file after the user clicks the Assimilate button. I've cut out the part that handles the file selector.

```
Sub AcquireFile ()
.
.
.
Open Selector.FileName For Binary As #1
byte& = 1
While EOF(1) = False
Get #1, byte&, charc$
If charc$ <> "" Then
    lastchar = Asc(charc$)
    seedchar$ = charc$
Else
    lastchar = Asc(" ")
    seedchar$ = " "
End If
byte& = byte& + 1
Nextchar:
    Get #1, byte&, charc$
    If charc$ = "" Then
        charc$ = " "
        byte& = byte& + 1
        GoTo Nextchar
    End If
    slot = Asc(charc$)
    If byte& > 1 Then
        probability(lastchar, slot) = probability(lastchar, slot) +
1
    End If
    lastchar = slot
    byte& = byte& + 1
    If Textuator.KeepCount.Value = True Then
        s$ = "Character # " + Str$(byte&)
        Textuator.Status.Caption = s$
        Textuator.Status.Refresh
    End If
Wend
Beep
s$ = Str$(byte&) + " characters assimilated."
ReDim strikearray(byte&)
Textuator.Status.Caption = s$
Close #1
End Sub
```

The very first character from the file is read into memory using a specific set of instructions. This is the only character that does not *follow* another one, so it doesn't fall within the loop. However, it provides what I call a "seed character" that starts the procedure's prediction recitation chain with a real character from the file rather than some unprintable garbage character.

The implied loop acquires characters from the open file. Each character's ASCII value is determined with the instruction slot = Asc(charc$). The procedure has kept track of the character it has just considered previously within the variable lastchar. Therefore, when the ASCII value slot is determined, the element denoting the probability that the lastchar previous character is followed by the slot current character is incremented.

Here is the procedure that processes all the characters in memory to determine which characters fall after other ones.

```
Sub GenerateFile ()
char = Asc(seedchar$)
Add char
For poke = 1 To byte&
    compchar = 0
    pnt = 0
    Do
oncemore:
        see = probability(char, compchar)
        If see > 0 Then
            hits = hits + see
            For strike = 1 To see
                strikearray(pnt) = compchar
                pnt = pnt + 1
            Next strike
            If compchar < 255 Then
                compchar = compchar + 1
            Else
                Exit Do
            End If
        Else
            If compchar < 255 Then
                compchar = compchar + 1
                GoTo oncemore
            Else
                Exit Do
```

```
            End If
         End If
    Loop Until compchar = 255
    rollchar = Int(Rnd(1) * hits)
    dart% = strikearray(rollchar)
    Add dart%
    char = dart%
    If Textuator.KeepCount.Value = True Then
        s$ = "Character # " + Str$(poke)
        Textuator.Status.Caption = s$
        Textuator.Status.Refresh
    End If
Next poke
Close #2
Beep
s$ = Str$(poke) + " characters generated."
Textuator.Status.Caption = s$
End Sub
```

This procedure starts by using the initial seedchar$ for its initial character prediction. The value of byte& is the length of the file just analyzed. At the start of the Do-Loop clause, an implied loop is started that tests for all 256 character possibilities compchar of the currently examined character char. If a probability exists, then exactly as many characters as followed char in the analysis are added to individual elements of strikearray(). This array later acts like a dartboard; the more instances of a particular following character that appear in the array, the more likely that character is of being "hit" by the random number generation given to rollchar. The random number has a value between 1 and the number of elements in strikearray(). The character beneath the randomly numbered element is retrieved; it is more probable that the value of dart% will be set to the ASCII value of a character that falls within strikearray() more times.

```
Sub Add (char As Integer)
charp$ = Chr$(char)
Textuator.Display.Print charp$;
If poke / 80 = Int(poke / 80) Then
    Textuator.Display.Print nl$
End If
Put #2, filepos, charp$
filepos = filepos + 1
End Sub
```

The retrieved character then is added to the current binary access file. If there's still room in the picture box, the character is added to the box. The conditional clause above checks to see whether the current count of characters is a multiple of 80, the linear length of characters in the picture box `Display`. If the division is nonfractional, a linefeed is sent and printing proceeds to the next line.

Conclusions Drawn Thus Far

For those of you who are curious, I've run a fair amount of tests on the Textuator program, especially on files made from chapters of this book (I'm wondering whether Visual Basic could predict the next chapter for me, you see). I've seen the Textuator generate some character combinations that revealed to me it was indeed capable of making interesting predictions. For fairly long documents, for instance, it generates an adequate space partition between "words." Also, the longer the chapter sample I feed it, the more that "Textuated" words tend to end in "e" after awhile.

I concluded, however, that if my algorithm for the Textuator was indeed sound, I would require about five or six human-composed sampled books the size of *Visual Basic for Windows Developer's Guide* before I could possibly have the Textuator generate some real stand-alone five-letter words or something at least as legible as an assembly language manual for the Zilog Z8000.

MAKING PROGRAMS APPEAR TO THINK

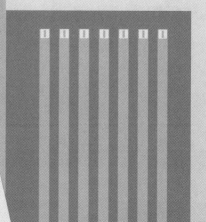

Far too much negative connotation has been given to the term "artificial" in the past few decades. For the most part, the term means "a product of humans"; however, the term lately has grown synonymous with "unreal."

13

Is "artificial intelligence" unreal? When a program is capable of reaching a conclusion that appears to have been rendered by way of insightful decision, is that not intelligence? Is not all intelligence, to some degree, artificial?

Is "artificial intelligence" oxymoronic?

Although the concept of artificial intelligence is quite ingenious in its design and execution, the term "artificial intelligence" itself is quite improper. Artificial sweetener is still sweet, although there would be considerable uproar if marketers instead began using the term "artificial sugar." "Artificial intelligence," likewise, is not intelligence. AI, more properly defined, is a rule-based system for employing mathematical symbols and algorithmic procedures to extrapolate logical conclusions.

The other term for this branch of computing is "heuristic logic." It would be more to the point if more people knew what "heuristics" is. In short, it's any set of encoded rules. If you as a programmer can describe the rules and behavior of a system to such a degree that you are able to extrapolate information that would otherwise have required human thinking to produce, then you are employing heuristics.

The Heuristic Arena

By far, the best arena for practicing the fine art of heuristic logical crafting is in the simulation of a board game. The rules of board games generally are fixed (not by the Las Vegas definition of "fixed," mind you) and are therefore more easily enumerable and quantifiable. For this book's *pièce de résistance*, I present my personal rendition of the game of Reversi, built especially so that you as a programmer and you as a *player* can see into the heuristic logic of the game system.

Situation #5: The "Glass-Sided" Reversi Game

The objective here is to craft a playable game of Reversi (also known in some circles as "Othello"). Using the limited tools provided by Visual Basic, the programmer crafts very-high-level algorithms and decision trees, and gives the would-be programmer and game enthusiast a way to examine the logical decision-making process of the game system itself.

Reversi is simpler than chess, and tactically speaking, it is arguably simpler than checkers. Having studied some text on recursive arrayed algorithms, I learned how crafters of algorithms are capable of building local-scope arrays for algorithmic procedures that place calls to themselves. The conclusions drawn from trial-and-error calculations may be drawn in this way without disturbing the state of the array that called them. A recursive procedure is capable of calling itself and also returning a function back to itself; recursion is effective in the art of building layered algorithms.

I was disappointed to learn that there is no way in Visual Basic that a recursive arrayed algorithm could be executed; there is no independently *and* procedurally local scope available for declaring arrays. The `Static` array type is as far down as scopes go; even though a VB procedure can be made to call itself, it cannot pass an independent array to itself by value. If the array is declared `Static`, then when the procedure calls itself, the array belonging to the calling procedure is exactly the same as the array belonging to the receiving procedure. Any change in one is made to the other; thus, they're not independent.

Visual Basic's lack of recursive array algorithm capability.

This causes the following problem in building board game models: The ideal board game system has the computer test out all the possible moves it can make in response to the human player. The image the computer has of the board is stored in an array in memory. If the computer player is to calculate all the possible moves the human player can make in response to all the moves it is capable of making itself, it would be nice if the testing procedure could pass itself a second copy of the game board, so that when it test-moves the human piece and evaluates the logical value of that move, the board the computer is currently considering would not be disturbed. This is why a recursive array algorithm system would be ideal for use in board game programming.

I realized that it isn't necessary to generate a table of possible moves, countermoves, and counter-countermoves only through recursive array passing. Instead, if there was a way to encode the current state of the board not as an array but as some other regulated data type—for instance, a string of decodable characters—the board could be passed between calculative procedures as a *unit* variable. The board could also be part of a static move tree that could be independently evaluated. What's more, a 64-element board represented as a 64-character string would result in a *savings of memory* over the more respected array structure.

Figure 13.1 shows the startup form for Visual Reversi. In deference to the former Burroughs Corp., which in the 1920s built with pride guaranteed-to-last, glass-sided adding machines, I have nicknamed Visual Reversi "the glass-sided board game." The game project described in this chapter is complete with a way for players to examine the actual decision-making processes of the game program.

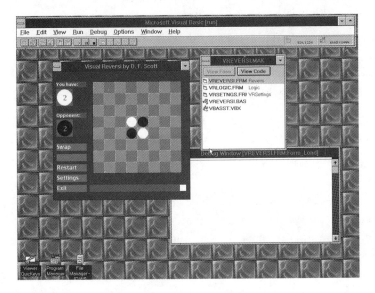

Figure 13.1. Heuristics you can feel.

Here are the vital property settings for this form:

VREVERSI.FRM Property Settings

```
Form Reversi
    BackColor     =   &H00400040&
    BorderStyle   =   1  'Fixed Single
    Caption       =   "Visual Reversi by D. F. Scott"
    Height        =   4956
    Icon          =   VREVERSI.ICO
    MaxButton     =   0   'False
    Width         =   5076
```

```
PictureBox Board
   AutoRedraw      =   -1  'True
   FillStyle       =   0   'Solid
   Height          =   3204
   Left            =   1440
   MousePointer    =   2   'Cross
   Top             =   360
   Width           =   3204
PictureBox YourScore
   BackColor       =   &H00C000C0&
   BorderStyle     =   0   'None
   FillStyle       =   0   'Solid
   FontName        =   "Lucida Bright"
   FontSize        =   12
   ForeColor       =   &H00808000&
   Height          =   600
   Left            =   120
   Top             =   600
   Width           =   600
PictureBox CompScore
   BackColor       =   &H00C000C0&
   BorderStyle     =   0   'None
   FillStyle       =   0   'Solid
   FontName        =   "Lucida Bright"
   FontSize        =   12
   ForeColor       =   &H00808000&
   Height          =   600
   Left            =   120
   Top             =   1680
   Width           =   600
Begin PictureBox Indicator
   BackColor       =   &H00808080&
   Height          =   252
   Left            =   4560
   Top             =   3960
   Width           =   252
Label Label1
   BackColor       =   &H00800080&
   Caption         =   "You have:"
   FontName        =   "Lucida Sans"
   FontSize        =   7.8
   ForeColor       =   &H00FFFFFF&
```

```
        Height      =    192
        Left        =    120
        Top         =    360
        Width       =    1092
Label Label2
        BackColor   =    &H00800080&
        Caption     =    "Opponent:"
        FontName    =    "Lucida Sans"
        FontSize    =    7.8
        ForeColor   =    &H00FFFFFF&
        Height      =    192
        Left        =    120
        Top         =    1440
        Width       =    1092
Label Swap
        BackColor   =    &H00FF00FF&
        Caption     =    "Swap"
        FontName    =    "Lucida Sans"
        FontSize    =    9.6
        ForeColor   =    &H00FFFFFF&
        Height      =    252
        Left        =    120
        Top         =    2520
        Width       =    1092
Label Pass
        Caption     =    "Pass"
        Top         =    2880
Label Restart
        Caption     =    "Restart"
        Top         =    3240
Label Settings
        Caption     =    "Settings"
        Top         =    3600
Label GameExit
        Caption     =    "Exit"
        Top         =    3960
Label Message
        BackColor   =    &H00800080&
        FontName    =    "Lucida Sans"
        FontSize    =    9.6
        ForeColor   =    &H0000FFFF&
```

```
Height      =   252
Left        =   1320
Top         =   3960
Width       =   3252
```

Initiating the Heuristic Process Model

No game program develops what can correctly be called a strategy for itself. It can detect a move that might be advantageous for "it" (the name given the program when it is playing a game with you), but only after it has spotted absolutely every other move there is and has witnessed the potential tragedies of all the bad moves it can make. It learns these lessons well during the evaluation phase. Like the well-structured computer program that it is, it forgets these lessons immediately because computers do not make plans of their own. That is simply the way computers work (or don't work).

The way that evaluative procedures of a heuristic logic program pass control to other procedures, or to themselves, is entirely reliant upon a conversational model of the game. In it, the current state of the board as the evaluator sees it—whether this state is real or *possible*—is represented as a node on a tree graph, as in Figure 13.2. The job for the evaluation process for any one node—any current state of the board—is twofold:

Defining heuristic logic.

- [ ] To evaluate and catalog all possible responses to the current state of the board.

- [ ] To render a viability rating for the current state of the board based entirely on the mathematical laws, or heuristics, currently given the program.

Notice how generically I've phrased some of the previous descriptions—notice I didn't say that the objective of the evaluator was to find the computer's best move. This is only half of the job; the other half is to find also the human's best move. The best way for the evaluator to do both is for it to be neutral—to place itself in the role of whoever's making the move at the time, whether it be the computer or human player.

Conceiving enumerable ratings for quantifiable possibilities.

This way, given the encoded laws of which plays are "good" and which plays are "legal," the evaluator routine can render results denoting which moves are viable for itself and which are equally viable for the human player, make those results quantifiable variables, and subtract one from the other to see how one balances the other out. If the ratings the evaluator has developed for a move are generated impartially, the ratings for the human and computer players have equal weight. Finding the difference between the two therefore results in a differential tilt. Here is a way for the overall evaluation process to determine for the computer-represented player a plan of action, a way of steering the moves in the direction that the evaluator shows gives the computer a ratings advantage over the human.

How Reversi Is Played

For those of you who have never played Reversi, here are its simple instructions. Figure 13.2 shows a Visual Reversi game in progress. The game is played with checker-like pieces having oppositely-colored sides. Like most other board games, each player has her own color. The game is played on an eight-by-eight square board; a chessboard will do well, though there is no pertinence in this game to the colors of the squares.

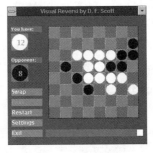

Figure 13.2. A Visual Reversi game in progress.

Your objective as a Reversi player is to fill the board with pieces that have your color turned face-up. A move is made by "capturing" pieces; in this case, by enclosing on two sides an uninterrupted line of pieces of your opponent's color with pieces of your color. You move by placing one piece of your color face-up on the board, but only in a square where a capture takes place. You cannot move in a square where none of your opponent's pieces are captured. To capture pieces, you flip them so that your color is now showing. For you to capture a line of your opponent's pieces, another piece of your color must already exist on the board. No pieces are ever removed from the board.

The game's opening position has four pieces on the board, with two pieces allocated for each player. As in chess, tradition has it that white moves first. Because a piece placed along the side can only be surrounded by pieces along that same side, there is a tactical advantage to placing pieces along the side. However, because the first four pieces are in the middle of the board and the rules state you must capture them first, you must first build from the middle outward toward the sides. The prizes of this game are the corners; they cannot be recaptured at all because they cannot be surrounded. Capturing the corners as early as possible gives you the best advantage because any of your own pieces adjacent to your corner piece also cannot be captured; and any of your opponent's pieces adjacent to your corner pieces are vulnerable to a less defensible attack.

The object of the game is to fill the board with as many pieces of your color as possible. The game ends when all 64 positions are filled, and the player with the most pieces wins. It is possible that the game can end in a 32/32 tie.

The Node Tree Structure

Before you start thinking you're reading Hoyle, it's time to put these principles into code. Here are the global variable declarations for Visual Reversi; these show you which tools you have to work with:

```
Global mainboard$, boardval$
Global whosemove As Integer, humancolor As Integer, compcolor
➥   As Integer, nummoves As Integer, lookahead
➥   As Integer, LogicOn As Integer
Global count As Integer, node As Integer, maxwidth As Integer,
➥   rate As Single
Global movetree(16, 100) As Integer, view$(16, 100),
➥   derived(16, 100) As Integer, arrate(16, 100) As Single
Global rating(64) As Single, legal(64) As Integer, booty(64)
➥   As Integer, candidate(60) As Integer, maxnodes(16)
➥   As Integer
Global direcx(8) As Integer, direcy(8) As Integer
```

At any one time during the game's evaluation process, there is one copy of the game board as it currently stands and one copy of the heuristically-derived ratings for the move. These are declared previously as `mainboard$` and `boardval$`, respectively. A flag variable `whosemove` denotes whose turn it is, though this is not a true/false flag but a positive one/negative one flag. This helps the evaluator examine the value of one player's moves as having the negative sign of the value of the opponent's moves; this in turn helps in combining the ratings together and reading the differential tilt. Respective color values corresponding to the current value of `whosemove` are given to variables `humancolor` and `compcolor`. This way the human player can choose colors or even switch sides in mid-game. (What does the program care? After all, it doesn't have an ego to bruise.)

The node tree for this game consists of four array variables with equally-declared dimensions. These equal dimensions serve to form a "record" of source in the internal database. Each possible move is represented as a node in the tree, the structure of which is depicted in Figure 13.3. The `movetree()` array contains the actual move that might be made by whosoever's turn it is at the time. This move consists of the square number where a piece is played. Remember, this is not representative of a move that has been made, but of a move that *might be made.*

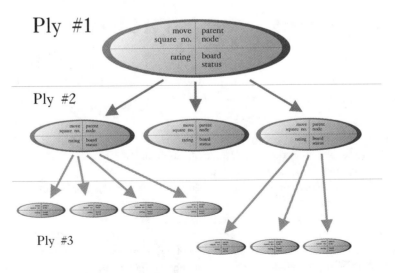

Figure 13.3. Loading your nodes.

Variable `view$()` contains the string description of what the board will look like once this move in `movetree()` is made. Because every move made is in response to a prior move, and any one move node *level* can contain as many as 100 branches—or avenues of response—linking the node to a prior move, the `derived()` variable ties the current move node to the state of the board for which this move is a response. It is `derived()` that establishes some semblance of a path between moves and gives the node tree a degree of continuity. Lastly, `arrate()` contains the current move rating given by the evaluator for this move. The move continues to be considered whether `arrate()` currently proclaims it "good" or "bad," because what appears now to be a bad move can turn out to be extremely advantageous three moves down the road.

For the sake of the evaluator, the next line defines data pertinent to the current state of the board. Variable `rating()` is the all-important proclamation of the fully-evaluated move. Variable `legal()` contains a series of flags denoting whether a move to this location is legal or illegal. The `candidate()` array is a sort of "top-ten list" for the sake of the evaluator. Depending on its mood, it can pick what might have been evaluated as the second-best move *intentionally*; this way, no two games you play with Visual Reversi are alike. Next, `maxnodes()` contains the current maximum number of branches for a node level that applies to the prior node level.

Finally, variables `direcx()` and `directy()` contain directional indicators that help the evaluator see the direction of a line of connected pieces.

The majority of evaluative functions have been delegated to the general module VREVERSI.BAS. The startup module here is assigned to whichever module has the `Sub main ()` procedure, and that is the sole general module in the application. Here is the first executing procedure:

VREVERSI.BAS

```
Sub main ()
Randomize
direcx(1) = 0
direcx(2) = 1
direcx(3) = 1
direcx(4) = 1
direcx(5) = 0
direcx(6) = -1
direcx(7) = -1
```

```
direcx(8) = -1
direcy(1) = -1
direcy(2) = -1
direcy(3) = 0
direcy(4) = 1
direcy(5) = 1
direcy(6) = 1
direcy(7) = 0
direcy(8) = -1
boardval$ = "ZTWVVWTZTAPMMPATWPRQQRPWVVWQMMQWVVWQMMQWVWPRQQRPWTAPM
➥   MPATZTWVVWTZ"
humancolor = 1
whosemove = 1
nummoves = 60
maxwidth = 100
lookahead = 2
LogicOn = True
Load Reversi
End Sub
```

Storing
heuristic code
as a string
array.

    The directional pointer arrays are loaded first. Next, note the magnificent way that the first set of heuristics is encoded in the variable `boardval$`. The purpose of this string is to steer the evaluator toward squares that it has proven are more advantageous to capture. I therefore have created an alphabetical scale of squares as depicted in Figure 13.4, where the corners are given the highest good rating `Z`, the inner corners next to them (that give away the corners to your opponent more often than not) are given the highest poor rating `A`, and some of the middle squares are given the mediocre rating `M`.

    Next, the human player is given piece code `1` (white), and the flag denoting who moves next is pointing toward `1` (white). If the human switches sides and plays black, the computer would become side `1`, the human side `-1`, and the computer would play next. Because four squares are already occupied, there are 60 moves left in the game; when `nummoves = 0`, the game is over. Next, the default maximum number of branches `maxwidth` is set to 100; this can be made narrower if you want the computer to play faster. The number of `lookahead` nodes is set to 2 (it can be increased) and the flag denoting whether the logic display board is showing is set to true. Actually, the presence of the logic board can detract from the game; if you're more serious at the moment about playing than about investigating, you can certainly turn off the logic board. (For slower computers, the logic board can make serious play unbearable, as one of my chief beta testers—Mom—will attest.)

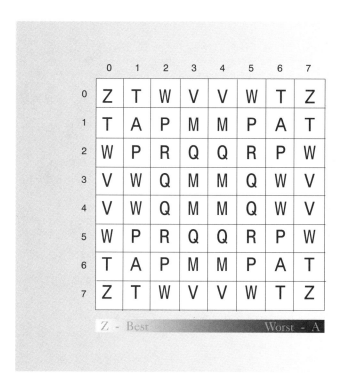

	0	1	2	3	4	5	6	7
0	Z	T	W	V	V	W	T	Z
1	T	A	P	M	M	P	A	T
2	W	P	R	Q	Q	R	P	W
3	V	W	Q	M	M	Q	W	V
4	V	W	Q	M	M	Q	W	V
5	W	P	R	Q	Q	R	P	W
6	T	A	P	M	M	P	A	T
7	Z	T	W	V	V	W	T	Z

Z - Best   Worst - A

Figure 13.4. The heuristic pattern code of boardval$ decoded.

The form module is loaded on execution of the last instruction in Sub main (). Here now is its first executing procedure:

VREVERSI.FRM

```
Sub Form_Load ()
Randomize
Board.Visible = False
Reversi.Show
Load Logic
tally = 1
For cubey = 0 To 7
    For cubex = 0 To 7
        If tally / 2 = tally \ 2 Then
            Board.Line (cubex * 400, cubey * 400)-
                (cubex * 400 + 399, cubey * 400 + 399),
                RGB(32, 128, 255), BF
```

```
        Else
            Board.Line (cubex * 400, cubey * 400)-
➡               (cubex * 400 + 399, cubey * 400 + 399),
➡               RGB(128, 128, 255), BF
        End If
        If cubex < 7 Then
            tally = tally + 1
        End If
    Next cubex
Next cubey
Board.Visible = True
mainboard$ = String$(24, " ") + "   XO      OX   " +
➡  String$(24, " ")
Plot mainboard$
scorenow
If humancolor = 1 Then
    Indicator.BackColor = QBColor(15)
Else
    Indicator.BackColor = QBColor(0)
    whosemove = -1
    Contrl
End If
End Sub
```

The visibility status of the game board is set to false while everything is being drawn for the first time. The two-tiered loop clause creates the checkerboard in slightly-varying shades of mid-range blue. Notice toward the bottom, the first assignment is made to the indicator of the current board state mainboard$. Here, letters X refer to white pieces, letters O to black pieces, and spaces to the lack of pieces. The string is 64 characters long and accounts for all the squares starting from left to right, top to bottom.

The procedure that acts now as the agenda-setter for what happens following the human player's move is also the procedure that detects that move when the player clicks the board square with the mouse:

```
Sub Board_MouseDown (Button As Integer, Shift As Integer,
➡  x As Single, y As Single)
squarex% = Int(x / 400) + 1
squarey% = Int(y / 400) + 1
If whosemove = -1 Then Exit Sub
If IsLegal(mainboard$, humancolor, squarex%, squarey%) > 0 Then
```

```
        PlacePiece mainboard$, humancolor, squarex%, squarey%
        Plot mainboard$
        Capture mainboard$, humancolor, squarex%, squarey%
        Plot mainboard$
        scorenow
        Board.Refresh
        nummoves = nummoves - 1
        whosemove = -1
        Contrl
    End If
End Sub
```

This procedure responds to the user's mouse click by placing a number of procedure calls, starting with one to Function IsLegal() that determines the legality of the move. The game doesn't respond at all if the chosen move is illegal—I don't believe in placing too many alert boxes in a program. Assuming the move is legal, a call is placed to Sub PlacePiece () which adds the appropriate characters to the proper spot in the string representing the current board. Next, Sub Plot () places the current contents of mainboard$ onto the screen. Notice no captures have been processed yet; this is so the human player can see the move he made, pause for a moment, and then see his captures. Obviously, Sub Capture () handles the capturing of pieces, and Sub Plot () is called a second time. Sub scorenow () evaluates how many pieces each player has on the board. The number of moves left is decremented, and the player-moving indicator whosemove is flipped.

From here, control is passed to the first entryway in the process model through the computer evaluation side of the game, at the "entry port" of Sub Contrl (). Keep this in mind because you'll return later to this point.

Here's the procedure which determines whether a move is legal; to some extent, this Function procedure could be considered algorithmic:

```
Function IsLegal (imageboard$, colr As Integer, x As Integer,
➡ y As Integer) As Integer
lookdown = piece(imageboard$, x, y)
If lookdown <> 0 Then
    IsLegal = False
    Exit Function
End If
For cycle = 1 To 8
    sx% = x
```

```
            sy% = y
            attack = 0
            Do
                sx% = sx% + direcx(cycle)
                sy% = sy% + direcy(cycle)
                If (sx% < 1 Or sx% > 8) Or (sy% < 1 Or sy% > 8) Then
                    Exit Do
                End If
                look = piece(imageboard$, sx%, sy%)
                Select Case look
                    Case 0
                        Exit Do
                    Case -colr
                        attack = attack + 1
                    Case colr
                        If attack > 0 Then
                            capt = capt + attack
                            cx% = x%
                            cy% = y%
inner_loop:
                            cx% = cx% + direcx(cycle)
                            cy% = cy% + direcy(cycle)
                            collect = collect + (Asc(Mid$(boardval$,
➠                               ((cy% - 1) * 8) + cx%, 1)) - 77)
                            If cx% <> sx% And cy% <> sy% Then GoTo
➠                               inner_loop
                        End If
                        Exit Do
                End Select
            Loop
        Next cycle
        IsLegal = capt
        booty(((y - 1) * 8) + x) = collect
        End Function
```

The first order of business is to determine whether there's already a piece at the location the player designated. This location is represented by the coordinates x and y; be careful here not to confuse the structure of the procedure header with that of a graphical event procedure such as Sub *Object*_DragOver (). The contents of the indicated square must be empty (0) in order for this procedure to go on; otherwise, the result of the function IsLegal is set to false.

When the loop clause counting for `cycle` is reached, the square must be empty. This clause will send a "stringer" of sorts in all of the eight directions of capture, starting with straight up. The coordinates of this stringer will be kept within `sx%` and `sy%`. Visual Basic is not by nature in tune with board games, so it really doesn't know at first which way is up (does that surprise you?). Therefore, at this point the game turns to the cycling arrays `direcx()` and `direcy()` to point each stringer's way to the next square. These arrays contain the horizontal and vertical directions, respectively, of each step to the next square. A stringer to the lower left, therefore, will be pointed out by a `direcx(6)` value of -1 and a `direcy(6)` value of 1.

The conditional clause within the `Do` loop checks to see if the stringer has strayed off the board; if it has, the loop is exited. Next, variable `look` is set to the color value of the piece pointed to by the stringer. If the square is empty, then there's no capture possible along this line—a capture line must be unbroken—so the loop is exited. If the color of the piece is the opposite of the player's color (`-colr`) then this may indeed become a piece that is eventually captured, so it is recorded within the tally variable `attack`. If the color of the piece matches the player's color, then the conditional clause checks to see if `attack` registers that any pieces are available for capturing. If there are pieces to be captured, then this move must be legal.

`Function IsLegal ()` doubles, however, as a function denoting just how great this move might be for which player the procedure is evaluating for, the computer or the human. The number of captured pieces found thus far is added to variable `capt`. The board rating for each captured piece is collected within the local variable `collect`; this will play a role a bit later. This collection is accomplished by sending out a *second* stringer for coordinates (`cx%`, `cy%`).

At the end of the procedure, the number of captured pieces is returned as the legality rating for the move. If this number is zero (`False`), then evidently this move is not legal. While this is going on, a separate "goodies" array `booty()` is assigned the board values of the captured pieces; this tells the evaluator how important the treasure is.

The evaluator for Visual Reversi maintains several images—perhaps even several hundred—in memory at any one time. When adding a test piece to one of these images, or even a real piece to the real game board, `Sub PlacePiece ()` in the general module puts the symbolic X or O into the image of the board passed as string `mainboard$`.

```
Sub PlacePiece (imageboard$, colr As Integer, x As Integer,
➥  y As Integer)
If colr = 1 Then
    token$ = "X"
Else
    token$ = "O"
End If
Mid$(imageboard$, (y - 1) * 8 + x, 1) = token$
End Sub
```

There's not a lot to this procedure but a simple assignment of a character to a designated position. Next, the new board state is plotted:

VREVERSI.FRM Property Settings

```
Sub Plot (imageboard$)
For char = 1 To 64
    py = ((char - 1) \ 8)
    px = char Mod 8
    If px = 0 Then px = 8
    piece$ = Mid$(imageboard$, char, 1)
    If piece$ = "X" Then
        colr& = QBColor(15)
    End If
    If piece$ = "O" Then
        colr& = QBColor(0)
    End If
    If piece$ <> " " Then
        Board.FillColor = colr&
        Board.Circle ((px - 1) * 400 + 200, py * 400 + 200),
➥  175, colr&
    End If
Next char
Board.Refresh
End Sub
```

This procedure counts by rows and columns, placing a circle of the appropriate color onto the Board device. Before the second call to Sub Plot (), we head to Sub Capture ():

VREVERSI.BAS

```
Sub Capture (imageboard$, colr As Integer, x As Integer,
➡  y As Integer)
If colr = 1 Then
    token$ = "X"
Else
    token$ = "O"
End If
For cycle = 1 To 8
    sx% = x
    sy% = y
    attack = 0
    footstep = 0
    Do While (sx% > 0 And sx% < 9) And (sy% > 0 And sy% < 9)
        sx% = sx% + direcx(cycle)
        If sx% < 1 Or sx% > 8 Then
            Exit Do
        End If
        sy% = sy% + direcy(cycle)
        If sy% < 1 Or sy% > 8 Then
            Exit Do
        End If
        look = piece(imageboard$, sx%, sy%)
        Select Case look
            Case colr
                If attack > 0 Then
                    GoSub loop2
                End If
            Case -colr
                attack = attack + 1
            Case 0
                Exit Do
        End Select
        footstep = footstep + 1
    Loop
Next cycle
Exit Sub
loop2:
    ssx% = x%
    ssy% = y%
```

```
    For collect = 1 To footstep
        ssx% = ssx% + direcx(cycle)
        ssy% = ssy% + direcy(cycle)
        look = piece(imageboard$, ssx%, ssy%)
        Select Case look
            Case -colr
                Mid$(imageboard$, (ssy% - 1) * 8 + ssx%, 1) =
➥                       token$
            Case Else
                Exit For
        End Select
    Next collect
Return
End Sub
```

The capture process uses much the same "stringer" system as did `Function IsLegal ()` presented earlier. The purpose of the `Do-Loop` clause is to search the current string of pieces beside the one just placed to see whether there's an uninterrupted string of the opponent's colors, terminated by an instance of the player's own color. The embedded `Select Case` clause does the actual checking. Notice that in the second subclause, if the search through the current line runs across a piece of the opposite color, one piece is added to the cumulative variable `attack` and the search for even more victims continues. Notice in the first subclause now, if the search through the current line runs across a piece of the player's own color and if the `attack` variable registers positive, you've officially struck gold. Branching now takes place to a subroutine (Get out your cameras, quick! A subroutine is an endangered species!) called `loop2`.

Later, down in the subroutine region, the capture process is afoot. Starting now from the beginning, the cycling variable gives the stringer coordinate variables `ssx%` and `ssy%` their marching orders. Where they see the opponent, they reverse its color; where they see the player's own color for the first time, they stop there. The subroutine ends here, past the executed end of the procedure `Exit Sub`.

You might have noticed a few calls placed earlier to a function procedure `Function piece ()`. This returns the character value of a piece in the designated location:

```
Function piece (layout$, x As Integer, y As Integer) As Integer
side$ = Mid$(layout$, (y - 1) * 8 + x, 1)
Select Case side$
```

```
    Case "X"
        piece = 1
    Case "O"
        piece = -1
    Case " "
        piece = 0
End Select
End Function
```

You might have noticed also the tendency for the course of execution to flip between modules—between the form module and the general module, to be specific. The way I divided my contexts for this application, those procedures that have bearing to both the human's and the computer's move evaluations are placed within the general module VREVERSI.BAS. Those functions dealing with how the user communicates with the application and how the board is plotted, however, are delegated to the form module VREVERSI.FRM. As I mentioned earlier, the procedure that passes the baton between the two so that the computer can come up with a move is called Sub contrl ():

VREVERSI.FRM

```
Sub Contrl ()
compcolor = -humancolor
If whosemove = -1 And nummoves > 0 Then
    If humancolor = 1 Then
        Indicator.BackColor = QBColor(0)
    Else
        Indicator.BackColor = QBColor(15)
    End If
    compmove% = Decision_Central()
    If compmove% > 0 Then
        y% = ((compmove% - 1) \ 8) + 1
        x% = ((compmove% - 1) Mod 8) + 1
        PlacePiece mainboard$, compcolor, x%, y%
        Plot mainboard$
        Capture mainboard$, compcolor, x%, y%
        Plot mainboard$
        nummoves = nummoves - 1
        Message.Caption = ""
        scorenow
```

```
        End If
        AssessGame
        whosemove = 1
        If humancolor = 1 Then
            Indicator.BackColor = QBColor(15)
        Else
            Indicator.BackColor = QBColor(0)
        End If
        For ly% = 1 To 8
            For lx% = 1 To 8
                look = look + IsLegal(mainboard$, humancolor, lx%, ly%)
            Next lx%
        Next ly%
        If look = 0 Then
            Beep
            Message.Caption = "You have no legal moves."
            Pass.Enabled = True
        Else
            Pass.Enabled = False
        End If
    Else
        AssessGame
    End If
End Sub
```

The very first thing that happens is that the sides are negated with one another just for safety's sake. The computer takes the negative side of the whosemove flag. The first conditional clause tests to see whether it's the computer's turn and whether there are any moves left. The Indicator control in the form showing whose move it is now flips colors. A call is placed to Function Decision_Central (); this is the chief evaluative procedure call in the entire application. When at long last a value is passed back to compmove%, it is processed and displayed in the same manner as Sub Board_Click () did for the human player's move.

After a move is officially made to the board that the human player actually sees (not all the trial boards the evaluator has been generating in memory), a call is placed to a procedure that evaluates the current score of the game. This is a chain-reaction process, though it runs rather quickly. First, a call is placed to this procedure:

VREVERSI.BAS

```
Sub AssessGame ()
scr$ = score$(mainboard$)
scorex = Val(Left$(scr$, 2))
scoreo = Val(Right$(scr$, 2))
If scorex > 0 And scoreo > 0 And nummoves > 0 Then Exit Sub
If scorex > scoreo Then
    msg$ = "You've won by" + Str$(scorex - scoreo) + " squares."
Else
    msg$ = "Computer wins by" + Str$(scoreo - scorex) +
➥          " squares."
End If
MsgBox msg$
r = MsgBox("Another game?", 4)
If r = 6 Then
    Unload Reversi
    nummoves = 60
    Load Reversi
Else
    End
End If
End Sub
```

The process model here is rather simple: All the pieces are added to one another, and if there are still moves left on the board, the game continues, otherwise the end-of-game routine is executed. The first instruction in this procedure places a call to this Function procedure:

```
Function score$ (imageboard$)
For char = 1 To 64
    chip$ = Mid$(imageboard$, char, 1)
    Select Case chip$
        Case "X"
            scx = scx + 1
        Case "O"
            sco = sco + 1
    End Select
Next char
If humancolor = 1 Then
    score$ = Right$(Str$(scx), 2) + Right$(Str$(sco), 2)
```

```
Else
    score$ = Right$(Str$(scx), 2) + Right$(Str$(sco), 2)
End If
End Function
```

It's fairly easy to see here that the loop clause counting for char checks the current textual contents of the board (remember, all 64 squares are kept in a collective string variable). The loop clause keeps count of each X and 0 it runs across.

Once the computer has moved, however, there's still work to be done. The first thing to do is see whether there are any legal moves for the human on the board; if there aren't, it's still the computer's turn. It's entirely possible that, although there are empty squares left on the board, a player will be unable to move. If this happens to the computer, the computer gives him the good news:

```
Sub Pass()
Beep
Reversi.Message.Caption = "Opponent must pass."
End Sub
```

The computer gets another piece once the human player acknowledges the awful truth that he can't move, and clicks the Pass button in the form. This triggers the following event procedure:

VREVERSI.FRM

```
Sub Pass_Click ()
whosemove = -1
If humancolor = -1 Then
    Indicator.BackColor = QBColor(0)
Else
    Indicator.BackColor = QBColor(15)
End If
Contrl
End Sub
```

All this procedure does is flip colors without a move being made, sending control back to procedure Sub Control ().

Welcome to Decision Central

The procedure `Function Decision_Central ()` is the nerve center for the entire evaluation process. It is a huge procedure, so in keeping with form, I'll break it down into bite-size components so you won't be flipping back and forth through pages.

VREVERSI.BAS

Part 1:

```
Function Decision_Central () As Integer
Dim ply As Integer, lcheck As Integer, rcheck As Integer,
➥   acheck As Integer
Logic.Cls
Logic.Switch.Enabled = False
If LogicOn Then Logic.Show
count = 1
legals = False
compcolor = -humancolor
Subplot mainboard$, 0, 0
```

The four declared variables are record finders, in a sense, for the four node variables you saw diagrammed earlier. If the logic board capability is enabled, then it will be shown now. The logic board `Logic` is a separate form that depicts in miniature the different board copies being considered by the computer. The `Subplot` procedure is for the sake of this logic board; it is the procedure that displays the miniature boards.

Part 2:

```
For lcheck = 1 To 64
    y% = ((lcheck - 1) \ 8) + 1
    x% = ((lcheck - 1) Mod 8) + 1
    legal(lcheck) = IsLegal(mainboard$, compcolor, x%, y%)
    If legal(lcheck) > 0 Then
        legals = True
        movetree(1, count) = lcheck
```

```
        boardrate = (Asc(Mid$(boardval$, lcheck, 1)) - 77) * 2
        rating(count) = legal(lcheck) + boardrate +
            booty(lcheck)
        view$(1, count) = mainboard$
        PlacePiece view$(1, count), compcolor, x%, y%
        Capture view$(1, count), compcolor, x%, y%
        If LogicOn Then Subplot view$(1, count), 1,
            rating(count)
        count = count + 1
    End If
Next lcheck
If legals = False Then
    Pass
    Decision_Central = 0
    Exit Function
End If
```

This is the part of the procedure that determines where all the legal moves are on the *current* board—not a copy of the board. Earlier the legals flag was set to False; if there are any legal moves found, this flag is set to True. If the IsLegal() function (the same one invoked earlier) returns a positive value, then when the move being considered is logged as legal, a node is created for it forthwith. A tally variable count keeps track of how many nodes are being considered. Keep in mind this count may not exceed 100; but for the first ply of the node tree, because there are never any more than 60 open squares in the first place, this overflow can never happen on the first ply.

The move being considered is rendered unto the movetree() array. Next, its positional rating is assessed. This is added to the legality value for the move (an illegal move is an *extremely* negative number, which figures quite poorly in the evaluation) to obtain an overall rating, which is assigned to the rating() array. A picture of the board at the state *before* the move is made is assigned to view$().

Employing Context-Independent Procedures

Next, the system actually processes a move and capture for the copy of the board that was just assigned to view$(). Notice the Sub PlacePiece () and Sub Capture () procedures are the same ones used to make the actual placement and capture on behalf of the human player; these procedures are *context-independent.* They pay no attention whatsoever to the current state of the game; they live, shall we say, in a hole. The calling body of the program has to give them a picture of the board along with instructions; it never tells these procedures whether this board is the real board or a copy under consideration.

At the bottom of Part 2 of Function Decision_Central () is a conditional clause that passes control back to the user if no legal moves were found for the first ply.

Part 3:

```
maxnodes(1) = count - 1
For ply = 2 To lookahead + 1
    rrate = 0
    rbest = 0
    count = 1
    For node = 1 To maxnodes(ply - 1)
        branchboard$ = view$(ply - 1, node)
        backmove = movetree(ply - 1, node)
        by% = ((backmove - 1) \ 8) + 1
        bx% = ((backmove - 1) Mod 8) + 1
        For rcheck = 1 To 64
            ry% = ((rcheck - 1) \ 8) + 1
            rx% = ((rcheck - 1) Mod 8) + 1
            legal(rcheck) = IsLegal(branchboard$, humancolor,
                rx%, ry%)
            If legal(rcheck) > 0 Then
                viewboard$ = branchboard$
                PlacePiece viewboard$, humancolor, rx%, ry%
                Capture viewboard$, humancolor, rx%, ry%
                boardrate = Asc(Mid$(boardval$, rcheck, 1)) - 77
                If piece(viewboard$, bx%, by%) = humancolor Then
                    If bx% = 1 Or bx% = 8 Or by% = 1 Or by% = 8
                        Then
                        mult% = 10
                    Else
                        mult% = 3
                    End If
                    backcapt% = ((Asc(Mid$(boardval$, backmove,
                        1)) - 77) + boardrate) * mult%
```

```
            Else
                backcapt% = 0
            End If
            rate = legal(rcheck) + boardrate + booty(rcheck)
➡                - backcapt%
            EnterArrays rcheck, node, viewboard$, rate,
➡                count, ply
            If LogicOn Then Subplot viewboard$, ply, rate
            count = count + 1
        End If
    Next rcheck
Next node
If count < maxwidth + 2 Then
    maxnodes(ply) = count - 1
Else
    maxnodes(ply) = maxwidth
End If
For backrate = 1 To maxnodes(ply)
    For carryup = ply To 2 Step -1
        parent = derived(carryup, parent)
    Next carryup
    rating(movetree(1, parent)) = rating(movetree(1, parent))
➡        + arrate(ply, backrate)
Next backrate
```

At this point, the evaluator is at the second ply of the node tree. A moment ago, `Function Decision_Central ()` was considering what the best computer move would be; now, it is busy considering what the best *human response* to that move might be. Counting for all the prior nodes in ply #1—the ply of the node tree for the actual computer move—variable `rcheck` starts evaluating the viability of moves for the human player's color. The pattern here is mostly the same as for ply #1, except for certain enhancements:

First, there's an arbitrary multiplier for situations where a legal move opens up for the human player to recapture the piece just played by the computer, and to place the recapturing piece along the sides or, worse, in the corner. This gives extra value to the human player's move. The board rating of the move, multiplied by this new factor `mult%`, is obtained and held for now. The overall rating for the computer's original move will now be counterbalanced by the legality of the human's move, plus its board rating, plus how many pieces are captured, *minus* that bonus for the human recapturing the computer's piece.

Backrating Explained

Some of my best ideas are sparked by the consumption, for some reason, of Mexican food. My substitute for recursive array algorithms is but one of them. Every time the procedure arrives at an overall rating for the current node below ply #1, I send this rating to Sub EnterArrays (). This is an algorithmic procedure that has been tweaked so that if the node width has been tightened by the player so that he can get more speed out of the game, those ratings that are the most mediocre—the ones that have the least effect on the overall outcome—are those that the algorithm will discard *first*.

The number of nodes generated for this move are determined and assigned to maxnodes(ply). Next, I start the backrating procedure that moves the rating value up the node tree until it reaches the move in ply #1 that led to this move. Depending on who made the move, this rating then counts for or against the computer move being considered for the *real* board.

Part 4:

```
ply = ply + 1
    count = 1
    For node = 1 To maxnodes(ply - 1)
        branchboard$ = view$(ply - 1, node)
        For acheck = 1 To 64
            ay% = ((acheck - 1) \ 8) + 1
            ax% = ((acheck - 1) Mod 8) + 1
            legal(acheck) = IsLegal(branchboard$, compcolor,
                ax%, ay%)
            If legal(acheck) > 0 Then
                viewboard$ = branchboard$
                PlacePiece viewboard$, compcolor, ax%, ay%
                Capture viewboard$, compcolor, ax%, ay%
                boardrate = Asc(Mid$(boardval$, acheck, 1)) - 77
                rate = legal(acheck) + boardrate + booty(acheck)
                EnterArrays acheck, node, viewboard$, rate,
                    count, ply
                If LogicOn Then Subplot viewboard$, ply, rate
                count = count + 1
            End If
        Next acheck
    Next node
```

```
      If count < maxwidth + 2 Then
          maxnodes(ply) = count - 1
      Else
          maxnodes(ply) = maxwidth
      End If
      For backrate = 1 To maxnodes(ply)
          For carryup = ply To 2 Step -1
              parent = derived(carryup, parent)
          Next carryup
          rating(movetree(1, parent)) = rating(movetree(1,
➡  parent)) + arrate(ply, backrate)
      Next backrate
Next ply
```

In this part, you probably know the process pattern well; this is the third time the same general pattern appears in the Function Decision_Central () procedure. This segment calculates the response to all possible *responses*; in other words, what the computer can do to respond to every (non-mediocre) human move generated thus far. Notice the end of the loop at Next ply; if there are any more node plies to be calculated, the evaluation can go back to the human response section in Part 3. Remember, though, that for every extra ply setting, the game process slows down exponentially.

Part 5:

```
bmove% = BestMove(maxnodes(1))
by% = ((bmove% - 1) \ 8) + 1
bx% = ((bmove% - 1) Mod 8) + 1
blegal% = IsLegal(mainboard$, compcolor, bx%, by%)
If blegal% > 0 Then
    Decision_Central = bmove%
    Logic.Switch.Enabled = True
Else
    m$ = "Illegal move generated at position" + Str$(bx%) +
➡        Str$(by%) + Chr$(13) + Chr$(10) + "Calculated rating
➡        of: " + Str$(rating(bmove%))
    MsgBox m$
End If
End Function
```

In this final part, the original node set for ply #1 is loaded with a well-considered set of ratings for the possible moves. The course of action now is to send control to a move selector procedure Sub BestMove () for a verdict. Notice I left in my old error-catching routine; if everything works right, the move selected by Function Decision_Central () will be legal; but during development of Visual Reversi, I had quite a few problems with selected moves being not only illegal but also completely impossible. On more than one occasion in early development, the generated move was off the board entirely.

Here's the move selector procedure I was telling you about:

```
Function BestMove (legals As Integer) As Integer
Dim best As Long
best = -32768
For examine = 1 To legals
    If rating(examine) > best Then
        best = rating(examine)
    End If
Next examine
For examine = 1 To legals
    If rating(examine) = best Then
        slot = slot + 1
        candidate(slot) = movetree(1, examine)
    End If
Next examine
BestMove = candidate((Int(Rnd) * slot) + 1)
End Function
```

This procedure checks the rating() array to see which moves are the best so far; in case of a tie, an extra slot is apportioned for the candidate() array. The BestMove final instruction then throws the proverbial dart at the candidate of choice.

> Selecting the best move from a backrated decision tree.

Stamp Out Mediocrity in Your Lifetime

Earlier, I also told you about Sub EnterArrays (), which is a procedure that throws out mediocre rating considerations if the number of nodes for a ply starts exceeding the maximum:

```
Sub EnterArrays (play As Integer, connect As Integer, look$,
➥rate As Single, num As Integer, ytree As Integer)
Static oldply, fill
Dim j As Integer, k As Integer, l As Integer, t As Single
If num = 1 Then fill = 1
If ytree <> oldply Then
    fill = 1
    oldply = ytree
End If
If fill < 101 Then
    movetree(ytree, fill) = play
    derived(ytree, fill) = connect
    view$(ytree, fill) = look$
    arrate(ytree, fill) = rate
    fill = fill + 1
End If
If fill = 100 Then
    For l = 1 To 100
        j = l
        For k = j + 1 To 100
            If arrate(ytree, k) >= arrate(ytree, j) Then
                j = k
            End If
        Next k
        If l <> j Then
            t = arrate(ytree, j)
            tp = movetree(ytree, j)
            tc = derived(ytree, j)
            ll$ = view$(ytree, j)
            arrate(ytree, j) = arrate(ytree, l)
            movetree(ytree, j) = movetree(ytree, l)
            derived(ytree, j) = derived(ytree, l)
            view$(ytree, j) = view$(ytree, l)
            arrate(ytree, l) = t
            movetree(ytree, l) = tp
            derived(ytree, l) = tc
            view$(ytree, l) = ll$
        End If
    Next l
    fill = fill + 1
    Exit Sub
End If
```

```
If fill > 100 Then
    If rate >= arrate(ytree, 50) Then
        For seed = 50 To 1 Step -1
            If rate <= arrate(ytree, seed) Then
                For seed2 = 49 To seed + 1 Step -1
                    arrate(ytree, seed2 + 1) =➡
arrate(ytree, seed2)
                    movetree(ytree, seed2 + 1) =
➡           movetree(ytree, seed2)
                    derived(ytree, seed2 + 1) =
➡           derived(ytree, seed2)
                    view$(ytree, seed2 + 1) =
➡           view$(ytree, seed2)
                Next seed2
                arrate(ytree, seed) = rate
                movetree(ytree, seed) = play
                derived(ytree, seed) = connect
                view$(ytree, seed) = look$
                Exit For
            End If
        Next seed
    ElseIf rate <= arrate(ytree, 51) Then
        For seed = 51 To seed
            If rate >= arrate(ytree, seed) Then
                For seed2 = 52 To seed - 1
                    arrate(ytree, seed2 - 1) = arrate(ytree, seed2)
                    movetree(ytree, seed2 - 1) = movetree(ytree,
➡                   seed2)
                    derived(ytree, seed2 - 1) = derived(ytree,
➡                   seed2)
                    view$(ytree, seed2 - 1) = view$(ytree, seed2)
                Next seed2
                arrate(ytree, seed) = rate
                movetree(ytree, seed) = play
                derived(ytree, seed) = connect
                view$(ytree, seed) = look$
                Exit For
            End If
        Next seed
    End If
    fill = fill + 1
End If
End Sub
```

This procedure might appear a little imposing at first. However, if you read the previous chapter on algorithmic logic, you should be able to recognize some of the patterns, as well as the inspiration, behind this algorithmic mediocrity extractor. When the arrays for the current ply reach 100 in length, they are immediately BubbleSorted using the rating as the key field. From that point on, when another element is to be added to the array, the portion of this procedure within the conditional clause starting with `If fill > 100 Then` will compare this value to the one in the middle of the array—presumably, the most mediocre element. The value of the new element will fall to one side or the other of this array; it is inserted there in order of rating. The rest of the array from the insertion point to the middle is then shifted toward the middle, with the middle element dropping off entirely. The result is a well-sorted array that has a big gaping hole where its mediocrity used to be.

The Logic Board

Certainly the unique feature of this game is the fact that you can see what it's thinking while it's thinking. Figure 13.5 shows what the logic board looks like in action. Following that is a list of its major property settings.

Figure 13.5. The face of logic.

VRLOGIC.FRM Property Settings

```
Form Logic
    BackColor       =   &H00400040&
    BorderStyle     =   1  'Fixed Single
    Caption         =   "Logic Board"
    Height          =   5136
    Left            =   6372
    LinkMode        =   1  'Source
    LinkTopic       =   "Form1"
    MaxButton       =   0   'False
    MinButton       =   0   'False
    ScaleHeight     =   4668
    ScaleWidth      =   4908
    Top             =   3828
    Width           =   5052

    PictureBox FirstPly
        BackColor       =   &H00400040&
        BorderStyle     =   0  'None
        FontName        =   "Lucida Sans"
        FontSize        =   7.8
        Height          =   852
        Left            =   1080
        Top             =   120
        Width           =   3732
    Label Label1
        BackColor       =   &H00800080&
        Caption         =   "Move Rating       Best Move
    Worst Move"
        FontName        =   "Lucida Sans"
        FontSize        =   7.8
        ForeColor       =   &H00E0FFFF&
        Height          =   204
        Left            =   1080
        Top             =   1080
        Width           =   3852
    Label MoveCount
        BackColor       =   &H00400040&
        FontName        =   "Lucida Sans"
        FontSize        =   7.8
```

```
        ForeColor        =    &H0000FFFF&
        Height           =    156
        Index            =    0
        Left             =    1080
        Top              =    1320
        Width            =    612
     Label MoveRate
        BackColor        =    &H00C00000&
        FontName         =    "Lucida Sans"
        FontSize         =    18
        ForeColor        =    &H00FFFFFF&
        Height           =    372
        Index            =    0
        Left             =    1320
        Top              =    1560
        Width            =    732
     Label BestMove
        BackColor        =    &H00008000&
        FontName         =    "Lucida Sans"
        FontSize         =    18
        ForeColor        =    &H00FFFFFF&
        Height           =    372
        Index            =    0
        Left             =    2520
        Top              =    1560
        Width            =    732
     Label WorstMove
        BackColor        =    &H00000080&
        FontName         =    "Lucida Sans"
        FontSize         =    18
        ForeColor        =    &H00FFFFFF&
        Height           =    372
        Index            =    0
        Left             =    3720
        Top              =    1560
        Width            =    732
     Label PlyNumber
        BackColor        =    &H00808000&
        FontName         =    "Lucida Sans"
        FontSize         =    9.6
        Height           =    228
```

```
        Index           =   0
        Left            =   4560
        Top             =   1644
        Width           =   252
Label MoveCount
        Index           =   1
        Left            =   1080
        Top             =   2280
Label MoveRate
        Index           =   1
        Top             =   2520
        Width           =   732
Label BestMove
        Index           =   1
        Top             =   2520
        Width           =   732
Label WorstMove
        Index           =   1
        Top             =   2520
        Width           =   732
Label PlyNumber
        Index           =   1
        Top             =   2604
        Width           =   252
Label MoveCount
        Index           =   2
        Top             =   3240
        Width           =   612
Label MoveRate
        Index           =   2
        Top             =   3480
        Width           =   732
Label BestMove
        Index           =   2
        Top             =   3480
        Width           =   732
Label WorstMove
        Index           =   2
        Top             =   3480
        Width           =   732
```

```
Label PlyNumber
    Index          =    2
    Top            =    3564
    Width          =    252
Label Switch
    Alignment      =    2   'Center
    BackColor      =    &H00800080&
    Caption        =    "Move Selected"
    Enabled        =    0   'False
    FontName       =    "Lucida Sans"
    FontSize       =    9.6
    ForeColor      =    &H00FFFFFF&
    Height         =    252
    Left           =    48
    Top            =    4320
    Width          =    4800
```

The form has three numeric display columns for current board rating, best rating found for the ply so far, and worst rating found so far. `Sub Subplot ()` keeps track of these on behalf of the `Logic` form.

VREVERSI.BAS

```
Sub Subplot (imageboard$, ply As Integer, rate As Single)
If LogicOn = False Then Exit Sub
Static bestrate(3), worstrate(3), movenum(3) As Integer
If ply = 0 Then
    For cler = 1 To 3
        bestrate(cler) = 0
        worstrate(cler) = 0
        movenum(cler) = 0
    Next cler
End If
If ply > 0 Then
    locale = ply Mod 3
    If locale = 0 Then
        locale = 3
    End If
    Logic.PlyNumber(locale - 1).Caption = Right$(Str$(ply),
➥ Len(Str$(ply)) - 1)
    Logic.PlyNumber(locale - 1).Refresh
End If
```

```
For char = 1 To 64
    py% = (char - 1) \ 8
    px% = char Mod 8
    If px% = 0 Then px% = 8
    sq$ = Mid$(imageboard$, char, 1)
    Select Case sq$
        Case "X"
            colr& = QBColor(15)
        Case "O"
            colr& = QBColor(0)
        Case " "
            colr& = RGB(0, 64, 255)
    End Select
    upleftx% = 100 + ((px% - 1) * 100)
    If ply = 0 Then
        yoff = 250
    Else
        yoff = 500
    End If
    uplefty% = (locale) * 920 + (py% * 100) + yoff
    Logic.Line (upleftx%, uplefty%)-(upleftx% + 88, uplefty% +
➡ 88), colr&, BF
Next char
If ply > 0 Then
    movenum(ply) = movenum(ply) + 1
    Logic.MoveCount(locale - 1).Caption = Str$(movenum(ply))
    Logic.MoveCount(locale - 1).Refresh
    Logic.Label1.Refresh
    Logic.MoveRate(locale - 1).Caption = Str$(rate)
    Logic.MoveRate(locale - 1).Refresh
    If rate > bestrate(ply) Then
        bestrate(ply) = rate
        Logic.BestMove(locale - 1).Caption = Str$(rate)
        Logic.BestMove(locale - 1).Refresh
    End If
    If Logic.WorstMove(locale - 1).Caption = "" Or rate <
➡ worstrate(ply) Then
        worstrate(ply) = rate
        Logic.WorstMove(locale - 1).Caption = Str$(rate)
        Logic.WorstMove(locale - 1).Refresh
    End If
End If
End Sub
```

Using conventional sort algorithms for unconventional purposes.

The procedure starts by declaring three `Static` arrays for each column in the logic form. Using modulo arithmetic, the procedure determines which row is available for displaying test plots. Once that's determined, the image of the board for the current ply and node is taken apart. The white characters are given white blocks, and the black characters black ones. The location of the board being plotted is also determined using modulo arithmetic, but the location of the pieces to be plotted is fine-tuned using the formula for `uplefty%`. Once the board is plotted, the column values are refreshed because the procedure has been keeping watch over the best and worst ratings it has seen thus far.

Since the mid 1980s, I've proclaimed in print that the programmer who had a keen mental grasp of the type of mind it takes to build a solid game program is among the highest order of programmers. By comparison to constructing the process model for Visual Reversi, the INVENT1 application was a breeze. Simple bookkeeping can be modeled by an application with hardly any difficulty because the contexts of the operation are already defined by the work environment.

With gaming, *you* as programmer are doing the defining. The game programmer requires a keen imagination coupled with an unflinching grasp of reality; a product from a programmer who leans too much in one direction or the other can well be declared mediocre and sorted out.

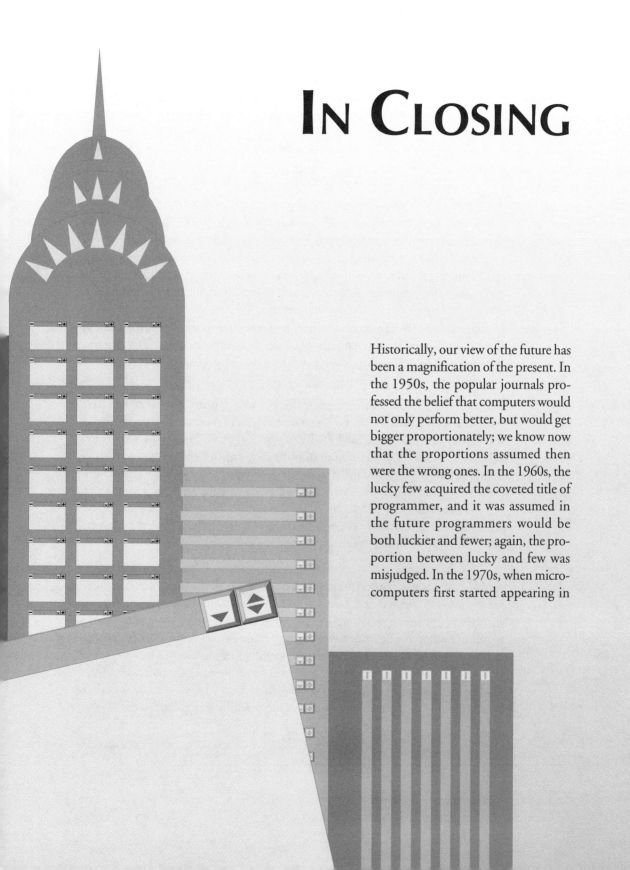

In Closing

Historically, our view of the future has been a magnification of the present. In the 1950s, the popular journals professed the belief that computers would not only perform better, but would get bigger proportionately; we know now that the proportions assumed then were the wrong ones. In the 1960s, the lucky few acquired the coveted title of programmer, and it was assumed in the future programmers would be both luckier and fewer; again, the proportion between lucky and few was misjudged. In the 1970s, when microcomputers first started appearing in classrooms, it was predicted that future schools would be delivering education by way of the computer; again, the proportions were misjudged. Today, more and more students are staying home from school in order to use the computer (which is at home), learn something useful, communicate with the world, and most importantly, *stay alive.*

In the 1980s, it was predicted that the "IBM-compatible" computer would become the standard for computing worldwide; and anybody who wanted a computer purchased *the* computer. Today, IBM itself no longer produces an IBM-compatible computer. The buyer has his choice of platforms now, along with his choice of operating systems and, atop that, operating environments. There's not just DOS in this world anymore; OS/2 is a real competitor. The Macintosh is still a viable, competitive platform, and to this day it shows users there is another way to work. Compatibility is not the catchword today; *connectivity* is. Again, the proportions of the prediction were incorrect.

If we are to spot the *real* and current trends for this business of computing, we should recognize that historically, our perceptions of those trends have been disproportionate. In any enterprise where the *people* are the driving force, the trend will be toward individuality, downsizing, and freedom of expression and choice. Visual Basic is a programming language for the people. It will not be the language of choice for creating large-scale applications, but this is immaterial—that has never been its stated purpose. Visual Basic brings people into the art of computing, making them mathematical craftsmen, empowering them with a new avenue for creative expression, and helping them to better comprehend the job processes of their own businesses.

If programming is to become a popular enterprise, then the companies that provide the tools for programming will need to accept the ideas, concepts, and methodologies created and brought to fruition by the people. Coalitions of manufacturers that seek to produce standards, specifications, and regulations without seeking the advice or voice of the people—the body of programmers at large—will have greater and greater difficulty finding acceptance among the people. Companies must make room for ideas submitted by the individual, from the field programmer who just may have discovered a better way to work than the companies' collective laboratories could possibly have conceived.

This book has been about the routes one takes to automate her business, to free it from the unnecessary restrictions imposed upon it by old methods and failed prospective solutions. It has also been about understanding the computing process, about seeing the work performed by the computer as symbolic at all times of that performed in reality, in the world outside of the microprocessor. If it has endowed but a few with the ideals and principles that will further shape the art of computing in the direction it must proceed—toward individual initiative and intercommunication between processes and people—then it will have fulfilled its mission.

-D.F. Scott
November, 1992

DOCUMENTATION AND ONLINE HELP

The industry of computing is, to a great extent, divided into two segments: service and support. For the most part, the role of the programmer is categorized as the service division; the provisions of applications to the general public is a service. Most programmers for large corporations rarely find themselves in a support role. They don't have to answer technical support questions over the telephone, and they don't have to write technical documentation for their users.

Yet programmers for large corporations are not most programmers. By far, the majority of working programmers are people who are held ultimately responsible for the integrity and applicability of their products. They face their public every day. Oftentimes, the user may rely upon preconceived notions of just who programmers are and what they do. When the user has a problem with an application—and that will happen, regardless of its quality—that user will most likely develop an impression of what to expect when she calls the programmer for assistance. What builds that impression is the quality of the documentation shipped with the product. An application's quality may be judged independently, but the producer of that application often finds himself judged by the quality of his documentation. It is one thing not to be able to speak BASIC. It is another thing to be unable to speak English.

How do you tell a user how to operate your application? There are several working methodologies; certainly, we at Sams abide by certain standards and guidelines. Corporations such as Microsoft and Xerox have published standards for the general public to read concerning how documentation should be written and laid out—in their respective opinions, of course. Corporate guidelines often state that use of language should be restricted to present tense and active voice, for ease of comprehension. In other words, rather than say, "The file icon is generally dropped into the save area," you might say, "You drag the file icon into the save area." Obviously there is a case for the latter construction; it's easier to read, and more to the point.

Yet for the same reason it turned out that not all computing concepts could be represented with icons, not all directions for computers and applications can be expressed in active voice and present tense. If everything followed the subject-verb-object structure, before long, you as *writer* would have documents that *do* things, dialog panels that *say* things, and command prompts that *talk* back to you. One day you will find yourself *authoring*, while the users of your applications go merrily about their business lawyering, dentisting, and plant supervisoring. You would forget that when describing the tools of your application, you are referring to machines and to symbols. In reality, symbols do not speak to you except in the poetic sense. It helps to be something of a poet when writing computer documentation, if only for the reason that a poet is most experienced at distinguishing metaphor from truth.

Instant Help

If you're a user of Microsoft Word for Windows, then you're in luck. Included with the disk supplied with your copy of this book is a series of Word for Windows document templates that will help you in the production of Windows Help files for your Visual Basic application. The Windows Help compiler is currently shipped with each copy of Visual Basic 2.0 Professional Edition; and every edition of the Visual Basic interpreter includes special new `.Help`-properties for graphic objects that allow you to link each important graphic object to a specific set of instructions you've written for it, to be shown using Microsoft's Windows Help hypertext file "player."

To better comprehend how these properties link to what is, for all intents and purposes, a compressed text file, you must better understand what a help file actually is. In much the same way that Visual Basic projects can incorporate ASCII text files and a "compiled" Visual Basic for Windows application is a compressed form of these text files, a Windows Help file is a compressed and compiled form of a series of textual documents. The native format of these documents is Rich Text Format (RTF), which is a current standard among software manufacturers for interchange of highly formatted published-quality text. Word for Windows recognizes Rich Text Format as one of its import/export formats.

The constitution of a Windows Help file.

A Windows Help file contains (or should contain) text that may be used to automatically reference other text, as though it were a book with pieces of string tying together related subjects across separate chapters. You may have read that a Help text file is organized differently from a standard text file, in that it consists of panels that have links to other panels in the text file, regardless of their distance. Quite frankly, as you'll see, the main text file in a Windows help system is not so unlike a standard document. You can write a simple text file with plenty of headers (not the attempts at humor that mine tend to be, but serious headers) and reformat it into a Help text file later.

Structuring a standard text file into a Windows Help file is a matter of calling out the important elements and renaming some of them so that the Help system will know which parts of your text relate to one another. You may decide later to add extra sections to help round out your coverage of the subject matter; but on the whole, a Windows Help file is a document with hooks. The template files this book gives you will help you take your ordinary text file and remodel it into self-referencing text.

There are some similarities worth noting between a Visual Basic project file scheme and a Windows Help file scheme. Both utilize separate ASCII text files containing lists of other files that comprise the collective project; for the Windows Help file, this is the .HPJ project file. Within a new type of Help file component called the *hypergraphic,* certain elements of graphics may be made to respond to "click events," shall we say, so that the reader may access certain elements of text by clicking a specific portion of a graphic with the mouse. The Help system also contains its own interpreted programming language for phrasing conditional instructions and creating limited animation. For now, however, this chapter deals with the primary component of the Windows Help project, the *topic file.*

To try out some of the ideas introduced in this appendix, you should first install the template files into your working copy of Word for Windows. These are .DOT files, so they belong in the home directory of the word processor. This way, when you select File/New from the Word menu, the list of available templates that follows will contain the name of the topic file template HELPTOPC. To bring up a new document using the Help topic file template, you would now simply click its template file name.

The Topic File

The division of elements in a Windows Help topic file.

A Windows Help topic file is also divided into separate *contexts*; the term means much the same here as it does in Visual Basic. Once you've written the directions to your application and grouped together the portions of those directions that naturally relate to one another, you place dividers into your text called *context strings* that signal the beginning of the next collective context (as well as the end of the last one).

To indicate and identify certain elements of the topic file for the sake of the Help compiler—such as topic headers and context strings—you place footnote indicators just *before* those elements in the topic file. Each specific type of element has its own footnote character; for instance, context strings are identified by a pound sign (#). Normally you manually place these footnote symbols into the topic file, but now that you have the Help templates, you can enter a context string through a Word menu selection. Here's how the topic file template works for context strings:

1. Place the cursor at the start of the title of a collective context in your help document.

2. From Word's Format menu, select Context String. This is not a selection native to Word for Windows; this is actually part of the topic file template. Selecting this menu item starts a Word macro that will place the pound sign before the context title in the main body of the text. Note that this pound sign is written in superscript. Next, Word's footnote pane will be displayed, and the pound sign footnote symbol will appear there as well. Footnote symbols within this pane appear in the same order as they appear in the main body of the text. The cursor will appear within the footnote pane beside the new pound sign.

3. Type the name of the context string beside the pound sign in the footnote pane. This string name should be phrased in the same way you'd phrase a Visual Basic variable—with any number of alphanumeric characters up to 255, the first being alphabetic, without space characters though allowing for underscore characters (_) if necessary. This string will be used elsewhere in the text of the topic file to refer back to the area pointed to by this footnote.

All text relating to a particular collective context appears on the same page as the # context header. This page, from the word processor's point of view, may be of any length, because the end-of-page in this case is officially marked by a "hard" (manual) page break. To insert a hard page break in Word for Windows, type Ctrl-Enter; this will officially denote the end of the collective context.

Titles for particular help panels are identified similarly using the $ footnote symbol. When the user of the Help system searches for a particular subject using the Bookmark menu (which is different from the Search button, mind you), those title lines identified with the $ character will appear within the list of available marked topic file locations by default. The user of the Help system can add her own bookmarks to this list.

By contrast, when the user clicks the Search button in the main Help window, a dialog panel shows a list of all available *keywords* relating to the help file. In this case, the term "keywords" is used loosely; entire *keyphrases* may be enrolled as keywords. Several keyphrases in this list may point to a single location in the topic file; when the user clicks one, the panel pointed to by the keyword is displayed forthwith. To enroll a series of keywords as pointing to a particular point in the text, place the cursor just before this point; using the topic file template menu, select Forma**t**/Keyphrases. A κ symbol is used in the footnote section to refer to a paragraph containing keyphrases. A keyphrase series may contain any number of characters up to 255, with any character accepted as part of the phrase except for the semicolon (;) which is used to separate keyphrases from each other. Each phrase in this paragraph will point to the portion of the topic file text indicated by the κ footnote marker.

A Calmer Way to Enter Hypertext

Implementing hypertext in Windows Help files.

What generally qualifies a passage of computerized text as being *hypertext* is the capability for certain parts of that passage to be referenced by other related parts simply by clicking those related parts. You'll see this definition hyperextended by advertisements and promotional literature to mean something else entirely. In the Windows Help system, a word or phrase that you intend to be "hot," so the reader can access a related panel by clicking that phrase, is made "hyper" by the following process:

1. Indicate the text that you want Windows Help to make "hot."

2. Format the characters for this indicated text to be double-underlined; in Word for Windows, type Ctrl-D. (If you're not using Word for Windows, Help will accept strikethrough text as well.)

3. Now place the cursor at the point following the end of the double-underlined characters.

4. You will be typing text that you don't want the Windows Help user to read, so set the current cursor mode for hidden text. In Word for Windows, type Ctrl-H.

5. Type the context string for the panel where the user will be sent when he clicks the hot text region. This text will appear with a single hazy underscore, if hidden text viewing mode is currently turned on.

Another way for the user to cross-reference text in a help file is to click and hold the mouse button over an area of text that brings up a definition window. This is a "pop-up" or "type 0" window that stays on-screen for as long as the index button of the mouse is depressed. The contents of a pop-up window are defined as follows:

1. Indicate the text that you want Windows Help to make "hot."

2. Format the characters for this indicated text to be single-underlined; in Word for Windows, type Ctrl-U.

3. Now place the cursor at the point just following the end of the under-lined characters.

4. You will be typing text that you don't want the Windows Help user to read, so set the current cursor mode for hidden text. In Word for Windows, type Ctrl-H.

5. Type the context string for the panel where the user will be sent when he clicks the hot text region. This text will appear with a single hazy underscore, if hidden text viewing mode is currently turned on.

The danger with this method of formatting is that a pop-up window is not defined within the topic file by any special characters, so the text belonging to a pop-up window may also effectively belong to a standard panel. You might be able to turn this into an advantage if you intend for the same collective context to be used for both purposes.

Armed with this information (once the general body of your directions have been written), you will probably want to write a "Table of Contents" or an "Index" panel to include as the front or "home" panel for your Help file. This panel will be displayed should the user want to browse leisurely through the file, or to look up a topic using the system's own index. The other way to invoke a Help file for most applications is to indicate the object that you want help using, and press F1; in such cases, the user of Help will not want to see the index again, but a panel that explicitly describes the indicated object. This type of referencing is called *context-sensitive help*; and as you can see, it is actually easy to implement.

The "home" or index panel of a Windows Help file.

Hooking Your Text File to Visual Basic

You've seen a quick demonstration of the primary elements of help file generation; just the basics, none of the tricks. I suggest that if you've never written documentation before, whether it be the online variety or the on-paper kind, try restricting yourself to the methods discussed here before you start constructing help macros, "hot" graphics, and animations.

Each major graphic object within a Visual Basic form, not counting lines and shapes but including the form itself, has been given access to the property `.HelpContextID`. The intent of this property is to relate each object to a particular collective context in the Windows Help topic file that describes its operation for the user. The trouble is that the setting of `.HelpContextID` can only be a number; so it's up to you as programmer to give each *named* collective context an associated numeral. No, you can't cheat and give collective context numerals to start with; Visual Basic is looking for an alias for the collective context strings.

These aliases must be written out within a special section of the Help project `.HPJ` file. As I mentioned earlier, this is an ASCII text file that contains special directives to the Microsoft Help compiler and may also contain macros for special operations. In this case, a special section is required within this file, headed by a line marked `[MAP]`. Divisions of a Help project file are not unlike those of an `.INI` file for Windows or its applications; the various divisions are marked, in no particular order, by sections enclosed within square brackets.

The syntax of alias statements within the `[MAP]` section is loose; all that's required for an alias instruction is the collective context string as you named it, followed by any number of spaces, and a numeral that will identify it for the `.HelpContextID` property setting. These numerals don't have to be in any particular order, nor do they have to start with 0 or 1 and work in sequence, though they must be integral.

For a simple Windows Help file for a Visual Basic application, the `[MAP]` section is really all that's necessary for the Help project file; as you grow more creative, I assure you, the size of your Help project files will grow exponentially.

Of course, this would not be enough for your Visual Basic application to be able to link to your Windows Help file, because it doesn't know yet which file you're linking it to. A direct link to the Windows Help file is accomplished through a declared function to the Windows API, written within your global declarations section as follows:

```
Declare Function WinHelp Lib "USER" (ByVal hWnd As Integer,
➥   ByVal lpzFileName As String, ByVal wCmd As Integer,
➥   dwData As Any) As Integer
```

In an earlier chapter, you saw how variable hWnd is used as a handle to Windows internal window number for the specified window. You should know by now that the window handle, like a handle to a device context, is never passed to the API by way of a VB variable, because Windows can change its handle numbers at any time without notifying anyone. Also in the above declaration, lpzFileName will stand for the filename of the Windows Help file itself. Parameter wCmd will contain a numeral which acts as a command; as you'll see momentarily, the Windows Help system receives a command through the application that calls it, through this parameter. The actual topic being requested by the call to Windows Help (and by the user of the application seeking help in the first place) is the numeral supplied as parameter dwData. This numeral may take any of several formats depending upon the type of search specified by wCmd; thus the declaration of the parameter As Any. Remember, nowhere else is the Any type for a variable accepted in Visual Basic but in the Declare statement.

For the sake of efficiency, you should also add to the global declarations section the following excerpt from the CONSTANT.TXT file:

```
'  Commands to pass WinHelp()
Global Const HELP_CONTEXT = &H1
            ' Display topic identified by number in Data
Global Const HELP_QUIT = &H2
            ' Terminate help
Global Const HELP_INDEX = &H3
            ' Display index
Global Const HELP_HELPONHELP = &H4
            ' Display help on using help
Global Const HELP_SETINDEX = &H5
            ' Set an alternate Index for help file with more
            '    than one index
Global Const HELP_KEY = &H101
            ' Display topic for keyword in Data
Global Const HELP_MULTIKEY = &H201
            ' Look up keyword in alternate table and
            '    display topic

Type MULTIKEYHELP
    mkSize As Integer
    mkKeylist As String * 1
    szKeyphrase As String * 253
End Type
```

The constant declarations will represent the command being sent to the Windows Help system by the application. Most of the time, the user will have implemented the "F1" method for invoking a Help screen (represented here by HELP_KEY), though perhaps the second most popular method is to pull up the index window first (represented here by HELP_SETINDEX). Finally, the composite variable Type structure for MULTIKEYHELP is reserved for cases in which you've compiled a separate text file that contains the list of keywords for the help topic file; this is in case the keywords list is too long within the help topic file itself to be manageable.

The Event Trigger

From this point on, it is up to you, the Visual Basic programmer, to define the Help access mechanism. Remember that the .HelpContextID property is just a convenience for remembering the alias number you gave a collective context; the property really has no real functionality in Visual Basic. Suppose the user has pressed F1 while a form named MachineParts is active; someplace within the form, the event procedure that handles keypresses should determine the identity and help context number of the graphic object that currently has the focus, by means of the property ActiveControl.HelpContextID. Assume for this example that this property setting is assigned to variable context%. The press of F1 apparently means the user wants a quick explanation of this control's operation, so the command sent to the Help system should be HELP_CONTEXT. The instruction that brings up the help screen now should read as follows:

```
helpnow% = WinHelp(MachineParts.hWnd, HelpFileName$,
➥  HELP_CONTEXT, context%)
```

On the other hand, assume the user has clicked a Help Index button within the active form. There should be only one index per help topic file, so the data parameter dwData in this instance will be ignored by the Help system. The trouble is, the parameter has to exist for the sake of the function call, ignored or not. Because default variable types are now variants and not values, it becomes necessary to assign a dummy variable a default value of 0, and pass that as a parameter to the help system. Here is the instruction that will bring up the index:

```
helpnow% = WinHelp(MachineParts.hWnd, HelpFileName$,
➥    HELP_INDEX, dummy%)
```

Because parameter `dwData` was declared `As` `Any`, it's safer here to assign a zero value to a variable `dummy%` and pass that as a parameter than it is to simply pass a zero.

TOPIC FINDER

As a new and exclusive feature, Sams Publishing presents the Topic Finder, a new and more commonsense way for you to find your way about this book. Along the margins of each chapter, you'll find margin notes which point the way to particular topics of interest. All topics covered in this book are listed in the Index, of course; but are you always so certain of what letter each topic begins with? Here, the margin notes are replicated and arranged in order of *subject*. To find a topic of interest to you, choose one from the list below and turn to the page listed here in the Topic Finder. The margin note will point the way to what you're looking for.

Topic Finder

continues

Topic Finder continued

continues

Topic Finder continued

continues

Topic Finder continued

A TERMINOLOGY GUIDE FOR THE MODERN ERA OF COMPUTING

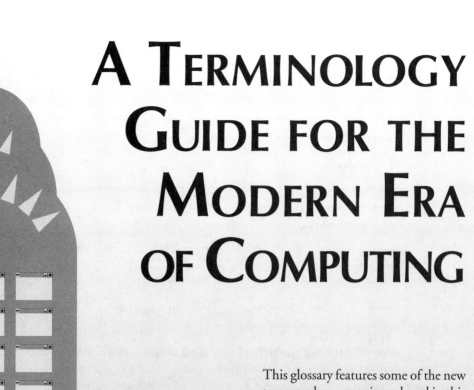

This glossary features some of the new terms and concepts introduced in this volume.

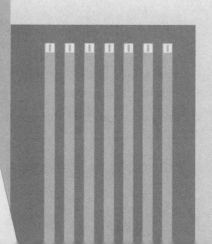

algebraic notation The usage model for a calculator designed to more closely approximate the way a formula is written.

algorithm A real-world process that is executed or simulated using a minimum of reiterative and often recursive code.

alphanumeric Having the quality of containing either letters or digits, or both.

antecedent The graphic object referred to by a property or method, generally written following the period that separates it from the graphic object with which it is associated.

application An operational program or set of cooperative programs within the computer environment having a work product that is a specific document or set of documents.

argument A value or variable used within a function or formula. This term is often synonymous with *parameter.*

array A list or set in memory of related values or alphanumeric contents, collectively referred to by a common term.

ASCII The American Standard Code for Information Interchange. This is the most widely used code for transmission and storage of alphanumeric data in a bitwise form within or between computers.

automation The ideal goal for a computing application; in other words, to perform real-world tasks on behalf of the user and in so doing integrate into the existing work environment, while adding as few new maintenance processes to that environment as possible.

backrating The distribution of data in a tree structure such that the changing of data referring to lower nodes in the tree is made to have direct bearing upon data in higher nodes.

binary Representable using as many as two digits. This term also refers to the base 2 numeral system.

binary access A method of storing data to and retrieving it from a device, whereby the structure of the data is not a factor, and data is interpreted only as single bits, bytes, or characters.

binary operator A symbol which represents a mathematical function combining, comparing, or equating two values.

binary state The minimum unit of value in a computer, which can be described as either true (–1 or 1, depending on the interpreter) or false (0).

bit Short for *binary digit,* which is the elementary unit of value within a computer, representing a logical state of true (1 or ON) or false (0 or OFF). Mechanically, it represents the presence of electrical current.

bitmap A group of related values which, when represented on the screen as pixels rather than characters, forms an image.

blit Short for *block transfer,* it is an instantaneous relocation of a grouping of memory contents from one region to another.

Boolean operator A term used to represent the comparison of one binary value to another, the intent being to derive a single binary value as a result. Named for George Boole, 19th century British mathematician.

branching To direct the interpreter to suspend execution of the normal sequence of instructions and resume the sequence at some other specified point in the program.

break A suspension of the operating state of the program.

breakpoint An instruction line temporarily scheduled to force execution of the program to be suspended immediately following the execution of that line.

broad time focus The structuring of the usage and process models of a component of an application such that all of its operations have bearing on future processes.

buffer A holding area in memory consisting of a fixed number of bytes, reserved for data that is to be sent to some device—often a disk file—at some later time, generally when the buffer is full.

bug The result of any process that failed to perform in the manner for which it was intended or designed, although it cannot be detected automatically by the interpreter or compiler. Thus by its nature, a bug allows logical program execution to continue along a potentially disastrous course.

button A control or graphic object used for passing directives or commands to the program.

byte The primary memory storage unit for all forms of data in a computer system, comprised of eight binary digits (bits).

caption A non-editable element of text appearing within a form or graphic object.

central administrator The primary module in a multi-modular application that initiates the other modules, and restricts user access to those modules.

channel 1. A logically interpreted device (in other words, not a tangible, physical entity) for maintaining the flow of data between the interpreter and an output device or storage unit. **2.** A logical device maintained in memory facilitating the transfer of data between applications.

check box A graphic control used to represent an on/off or true/false state, the setting of which is chosen by the user.

child Also called a "subordinate." An object or element belonging to, or residing within, a broader *parent* element.

clause 1. A compound instruction that contains one or more subordinate instructions and is distributed in a single group over more than one line. **2.** Any set of instructions, the execution of which is dependent on the value of a variable in a mathematical expression.

client The primary receiver of functionality and data in a computing network, or in an environment in which programs and processes communicate with one another.

clipboard The logical device maintained by Escher, which retains an element of text being transferred between forms or graphic objects.

combo box A control that enables a user to choose an item from a list or type a choice that may not appear on that list.

Common User Access The written set of standards for user/application visual interchange subscribed to by a consortium of computing manufacturers, publishers, and vendors led by IBM Corp.

communications model Any physical or mental diagram of a real-world process in which information is interchanged between parties.

compiler A program which takes high-level source code and breaks down that code into its most primary logical components, resulting in a machine code executable file that requires no pre-interpretation by any other program.

composite variable A container for multiple numeral, string, or other composite variables, addressed together as one unit using a single, arbitrarily defined term and invoked within an instruction using object-oriented syntax.

concatenation The process of joining elements of data together, especially with respect to strings.

condition 1. The test of whether an instruction will be executed. 2. A mathematical test, stated in the form of an expression, used to determine the order of execution of the program.

constant A term that stands in place of a value in an expression, having its value set once and only once.

context The definable relationship between a structure of data or functionality, and the larger structure of which it is a component.

context-independence Referring to a routine, process, or procedure whose functionality has been constructed with a lesser degree of regard to the specific situation of the application to which it belongs, such that the procedure may be easily ported to another application entirely without loss of functionality.

control A graphic object placed on a form specifically for purposes of data acquisition and display, in a manner that easily can be made familiar to the user.

control array A set of similar, related controls in a form that are referenced together as a group, and the operation of which is jointly defined by a single procedure in the source code.

cross-modular variable A variable declared at the module level, whose scope extends between the various modules in the project, but does not extend to any procedures in the project.

cross-reference In data processing, the act of searching for a record or records of data within a set or database wherein one or more elements correspond to those from another set or database within the same schema.

cursor A marker indicating the point within a document or textually oriented control where new characters will appear after they are typed; also called the *caret*.

data The carrier(s) of information within a computer.

data set A structure of data in memory that does not carry with it code defining that structure.

database Any stored group of data elements containing the structure by which those elements are related to each other.

decimal A number that can be represented using as many as 10 digits. The term also refers to the base 10 numeral system.

declaration 1. The first statement in a program to assign a legitimate value to a variable. 2. An instruction that introduces a procedure or process and defines the context of that process.

default The state of an object, device, or memory construct that is presumed beforehand if no instructions to alter that state have been processed.

delimiter A character of punctuation used to distinguish elements of an expression from each other, or to separate them from each other.

device context The extent to which a simulated mechanism in the computing environment applies to the overall job.

dialog box A window having the purpose of obtaining at least one element of user input. It is often abbreviated as *dialog*.

directive The second division of the input level of a usage model, in which command instructions are given by the user to the computer.

disclosure The first division of the input level of a usage model, in which data is transferred from the user to the computer.

document The primary data product of an application as it is represented in memory and presented to the user.

double-word raster A system of representing graphics using a 16-bit element representing the color and characteristics of a set of pixels.

drag When forms are active, to move an image of a graphic control using the mouse.

dynamic array An array whose assigned amount of elements may be set or changed on demand.

Dynamic Data Exchange The system employed by Microsoft Windows for establishing a communications link between applications and transferring data over the channels comprising that link.

environment The logical and often graphical facilities one program provides another for easier, more efficient operation.

equation A statement of equality that assigns a value—whether it is a numeral or an arithmetically derived value—to a variable.

error The result of any process that fails to perform in the manner it is intended or designed, and which by its nature or in the interest of preventing disaster prevents logical program execution from continuing.

event A unit of user input, utilizing any of the available devices attached to the computer system, which triggers the execution of a procedure in response.

event procedure A portion of a form module that is executed once a graphical event is recognized by the system.

executable file A file recognized by MS-DOS as being comprised of instructions to the CPU, and not data.

expression 1. An arithmetic comparison between two values, the result of which is expressed logically as a binary state. 2. One or more values or variables arithmetically joined by functions or functional operators. 3. An assignment of value to a variable with another value, variable, or another expression.

field Any container for an element or item of data, whether it be a graphic object for the display of that datum, a region of memory reserved for that datum, or a region of a file reserved for that datum.

flag variable An integer variable whose possible values are limited to logical true (–1) and logical false (0), in order that the variable may represent a binary state.

floating-point The storage format for a possibly fractional value, having its decimal point position stored in memory as a separate value.

focus The state of a graphic object indicated on-screen by a hazy rectangle, which designates that the control is active or awaiting input from the user.

form The input/output window for Escher applications, and the container for graphic objects that act as controls.

formula An algebraic expression of equality that states the relationships between qualities, quantities, or other such values, whether they are known or unknown.

frame A subdivision of a form that divides groupings of elements, such as options, from groups in other frames and elsewhere on the form.

function An arithmetic operation performed on a value, variable, or expression, the result of which is returned in a single variable.

functionality Used to describe the quality of performance of the components of a computing process.

global Extending in scope or context to all parts of an application.

graphic device Any mechanical or logical unit having the purpose of displaying data as both characters and images.

Graphic Device Interface The division of Microsoft Windows that processes graphic instructions and maintains a division of graphical contexts between different independent regions of the screen.

graphic object A data structure that can be represented visually and behaves to some degree as a device that receives user input and displays result data.

graphics array The method for interpreting graphic images to be displayed on the screen, as a map of binary code.

handle The accession number given a logical device by the operating system or environment, used to identify that device within the program.

heuristic logic Also called "artificial intelligence." The use of a rule-based system to simulate real-world situations in which the role of the application is to logically deduce a proper course of action, thus appearing to have made a decision.

heuristics The practice of describing rules for the behavior or operation of a system as code.

hexadecimal A number that can be represented using as many as 16 digits. This term also refers to the base 16 numeral system.

high-level language A computing language which is designed to be more interpretable by the human reader, and which is generally reinterpreted into lower-level machine code.

icon A functionally symbolic representation of a form, window, device, or application.

iconography Any system of written communication whereby the symbology used to portray the message has a direct correlation to the message itself; i.e., the opposite of orthography. Pictograms and hieroglyphs are iconographies.

image The visual interpretation of a segment of values in memory.

index The value represented by a subscript of an array.

indicator node A box, generally black or a reverse color, and one of eight such items, surrounding a graphic object when the user clicks on it, serving to convey to the user that this object will be the focus of any command or directive given forthwith.

information Any symbol or message that is meaningful to people.

instance array An independent quantifiable structure in memory defining how data from a shared schema is to be accessed.

instruction Any complete directive made within a program, comprised of a keyword and any parameters, terms, or delimiters associated with that directive.

integer Any whole number that has no fractional value.

integrity The measure of the logical correspondence between data and the information it is intended to represent.

interface Any physical or written model which depicts how an electronic device connects and transmits data and functionality to another electronic device.

internal variable A variable whose name is recognized by the interpreter as a keyword, and whose purpose has been defined beforehand by the interpreter.

interpreter Any program that receives a set of compound, high-level instructions from the programmer and instantly translates them into more rudimentary instructions that are easier for the computer to understand and execute.

iteration One repeated cycle of execution of the instructions in a loop clause, or any repetitious body of instructions.

key field The most pertinent element of a data structure, generally serving as the subject for a sorting operation.

keyword A term having its use reserved for instructions. It cannot be used for variables or labels.

label A non-instruction written on a line by itself and succeeded by a colon, designating a branching point.

layer Any grouping of modules or procedures belonging to a division of the process model which may operate and interact independently of the whole application.

lexeme A unit of representation in a high-level language representative of exactly one programmer directive; i.e., the minimum quantifiable component of an instruction.

library A set of process names that are treated as procedure names by Escher, but which are actually calls to processes within an executable outside of Escher, that may be linked to or compiled with the Escher application.

list box A control that allows one or more items to be chosen from a list, often a scrollable list.

local The minimum scope of a variable or composite structure, which limits its references to the confines of a single procedure.

logical context A program structure that simulates an electronic device for the sake of any routine that directs data to it for output.

logical reduction The act of obtaining the solution value to an expression by reducing the elements of that expression through arithmetic combination.

loop A sequence of instructions that are executed repetitively either for a specified count or until a condition is evaluated true.

low-level language A set of computing symbols that is designed to be readily interpretable more by the computer than by the human programmer.

map A large block of code in memory whose contents numerically encode in another form the contents of some other block—generally a larger one—or the contents of the screen.

maximize To bring a reduced icon back into the workspace, as the form or window associated with that icon.

memory map A database table in memory specifically for the operating system's use, which regulates the storage of object code, of intermediate Escher p-code, and of variable values and contents.

menu bar The area of a form or window below the title bar where categorical command or directive choices are listed.

meta-application A single task formed by the cooperation of several application components working in conjunction within the same environment.

metafile A method of representing vectored, object-oriented graphics within the Windows environment.

method An instruction that directs the interpreter to perform a programmed action on a graphic object.

minimize To reduce a form or window to its associated icon temporarily, thus suspending its primary execution.

modal An attribute of a window which suspends the operability of every other window until it is exited.

modular variable A variable declared at the module level, whose scope does not extend to procedures within that module.

module The core component of an Escher application, comprising routines and procedures, and possibly comprising form contents and properties, stored within a single file.

module-level code That portion of the source code in a module that exists outside of the framework of a formal procedure.

Multiple Document Interface Microsoft's specifications for the representation of multiple collected visual data structures in a Windows application.

multitasking The planned or scheduled cooperation of multiple programs within a single computer system, with the capability for single elements of data to be recognized by those multiple programs during the same session.

narrow time focus The structuring of an element of the process model of an application whereby a process has little direct bearing upon future processes in the model.

nest The special indentation of typesetting optionally given to a set of dependent instructions within a clause.

node A record of data in a tree structure that may have any number of other records directly pertaining to it, and that is directly pertinent to one and only one record.

object In object-oriented syntax, a data structure that combines the contents and attributes of the data, along with the encoded form of its function.

object code A file on disk or in memory comprised of CPU instructions that are not symbolized in any way for human interpretation. Also called *machine code*.

Object Linking and Embedding The system employed by Microsoft Windows whereby a visible record of data may appear within the document of one application, while its appearance, structure, and maintenance functions are simultaneously being provided by another application.

objectified data The hierarchical structuring of data such that the relationship between elements of data in a database, both to each other and to a broader collective topic, may be stated linguistically, in a manner uniform among more than one application in the system.

octal Numbers that can be represented using as many as eight digits. This term also refers to the base 8 numeral system.

opcode The minimum quantifiable element of instruction or directive made by a program to a computer.

operand A unit of data that is the subject of an instruction defined by an opcode.

operator A symbol that represents a mathematical function combining, comparing, or equating two values.

option dot A control, generally one of a set of such controls, used to represent the user's single choice of all the elements within a collected set.

orthography Any system of written communication whereby the symbols used to represent the message do not have direct correlation to the message itself; i.e., the opposite of iconography. Alphabetic language is an orthography.

parameter A value or variable passed to a procedure from outside that procedure.

parent The encompassing object or element with which another object or element is related, and to which that element is subordinate, such as a document window within an application window.

parser The portion of an interpreter in computing that decodes and defines a linguistic instruction.

peripheral context The relationship between those elements of an application which provide extra functionality to the more useful and purposeful elements.

phrase Any functional combination of terms within an instruction or routine.

pixel The minimum unit of measurement or plotting in the physical screen coordinate system.

pointer *1* The logical device operated by the mouse, used for indicating elements on the screen.

pointer *2* 1. A value that represents the location in memory where a value or contents of a variable are stored. 2. Any logical value that represents the location or position where another value can be obtained.

precision Refers to the number of bytes used to represent a variable's value.

primary context The relationship between those elements of an application that perform that part of an application most pertinent to its overall purpose.

procedure The component of an Escher application whose purpose is to logically describe or model at least one task or mathematical function, passing its results to some other component.

process 1 The act of performing real work.

process 2 The work performed by an application, module, procedure, or routine, usually perceived independently of the specific instructions comprising that routine.

process model Any physical or mental diagram which depicts how a computing application performs real work on behalf of the user, given data as an input.

program The symbolic form of a task, or any computing process that is described logically in a uniformly interpretable code.

project All the files that collectively comprise an Escher application.

prompt A symbol used to represent the point on the screen where the user enters lexical directives to the application or system.

property An attribute of a graphic object that is addressable by name using object-oriented syntax, and can be described by a value or term.

pseudocode Written language designed to approximate the activity of a high-level computing language, without obeying the specifications of that language.

quantifiable Used to describe a unit indivisible within its native frame of reference, and collectible in multiple units; for instance, a datum, a lexeme, a neuron, a moment.

query A request for elements from a database or data set that match a specified pattern or structure.

random access A mode for storing data to and retrieving it from a device, either physical or logical, whereby data can be written to or read from a region or file at any specifiable point, at any time.

record A logical grouping of related elements of data within a data file or database.

recursion The capability of a procedure or routine to call and pass parameters to a copy of itself.

recursive array algorithm A process which is capable of passing control to an independent copy of itself, and in so doing generates an independent copy of its entire data structure.

redundancy 1 With respect to data, an indicator of repetition that can be defined by formula, and that is used in error checking.

redundancy 2 With respect to the usage model of an application, the provision of the same command functions using multiple methods. Also called *redundant control*.

reference passing The transfer of a variable's value between two procedures, such that the value of the variable denoted in the passing instruction is changed in concordance with the value of the variable in the receiving procedure.

relation The mathematics that symbolically joins two or more elements or fields of a database.

resource In database technology, that part of a data structure which describes its construction and content.

Reverse Polish Notation (RPN) The usage model for a calculator designed to correlate with the order in which that calculator actually processes functions.

RGB Refers to a method of mixing red, green, and blue colors optically.

routine Any arbitrarily bounded sequence of instructions within a body of source code.

run time The period in which instructions within the source code of the program are executing.

schema Any structure of data which combines related databases; i.e., an overall frame of reference for all databases pertinent to an application.

scope The extent to which the reference of a variable is applied across the various divisions of the source code of a program.

scroll bar A sliding graphic device having the purpose of representing a value within a minimum and maximum range.

sequential access A mode for storing data to and retrieving data from a physical device in an absolute, specifiable sequence.

server The core supplier of functionality and data in a computing network, or in an environment where programs and processes interact.

setting A term that represents the state, appearance, or some aspect of a graphic object.

source code The written text of a program in its native language.

startup module The module within a project slated to begin execution first.

statement An instruction that specifies a change or deviation in the operating status of the program.

static Used to describe a variable or structure local to a procedure, having its value or contents maintained by the interpreter on exiting that procedure, for use when the procedure is entered again.

static array An array whose size in elements is fixed throughout the execution of the application.

string A sequence of any number of bytes that are interpreted jointly as text or alphanumeric characters.

subordinate module One whose procedures are called by the main startup module.

subroutine A set of instructions within a procedure that is executable repetitively, is callable by name, and at whose end forces a branch back to the instruction just past the one that called it.

subscript An integral value or variable within an array variable which represents the place or position of a value in the array's list or table.

symbological Referring to the directly correlative relationship between concept and symbol.

syntax The arrangement of terms within an instruction or clause.

tab sequence The arbitrarily designated order of graphic objects within a form, representing the sequence in which the focus passes through those objects during run time, when the user presses the Tab key.

table A stored database component consisting of data, along with the structure of that data, such as field names and relations.

table route A set of data which acts symbolically as a map denoting how that data relates to the components of an application.

tag Refers to the alias name arbitrarily given to a graphic object.

time focus The degree of bearing a process has upon the execution of a future process.

title bar The uppermost bar of a form or window, which generally contains the title of that window.

transparency The degree to which an application manages to shield the user from seeing the mechanics of its operation.

tree structure Also called "hierarchical tree structure." The organization of related records of data in memory or in a database, such that each record forms a node with multiple branches linking it to related subordinate nodes, and that each node is subordinate to one and only one "higher node."

usage model Any physical or mental diagram which depicts how human beings interact with a computing application. (Suggested replacement term for "user interface.")

user program The original name for what later became known as the "operating system."

variable An arbitrarily named term that represents a unit of data in memory that can be altered by the program.

viewport A rectangular subdivision of a graphics screen, to which graphic output is restricted.

virtual pen A representation in memory of the point in which a graphical plot will occur, and the direction taken by that plot.

virtual terminal Any graphic object capable of receiving input and output in the manner of a standard computer terminal.

virtuality The simulation of a real-world object or element through approximating the characteristics of that element.

visible record A record containing related information from the viewpoint of the user, though hiding from that user the multiplicity of databases and cross-referencing of records necessary to produce the record.

watchpoint A program line designated by the programmer to send an extra signal to a special window, containing the value or contents of a specific variable being watched.

window **1.** The graphical rectangular container for all subordinate graphic elements in an application containing forms. **2.** A portion of the graphics screen which logically displays a different magnification of the physical graphics array.

workspace The area of the screen where forms and tools reside—but may not necessarily appear—during an application's run time.

INDEX

Symbols

A

C

Q

R

What's On The Disk

The disk included with this book contains:

- The program code discussed in the book, including compiled executable programs.

- vxBase, a dynamic link library (DLL) of database functions that has been customized for use with Microsoft Visual Basic for Windows.

Installing The Floppy Disk

The software included with this book is stored in a compressed form. You cannot use the software without first installing it on your hard drive.

1. From a DOS prompt, set your default drive to the drive that contains the installation disk. (For example, if the floppy disk is in drive A:, type **A:** and press Enter.)

2. Type **INSTALL** *drive* (where *drive* is the drive letter of your hard drive), and press Enter. (For example, to install the files to drive C:, type **INSTALL C:** and press Enter.)

The code and programs from the book are now installed in a directory called \VB-DEVGD on your hard drive.

The vxBase DLL and EXE files are in your Windows directory. The other vxBase files are located in the \VB\VXBASE directory. Documentation is in the DOCS subdirectory and sample data files are located in the AIRPLANE and SAMPLE subdirectories. Read the documentation files for more information on running vxBase.

NOTE: To install all the files, you'll need at least 2.8M of free space on your hard drive.